Paulraj Lourdusamy

Meditations on the

Forty Names of Jesus

Llumina
Christian
Books

© 2006 Paulraj Lourdusamy

All rights reserved. No part of this publication may be reproduced or transmitted in any form or by any means electronic or mechanical, including photocopy, recording, or any information storage and retrieval system, without permission in writing from both the copyright owner and the publisher.

Requests for permission to make copies of any part of this work should be mailed to Permissions Department, Llumina Christian Books, PO Box 772246, Coral Springs, FL 33077-2246

ISBN: 1-59526-582-1

Printed in the United States of America by Llumina Christian Books

Library of Congress Control Number: 2006920254

FOREWORD

This book is an invitation to contemplate the mystery of Jesus Christ who came into our world as God in human flesh. Jesus is 'the Son of God' (Mk 15:39) - God made visible, the 'thought' of God made audible to us. Jesus Himself said, 'Anyone who has seen me has seen the Father' (Jn 14:9). God is a mystery. His divine life is beyond human comprehension. A complete understanding of the inner life of God is not within our reach. As intelligent and rational creatures, we can reflect and make an examination of the observable things and conclude that there exists a Supreme Being, whom we call 'God'. Thus, we may reach the knowledge of God as the uncreated source of all that exists. However, it is impossible for us to know conclusively what 'He is like' unless He takes the initiative and reveals Himself to us. It is God Himself, out of His own infinite goodness and love, at various times and in numerous ways, revealed to us His divine plan of our salvation. In the fullness of time, God sent His only Son to the world as the bearer, revealer and communicator of His infinite love and blessings for us. The eternal Son of God became Jesus Christ, the Lord and Savior of the world, the center of salvation history and the architect of human destiny to grant us, unworthy sinful human beings, a share in His divine glory and to make us the heirs of God's everlasting kingdom.

The names of Jesus

For the ancients, a name was not simply a conventional designation. It expressed the man's destiny and activity. The name was not simply an artificial tag that distinguished one person from another but had a mysterious identity with the bearer. It could be considered as a substitute for the person, as acting or receiving in his place. The name had a definite meaning and told something of the kind of person he/she was. Some people, especially the great ones, had several names given to them as their titles or designations. These names revealed what those persons stood for, the substance of their character and their authority, power and glory. Jesus Christ has several names that we find in the pages of the New Testament. Meditating on those names of Jesus can draw us to the very source of divine revelation that can enlighten us about the infinite love of God for us, about our dignity as God's loving children, about the goodness of the entire creation and above all, God's mysterious yet glorious plan of salvation to gather all things in the fullness of the divine splendour of Jesus Christ, His only Son. Then, it is spiritually very useful and much rewarding for us to reflect upon the forty names or the titles of Jesus and thereby contemplate His divine glory and majesty as well as His infinite and steadfast love for us.

Forty Names for Forty Days

Through the entire Bible, 'forty days' appear as a spiritually significant time to receive the favor of God and His blessings. Rick Warren in his memorable book, 'The Purpose Driven Life' states: 'Noah's life was transformed by 40 days of rain. Moses was transformed by 40 days on Mount Sinai.

The spies were transformed by 40 days in the Promised Land. David was transformed by Goliath's 40-day challenge. Elijah was transformed when God gave him 40 days of strength from a single meal. The entire city of Nineveh was transformed when God gave the people 40 days to change. Jesus was empowered by 40 days in the wilderness. The disciples were transformed by 40 days with Jesus after His resurrection'. Therefore, meditating on the forty names of Jesus during 40 days, especially during the holy season of Lent, will enable us, first of all, to know Him more. Knowing Him more will inspire us to love Him more. Loving Him more will empower us to serve Him more. God created us in this world to know Him, love Him and serve Him. Then, knowing, loving and serving Jesus, the only Son of God, will bring us happiness, peace and countless divine blessings in this world and after our death, will reward us with eternal joy in the everlasting kingdom of Heaven.

I have presented reflections on the forty names of Jesus following the order of the revelation of the mystery of Jesus in the New Testament. Jesus, the eternal Word, above all else and first of all, is God (Jn 1:1). He became man for our salvation. During His public ministry, Jesus revealed His divine identity progressively. The ordinary rural folk of Galilee saw Him as another Rabbi or Teacher and perhaps a Prophet. The Disciples accepted Him as their Master. Jesus enabled the believers 'to see Him with their eyes, to touch Him with their hands' (1 Jn 1:1) and to experience His glory as the 'Son of God' so that they may 'testify and proclaim to the world that 'the eternal life' that was with the Father has appeared as Jesus, the Lord' (1 Jn 1:2). I begin our meditation with reflection on Jesus' name as 'God' and end it with the reflection on Jesus' designation as 'Lord'. Every title of Jesus reveals an aspect of the great mystery of the 'Son of the living God'.

I am very grateful to my superior, Dr. A.M. Chinnappa, present archbishop of Madras-Mylapore for his encouragement and valuable support. At this time, I also remember with gratitude his predecessors under whom I exercised my pastoral ministry: Dr. Aruldas James, Dr. Casimir and Dr. Arulappa. With profound thanks, I gladly acknowledge the support of Mgr. John M. Quinn, the auxiliary bishop, Mgr. Michael Lefevre, the Director of Priests' Personnel as well as Mgr. William Sherzer, Rev. Raymond Bucan and Rev. James McNuity- of the archdiocese of Detroit. I am indebted to Maria Gomes, Dorothy Byrne, Tyndale Martin, Ray Keller, Jeevaratnam, Albert John and Dhanamsezhiyan for proofreading the manuscript. I would like to thank Ms. Deborah Greenspan of the Llumina Press and her team for their excellent work. With profound love, I dedicate this book to my beloved parents Lourdusamy and Amalorpavamary. 'There is no other name under heaven given to men by which we must be saved except the name of Jesus' (Acts 4:12). It is my sincere hope that this book that presents meditations on the forty names of Jesus may become a rewarding spiritual exercise for the Christian people of all the denominations by leading them to a profound appreciation of the supreme sacrifice of the only 'Son of God who loved us and gave Himself for us' (Gal 2: 20) and inspiring them to love and serve Him with thankful and joyous hearts.

Abbreviations of Books of the Bible

Acts	Acts of the Apostles	Jos	Joshua
Am	Amos	Jude	Jude
Bar	Baruch	Jgs	Judges
1 Chr	1 Chronicles	Jdt	Judith
2 Chr	2 Chronicles	1 Kgs	1 Kings
Col	Colossians	2 Kgs	2 Kings
1 Cor	1 Corinthians	Lam	Lamentations
2 Cor	2 Coronthians	Lv	Leviticus
Dn	Daniel	Lk	Luke
Dt	Deuteronomy	1 Mc	1 Maccabees
Eccl	Ecclesiastes	2 Mc	2 Maccabees
Eph	Ephesians	Mal	Malachi
Est	Esther	Mk	Mark
Ex	Exodus	Mt	Matthew
Ez	Ezekiel	Mi	Micah
Ezr	Ezra	Na	Nahum
Gal	Galatians	Neh	Nehemiah
Gn	Genesis	Nm	Numbers
Hb	Habakkuk	Ob	Obadiah
Hg	Haggai	1 Pt	1 Peter
Heb	Hebrews	2 Pt	2 Peter
Hos	Hosea	Phlm	Philemon
Is	Isaiah	Phil	Philippians
Jas	James	Prv	Proverbs
Jer	Jeremiah	Ps	Psalms
Jb	Job	Rv	Revelation
Jl	Joel	Rom	Romans
Jn	John	Ru	Ruth
1 Jn	1 John	1 Sm	1 Samuel
2 Jn	2 John	2 Sm	2 Samuel
3 Jn	3 John	Sir	Sirach
Jon	Jonah	Sg	Song of Songs
1 Thes	1 Thessalonians	Tb	Tobit
2 Thes	2 Thessalonians	Wis	Wisdom
1 Tim	1 Timothy	Zec	Zechariah
2 Tim	2 Timothy	Zep	Zephaniah
Ti	Titus		

TABLE OF CONTENTS

Day 1 : GOD   1
Day 2 : SON OF GOD   10
Day 3 : ETERNAL WORD   18
Day 4 : JESUS   26
Day 5 : EMMANUEL   34
Day 6 : SON OF DAVID   42
Day 7 : SON OF ABRAHAM   50
Day 8 : NEW ADAM   58
Day 9 : NAZARENE   65
Day10 : RABBI   73
Day 11 : PROPHET   81
Day 12 : MASTER   89
Day 13 : SON OF MAN   96
Day 14 : LAMB OF GOD   103
Day 15 : TEMPLE   110
Day 16 : WITNESS   118
Day 17 : CHRIST   125
Day 18 : SAVIOR   132
Day 19 : JUDGE   139
Day 20 : BREAD   146
Day 21 : LIGHT   153
Day 22 : GATE   160
Day 23 : SHEPHERD   167
Day 24 : RESURRECTION   174
Day 25 : LIFE   181
Day 26 : SERVANT   188
Day 27 : WAY   195
Day 28 : TRUTH   202
Day 29 : VINE   209
Day 30 : KING   216
Day 31 : CORNERSTONE   224
Day 32 : HEAD OF THE BODY   231
Day 33 : HIGH PRIEST   238
Day 34 : MEDIATOR   247
Day 35 : PEACE   253
Day 36 : POWER OF GOD   260
Day 37 : WISDOM OF GOD   267
Day 38 : DIVINE FULLNESS   276
Day 39 : ALPHA AND OMEGA   284
Day 40 : LORD   292
CONCLUSION   299

GOD

*E*ncountering the risen Christ, Thomas, the Apostle, makes a profession of faith in Jesus, addressing him as 'my God' (Jn 20:28). Jesus is, first of all, and above all else, 'God'. That is what He IS. We go back 2,000 years to a small village called Bethlehem in Palestine. There a male child was born in a stable. He was named Jesus. He grew up in obscurity in a Galilean village called Nazareth until He was thirty, and then began a public ministry that lasted only three years. But, He was destined to change the course of history forever. In human appearance, he was a kindly person and we're told in the pages of the Gospel that the common people heard Him gladly. He taught as one who had authority, and not as the teachers of the Law (Mt 7:29). It soon became apparent, however, that He was making shocking and startling statements about Himself. Jesus of Nazareth began to identify Himself as far more than a remarkable teacher or a prophet as the ordinary rural folk of Galilee thought He was. At the end of His public ministry, during which time He attracted much attention for His miracles and teachings, Jesus put the all-important question, 'Who do you say I am?' to those who closely followed Him as apostles. When Peter answered and said, 'You are the Christ, the Son of the living God' (Mt 16:15-16), Jesus was neither shocked nor did he rebuke Peter. On the contrary, He commended him and clarified the true meaning of His title, the Christ, in due course.

Jesus made His claims explicitly and His Jewish hearers got the full impact of His words. John testifies: 'The Jews tried all the harder to kill Him; not only was He breaking the Sabbath, but He was even calling God His own Father, making Himself equal with God' (Jn 5:18). When Jesus said, 'I and my Father are One' (Jn 10: 30), the Jewish people, who were strongly nourished in strict monotheism, could not tolerate such a claim and hence wanted to stone Him as per their tradition. Jesus asked them for which good work they wanted to kill Him and they replied: 'We are not stoning you for any of these but for blasphemy, because you, a mere man, claim to be God' (Jn 10:33). During His earthly life, Jesus not only manifested but also clearly claimed attributes that only God has. When a paralyzed man was let down through the roof wanting to be healed by Him, Jesus said, 'Son, your sins are forgiven' (Mk 2: 5). This caused a great stir among the religious leaders, who said in their hearts: 'Why does this fellow talk like that? He's blaspheming! Who can forgive sins but God alone?'(Mk 2:7). At the critical moment when His life was at stake, the high priest put the question to Him directly: 'Are you the Christ, the Son of the Blessed One?' and Jesus' reply was: 'I am'. He further said: 'And you will see the Son of Man sitting at the right hand of the

Mighty One and coming on the clouds of heaven'. The High Priest tore his clothes and told others in the Jewish Council, 'Why do we need any more witnesses? You have heard the blasphemy' (Mk 14:61-64). Jesus clearly equated a person's attitude to Himself with the person's attitude toward God: to know Him was to know God (Jn 8:19; 14:7). To see Him was to see God (Jn 12:45; 14:9); to believe in Him was to believe in God (Jn 12:44; 14:1); to receive Him was to receive God (Mk 9:37); to hate Him was to hate God (Jn 15:23) and to honor Him was to honor God (Jn 5:23).

Evidence from the Life of Jesus

Jesus had the credentials to authenticate His claim. He said: 'Even though you do not believe me, believe the evidence of the miracles that you may learn and understand that the Father is in me, and I in the Father' (Jn 10:38). He showed His power and authority over natural forces that belonged only to God, the author of these forces. He stilled a raging storm of wind and waves on the Sea of Galilee. In doing this, He provoked from those in the boat the awestruck question: 'Who is this? Even the wind and waves obey Him!' (Mk 4:41). He turned water into wine, fed thousands from five loaves and two fish, gave a grieving widow back her only son by raising him from the dead, and brought to life the dead daughter of a shattered father. To an old friend, He said, 'Lazarus, come forth!' and dramatically raised him from the dead. It is most significant that His enemies did not deny this miracle. Rather, they tried to kill Him. 'If we let Him go on like this', they said, 'everyone will believe in Him' (Jn 11: 48). Jesus demonstrated the Creator's power over sickness and disease. He made the lame walk, the dumb speak and the blind see. We may point out the case of the blind man. Though he couldn't answer his speculative questioners, he spoke with firm conviction: 'One thing I do know. I was blind but now I see'. He was astounded that his friends and interrogators didn't recognize his healer as the Son of God: 'Nobody has ever heard of opening the eyes of a man born blind', he said (Jn 9:25-32). Jesus' supreme credential to authenticate His claim to deity was His resurrection from the dead. In the course of His life He predicted that He would die. He also predicted how He would die- crucified on the cross. He foretold also that three days later He would rise from the dead. Jesus rose from the dead and appeared several times to His disciples proving His divinity to them.

The moral character of Jesus coincided with his claims as divine. Jesus Christ was sinless. The caliber of His life was such that He was able to challenge His enemies with the question, 'Can any of you prove me guilty of sin?' (Jn 8:46). He was met by silence, even though He addressed those who would have liked to point out a flaw in His character. We read about the temptations of Jesus in the Gospel narratives, but we never hear of a confession of sin on His part. He never asked for forgiveness, though He told his followers to do so. This lack of any sense of moral failure on Jesus' part is astonishing because it is completely contrary to the experience of the saints and the mystics in all ages and in all religious traditions. The closer men and women draw to God, the more overwhelmed they are with their own failures, infirmities and shortcomings. It is striking that Peter, John and Paul, all of whom, trained from earliest childhood as Jews to believe in the universality of sin, spoke of the sinlessness of Jesus: 'He committed no sin, and no deceit was found in His mouth' (1 Pt 2:22).

The divinity of Jesus affirmed by the early Church

The single most important development within the early church was the rise of cultic worship of the exalted Jesus within the primitive Palestinian Church. The first category of devotional action is Christian prayer practice, wherein God and Jesus were addressed and invoked together as seen in the earliest writings of the New Testament (1 Thes 3:11-13; 2 Thes 2:16-17; 3:5). In the earliest gatherings of Christian worship, it was a common practice to link Jesus with God and invoke them together as the source of all the divine blessings. Baptism was given in the name of Jesus, thus making Jesus the fundamental reference of the rite. Also the celebration of the Eucharist was associated with Jesus. It was not a memorial meal for a dead hero but for the risen Christ. Jesus is perceived as the living and powerful Lord who owns the meal and presides at it and with whom believers have fellowship as with God. Hymns, that formed a characteristic feature of Christian worship, were numerous in honor of Jesus, similar to the hymns honoring God. Prophecy in Christianity was associated with Christian worship and Jesus is identified as the source and authority of prophetic speech. In early Christianity we see a remarkable overlap in functions between God and Jesus as well as in the honorific rhetoric used to refer to them both. This cultic practice was well developed already by the 50s, just twenty years after the death and resurrection of Jesus and is taken for granted by Paul, as evidenced in his epistles. There seems to be no controversy about the divine titles to Jesus.

The key distinguishing feature of the early Christian communities was the prominent place of Jesus Christ in their religious thought and practice. From the beginning, devotion to Jesus as a divine figure constituted the religious life and thought of early Christianity. It was their firm belief that God has exalted Jesus to unique authority and status as 'Christ' and 'Lord'. So pronounced was this conviction that the term 'Christ' quickly became another name for Jesus in early Christian usage, as it continues to be the popular usage to this day. The exalted significance of Jesus appears astonishingly early in Christian circles. Jesus was treated as a recipient of religious devotion and was associated with God in striking ways. Devotion to Jesus emerges phenomenally early in the circles of His followers and can not be restricted to a secondary stage of religious development or explained as the product of extraneous forces. Also, devotion to Jesus was exhibited in an unparalleled intensity and diversity of expression for which we have no true analogy in the religious environment of the time. There is simply no precedent or parallel for the level of energy invested by early Christians in expressing the significance of divine Jesus for them in their religious thought and practice.

The uncompromising Jewish Monotheism

Christianity began as a movement within the Jewish religious tradition of the Roman period. The chief characteristic of Jewish religion in this period was its defiantly monotheistic stance. The Hebrew Scriptures present the nation of Israel as summoned to an exclusive worship of Yahweh, the one and true God. They also condemned the worship of other deities. Jewish faith was strictly monotheistic and the daily prayer, known as 'the Shema' began with the assertion: 'Hear, O, Israel, the Lord thy God is one God'. The Jews affirmed the belief in one God in distinction to the Hellenistic polytheistic concept of divinity as several gods. The earliest and clearest expression of a genuinely monotheistic belief which is a denial of the efficacy or reality of any other deity is found in Isaiah 43-48. This is a section of the book that is widely seen among the scholars as coming from the period of the Babylonian exile (sixth century BC). This suggests that although monotheism was always the firm belief of the people of Israel for whom Yahweh, their God, alone was the one and the only God and there was no other, it may have been the difficult and scandalous encounter with the many gods of other nations, during their painful exile that would have greatly solidified the exclusive and uncompromising monotheism of Judaism. In the Persian period and thereafter, this exclusive and uncompromising monotheism became fully identified with Jewish piety. Later, the religious crisis generated by the persecution of Antiochus IV further strengthened the strict monotheistic belief of the Jews. By the Roman period, failure to maintain such a monotheistic stance was perhaps the greatest sin a Jew could commit. In the time of Jesus, the Jewish people were very sensitive to any challenge to the exclusivity of the God of Israel. They also condemned the worship of many deities of the non-Jewish religions and of the human rulers like the Roman emperors as sheer stupidity and as the worst of many corrupt features of idolatrous Gentiles.

In numerous other matters, many (perhaps most) Jews showed a readiness to accommodate themselves, though in varying ways and degrees, to the Hellenistic culture. Language, dress, dining practices, intellectual categories and themes, sports and many other things were widely adopted. But there could be no negotiating away the monotheistic posture of Jewish religion. For devout Jews, the core requirement of Judaism was the exclusive worship of Yahweh, the one and the only true God. They refused any form of worship not only to the deities of other peoples and religious traditions but also to the 'divine agents' of the God of Israel. Even the angelic figures that formed part of God's vast heavenly entourage and the great human heroes in the Bible like Moses were not treated as rightful recipients of cultic worship in any known Jewish circles of the time. This shows that the Jews did not merely carry a negative attitude toward the deities of foreigners but faithfully practiced a genuinely exclusivist 'monotheism'. Of course, they certainly saw the heavens full of angels and made ample space for the involvement of various figures from God's heavenly entourage. However, the Jewish people were quite scrupulous in restricting full worship to the God of Israel alone. Their monotheistic commitment was always unwavering. God's universal sovereignty as creator and ruler over all, even over the evil forces that oppose God, was firmly upheld in Jewish belief. In the second temple Jewish tradition, especially during the time of Jesus and of the early Church, worship was withheld from others and was reserved exclusively to the one and only true God, Yahweh.

Devotion to the divine Jesus

The cultic worship practices express thanksgiving, praise, communion and petition that directly represent, manifest and reinforce the relationship of the worshipers with their deity. All the first Christians were Jews who were brought up in the strong exclusivist, uncompromising monotheism of their traditional faith and thus were used to worshiping Yahweh alone. That is why their accommodation of Christ as a recipient of their cultic devotion was a most unusual and significant step that cannot be easily accounted for, except by their strong belief in the divinity of Jesus. To accommodate Jesus with God as rightful recipient of worship is something unique among the early Christians, all of them Jews, and this practice existed right from the very first decade of the early Church as seen in Phil 2:6-11. As regards other deities, the early Christians had the same uncompromising attitude as their Jewish brethren. Thus, Paul refers to the pagan religious ceremonies as the worship of idols (1 Cor 8: 1, 4). He has scornful attitude toward the pagan deities which is characteristic of his Jewish background. Paul demands that his converts completely avoid participation in the worship of idols insisting that participation in the Christian meal (the cup of the Lord and the table of the Lord) is incompatible with joining in religious festivities devoted to other deities (1 Cor 10: 14-22). In fact, he calls those deities demons (1 Cor 10: 20-21). He has only contempt for the pagan deities that were worshipped in the Roman religious environment (Rom 1:18-25). Paul freely states a willingness to adapt himself to those Gentiles outside the law on a number of matters (1 Cor 9:21). However, he maintains a totally negative stance toward worship of anything or anyone other than the one God of Israel.

No doubt, Paul is firm in his faith in 'one God, the Father, from whom all things came and for whom we live' (1 Cor 8: 6). However, to his worship of one God, Paul also adds the worship of one Lord, Jesus Christ, 'through whom all things came and through whom we live' (1 Cor 8: 6). To Paul and to other Jewish Christians of his time, devotion to Christ was compatible with a vigorously monotheistic faith and practice. In the Book of Revelation also, we see a contrast between the worship of God (4-5) and the improper worship of the idols. There is a clear prohibition against the worship of the heavenly representatives of God as well as the demons and the idols that 'cannot see or hear or walk' (9:20-21). In this background, the scene in Revelation 5 is quite remarkable. The Lamb is pictured as receiving the idealized worship of the saints in heaven. What is evident to us is that the early Church, while it made a strong affirmation of exclusivist monotheism in belief and practice, yet at the same time included Christ along with God as rightful recipient of cultic devotion. Jesus is not reverenced as another deity of independent origin or significance. Instead, devotion to Him is characteristically expressed in terms of His relationship to the one true God, as His only Son. The New Testament claim is that it is the one God who has exalted Jesus to an exceptional position of reverence and given Him a name of divine significance (Phil 2: 9-11). It is God who requires that Jesus be reverenced as the divine Kyrios, the 'Lord'. According to Paul, reverence to Jesus brings glory to God, the Father (Phil 2:11). John would insist that to fail to give reverence to the 'Son' is to fail to give proper reverence to God, the Father (Jn 5:23; 1 Jn 2:22-23; 5:9-12). God and Jesus are positioned in a relation to each other that seems intended to avoid a worship of two gods. The accommodation of Jesus as recipient of cultic worship with God is unparalleled and signals a major and unique development in the monotheistic belief and the cultic worship of the early Church.

Jesus Himself revealed His identity as 'God'

How can we understand and account for the devotion to Christ among the early Jewish Christians? In Jesus' own lifetime, people were strongly polarized over His claims. At one end, ordinary Jewish people saw Jesus as only a teacher/rabbi or a prophet, in the model of Elijah or John the Baptist. At the other end, the Pharisees saw him as a false teacher or a magician. The powerful chief priests and the elders of the people usually opposed Him and insulted Him by calling Him names. The religious establishment considered Him a dangerous agitator against their Temple system and handed Him over to the Romans to be crucified. The execution by the inhuman and cruel crucifixion indicates a clear intent on their part to humiliate and eliminate an offender by the strongest available measure in Roman judicial usage. However, Jesus had many followers, all of them Jews, including some who were closely attached and keenly devoted to Him. They were also fully involved in His activities during His public ministry. Some followers, who were inspired by and drawn to Him, even left their normal occupations and their familial ties and formed a small band around Him as the apostles. These followers were committed to His teachings. To them, Jesus revealed His identity progressively as the circumstances arose like the healings and the exorcisms. It is revelation, first of all, by Jesus Himself about His identity as 'God' that constituted the basis of 'Jesus devotion' within the early Church. Of course, the early Jewish followers of Jesus were further enlightened and strengthened in their faith in Jesus as God after His resurrection and the reception of the Holy Spirit during the Pentecost.

Without doubt, devotion to Jesus as 'God' was an unparalleled innovation in the sense that a second figure was included with God in the devotional pattern of Christian groups who were at the same time strictly and firmly monotheistic. The encounters of the apostles with the Risen Christ were crucial for a correct understanding about the divinity of Jesus, but it only confirmed what Jesus has been teaching them all along about His identity as the beloved 'Son of God'. While confirming that God raised Him to an exalted status and clothed Him in glory and power, the encounters with the risen Jesus affirmed beyond doubt the revelation of Jesus about Himself as the one and only 'Son of God'. As a result, the early Jewish Christians did not hesitate to have devotion to the divine Jesus, along with their devotion to the God of Israel. For Paul also, the revelatory experience on the road to Damascus was very important for understanding the identity of Jesus as a divine person and promoting cultic devotion to Him among his converts.

Personal reflection - 'The descent of the divine'

The Gospels proclaim not an ascent of a man to the heights of divine, but a descent of Godhead to the human state with all its limitations, even death, so that humans may become the sons and the daughters of God. This is the kernel of the Gospel as good news. The Word was made flesh and dwelt among us (Jn 1:14). He emptied Himself, taking the form of a servant, being made in the likeness of man (Phil 2:6-7). Jesus possessed a human body, a human soul, a human will and a human consciousness, a human emotional life in the full and true sense. He became one of us, yet this man Jesus was always God. The majesty of God shone in Christ's countenance. In Jesus, God became true man, eternity broke through into time, the super-historical into the level of history and the divine into the human. Jesus became a man among men, and yet their king, their judge, and their savior, a man from heaven, yet a man - a man with body and soul, with a human mind, with a human will and emotions. Jesus was truly a human being yet also truly God. He made human nature so intimately and so utterly a part of Himself that it had no separate existence independent of the eternal Word of God. Its human consciousness, its human freedom and its human resignation were assumed into the unity of the person together with His divine nature, with its divine knowledge and its divine will. Being in the form of God, Jesus nevertheless emptied not His divinity in order to assume the form of a servant and become one of us. God appearing in human form is not unique to Christian faith. Indeed there are many mythologies in numerous religious traditions about 'avatar' or 'appearance' of gods in human form on earth in order to make the divine 'visible' to mankind. The incarnation of Christ is quite different from the 'avatar' because the humanity of Christ is not an illusion but real and true fact. By His incarnation, Christ became fully man. In being totally and fully one with mankind, He became the way and the sacrament by which God draws near to us and redeems us. In the entire religious history of mankind, there is no analogue to this fundamental Christian belief of the incarnation of Christ and the redemptive significance of Christ's humanity. He, who was perfectly divine with God, His Father, became perfect and complete man and in His humanity and by virtue of it, became the source and mediator of all divine blessings and offers the gift of salvation to the fallen mankind.

God is with us in Jesus Christ

God's own Son took to Himself human nature and entered (sin excepted) into solidarity with the human race. By becoming man, He became our brother, indeed the first-born of our brothers, not merely a man like us, but the man, the new man, the last Adam. We are linked with the incarnate God by the mysterious process of baptism. To be a Christian means to be taken up into participation in His life, passion and resurrection. The incarnation of the Eternal Word stands at the center of Christian faith. The pre-existent Son of God became truly man and through this mysterious union of the Godhead and manhood in His person, has become the mediator, redeemer and savior of mankind. In this mystery of Christ, whenever His human or divine nature is exclusively or falsely stressed, the whole of Christian faith is distorted or misdirected. There is one Jesus Christ, who is perfect man as well as perfect God. Hence He is not only with God but also with men. Precisely because He is at once perfect God and perfect man, He is able to be the perfect mediator through whom we come to God, the Father. Since the eternal word came down to us not in the form of God, but in that of a man and a servant, He becomes the creative principle of the new humanity. Before the coming of Jesus Christ, the existence of the entire human race languished and withered under the weight of original sin and inherited guilt. In the humanity of the only begotten Son, we received a new life. In Him, our human nature is brought into relation with Godhead and through union with Him is filled with divine glory. Hence Christ is redeemer, not in so far as He is God, nor in so far as He is Man, but because He is God-Man. That is why, in our Christian faith, we have to keep our focus on Jesus Christ as 'God made Man', wherein both His divinity and humanity are fully recognized and honored. The divine Savior joins, in space and time, new members to Himself, as the divine Head of the Body, the Church, until the end of age, when we, the ordinary mortals, will share in His divinity and thereby inherit everlasting glory as the children of God.

My brother is never too heavy for me to carry: A seven-year old boy used to carry his three-year old younger brother to church for the evening prayer almost every day. The distance from his house to the church, though a walking distance, was quite considerable. One day, as pastor, I asked him whether he found it hard to carry his younger brother to the church. He responded: 'My brother is never too heavy for me to carry'. Jesus, who was with God and who was God (Jn 1:1) found not the human form too heavy to carry for our salvation. He emptied himself of His glory as God and became a man and died on the cross. The descent of the divine Jesus is for the ascent of us, the human beings.

Quote: What does the Church think of Christ? The Church's answer is categorical and uncompromising, and it is this: That Jesus, the Carpenter of Nazareth was in fact and in truth, and in the most exact and literal sense of the words, the God 'by whom all things were made'. His body and brain were those of a common man; His personality was the personality of God, so far as that personality could be expressed in human terms. He was in every respect a genuine living man. However, He was not merely so as to be 'like God'- He was God - ***Dorothy L.Sayers***

Scripture reading for Day 1: Phil 2: 6-11

Prayer for Day 1: Heavenly Father! We thank you for Jesus your Son, who was God with you but became man for our sake. Fill us with your love and help us to be always grateful to you. Bless us and guard us as we strive to live in your love and journey towards our heavenly home. May Jesus Christ, your only Son, be always our light and life, our way and truth, during our earthly journey! Amen.

2

SON OF GOD

*W*e have seen that the early Christians had devotion to Jesus as 'God' which was an unparalleled innovation within the uncompromising monotheistic background of their Jewish tradition. They included the second figure of Lord Jesus Christ, along with God, in their cultic/devotional practices of worship. They honored Jesus as 'divine', even while they remained strictly and firmly monotheistic at the same time. As the result of their unwavering faith in the divinity of Jesus, they had to reconcile their traditional Jewish belief in one God with their faith in the divinity of Jesus. They did this, by honoring Jesus as the 'Son of God' which enabled them to preserve their monotheistic faith in one God, without in any way denying the divinity of Jesus. This does not mean that the title 'Son of God' is something these early Palestinian Jewish Christians invented for Jesus. Rather it was a title very much in vogue both in pagan and Jewish traditions. What the early Christians did was apply this title in a very unique way to Jesus, quite different from their own Jewish tradition as well as from the pagan environment. In this, they were guided by their own personal experiences with Jesus during His earthly ministry (1Jn 1:1-3), by their extraordinary encounter with the Risen Lord and above all, by the gift of light from the Holy Spirit. The disciples made a progressive understanding of the identity of Jesus as the 'Son of God' and perceived its full implications for their faith only after the resurrection of Jesus and the reception of the Holy Spirit. However, as we shall see later, already during His public ministry, Jesus was addressed many times as the 'Son of God'. This title is applied to Jesus 31 times in the Synoptic Gospels, 42 times in the Epistles, 23 times in John, where the title is most frequent, 3 times in Acts of the Apostles and once in the Book of Revelation. We present the pagan as well as the Jewish understanding of this title, before we explain the unique meaning of this title as applied to Jesus.

In the pagan traditions

Human or part-human offspring of the deities, quite commonly venerated in many religions and their mythologies, were called as the 'sons of God' among the pagans. For instance, in the Epic of Gilgamesh, one of the earliest recorded legends of humanity, Gilgamesh claimed to be of both human and divine descent and hence honored as a 'son of God'. Another well-known son of a god and a human is Hercules. A great many pantheons also included genealogies in which various gods were descended from other gods, and so the term 'son of a god' may be applied to many actual deities as well. Thus, this title was given frequently to demigods, heroes, kings and even priests. In Egypt, the kings called themselves the 'sons of God' and by the time of Jesus, the Roman emperors had taken over this Near Eastern practice and called themselves as the 'sons of God'. Evidently, the divine sonship was an accepted category in the pagan religious environment of the Roman era and those referred to as the sons of the gods were treated and venerated as divine beings.

In the Jewish tradition

The word 'son' was employed in the Jewish tradition to signify not only filiation but also other close connection or intimate relationship. Used in this way, the title 'son of God' is frequent in the Old Testament and was applied to persons having any special relationship with God. The angels were called the 'sons of God' (Gn 6:2-4; Jb 1:6; 2:1; Ps 29:1; 89:7). As heavenly creatures, they were considered as members of the divine order of being. The title was also given to the people of Israel (Dt 14: l), in virtue of Yahweh's choice, deliverance and covenant with them. For instance God says to Moses: 'Thou shall say to Pharaoh: Thus says the Lord: Israel is my son, my firstborn. I have said to thee: Let my son go, that he may serve me' (Ex 4: 22). God also declares: 'Israel is my son' (Hos 11:1. Is 63:9; Jer 31:9). In this way, the title 'son of God' expressed the unique covenant relationship of Yahweh with the people of Israel and implied that through His covenant, Yahweh adopted the people of Israel as His own children. In later usage, the title, 'son of God' referred to any devout Israelite as an individual person (Ps 73:15; Wis 2:13). Thus, a just man who practiced the virtues, especially generosity to the poor was 'like a son to the Most High' (Sir 4:10). What is of interest to us is that while the ancient Near East celebrated the divine filiation of kings and thus divinized the monarchs, the Old Testament honored not only the kings but also the angels, powerful persons, above all, the pious individuals as 'sons of God'. However, the people of Israel were very clear that divinity belonged only to God and to God alone. The king or emperor was no more than one man among others, subject to the same divine law and answerable to the same divine judgment as any human person. Thus, the kings of Israel were considered ordinary mortals. Only as leaders and representatives of the chosen people of Israel, they stood in special relationship to God. As the figurehead representing Israel, the king was decreed to be God's son. In the same way, the leaders of the chosen people like the judges, the princes and the priests were considered as holding authority from God and hence were called the sons of God.

In view of the special election and promise, David, especially was called as 'son of God' (2 Sm 7: 14; Ps 139: 27, 28). This royal birthright was passed on to Solomon and, by implication, to all future successors of the House of David. Thus, all the Davidic kings were honored with the title 'son of God'. The expected Messiah from the lineage of David, the Chosen One, the Elect of God was called the Son of God par excellence (Ps 2: 7). However, in the Hebrew Bible, the term 'son of God' does not connote any form of physical descent from or essential unity with God. Even the Messiah, as the 'son of God' par excellence was not given any preexisting heavenly traits in the Old Testament. When the Rabbis said that Messiah existed eternally with God, they meant merely that God knew who the messiah was from all eternity. In the Jewish tradition, the title 'son of God' indicated only a special status and relationship to God, without any indication of possessing divine nature. For Israel, it signified only the special acceptance by Yahweh, who assures His love and care, yet at the same time demands responsibility and obedience from His people and from His chosen instruments, such as the kings.

In the Christian tradition

The Gospels, in conformity with the Jewish tradition, used the expression 'sons of God' or 'children of God' to refer to anyone who enjoyed a special relationship with God. We present two examples: 'Blessed are the peacemakers, for they shall be called sons of God' (Mt 5:9); 'The son of Enosh, the son of Seth, the son of Adam, the son of God' (Lk 3:38). The Gospel of John declares that Jesus gave the right to become 'the children of God' to those who received Him and believed in His name (Jn 1: 12-13). Paul also makes a similar statement: 'The Lord Almighty says, 'I will be a Father to you, and you will be my sons and daughters' (2 Cor 6:18). However, both in the Gospels and in the Epistles, the title 'the Son of God' is applied, in a very special and unique way, only to Jesus Christ. As we have already mentioned, the first Christians, who were all Jews, in their attempt to preserve their monotheistic faith in one God without, at the same time, denying the divinity of Jesus, called Him, 'the Son of God'. Drawing from their own Jewish heritage, they expressed their firm belief in the special and unique relationship of Jesus with God, as His only Son. Does it mean that the conception of Jesus' divine sonship is derived uniquely and only from the faith of the early Christian community and not from Jesus? This question is relevant especially if we remember that in the Synoptic Gospels, Jesus calls Himself only 'the Son of Man', and never applies to Himself the title 'Son of God'. Every time this title is applied to Jesus in the Synoptic Gospels, only others call Him the 'Son of God': we see this, 9 times in Matthew, 5 times in Mark and 6 times in Luke. For instance, the angel Gabriel announced to Mary: 'He shall be great, and shall be called the Son of the Most High (Lk 1:32). Another clear instance of the application of the title to Jesus was the confession of Peter: 'Thou art Christ, the Son of the living God' (Mt 16:16). The devils called Him by the same name (Mk 5:7). In all these cases its meaning was equivalent to the Messiah, at least.

The Gospel according to Mark, the earliest of the Gospels, begins with the statement: 'The beginning of the Gospel of Jesus Christ, the Son of God' (Mk 1:1). According to Mark, no human being could know and proclaim in faith that Jesus is the Son of God before the ultimate act of mysterious revelation- Jesus' death on the cross. Only then could a human being, in this case, an outsider, a Gentile centurion involved in Jesus' execution, proclaim the most fundamental yet awesome Christian truth: 'Truly this man was Son of God' (Mk 15:39). Before that, only God, who knows the true identity of all, speaking from heaven at Jesus' baptism and transfiguration, could voice this truth of Jesus' divine sonship. We have the testimony of the Father, first at the Baptism of Jesus: 'Behold! a voice from heaven said, 'This is my beloved Son, in whom I am well pleased' (Mk 1: 11). The second was at Jesus' Transfiguration: 'And a voice out of the cloud said, 'This is my beloved Son, in whom I am well pleased' (Mk 9: 6). At Baptism, it is probable that only Christ and John, the Baptist, heard the voice from heaven. At the transfiguration, the three apostles heard the voice. We are told that they did not fully understand the significance of the heavenly declaration. The devils also, as supernatural beings, knew the true identity of Jesus, as the 'Son of God' as seen in the shouting of the man possessed by an evil spirit (Mk 5:7).

Testimony of Jesus Christ - in the Synoptic Gospels

Our interest is whether Jesus applied this title to Himself. First we examine the references in the synoptic Gospels. The only time He uttered the word 'our Father' was when He taught His disciples how to pray (Mt 6:9). Otherwise He always made a distinction between God as His Father (my Father) and God as the Father of all creatures (your Father). His claims to unique divine sonship are contained very clearly in the Synoptic Gospels, though not as frequently as in John. Even as a twelve year old, He asks His parents: 'Did you not know that I must be about my Father's business?' (Lk 2: 49). During His public ministry Jesus declares: 'Not every one that says to me, Lord, Lord, shall enter into the kingdom of heaven: but he that does the will of my Father who is in heaven, he shall enter into the kingdom of heaven' (Mt 7: 21-23). 'Everyone therefore that shall confess me before men, I will also confess him before my Father who is in heaven' (Mt 10: 32). 'I praise you, Father, Lord of heaven and earth, because you have hidden these things from the wise and prudent, and have revealed them to little children. Yes, Father; for this was your good pleasure. All things have been committed to me by my Father. No one knows the Son except the Father and no one knows the Father except the Son and those to whom the Son chooses to reveal Him' (Mt 11: 25-30; Lk 10: 21- 22). In the parable of the wicked tenants, Jesus speaks about Himself as the Son: 'This is the heir; come let us kill him' (Mk 12: 6-7). Jesus confessed before Caiphas that He was the Son of the blessed God (Mk 14: 61-2). In the final commission, Jesus asked the disciples to baptize also in the name of the Son: 'Go therefore, teach all the nations, baptizing them in the name of the Father and of the Son, and of the Holy Ghost' (Mt 26: 19- 20). From the above evidence, it is clear that Jesus, in fact, applied the title 'Son of God' to Himself, during His entire life on earth.

In the Gospel according to John

Throughout the Gospel according to John, Jesus always spoke of 'my Father', never of 'our Father'. We shall refer to a few passages from the Gospel: 'For the Father loves the Son, and shows Him all He does. Yes, to your amazement, He will show Him even greater things than these. Moreover, the Father judges no one, but has entrusted all judgment to the Son so that all may honor the Son, just as they honor the Father' (5: 20-23). 'And this is the will of my Father who sent me: that everyone who sees the Son, and believes in Him, may have life everlasting' (6: 40). 'Father, the hour has come, glorify your Son, that your Son may glorify you. And now, Father, glorify me in your presence with the glory I had with you before the world began' (17:1, 5). We see Christ referring specifically to Himself as the unique Son of God in the most famous verse of the Bible: 'God so loved the world that He gave His one and only Son' (3:16). Nathanael, one of the disciples, tells Jesus: 'Rabbi, you are the Son of God; you are the King of Israel' (1: 49). When Jesus was brought before Pilate, the Jews said, 'We have a law, and according to that law He must die, because He claimed to be the Son of God' (Jn 19:7). Death was the penalty for blasphemy (Lv 24:16). If Jesus were only speaking metaphorically, the Jews would not have brought Him to trial on such a serious charge as blasphemy. The Jews knew and understood Ps 82: 6: 'You are gods. You are all sons of the Most High'. They had no problem with metaphorical statements. The Jews objected to Jesus claiming to be the unique, eternal, 'Son of God' and condemned Him to death on the grave charge of blasphemy. Jesus paid with His life for His declaration about His true identity. There is no doubt that when Jesus called Himself as 'Son of God' He did not mean it in a metaphorical sense, but rather in a very real and authentic way.

Personal reflection - 'You are my beloved Son'

The names 'the Beloved' and 'My beloved Son' as addressed by the Father from heaven during the baptism and transfiguration of Jesus indicate an intimate relationship between the Father and the Son which transcends all that is true of man's communion with God. Jesus is 'Son of God' in a very unique way, beyond our simple human understanding. It took the Church several centuries to understand, though only a little, the great mystery of the divine sonship of Jesus and make a doctrinal statement in the Council of Chalcedon in 451 AD: 'One and the same Christ, Son, Lord, only-begotten, proclaimed in two natures, without confusion, without change, without division, without separation'. The philosophical concepts of 'Person' and 'Nature' were used in the above statement and the title 'Son of God' was explained to mean that Jesus exists as one divine person but has two natures, divine and human. The Church proclaimed this statement as undisputable doctrine to be accepted and believed by all the members of the Church. Beyond this doctrinal declaration about Jesus as the 'Son of God', our interest is how Jesus personally experienced His own unique relationship to God as

His Son during His earthly life. Let us examine the first public declaration of the Father during the Baptism of Jesus. Luke records that Jesus was sitting by the river praying when He saw the heavens torn open, and the Spirit descend upon Him like a dove, and that a voice then came from the heavens, saying, 'You are my beloved, with you I am well pleased' (Lk 3:22). There is no doubt that those most consoling words reflect the intimacy between the Father and the Son. A person of profound prayer and contemplation, Jesus must have always searched, from His early youth, to know who He was and what He was supposed to do. Then, after His baptism, He heard these words of affirmation and confirmation, when God declared to Jesus: 'You are my beloved Son'. He was so lovingly confirmed by the Father in His true identity, His vocation and His calling. He is 'the Beloved Son of God'.

For the rest of His life, He would understand about Himself and His mission in the light of this great revelation from His Father. He accepted His special identity, welcomed it and honored it. He would never deny His identity even at the cost of His life when He was accused of blasphemy. When asked by the Jewish Council, 'Are you then the Son of God?' Jesus unhesitatingly answered: 'You are right in saying I am'. Those in the Council said: 'Why do we need any more testimony? We have heard it from His own lips' (Lk 22: 70-71). What a scene! Stripped of everything and facing His terrible death, Jesus kept His claims intact. Jesus remained true to His identity until His final breath on the cross. Always faithful to His calling and mission that His Father gave Him, Jesus lived His entire life in a relationship of intimate love with His Father. He accepted all the consequences of total obedience to God's will, which led Him to the way of the cross and crucifixion and finally a disgraceful death like a criminal. After Jesus was confirmed as God's beloved Son at Baptism, He went forward into the world and called people to trust God and love Him, as He proclaimed the unconditional and everlasting love of His Father that He Himself was experiencing every moment of His life, as His only Son. He would trust God even when everything seemed to fall apart and His death approached near. Jesus lived His whole life on earth within the framework of His core identity as God's beloved Son.

The obedient Son of God

The title 'Son of God' is a messianic title and as such it had messianic implications for the Jews. They waited for the Messiah whom they expected to be a political ruler with mighty power. It was given to Jesus to clarify the role of Messiah in the history of salvation. During the temptation, Satan offered Jesus the guarantee of stupendous power and glory (Mt 4: 3-6). Jesus rejected Satan and chose to follow God's plan for Him. He came to the world to do God's will alone, which meant not enjoying power and glory as offered by Satan, but suffering the humiliation of death on the cross, for the love of the Father. When Peter made the profession of faith identifying Jesus as the 'Son of the living God', Jesus would immediately affirm that He should suffer and die to be the 'beloved Son' of the Father (Mt 16:16-21). The Heavenly Father, in His turn, would affirm for the second time, during the transfiguration of Jesus that He was well pleased with the total obedience of His 'Son' (Mt 17:5). After seeing how Jesus died on the cross, the centurion would declare, 'Surely this man was the Son of God' (Mk 15: 39). Only by doing God's will, till His death, did Jesus affirm His divine sonship before the world. But the cross was not the end for the 'Son'. Through resurrection, the Father confirmed the claims of Jesus, especially before Caiphas and the Jewish Council that He was indeed the 'Son of God'. The Father authenticated His unique and profound relationship with Jesus by exalting Him to glory and establishing Him in power. Seated at the right hand of the Father, Jesus communicates to men the eternal life that comes from the Father (1 Jn 5:11). He who believes in the 'Son' has life everlasting (Jn 6:40) and he who does not believe is condemned (Jn 3:18). Now, to the Christians, as believers in Jesus, who is the one and only 'Son of God', is granted the privilege of becoming the adopted 'sons' and 'daughters' of God (Gal 3:26; Eph 1:5). The people of Israel enjoyed this honor through election and covenant. Now, through faith in Jesus and through rebirth in baptism, the Christians are granted the blessing of being the children of adoption through the power of the Holy Spirit, by the union with the only Son of God (Rom 6:4). Jesus revealed to us that His Father, the Creator of the universe, invites each one of us to be 'the beloved child of God'. We understand that, in and through Jesus, especially through the sacrament of baptism, all of us have become the beloved sons and daughters of God. As we are aware of our true identities, like Jesus, let us remain faithful to our noble calling to be God's beloved children. Let us seek to do God's will everyday of our lives, whatever it may entail. Living as the beloved children of God means, above all, that we live always rooted in the intimate relationship of love with our beloved heavenly Father, just as Jesus did. It also means loving and serving others, our neighbors, as God's beloved children, following the good example of Jesus Christ, the only 'Son of God'.

He is always my beloved son: In a poor peasant family of a rural parish where I served as pastor, the oldest and the only son went to the Christian University in the nearby city. The parents labored all day long in the fields in order to pay for the high cost of the university education. It was their hope that after graduation he would get good employment and earn well in order to take care of the family and meet the huge expenses of the marriage of his three younger sisters. But the son wasted the hard earned money and precious time in the luxuries of the city and failed in the examination. When this report from the University reached the illiterate parents, the father came to me for the explanation of the report. When I told him about the failure of his son and how it happened, I thought he would be very angry with his son. Quite calm, he told me: 'He is always my beloved son. I will encourage him to do better next time'. God always loves us. Even when we fail, He forgives us and lovingly calls us to repentance and conversion, saying to us: 'You are always my beloved children'.

Quote: Behold the amazing gift of love the Father has bestowed on us, the sinful sons of men, to call us the 'sons of God'- ***Scottish Paraphrases***

Scripture reading for Day 2: Gal 3: 26-29 & 4: 1-7

Prayer for Day 2: Loving Father, through your Son, you have made us your adopted children. We thank you for accepting us as your sons and daughters. Open our hearts to your love and fill us with the gifts of your Holy Spirit. Make of us the instruments of your compassion and love in this world! Amen.

3

ETERNAL WORD

B y 'Word', we may imply many things, but they are fully related to one another. Thus, word signifies the external sound that communicates an idea as speech, the internal thought or concept communicated by that sound, above all, the very thought itself that comes to us through the use of our reason or intelligence. We owe to the great ingenuity of John, the author of the fourth Gospel, for naming Jesus as the eternal 'Word', 'Logos' in Greek language, in which he wrote his gospel. No doubt, 'logos' was the greatest philosophical title applied to Jesus in the New Testament. The name of Jesus as 'word' is used only by John, in the Prologue to his Gospel 1:1-18, and in the opening words of his first letter, where he states: 'we proclaim concerning the Word of life' (1Jn 1:1). Paul, without using this title, attributes to Jesus eternal preexistence, as does John. For instance, we see this attribution in his beautiful hymn in his letter to the Colossians 1:15-20. The writer of the letter to the Hebrews also affirms, like John, that God created the universe through His Son, thereby assigns preexistence to Jesus: 'In these last days, God has spoken to us by His Son, through whom He made the universe' (Heb 1:2). However, it was given to John alone, to use the title 'the eternal Word' to express his Christology or his understanding of Jesus. In doing so, was John influenced by the non-Jewish, Greek, more specifically the Stoic philosophical system that conceived 'logos' as an intelligent principle, an intermediate being separate from God? It is quite possible that John might have been impacted by the Stoic philosophy, since he wrote his Gospel and his letters to the Gentile converts, who were familiar with Greek philosophy. He might have communicated his understanding of the preexistence of Jesus in non-Jewish Hellenistic philosophical categories. However, his inspiration came from the biblical/Jewish traditions, as presented in the Old Testament literature. As a pious Jew, he drew from his Jewish religious heritage and Jewish sacred scriptures to explain the preexistence of Jesus and His role in the creation and in the redemption of the world.

John presents the faith of the early Jewish Christians

In the Old Testament, the 'Word of God', that comes as His personal and divine 'communication' to human beings, assumes a sort of quasi-independent existence as seen in: 1 Kgs 17:2; 18:1; Is 38:4; Jer 1:2, 4; 2:1; 11:1; Ez 3:16; 11:14; 12:1 ; Ps 148:18. The personification of Wisdom (Prv 8: 22-31; Wis 7:22-8:1; Sir 1:24; Bar 3-4) and the depiction of Wisdom as both independent of God and identical with God, above all, as God's companion in creation (Prv 8; Sir 24:1-22; Wis. 9:9) seem to be the direct
18

inspiration for John's presentation of Jesus as God's eternal Word. The Creation narrative of Genesis 1, with its focus on the Word of God that brought order out of chaos, appears to be the background to the famous Prologue of John, which declares that the Word existed 'in the beginning', 'with God', and was as indeed 'divine' (Jn 1:1). When John presents Jesus as the Word, it is more than the personification of a divine attribute of God. The 'Word' is a person, and the activity of the Word is personal: He is the agent in creation and the source of life and light (Jn 1:3). The Word existed outside the limits of time and place, neither of which existed in the beginning. The Word preexisted human history. It did not preexist for its own sake, but in relationship with God, as God's own Word. God and the Word are distinct and not the same, yet they are inseparably united in love. They retain their uniqueness despite the oneness that flows from their intimacy. Never denying the divine status of the 'Word', at any time, John presents the 'Word' as a definite entity that existed separately from God. That is how the 'Word' that descended from heaven, could take flesh and establish residence among us (Jn 1:14). The first Christians believed without any hesitation that Jesus had come from God for the redemption of all mankind and that the final salvation of the human race was to be realized only through Jesus Christ.

John firmly insists that Jesus, as the preexistent Word, always existed with the Father (Jn 1:1). He did not come into being only after being born in Bethlehem as a child. He was present throughout all the endless ages of past eternity. John also declares that Jesus is also the creative Word, the energy behind the creation of the universe (Jn 1:3). Here, John only affirms the strong belief of the early Church. In line with Jewish apocalyptic literature that spoke of the end of age, the first Christians looked forward to the return of the Lord Jesus, as He promised in several discourses, at the end of time. From reflecting on the role of Jesus at the end of time, it was just another small but very natural step for the early Christians, all Jews, to contemplate the role of Jesus at the beginning of time. In this way, they acquired a very strong belief that Jesus was also in some way 'there' with and in God before the creation of the world. They attributed to Jesus not only preexistence but also an active role, as divine agent, in the process of the creation of the universe. In his Prologue, John explains this firm belief of the early Christians to the predominantly Gentile converts under his pastoral care, especially in Ephesus, where he lived most of his life, until his death. By the time John was writing the fourth Gospel, around 90-100 AD, the Church, initially made up of the Jewish Christians of Palestine, had already reached out to the corners of the vast Roman Empire and its membership had become predominantly Gentile. The extraordinary ministry of Paul, the apostle, contributed in no small measure, along with numerous other dedicated ministers of the Gospel, to the speedy spread of the Christian faith throughout the territories of the Roman Empire and far beyond. To the Gentile converts, John presented the faith of his fellow Jewish Christians who constituted the primitive Church.

19

The Gentile converts and the Greek Philosophy

The Gentile converts, like other Gentiles in the Roman Empire, were familiar with Greek philosophy, and for them, especially for the Greeks, 'Logos' meant 'Reason'. Any keen observer looking at nature can easily see the unvarying patterns of dependable order. Night and day come with unfailing regularity. The year keeps its seasons in unvarying course. The stars and the planets move in their unaltering path. Who created this 'order' and now maintains it in the universe? The Greeks answered that 'logos', the mind of God, brought 'order' to the world and keeps it going. It is the same 'logos' that gives man intelligence and power to know, to think, to analyze and to reason, thereby making man a 'rational' and 'intelligent' being. John would declare to the Gentile converts who were familiar with the concept of 'logos' that Jesus, the Lord, is, in fact, the 'logos' of God. The Greek concept of 'logos', by strange coincidence, originated in Ephesus, the same city where John wrote his Gospel, some 650 years later. In 560 BC, an Ephesian philosopher, named Heraclitus, spoke about 'logos' for the first time. According to him, everything in the universe was in a state of flux. Things changed moment to moment. He illustrated this principle by pointing out that in a river, a person cannot step into the same water twice, as water is continuously moving. In the same way, in the universe, everything is in a state of flux and things change constantly. Then how is there stability and order, preventing chaos and disorder in the universe? Heraclitus explained that 'logos' assured the stability of the universe by maintaining 'order' in the midst of change. As a result of 'logos', there is a design and a pattern in the universe, revealing a definite plan and purpose. Heraclitus called the logos the 'universal reason'. The same 'logos' dwelling within man gave him the ability to judge right and wrong, good and bad. The Stoic philosophers further elaborated Heraclitus' thinking by proposing that the 'logos' pervaded the entire universe, remaining within it as the power that maintained order, the reason that gave purpose and the intelligence that brought stability. For the Stoics, 'logos' contained the germ of all things.

A Jewish philosopher living in Alexandria in the first century AD, Philo Judaeus, a great scholar who combined the great insights of both the Jewish and the Greek worlds, brought together under the single concept 'logos' both the Jewish understanding of 'word' and the Greek understanding of 'reason'. In the writings of Philo, the two meanings of 'logos' as 'Word' and 'Reason' come together and remain closely intertwined. For Philo, the 'logos' was the aggregate of ideas in the Divine Mind. According to him, 'logos' was the thought of God stamped upon the universe. God made the universe and all the things that exist, through 'logos'. Man's mind was also stamped with 'logos' and thus 'logos' gave man the power to know and to think as an intelligent and rational being. According to him, the 'logos' is the intermediary between God and the world. To the Gentile converts and to other Greeks interested in the Gospel, John declared that the same eternal 'logos' which they know as the power through whom the world was created, the power that keeps order in the universe, the power that gives man the ability to know right and wrong and good and bad, came to the world, in the person of Jesus Christ. Indeed, the 'logos', the mind of God, lived and walked in the world as a human being and spoke the truth of the Gospel in the person of Jesus of Nazareth. John makes a profound proposition to his Gentile converts using their own Greek philosophical categories. At the same time, he also brings them the wonderful insights from his Jewish heritage about the 'Word' of God.

Yahweh, the only God who speaks

We see that many peoples of widely scattered cultures around the world have a belief in the distinct reality of the spoken word as a dynamic entity. The spoken word is especially important in a culture which writes little or not at all. Sometimes, this belief in the efficacy of the word degenerates into magic. The word is manipulated resulting in the perversion of a genuine belief in the power of the word. Even in our ordinary use, we understand the efficacy and the power of the word: It is the word that gives intelligibility to things; a thing does not acquire full reality and meaning until it is given a name and only then does it become intelligible to us. Words uttered with solemnity such as the words of vows and promises carry great responsibility and obligation because the words are 'to be kept' as a mark of sincerity and honesty. Words that reach out from the present to the future, such as blessings and curses, carry power. Belief in the power and efficacy of the word was very strong in the ancient Semitic world of the Near East and Egypt and the people of Israel were no exception. For instance, we see in Genesis 27 that the words of blessing, reserved to be conferred upon the firstborn, could not be withdrawn once spoken by Isaac to Jacob and as a result, Esau, the firstborn, suffered a terrible deception and wept (Gn 27: 30-38).

The people of Israel became monotheistic not because of human reason and philosophical speculation but because 'Yahweh, their one true God, spoke to their Fathers, then to Moses, in order to make Himself known as the 'only God' (Ex 3: 3-15). 'They have mouths and they do not speak' (Ps 115:5). This mockery of the 'mute' idols, the pagan gods, brings to focus one of the most important characteristics of the living God of Israel, the 'God who speaks' as portrayed in the Old Testament. The Hebrew Scriptures affirm this important and unique religious experience of the people of Israel: Yahweh communicated with His chosen people by speaking to them. His Word, in turn, became their law and rule of life. At the time of the covenant on Mount Sinai, God gave His people, through Moses, a moral and religious charter that was summed up in 'ten words', the Decalogue (Ex 20:1-17). As they stood before the presence of God on Mount Sinai and heard Him speak directly to them from the center of the cloud (Ex 20:1), the first and foremost realization of the people of Israel about their God was that Yahweh was someone who 'speaks' and 'reveals' Himself. His voice thundered as He spoke: 'I am Yahweh, your God, who has brought you out of the land of Egypt' (Ex 20:2). In their history as the people of the covenant and nation of election, they heard the 'Word' of Yahweh not only as an intelligible message directed to men and their affairs, but also as a dynamic reality that infallibly achieves the effects that Yahweh aims to accomplish: 'My word that goes forth from my mouth shall not return void but do my will, achieving the end for which I sent it' (Is 55: 11). 'Not a single word has gone unfulfilled' (1 Kgs 8:56). The very first verses of their Holy Scripture declare that God spoke and the universe came into being. The people of Israel present their entire religious experience with the firm conviction: 'Yahweh spoke and it was' (Gn 1). 'By the word of the Lord were the heavens made, their starry host by the breadth of His mouth' (Ps 33: 6). Since the time of creation, the very same Word has remained active in the universe, ruling the stars (Is 40:26), the waters of the deep (Is 44:27) and all natural phenomena (Ps 107: 25). The Word of God lives forever (Is 40 8). The Rabbinic literature, whenever it referred to the word of God, used the Aramaic word 'Memra' which was a personified attribute of God.

Yahweh spoke to His chosen people through His messengers- the patriarchs, the judges and the prophets whom He appointed and sent to His people on His behalf. The divine word was not given to these chosen instruments of God as an esoteric teaching to be hidden from others. Rather, His 'word' was a message to be transmitted, not to a small circle but to the entire people of God, to whom God wished to communicate His word through His chosen spokesmen in order to provide guidance and to demand fidelity to His covenant. So, the experience of Word of God was not the privilege of a small number of mystics, but the blessing for the entire community, as all of Israel was called to listen to God's word. As He put His own words into the mouth of His messengers, God gave them sufficient power to fearlessly transmit the message entrusted to them (Jer 1:6-10). As for the hearers of the Word, they had to prepare a confident and docile reception in their hearts and welcome it. Israel received the divine Word under three aspects: Law, Revelation and Promises. God spoke and gave them the 'Law', their rule of life. God revealed to them His plan of salvation, assuring them that He would carry out His plan in all its fullness. God's plan consists of His promises for the salvation of mankind. In fact, all of human history can be conceived as the fulfillment of God's promises (Dt 9:5; 1 Kgs 2:4; Jer 11:5). God assured Israel again and again that He would always remain faithful and always keep His promises.

Jesus, the 'Word of God'

The early Christians, all of them Jews, saw in Jesus the final utterance of the 'Word' of God: 'God spoke to our fathers at many times and in a multiplicity of ways. But in these last days, He has spoken to us through His Son (Heb 1:1-2). In Him and through Him, the creative Word of God came as a person to speak and to work among human beings and to accomplish their salvation here on earth. He is the true light that reveals God to the world (Jn 1:4). His words have spirit and life (Jn 6:63). He speaks with authority and certitude (Mk 1:22). Jesus proclaimed the 'word' as the Gospel of the Kingdom of God (Mk 4:33), making known through parables the mysteries of the Kingdom. By His 'word', Jesus accomplished the miracles as the signs of arrival the kingdom in His own person (Mt 8:8, 16; Jn 4: 50-53). By His 'word', He forgave sins (Mt 9:1-7). By His 'word', He gave His powers to the twelve (Mt 18:18; Jn 20:23). By His 'word' He instituted the sign of the new covenant, the Eucharist (Mt 26: 26-29). 'His words will not pass away' (Mt 24: 35), as 'they are the words of eternal life' (Jn 6:68). However, His words are received differently by the listeners, as illustrated in the parable of the sower. All hear the word, but only those who understand it (Mt 13:23) or accept it (Mk 4:20) or keep it (Lk 8:15), see its fruit in them. At the conclusion of the Sermon on the Mount, where He has just proclaimed the new Law, Jesus contrasts the condition of those who hears His words and put them into practice and those who hears them but do not put them into practice (Mt 7: 24-26). The first is a house built on rock and the second a house built on sand. These metaphors introduce a perspective of judgment. Each person will be judged according to his attitude toward the Word: 'Whoever shall be ashamed of me and my words, the son of Man shall also be ashamed of him when He comes in His Father's glory (Mk 8:38). John shows that a division is brought about by His words (10:19). On the one hand are those who believe (2:22) who hear His word (5:24) who keep it (8:51), who dwell in it (8:31) and in whom it dwells (15:7). These have eternal life (5:24), and they shall never see death (8:51). On the other hand, there are those, who find this Word too hard (6:60) who cannot hear it (8:34) and who by this fact refuse it and reject Christ. These will be judged by the very Word of Jesus on the last day (12:48) because it is not His word, but that of the Father (12:49), who is truth (17:17). It is therefore one and the same thing to take a position regarding the word of Jesus, regarding His person, and also regarding God.

Personal reflection- 'the Word of eternal life'

John gives us a profound insight about the mystery of the divine Word, by identifying it in the strictest manner with the very mystery of Jesus, the Son of God. Insofar He is god's Son Jesus is the subsistent Word, the 'eternal Word' of God. It is from Him that every manifestation of the divine Word in creation, in history and in the final work of salvation is ultimately derived. In Old Testament times, He was already manifesting Himself secretly under the guise of the creative and revelatory Word of God and Wisdom. Finally, in the fullness of time, this Word entered openly into history: 'After having spoken to our fathers through the prophets, God speaks to us through His Son' (Heb 1:1). The Word was made flesh and dwelt among us (Jn1:14). He then became the object of man's concrete experience (1Jn 1:1-2), in such a way that 'we have seen His glory' (Jn 1:14). As 'the Son', He has made the Father known to men (Jn 1:18) in order to save men. He has brought grace and truth into the word (Jn1:14-16). Henceforth the Word, manifested to the world as Jesus Christ, is at the very heart of human history. Before His coming, history looked towards His incarnation. After His coming, history looks to His final triumph. In the fullness of time, according to God's plan and His promise, He will manifest Himself in the last days and engage Himself in the final battle to end the workings of the evil powers and assure the definitive victory of God here on earth (Rv 19:13).

Until then, during the course of human history, the attitude of the human beings regarding His word determines their openness towards God and brings about an effective division in mankind as those who receive and those who reject the word. On the one hand, the darkness has not received Him (Jn 1: 5) and the evil world has not known Him (Jn 1: 10) and the leaders of the chosen people rejected Him (Jn 1:11) leading to His passion and death. The event of the death and resurrection of Jesus becomes the 'word'of good news, the Gospel, that has to be preached to all the nations until the end of time (Mk 16:15). To those who receive the Gospel and believe in His holy name (Jn 1:12), He, who is the Son of God by nature (Jn 1:18) gives the power to become the children of God by adoption (Jn 1:12). His 'word' becomes the 'Holy Scripture', that ' is God-breathed, and is useful for teaching, rebuking, correcting and training in righteousness, so that the children of God may be thoroughly equipped for every good work (2 Tim 3:16). Molded by God's word, they receive from the fullness of His grace blessing after blessing (Jn 1:16) in this life and the heavenly inheritance in the life to come.

I have to keep my word: Some years ago I was serving in a very poor rural parish. The parish had long suffered from disunity because of numerous factions. In order to promote unity and fellowship and at the same time increase devotion to the crucified savior, I proposed to build a Calvary near the Church. I asked the people to donate cement, stones and other required material. A young man from the parish, working in a far away city more than a thousand miles away who happened to have come home for holidays, promised me that he would buy a huge crucifix to be at the center of the Calvary. The construction of Calvary was nearing the end. I did not hear from the young man either about the crucifix or about the amount to buy it. On the very last day, suddenly there he appeared with a huge beautiful crucifix. He told me: 'I have to keep my word at all cost'. I thought at that time: 'If human beings are so much concerned about their 'word', what about God and His 'eternal Word'!

Quote: 'What God's Son has told me, take for true I do. Truth Himself speaks truly or there is nothing true' - ***Thomas Acquinas***

Scripture reading for Day 3:Mt 13: 1-23

Prayer for Day 3: Loving Father! Guide your people that we may always reject what is displeasing to you and seek to do what is pleasing to you. May we become your loving children by hearing the words of Jesus and keeping them in good and docile heart! Help us to find pleasure in understanding your words and keeping them in our lives! Amen.

JESUS

4

To the Hebrews, like other Semitic people, a name was more than just an identifying title for a person. A name carried with it the essence of a person - the character, reputation, especially reputation by inheritance, authority, worth, ownership, and many other attributes descriptive of the person and all that the person represents. Numerous examples in the Bible show that a name was considered descriptive of the nature and the character of the person. A name signified what the person or being represented. God named or changed the names of individuals to reflect the purpose for which He used them. Those names tell us of the individual's role and purpose in God's great plan.

God gives names people to signify His purpose

God changed Abram's name to Abraham when he became a friend of God by faith. God, through His covenant with him, made Abraham the founder of the nation of Israel. Abram meant 'exalted father' and Abraham meant 'father of a multitude'. God said: 'My covenant with you is this: you are to become the father of a host of nations. No longer shall you be called Abram; your name shall be Abraham, for I am making you the father of a host of nations' (Gn 17:5). Earlier, God named Hagar's son, whom she bore to Abraham, 'Ishmael'. God said to Hagar: 'You are now pregnant and shall bear a son; you shall name him Ishmael. For the Lord has heard you, God has answered you' (Gn 16:11). In Hebrew, Ishmael means 'God has heard'. God changed the name of Abraham's wife from Sarai to Sarah. Both are variant forms of the same name and the meaning of both names was a 'princess'. God said to Abraham: 'As for your wife Sarai, do not call her Sarai; her name shall be Sarah. I will bless her and I will give you a son by her' (Gn 17:15-16). God named their son 'Isaac', which means 'laughed'. God said to Abraham: 'You shall call him Isaac. I will maintain my covenant with him as an everlasting pact, to be his God and the God of his descendants after him' (Gn 17: 19).

God changed the name of Jacob to Israel. He said to Jacob: 'You shall no longer be spoken of as Jacob, but as Israel, because you have contended with divine and human beings' (Gn 32: 28; 35:10). Israel actually means 'you contended with the divine beings'. God named Solomon, the son of David, Jedidiah: 'The Lord sent the prophet Nathan to name him Jedidiah, on behalf of the Lord' (2 Sm 12: 25). God gave a name to the son of the prophet

Isaiah to warn of the imminent Assyrian invasion: 'The Lord said to me: Name your son Maher-shalal-hash-baz. For before the child knows how to call his father or mother by name, the wealth of Damascus and the spoil of Samaria shall be carried off by the king of Assyria' (Is 8:3-4). God asked the prophet Hosea to name his children Jezreel, Lo-ruhama and Lo-ammi' (Hos 1:4), as a sign of punishment for the bloodshed at Jezreel (2 Kgs 15: 8-10) and His rejection of Israel, as shown in the names: Lo-ruhama means 'she is not pitied' and Lo-ammi means 'not my people'. The name 'John' was given by the angel to the son of Zechariah and Elizabeth (Lk 1:13), who would later be called John the Baptist. We are quite familiar with how Saul became Paul after his encounter with the Risen Lord. Saul was the Jewish name of the Apostle, meaning 'desired'. Paul, his Greek name, means 'small or little'. In the service of the Lord Jesus Christ, Paul chose to be a small and humble servant for the glory of His holy name.

The name 'Jesus' in Jewish history

The name 'Jesus' tells us a great deal about His mission in God's great plan. It was the name given by God Himself. The angel told Joseph: 'You are to give Him the name Jesus, because He will save His people from their sins' (Mt 1: 21). The angel also told Mary: 'You will be with child and give birth to a son, and you are to give Him the name Jesus' (Lk 1:31). The name, 'Jesus' is derived from the Hebrew 'Yeshuah' which means 'God is Salvation'. Yeshuah was not uncommon in the days of Jesus. To the Hebrew mind, so eagerly expecting God's salvation which the Messiah would bring, the name held much significance. The angel's message to Joseph implied that 'God's salvation' was coming to the world through his child. The name revealed Jesus' mission in God's plan: it was through Him that God would offer His salvation to the world and save mankind from sin, evil and death and their source, the Devil, the author of corruption and destruction.

The Hebrew original of the name 'Jesus' comes from Joshua, son of Nun, who became Moses' assistant (Ex 33:11) and successor. The name of Joshua was originally 'Hosea' or 'Howshea' meaning 'deliverer'. Moses modified his name to 'Yehoshua' meaning 'Yahweh saves' (Nm 13: 16). During the Babylonian captivity, the name was shortened to 'Yeshua' meaning 'he will save' (Neh 8:17). The name is exactly the same in Aramaic: 'Yeshua' is found in an Aramaic portion of the book of Ezra (5:2). Though this name in one form or another occurs frequently in the Old Testament, it was not borne by any person of prominence between the time of Joshua, the son of Nun and Joshua, the son of Jozadak. The latter built the temple of Jerusalem with Zerubbabel (Ezr 5: 2), after the return from the exile of Babylon. It was also the name of the author of the book of Ecclesiasticus (Eccl 50:27), perhaps, one of the ancestors of Jesus, mentioned in the genealogy found in Luke's Gospel (Lk 3:29). One of

Paul's companions was called by this name (Col 4:11). During the Hellenizing period, Jason, a purely Greek version of the name 'Jesus', appeared to have been adopted by many (1 Mc 8:17; 12:16; 14:22).

Greek and Latin translation of the name 'Jesus'

Two hundred years before Jesus was born, Jewish scribes translated the Old Testament into Greek. They transliterated the Hebrew 'Yehoshua' and 'Yeshua' into Greek as 'Iesou' (Yay-soo). The Jewish scribes who translated the Septuagint or LXX, in order to conform to proper Greek grammar, added the 's' ending to Joshua's name, as 'Iesous' (Yay-soos). Later, the entire New Testament was written in common Greek, and the name of Jesus was always written as 'Iesous'. As the gospel spread into areas where Greek was not spoken, missionaries made translations in other languages such as Latin, Coptic, and Slavic. By the end of the second century AD, many different Latin versions of the Bible were in circulation. In 382 AD, Jerome translated a standardized Latin Bible called the 'Vulgate' or common Bible. The Latin Bible transliterated the Greek name of Jesus by bringing across all of the Greek sounds in His name 'IESOUS' and thus His name was written in Latin as 'IESUS'. The Latin spelling and pronunciation, 'Iesus' dominated the Western Christian world for almost 1,000 years. In both Greek and Latin, the 's' ending (Iesous -Greek) and (Iesus -Latin) is added in the nominative case only, when the name 'Jesus' stands alone or is the subject of the verb. The 's' ending is not used in other cases. Thus, we see, in Exodus 17:9,10 of the Greek Old Testament (LXX), the name of Joshua as 'Iesou' in verse 9 (Joshua not being the subject of the verb) and 'Iesous' in verse 10 (Joshua being the subject of the verb). This is also true of all the New Testament books and of their early Latin translations, as they wrote the name of Jesus in Greek or Latin. When Pilate wrote 'Jesus of Nazareth, the king of Jews', on Jesus' cross, it was written in Hebrew (Aramaic), Greek and Latin (Jn 19:19-20) and would have appeared as Yeshua (Hebrew), Iesous (Greek) and Iesus (Latin). As the distinction between subject and object is not made in English grammar the 's' ending is retained in all cases. So normally, we should write and pronounce the name in English with 's', as 'IESUS'.

The name 'Jesus' in English language

The Norman invasion of 1066 introduced the letter 'j' to England but the sound of the letter did not exist in the Old English language until the early 1200's. Over the next 300 years, the hard 'J' sound started to appear in male names that began with I or Y because this sounded more masculine. Names like Iames became 'James', Iakob became 'Jacob', and Yohan became 'John', and naturally IESUS became JESUS. During the time when the letter J was starting to gain acceptance, John Wyclif became the first person to translate the New Testament from Latin into English, in 1384. He preserved the Latin spelling and pronunciation of IESUS. His translation was not available to the common man because only a few hand-written copies of his Bible were produced. When Gutenburg invented the printing press the Latin Vulgate Bible became the first book ever printed, in 1455. The German Mentel Bible was printed in 1466 followed by the Martin Luther's Bible in 1522. After William Tyndale was denied permission to print an English Bible, he went to visit Martin Luther and completed his translation of the New Testament in 1525. Tyndale had 18,000 copies printed at Worms and smuggled into England of which only two copies survive. By the year 1611, the King James Bible was printed along with pronunciation guides for all proper names like Jesus, Jew, Jeremiah, Jerusalem, Judah, and John. The name 'Jesus' has been in regular use ever since. But whatever was the writing or the pronunciation of the name over the centuries, the meaning always remained the same: God is salvation and this salvation is offered to mankind through Jesus.

Jesus saves us from our sins

To be saved means to be taken out of a dangerous situation in which one risked perishing. According to the nature of danger, the act of saving or salvation manifests itself in protection, liberation, ransom, health, healing, victory, life and peace. One of the most essential aspects of God's action on earth is 'salvation'. The name of Jesus as 'God is salvation' affirms this particular truth about God. Jesus revealed Himself as somebody through whom God saves. We have so many incidents of healing reported in the pages of the Gospel presenting Jesus as the healer who saved the sick by curing them. But Jesus is, above all, the divine instrument that saves human beings from their sins. We see that one of the most distinctive features of Jesus' ministry was His offer of forgiveness to those who repented and sought His grace for their restoration to the love of God. He preached conversion, a radical change of heart that puts man in a disposition to receive divine favor and thereby permit God's grace to act on him: 'The Kingdom of God is at hand; repent and believe in the good news' (Mk 1: 15). He revealed God as a loving and forgiving Father who delights to pardon and wills that no man be lost (Mt 18:2).

During His public ministry, Jesus offered forgiveness to sinners and exercised the power of pardon that belongs to God alone (Mk 2: 5-11). However, to those who refused the light (Mk 3: 29) or imagined that they had no need of pardon, like the Pharisee in the parable (Lk 18: 9), Jesus could not offer the grace of forgiveness and reconciliation at all. But to the contrite of heart, He offered God's infinite mercy and compassion. He crowned His work of saving the sinners by His death on the cross and obtained the pardon of His Father for the entire human race (Mt 26: 28). A true servant of God, He brought justification to mankind by taking the sins of the world on Himself (Mk 10:45; 1 Pt 2: 24). Indeed, it is by His precious blood that we are purified and cleansed from our sins (1Jn 1: 7). After His resurrection, the Risen Lord communicated the power to forgive sins to the Apostles and through them to the Church (Jn 20: 22). The remission of sin is to be granted, first of all, to those who believe in Him and are baptized in His name (Mt 28:19). As His name signifies, Jesus is indeed God's salvation and He offers this salvation by the forgiveness of all our sins through His precious blood shed on the cross.

Personal reflection - 'Jesus', the name above every name'

In contrast to the early biblical period, during the epoch of the Second Temple, especially during the time of Jesus, there were relatively few different names in use among the Jewish population in Palestine. In fact, when Jesus lived in Galilee, His name 'Yeshua' was one of the most common male names and it was tied with Eleazer for fifth place behind Simon, Joseph, Judah, and John. Nearly one out of ten persons was named Yeshua at that time. It is evident that Jesus was not an unusual name in His time. Josephus, the famous Jewish historian, mentions twenty different Yeshuas (Jesuses) of whom ten were contemporary of Jesus. The name 'Jesus' points to Jesus' commonness. God came among us as an ordinary man and took upon Himself a very common name as He dwelt among sinful men. However, to those who believe in Jesus, His name is unique.

The name Jesus is found nearly 700 times in the New Testament. It testifies to the supreme position the name occupies in the religious devotion of those who believe in Jesus. To the believer, the name 'Jesus' expresses both Jesus' identity and His mission. Since God alone can forgive sins, in the person of Jesus, the eternal Son who became man, it is God Himself who has come down to be with His people, to save them from their sins. Through his Incarnation, Jesus united Himself to all men to take away all their sins. His death on the cross became the atoning sacrifice for the salvation of the world. In raising up Jesus and making Him sit at His right hand, God has given Him the name above every name (Phil 2:9; Eph 1:20). Henceforth all can invoke His name for their salvation. The name of Jesus is at the heart of Christian prayer. All our liturgical prayers conclude with the words 'through our Lord Jesus Christ'. Christians are defined as those who invoke the name of Jesus. They invoke it in the confession of their faith and in ritual invocations of which the most important is baptism that is performed in the 'name of Jesus'. Peter says, 'Be baptized every one of you in the name of Jesus Christ for the forgiveness of sins. And you will receive the gift of the Holy Spirit (Acts 2: 38). Paul asks, 'Don't you know that all of us were baptized into Christ? (Rom 6: 3). The believers obtain eternal life, in the name of Jesus: 'whoever believes in Him is not condemned, but whoever does not believe stands condemned already because he has not believed in the name of God's one and only

Son' (Jn 3: 18). John testifies: 'I write these things to you who believe in the name of the Son of God so that you may know that you have eternal life' (1Jn 5: 13). As Christians, we gather in the name of Jesus: 'For where two or three come together in my name, there am I with them' (Mt 18: 20).

In the Holy Name of Jesus

We give thanks to God in the name of Jesus: 'always give thanks to God the Father for everything in the name of our Lord Jesus Christ' (Eph 5: 20). 'And whatever you do, whether in word or deed, do it all in the name of the Lord Jesus, giving thanks to God the Father through Him' (Col 3: 17). We have to conduct ourselves in such a way that the name of Jesus is glorified: 'We pray this so that the name of our Lord Jesus may be glorified in you and you in Him, according to the grace of our God and the Lord Jesus Christ' (2 Thes 1: 12). By appealing to the name of Jesus the disciples healed the sick. Peter told the crippled man, 'Silver or gold I do not have, but what I have, I give you. In the name of Jesus Christ of Nazareth, walk!' and the man began to walk (Acts 3: 6). They also cast out the demons in His name (Mk 9:38; 16:17), because the evil spirits feared His name. The Seventy-two disciples returned from their mission with joy and said: 'Lord even the demons submit to us in your name' (Lk 10:17). Paul said to the spirit that possessed a girl: 'In the name of Jesus Christ I command you to come out of her'. At that moment, the spirit left her (Acts 16: 18).

In the name of Jesus, the disciples could perform all kinds of miracles (Acts 4:30) because the Father grants all they ask in His name. They are said to have been full of joy for having been 'accounted worthy to suffer for the name of Jesus' (Acts 5:41). Apostolic preaching has its object the proclamation of His name (Acts 4:17, 5:28, 40). Missionaries have gone forth to proclaim the Gospel 'on behalf of the name of Jesus' (3 Jn 1: 7). They will have to suffer for His name (Mk 13: 13). Paul has pledged his life to His name (Acts 15:26). He says: 'I am ready not only to be bound, but also to die in Jerusalem for the name of the Lord (Acts 21: 13). In His name, all sins are forgiven: 'All the prophets testify about Him that everyone who believes in Him receives forgiveness of sins through His name' (Acts 10: 43). John states: 'Your sins have been forgiven on account of His name' (1 Jn 2:12). Paul affirms: 'You were washed, you were sanctified and you were justified in the name of the Lord Jesus Christ' (1 Cor 6: 11). Indeed, 'salvation is found in no one else, for there is no other name under heaven given to men by which we must be saved, except in the name of Jesus Christ of Nazareth' (Acts 4:12). However, we should be careful not to attribute any sort of mystical power to the name of Jesus, as in a magic. Rather, it is only the faith in the name of Jesus that brings the blessings of God for humanity. In the case of the seven sons of Sceva, a Jewish chief priest, we see what happens when people use the name of Jesus without any faith and turn His name into a mere magical formula: In Ephesus, these seven men were attempting to cast out evil spirits in the name of Jesus. They tried to imitate Paul who was casting out the demons and healing the sick. One of the demons replied: 'Jesus I know and I know about Paul, but who are you? Then the man who had the evil spirit jumped on them and overpowered them all. He gave them such a beating that they ran out of the house naked and bleeding (Acts 19:13-16). From this event, we can safely conclude that real faith in Jesus is absolutely necessary as a precondition to invoke His holy name. Has not Jesus told us? 'Truly I tell you. If you have faith as small as a mustard seed, you can say to this mountain, 'Move from here to there' and it will move. Nothing will be impossible for you' (Mt 17: 21). For those who believe in Him, Jesus becomes what His name signifies-He who saves (Mt 1:21); He becomes God's salvation.

We have pointed out, at the beginning of our reflection, that 'Jesus' was an ordinary common name, quite prevalent in the Jewish society of Jesus' time, so that every tenth male would have been called by that name. However, the same ordinary common name has become the singular name of salvation, a name above every name, that 'at the name of Jesus every knee should bow in heaven and on earth and under the earth' (Phil 2: 10-1). We are also ordinary people or common people, just like everyone else. We may have nothing at all to glorify in this world. When we are in that situation, there is no need to feel worthless, unworthy or ashamed. From the common people, God makes authentic heroes, as He has clearly shown with the name of Jesus, His only Son. Let us always trust Jesus and always walk faithfully in His ways. Jesus knows how to glorify our ordinary common names as well as our ordinary human lives.

We have never seen anything like this: Once during a dry and terrible summer, the monsoon that should have come in the beginning of May failed. As a result, all the wells dried up. People in my rural parish were suffering without water to drink. The month of May was over and still there was no sign of rain at all. The misery of the people grew worse day by day. I proposed to the people to pray in small groups and to take turns for forty hours to pray continuously and to call upon the name of Jesus unceasingly during those forty full hours. The number 'forty' brought to our mind the biblical notion of 'being' with the Lord in complete surrender. Exactly at the fortieth hour, the rain came pouring down and never stopped for a full day, filling up all the reservoirs of drinking water. It was a great manifestation of faith on the part of the Christians that many people in that region witnessed. Seeing this extraordinary event, the majority Hindus exclaimed: 'we have never seen anything like this'. Along with the Christian community, I gave all praise to the holy name of Jesus.

Quote: 'Apart from Jesus, we know neither what our life nor our death is; we do not know what God is nor what we ourselves are'- ***Blaise Pascal***

Scripture reading for Day 4: Mk 16: 14-20

Prayer for Day 4:   Yours, O, Lord, is the greatness, the power, the glory, the splendor and the majesty; for everything in heaven and on earth is yours! Pour into our hearts such love toward you that we may love you above all things and obtain your promises, which exceed all that we can desire! Amen.

5

IMMANUEL

*T*he name of Jesus as 'Immanuel' comes from the Hebrew original 'Immanu-el', which is a compound of two Hebrew words meaning 'accompanying God'. As a compound word it means 'God is with us' or 'may God be with us'. This word was transliterated and not translated, as was the practice with names, when the Old Testament was translated into Greek. In the transliteration, the phonetic sound of names is retained as much as possible from the Hebrew by using Greek characters. That is how the Hebrew name 'Immanuel' was retained in the Greek translations also as 'Immanuel', the name of the mysterious child about whom the prophet Isaiah foretold: 'Behold a virgin shall conceive, and bear a son, and his name shall be called Immanuel' (Is 7: 14).

The background of the oracle

The crisis of 735 B.C., when Judah was threatened with attack by Pekah of Israel and Rezin of Damascus in order to force Judah into an alliance against Assyria, forms the background to this oracle. Faced with this difficult situation, immediately after his accession, Ahaz, the king of Judah (735-715 BC) planned to invoke the assistance of Assyria, which he eventually did. Against this intention, Isaiah called upon him to trust the Lord, rather than a foreign power and offered the king a sign: 'Ask for a sign from the Lord, your God. Let it be deep as the nether world, or high as the sky! But Ahaz answered, 'I will not tempt the Lord' (Is 7: 10-12). Ahaz, more by unbelief rather than piety, refused the sign. Then Isaiah said: Listen, O house of David! Is it not enough for you to weary men, must you also weary my God? Therefore the Lord himself will give you this sign: the virgin shall be with child and bear a son and shall name him Immanuel. He shall be living on curds and honey by the time he learns to reject the bad and choose the good. For before the child learns to reject the bad and choose the good, the land of those two kings whom you dread will be deserted (Is 7:13-16). What the prophet was telling was before even the child grows up to adolescence and learns to distinguish between good and evil, the territories of the kingdoms of Israel and Syria would no longer exist. In short, Ahaz should not fear the campaign of Pekah of Israel and Rezin of Damascus against Judah.

Before we move further, let us see how the single kingdom of David and later Solomon came to be divided as the northern kingdom of Israel and the southern kingdom of Judah, who fought each other during the time of the prophet Isaiah. God promised David through the prophet Nathan: 'When your days are over and you go to be with your fathers, I will raise up your offspring to succeed you, one of your own sons, and I will establish his kingdom. He is the one who will build a house for me, and I will establish his throne forever. I will be his father, and he will be my son. I will never take my love away from him, as I took it away from your predecessor. I will set him over my house and my kingdom forever; his throne will be established forever' (2 Sm 7: 11-16; 1 Chr 17:11-14). This prophecy has been understood as having a double fulfillment: the first part concerning the construction of the temple was fulfilled in the person of the king, Solomon, who built the first Temple. The second part was regarding the perpetuity of the Davidic dynasty that can be fulfilled only in the future Messiah. Solomon, who initially enjoyed the favor of Yahweh, later did that which God had forbidden - he amassed a fortune and married foreign wives who led him to idolatry. As punishment, within a few years of his death, his kingdom broke apart into the northern and the southern kingdoms. During one of the feuds between the two kingdoms, Pekah of Israel joined Rezin of Syria to attack Judah. When promising Ahaz, the king of Judah, that if he would place his trust in Yahweh, the campaign against him would be unsuccessful, Isaiah speaks about a mysterious 'young woman and her child', whom he calls 'Immanuel'. The Septuagint translation renders the Hebrew word 'alma' which means a young woman by 'parthenos', the Greek technical term for a virgin.

Who is this child?

The foremost question is who is this child? First of all, the child is not merely an ideal or metaphorical person and thus he cannot be identified with the people of Israel because he is an individual. Both the text and the context make it clear that the prophet does not refer to a child in general; rather, he points to an individual: 'he shall eat butter and honey' the supposed food of the gods as believed by the pagans, during his infancy. However, the child is not a son of the Prophet Isaiah. Isaiah 8:1-4 shows that the prophet's son has a name different from that of Immanuel. The child also does not seem to be a son of Ahaz. In fact, Hezekiah, a son of Ahaz who succeeded him to the throne, was already five years old, when the prophet made the oracle. Moreover, though Hezekiah was a good king, yet, he did not possess all the characteristics of Immanuel as described by Isaiah. What is certain is that the identity of the child appears to be ambiguous and mysterious to the point of being incomprehensible. The oracle of the prophet seems to foretell a 'future dramatic event' in the history of Israel. It is given to Matthew to point out to us who the child is. As he recounts how Jesus was conceived in the womb of His mother Mary, by the power of the Holy Spirit, Matthew declares: All this took place to fulfill what the Lord had said through the prophet: Behold, the virgin shall be with the child and bear a son, and they shall name Him Immanuel' (Mt 1:21-23).

Threat to the kingdom of Israel

The oracle of the prophet contains both threats and promises. Let us investigate first what were the threats or warnings of the prophet and how they came to be fulfilled. The first threat was 'before the child learns to reject the bad and choose the good, the land of those two kings whom you dread will be deserted' (Is 7:16). The same threat was repeated again: 'The Lord said to me: Take a large cylinder-seal and inscribe on it in ordinary letters: belonging to Maher-shalal-hash-baz. And then the Lord said to me, 'Name your son Maher-shalal-hash-baz' for before the child knows how to call his father or mother by name, the wealth of Damascus and the spoil of Samaria shall be carried off by the king of Assyria' (Is 8: 1-4). The name of Isaiah's child means 'quick spoils' or speedy plunder'. We know that the fall of Damascus in 732 B.C. (2 Kgs 16:9) and the fall of Samaria (2 Kgs 18: 9-11) in 721 B.C. at the hands of the Assyrians are firmly dated events and thus, we know that the threat of the prophet indeed came true. The reason for the punishment of the northern kingdom is explained elsewhere as 'this came about because they (the king and the people) had not heeded the warning of the Lord, their God. They violated His covenant, not heeding and not fulfilling the commandments of Moses, the servant of the Lord' (2 Kgs 18: 12). After the fall of the northern kingdom, the king of Assyria deported the Israelites and settled them in Halah, at the Habor, a river of Gozan, and in the cities of Medes (2 Kgs 18:11). The Israelites deported from the northern kingdom disappeared as a group from history. The practice of removing conquered peoples on a large scale was ancient in the Near East. It appears that Tiglath-pileser III of Assyria (745-727 BC) was the first to refine this simple enslavement by resettling the peoples in different parts of the empire. The policy was devised to detach people from their land and thus to destroy the spirit of resistance and rebellion, by suppressing their sense of national identity. Deportation did not, as a rule, include the entire population. Those selected for removal included the royal and noble families, the wealthy, the landowners and the skilled artisans. These were the people who normally have the capacity to organize the possible resistance. Hence they were displaced in foreign lands in order to thwart their efforts at rebellion.

Threat to the kingdom of Judah

The oracle contains a threat concerning the kingdom of Judah also. The prophet was not pleased with the unbelief of Ahaz. The prophet warns Ahaz not to place his confidence in the alliances with earthly kingdoms, but rather to seek the help of God. Isaiah says: 'For thus said the Lord to me, 'Call not alliance what this people calls alliance, and fear not, nor stand in awe of what they fear. But, you make your alliance with the Lord of Hosts, for Him to be your fear and your awe (Is 8: 11-13). But Ahaz, in spite of such encouragement from the prophet, would seek the assistance from Assyria, a foreign power that had no reverence for Yahweh, the one true God. The unbelief of Ahaz was only a clear example of the betrayal of the successive kings of Judah who did evil in the sight of God. There were only two exceptions. The first was Hezekiah, the son of Ahaz, who was very devout to God: 'His piety won God's favor, for he pleased the Lord, just as his forefather David had done.He put his trust in the Lord, the God of Israel; and neither before him nor after him was there anyone like him among all the kings of Judah. The Lord was with him and he prospered in all that he set out to do' (2 Kgs 18: 3-7). The Lord protected him from the king of Assyria in a very miraculous way: 'The angel of the Lord went forth and struck down one hundred and eighty-five thousand men in the Assyrian camp. Early the next morning, there they were, all the corpses of the dead. So, Sennacherib, the king of Assyria, broke camp and went back home to Nineveh' (2 Kgs 19: 35-36). Another king who 'pleased the Lord and conducted himself unswervingly just as his ancestor David had done' (2 Kgs 22:2) was the king Josiah. In recognition of his piety and devotion, the Lord promised him: 'you shall go to your grave in peace and your eyes shall not see all the evil I will bring upon this place' (2 Kgs 22: 20). But the rest of the kings of Judah, just like the kings of the northern kingdom, did what was displeasing to God. We present a few examples: Manasseh, the son of Hezekiah, 'did what is evil in the sight of the Lord, following the abominable practices of the nations whom the Lord had cleared out of the way of the Israelites. He rebuilt the high places which his father Hezekiah had destroyed. He erected altars to Baal, and worshiped and served the whole host of heaven' (2 Kgs 21:2-5). His son Amon who succeeded him also 'did evil in the sight of the Lord. He worshipped the idols his father has served. He abandoned the Lord, the God of his fathers, and did not follow the path of the Lord' (2 Kgs 21:21-22). Jehoahaz, son of Josiah, also 'did evil in the sight of the Lord just as his forefathers had done' (2 Kgs 23:32). His brother, Jehoiakim, who succeeded him also 'did evil in the sight of the Lord as his forefathers had done' (2 Kgs 23:37). As successive kings had done evil, the wrath of the Lord was approaching near. The Lord said: 'Because they have forsaken me and have burned incense to other gods, provoking me by everything to which they turn their hands, my anger is ablaze against this place and it can not be extinguished' (2 Kgs 22: 17).

As He Himself insists, God inspired Nebuchadnezzar, the king of Babylon, to move against Judah and deport Jehoiachin, the king of Judah, together with his mother, his wives, ministers, officers, functionaries and the chief men of the land in 597 BC. None were left among the people of the land except the poor (2 Kgs 24: 12-16). When Zedekiah, the uncle of Jehoiachin, whom Nebuchadnezzar appointed as king of Judah, revolted against Babylon in the ninth year of his reign, Nebuchadnezzar invaded Judah again and burnt Jerusalem including the temple in 587 BC. He led into exile the last of the people remaining in the city, leaving only some of the poor as vinedressers and farmers (2 Kgs 25: 1-12). Thus came to be fulfilled another threat in the oracle of prophet Isaiah, that was concerning the fall and destruction of the kingdom of Judah: 'The Lord shall bring upon you and your people and your father's house, days worse than any since Ephraim seceded from Judah (Is 7: 10-17). The prophet also said: 'Again the Lord spoke to me: Because this people has rejected the waters of Shiloah that flow gently and they melt with fear before the loftiness of Rezin and Ramaliah's son, therefore the Lord raises against them the waters of the River, great and mighty. It shall rise above all its channels and overflow all its banks. It shall pass into Judah and flood it all throughout: up to the neck it shall reach; It shall spread its wings the full width of your land' (Is 8: 5-8). The 'waters of Shiloah' refer to the stream that flows into the pool of Shiloah in Jerusalem. Its slow current symbolizes the silent divine protection. According to the prophet, Judah has rejected God's help and sought the assistance of a foreign power. God would therefore summon the mighty army of Babylon across Eupharates, to devastate Judah.

Promise of the perpetuity of the Davidic dynasty

On the one hand, the threat of the prophet in the oracle foretells the end of the Davidic dynasty with the destruction of Jerusalem in 587 BC. By the destruction of the southern kingdom, the Davidic dynasty had apparently come to an end. On the other hand, the promise assures the perpetuity of the Davidic dynasty, 'in the child to be conceived by a young woman'. As we know, God had promised David, the perpetuity of his dynasty (2 Sm 7: 16). The oracle of the prophet Isaiah contains the promise of 'a child' that can be understood only in relation to the assurance of God regarding the perpetuity of the Davidic dynasty. The promise of the prophet Isaiah is evidently messianic and points to the future coming of the Son of God par excellence as 'God with us'. If we trace the history of the kings of Israel, we know that God was hesitant to give the people of Israel a king. When the people of Israel asked Samuel for a king, in the place of the judges, the Lord said: 'Grant the people's every request. It is not you they reject, they are rejecting me as their king. They deserted me and worshipped strange gods' (1 Sm 8: 6-9). God hesitatingly yielded to the request of the people of Israel, even though He was not very pleased about it. As God had forewarned, most of the kings who ruled over the people of Israel did not follow the ways of the Lord and did what was evil in His sight. Their infidelity brought the land and the people of Israel terrible sufferings as the result of God's anger. Always the One to take His own initiative for the relief and salvation of His people, in spite of their failures, God chose to send His only Son who would be the 'eternal King' over God's people: 'The Lord God will give Him the throne of David, his father, and He will rule over the house of Jacob forever, and His kingdom will have no end' (Lk 1: 32-33). The prophet Isaiah makes it clear that the birth of 'the child' assures the permanence of the Davidic dynasty in spite of the unbelief of its present representative, king Ahaz, and in this wonderful child, Israel will have their perfect king who will fully please God.

In the coming of Immanuel, as the ideal king, God Himself would personally enter human history to be with His people, and that is why this future king is called Immanuel, 'God with us'. According to the prophet Isaiah, in 'Immanuel', 'the people who walked in darkness would see a great light. Upon those who dwelt in the land of gloom a light would shine'. The prophet insists: 'A child is born to us, a son is given us: upon his shoulder dominion rests. They name him Wonder-Counselor, God-Hero, Father-Forever and Prince of Peace. His dominion is vast and forever peaceful! From David's throne, and over His kingdom, He confirms and sustains by judgment and justice, both now and forever' (Is 9: 1-6). The prophet assures us that the future 'eternal King' would be a Wonder-Counselor, remarkable for his wisdom and prudence. He would be a 'God-Hero' always a defender of his people. As 'Father-Forever' He would be ever devoted to His people and His reign would be characterized by peace, since He is the Prince of peace: 'The Spirit of the Lord shall rest on Him. Not by appearance shall He judge. Nor by hearsay shall He decide. But He shall judge the poor with justice and decide aright for the Land's afflicted. Justice shall be the band around His waist, and faithfulness a belt upon His hips' (Is 11:1-5). In 'Immanuel', God will be truly with us, in order to accompany us in our 'life-journey'.

Personal reflection – 'Jesus, the Immanuel - God with us'

In the midst of great historical events of far reaching implications, when kingdoms were falling and empires were rising and the human drama of success and failure of the kings and peoples were decided by wars and alliances, God announced, through the prophet Isaiah that a 'child' would be born whose birth would become the most important event in the history of the world. Moreover, in this 'child' God promises to be with us to accompany us in our journey in the world, and thus we become 'God accompanied'. Centuries later, after the prophet made the promise, Matthew writes in the Gospel that Isaiah's prophecy was fulfilled in the birth of Jesus. He gives us the good news that in the tiny helpless baby, born of the poor and humble peasant parents in a manger of a stable in the backyard, since there was no room for Him in the inn, God entered human history in a very decisive way. Through the Babe of Bethlehem, called Immanuel, the One whose name is Wonderful Counselor, Mighty God, Everlasting Father, Prince of Peace, God is with us. We are no more orphans, but are truly 'God-accompanied' people in this world.

Sometimes, for us, life may make no sense at all, as it was when the people of Israel encountered terrible calamities like the destruction of Jerusalem and the exile into foreign countries. In the face of difficult circumstances, just like the chosen people who suffered terrible national tragedies, we may feel that God does not care for us at all. In those hours, we may go through the terrible pain that the Psalmist felt, when he cried, 'I have no refuge; no one cares for my soul' (Ps 142: 4-7). It is a terrible thing to feel alone, separated from those who love us, at times, even from God. But let us remember that through Jesus, who is Immanuel, God is always with us. Through Him, God sees us in the midst of our hardships. He comes to us and He delivers us from our sufferings and hardships, so that we may praise His holy Name. Life is not easy for any of us. Throughout our lives we must face cruel circumstances, hard choices, sickness and at times incurable diseases, even terrible suffering and inevitable death. God wants to be Immanuel to us, to be with us and help us handle our difficulties. Without Him, we are miserable! Without Him, we are hopeless! But the Good News is that we do not have to live without Him. We can talk with Him and walk with Him as He goes along with us in our journey as a friend, to share our joys and sorrows. We can confidently feel that during a crisis in our lives, God is certainly with us in our midst. As He accompanies us to help and comfort us, He also sends us to comfort others, our neighbors, as they face hardships and sufferings. In this world, God offered us the great privilege of walking in the company of Jesus, whom He sent to the world to save us. In Him, God will not fail us, nor will He leave us (Heb 13:5), since in Jesus Christ, we have become 'God-accompanied'. Let us always remember the parting words of Jesus in the same Gospel of Matthew who spoke about Immanuel: 'And behold, I am with you always, until the end of the age' (Mt 28:20). As human beings we shall never be able to make sense of all the historical events and understand their significance for us and also for others. But we can trustingly encounter human history as it unfolds before us and walk with Jesus hand in hand, entrusting ourselves totally to our Heavenly Father, the supreme source of love and wisdom. Praise and thank God, for in Jesus, His only Son, God is with us always and forever!

I am with you always: During his long journey alone towards his new residence in another monastery, a monk, who rarely went out, made a plea to Jesus to walk with him. For a person who always remained inside the safe walls of the monastery, a tedious walk through rough terrain seemed quite frightening. He especially feared the muddy path through the forest where some wild animals roamed and was afraid of the thieves who killed people even for a little money. As he walked towards his new place, he always noticed two pairs of steps and he realized that Jesus was accompanying him on his way. However, he saw only a single pair of steps through the most dangerous muddy path in the thick of the forest. After fearfully crossing it, he asked Jesus why He left him during the most frightening time of the journey. Jesus assured him that He was always walking with him. He told the monk that during the most difficult part of the journey in the muddy path, He made sure to carry the monk over His shoulders and that is the reason the monk found only a single pair of steps.

Quote: Never forget that you are not alone. The Divine is always with you, helping and guiding. He is the companion who never fails, the friend whose love comforts and strengthens. Have faith in Him and He will do everything for you - *Aurobindo*

Scripture reading for Day 5:Is 11: 1-9

Prayer for Day 5: O God, you know that we are set in the midst of many and great dangers. You can also understand that by reason of the frailty of our nature we donot always stand upright. Grant to us strength and protection and support us in all dangers and carry us through all temptations. Be with us always! Amen.

6

SON OF DAVID

*T*he Gospels are careful to point out that Jesus has descended from David through both of His parents, Joseph and Mary. Matthew opens his book this way: 'The book of the genealogy of Jesus Christ, the Son of David' (Mt 1:1). In Hebrew the name 'david' meant 'beloved' or 'prince'. David was no doubt Israel's greatest king, who conquered her troublesome enemies and established the nation in security. He successfully united the tribes of Israel in an acceptable monarchy. He was also a man after God's heart, in the sense that he remained grateful to God for His many blessings. He always recognized that it was God who gave him all his victories and the prosperity that came to his people during his reign. He tried to please God in all his ways, though he failed many times from his personal weaknesses. He is a central figure in the history of Israel both historically and theologically. He became the kingly type of the Messiah, Israel's hope for salvation. His was the wonderful story of a shepherd boy who became the greatest king of Israel through the election, blessings and guidance of Yahweh, the God of Israel.

David, the ideal king of Israel

David was the youngest of eight sons of Isai or Jesse (1 Sm 17: 12). At God's command, Samuel came to Bethlehem to anoint one of the sons of Isai as Saul's successor. At Bethlehem, as God had told him, Samuel chose David and anointed him. Pointing to David, the Lord said to Samuel: 'There---anoint him, for this is he'. Then Samuel, with the horn of oil in his hand, anointed him in the midst of his brothers; and from that day on, the Spirit of the Lord rushed upon David' (1Sm 16:1-13). David came to court of Saul to dispel Saul's melancholy by his music (1 Sm 16: 14-23). His victory over the giant Goliath so impressed Saul that he appointed him commander over some of his soldiers (1 Sm 17: 1- 18: 5). However, the youth's bravery and his popularity for slaying Goliath aroused Saul's jealousy (1 Sm 18: 6-9). Saul made repeated attempts to slay David (1 Sm 18: 10-30). Aware of Saul's jealousy and enmity, David fled and sought refuge in the desert of southern Judea. After Saul's defeat at the hands of Philistines and his subsequent death, David accepted the kingship of Israel and took his residence in Hebron (2 Sm 2:1-4) at the age of thirty, about 1000 BC. The most important steps in the consolidation of David's monarchy were the capture of Jerusalem and the defeat of the Philistines. In spite of his many shortcomings, David was considered the ideal king. He did far better than any other king in the Hebrew history, regarding what a king was expected to do. He best realized the ideal of kingship and none of his successors could equal him. He created a united Israel. His military successes removed external danger and greatly enriched his people. He made it possible for the Israelite 'to sit under his vine and fig tree with none to terrify'. It can be said that David established a little Israelite empire.

A man after God's own heart

David was a man after God's own heart: 'The Lord has sought a man after his own heart and has appointed him commander of His people' (1 Sm 13:14). This judgment does not imply that David was sinless, but refers rather to his docile and sincere heart. It is his sincere love and profound devotion to God that motivated him to build a fitting temple for Yahweh (2 Sm 7:1-3). The book of Sirach gives a more detailed description of David's qualities: 'With his every deed he offered thanks to God the Most High, in words of praise. With his whole being he loved his Maker and daily had His praises sung. The Lord forgave him his sins and exalted his strength forever. He conferred on him the rights of royalty and established his throne in Israel' (Sir 47:1-12). No doubt David was a great king and later writers of the history of Israel idealized him considerably holding him up as the model for subsequent kings; that is best seen in the chapters 11- 29 of the first book of Chronicles. God promised an eternal dynasty to David (2 Sm 7: 8-16). This oracle is preserved at greater length in Ps 89: 'I have made a covenant with my chosen one; I have sworn to David my servant: I will make your dynasty stand forever and establish your throne for all ages' (Ps 89: 4-5). This promise led to the belief that a deliverer from David's house would effect the final and lasting deliverance of Israel. His house would endure even if his successors were unworthy. The covenant of Yahweh with David would stand until it was fulfilled in another ruler who would be a greater David and who would establish the ideal kingdom of Yahweh. This idea grew with the progress of time, attested to and confirmed by the prophets who saw the messianic king as a descendant of David.

The promise and its fulfillment

The promise of God stresses the continuity of kingship in the House of David. Even when the House of David was still ruling, the prophets began to foretell the coming of one particular ruler, a descendant of David: 'There shall come forth a Rod from the stem of Jesse (David's father), and a branch shall grow out of his roots. The Spirit of the Lord shall rest upon Him. In that day there shall be a Root of Jesse, who shall stand as a banner to the people; The Gentiles shall seek Him' (Is 11:1-10). 'Behold, the days are coming, says the Lord, when I will raise up a righteous shoot to David; As king he shall reign and govern wisely, he shall do what is just and right in the land' (Jer 23:5). 'In those days, in that time, I will raise up for David a just shoot' (Jer 33:15). 'Then the people of Israel shall turn back and seek the Lord, their God, and David, their king; they shall come trembling to the Lord and to his bounty, in the last days' (Hos 3:5). 'My servant David shall be prince over them, and there shall be one shepherd for them all; they shall live by my statutes and carefully observe my decrees' (Ez 37:24). Through their promises, as seen above, the prophets created among the people of Israel a fervent hope in the future 'Son of David' whose kingdom would last forever and through whom the Davidic dynasty would endure forever.

In the Gospel according to Matthew

When Matthew wrote that Jesus was the 'Son of David', his words brought a deep and profound theological message to the Jews of the first century AD. He stated to them in clear terms that Jesus was the fulfillment of the promise of God to David to establish an enduring kingdom for his dynasty. Matthew identifies Jesus as the long-awaited Messiah, who would rule forever over the throne of David. Establishing clearly that Jesus descended from king David is one important way for Matthew to prove that He is indeed the promised Messiah. In Matthew's division of Israel's history, there are 14 generations from Abraham to David, 14 generations from the David's reign to the Babylonian captivity, and 14 more after it, until Jesus comes as 'the Messiah' (Mt 1:17). We may note also that, in the genealogy, only Jesus and David are identified by their titles: David as King (1:6) and Jesus as Messiah (1:16). According to Matthew, Jesus receives His royal birthright through Joseph, 'the husband of Mary', and the 'son of David' (Mt 1:16-18). He begins his Gospel with a genealogy that has long list of names to prove the Davidic descent of Jesus, the Messiah. Matthew writes from Joseph's point of view. He records the angel's appearance to Joseph. The ancestral line is that of Joseph. 'And Jacob begot Joseph the husband of Mary, of whom was born Jesus who is called Christ' (Mt 1:16). Jacob (not Heli) was the father of Joseph. Joseph was not the father of Jesus, but only 'the husband of Mary, of whom was born Jesus'. Both Mary and Joseph were presented as belonging to the house of David and hence Jesus was doubly the Son of David: physically through Mary and legally through Joseph, his step-father.

In the Gospel according to Luke

There is also another genealogy presented in the Gospel according to Luke. From Abraham to David, the two lists are identical; but, from David to Jesus, they differ. How can that be? What is shown is the involvement of both Joseph and Mary in assuring the Davidic descent to their son, Jesus. As for Mary, she was Jesus' physical mother. Luke tells the account of Jesus' conception from Mary's viewpoint as he records the angel Gabriel's appearance to her. Luke's genealogy begins: 'Now when Jesus began His ministry He was about thirty years of age. He was the son, as was thought, of Joseph, the son of Heli' (Lk 3:23). With the Jews, the legal ancestral line was that of the father. Thus Joseph is mentioned.

But the key is in the words 'as was thought'. Jesus supposedly, to the world's eye, was Joseph's son. But in reality, He was not. He was Mary's son. Some scholars say that Mary was the daughter of Heli, since Jacob is the father of Joseph (Mt 1:16). The ancestral line presented by Luke in the genealogy is that of Mary. Apart from their genealogies that affirm the Davidic ancestry of Jesus, both Matthew and Luke make sure to point out, in numerous references, that Jesus was born into the family of David. For example, in Matthew, the angel addresses Joseph as 'Joseph, son of David' (Mt 1:20). In Luke, we find: 'Joseph went up to the city of David, which is called Bethlehem, because he was of the house and lineage of David' (Lk 2:4). Matthew and Luke are at pains to give factual details regarding what the New Testament asserts many times: 'Jesus is of the line of the king David'.

Jesus is hailed as the Son of David

The Jews had been waiting for the Messiah for centuries. Jesus' great healing powers and other such miracles gave testimony to Him about being someone very special, perhaps the Son of David himself! One day in the temple of Jerusalem, the Jews were debating whether Jesus was the Christ. Therefore, some said, 'Will the Christ come out of Galilee? Has not the Scripture said that the Christ comes from the seed of David and from the town of Bethlehem (Mi 5:1), where David was?' (Jn 7: 41-42). No doubt, the Jews knew the Old Testament prophecies and were correct in what they affirmed. What they did not know was that Jesus indeed was born in Bethlehem and that He was, indeed, a descendant of David! Another time, when Jesus miraculously healed a man both blind and mute, 'all the multitudes were amazed and said, 'Could this be the Son of David?' (Mt 12:22-23). Later, a woman with a demon-possessed daughter cried out to Jesus: 'Have mercy on me, O Lord, Son of David!' (Mt 15:22). Sometime after, when two blind men heard Jesus was passing by near Jericho, they cried out, 'Have mercy on us, O Lord, Son of David!' (Mt 20:30). Shortly thereafter the triumphal entry of Jesus into Jerusalem took place. Multitudes surrounded Jesus and cried out, 'Hosanna to the Son of David! Blessed is the kingdom of our father David! Blessed is the King who comes in the name of the Lord! (Mt 21:9; Mk 11:10; Lk 19:38). It was a very large crowd. As they made their way from the Mount of Olives to the city of Jerusalem, they spread garments and palm branches on the ground. When they arrived in Jerusalem, the whole city was stirred and wanted to know who it was. 'This is Jesus, the prophet from Nazareth of Galilee'. All this was to fulfill the prophecy: 'Behold, your King is coming to you, lowly, and sitting on a donkey' (Mt 21:1-11). What an emotional time for the Jews! Here was Jesus, the Son of David, riding triumphantly into their capital city! Prophecy was being fulfilled before their very eyes. The long-awaited Messiah had at last arrived! The eagerly expected 'Son of David', King of Israel, was indeed in their midst. The last healing by Jesus, as presented by Matthew, evoked the difference between Jesus and David. When David conquered Jerusalem, he mockingly called his enemies 'the lame and the blind'. David had said on that day, 'All who wish to attack the Jebusites must strike at them through the water shaft. The lame and the blind will be the personal enemies of David. That is why, it is said, 'The blind and the lame shall not enter the palace' (2 Sm 5: 8). The Son of David as healer is contrasted with his father David. David was a powerful warrior who killed the figuratively blind and lame and excluded them from his 'house'. His son Jesus is a powerful healer who cures the literally blind and lame within His 'house', the temple. 'The blind and the lame approached him in the temple and he cured them' (Mt 21:14).

The loyalty of David

David was chosen by God to be the king of Israel and he answers this calling with a deep attachment to God. He allowed himself to be entirely ruled by God's will and was ready to accept whatever came from Him (2 Sm 15:25). He had utter confidence in God and trustingly hoped that the Lord would change all the evils he had to undergo into blessings (2 Sm 16:10). David's fame as the greatest king of Israel should not make one overlook the man. He had his weaknesses along with his great qualities. He was a relentless soldier engaged in violence and bloodshed, and was deceitful too (1 Sm 27: 10). However, David remained the lowly servant of Yahweh, overwhelmed by the privileges God gave him: 'Who am I, Lord God, and who are the members of my house that you have brought me to this point?' (2 Sm 7: 18-29). Hence he is the model of the 'poor of Yahweh' as seen in his surrender to God and in his most certain hope in Him. The praises and petitions of the Psalter reflect very well the attitude of surrender and trust of David towards God. To David, the 'singer of Israel's songs' (2 Sm 22) is attributed, besides numerous psalms, the plan of the temple (1 Chr 22-23) as well as the organization of the cult (1 Chr 24-29). Recognizing the devotion and piety of David, God promised him a perpetual dynasty.

Davidic Messianism

The people of Israel, trusting in the promise of God, expected the Davidic rule, by his descendants, to bring them peace, justice and prosperity. But, what they experienced actually was poverty, conflict, oppression, colonization, and exile, especially as the result of the failure of most of the kings, all of whom came from the dynasty of David. Promise clashed with fulfillment, resulting in a tension, which the people resolved by projecting the expected fulfillment of the divine promise to the future. What Israel believed was that the promises of the God would 'one day' be definitely fulfilled. Davidic kingdom, as a definitive saving act of God, would 'one day' certainly be established. We may call this hope as Davidic Messianism. It looks forward to the realization of God's promise of everlasting peace and prosperity through a descendant of David, i.e. a son of David, who will be raised up by God as the 'Messiah', the anointed one or the king par excellence. The Messiah was expected to establish a world-wide kingdom of justice, peace and prosperity in which all the promises of God will finally be realized. Davidic Messianism presents the future Messiah as the ideal king and his kingdom is seen as the restoration of a lost golden age of perfect freedom, peace and prosperity, which prevailed on the earth during the time of the first parents, Adam and Eve, who once reigned over paradise (Mi 5: 2-3; Is 11:2-9). Man will be reconciled with man and nature and thus humanity will live in perfect harmony. But, the hope, expressed in Davidic messianism, is a thoroughly worldly and political one in the sense that God's promises are to be realized in a worldly kingdom to be established on earth and within history. Davidic messianism relies on political power of the ideal king. Jesus, on the contrary, proposes a spiritual kingdom. For him it is not power, but God's love which is the key for man's salvation and that is what Jesus offers when He proclaims the arrival of God's kingdom. Drawing from His own experience of God as 'abba', the dear Father, He proclaims God's unconditional love for men. The Kingdom of God, proclaimed by Jesus, then, is ultimately His revelation of God's unconditional love for humanity and its realization in the lives of the individuals and communities. When we encounter and accept the love of God and respond to it appropriately in trusting and total surrender, we experience true freedom, peace, justice and prosperity in our hearts as individuals and in our relationships with others people in our community and in the larger society.

Personal reflection- 'Hosanna to the Son of David'

'Son of David' was an inspiring concept to the Jews of the time of Jesus. However, they had the false perspective of an earthly king, earthly throne and earthly kingdom- all like David's. They were thinking of military action and political solutions. Once, indeed, 'they were about to come and take Jesus by force to make Him king' (Jn 6:15). Jesus escaped from their hands and walked away! To conceive of Jesus as only or principally the physical Son of David and an earthly king was quite an inadequate perception. It missed the mark. Jesus Himself once clarified the meaning of the 'Son of David' prophecies. Shortly after the triumphal entry, people posed a lot of questions to Jesus in the temple. This was Jesus' final week before His death on Calvary. The Pharisees, the Sadducees and the Scribes challenged Jesus with difficult questions. Jesus' replies were so brilliant, that 'after that no one dared question Him' (Mk 12:34). Then it was Jesus' turn to ask them a question: 'What do you think about the Christ? Whose Son is He? They said to Him, 'The Son of David'. He asked them, 'How then does David in the Spirit call Him 'Lord', saying: 'The Lord said to my Lord, 'Sit at my right hand, till I make your enemies your footstool? 'If David then calls Him 'Lord', how can He be his Son? and no one was able to answer Him a word' (Mt 22:41-46). This way, by asking them to reflect whether the Messiah was the Son of David or the Lord of David, Jesus raised questions to them about the political and spiritual role of the expected Messiah. They did not know what to answer Him. Jesus was not denying that He was the 'Son of David'; that would be contradicting the Scripture. Rather, Jesus explained to them the difficulty of assigning a particular role to Messiah so that the people could think more clearly and understand the deeper significance of the promise of God regarding His Messiah. Jesus was striving to get them to understand that there is more to Messiahship than a physical relationship to David or an earthly king. No doubt, the physical relationship did indeed exist between Jesus and the family of David. However, Jesus is also divine! His Kingship is far above any mere earthly kingship of David and His kingdom is not political or territorial, because He is not only the Son of David, but also the only begotten Son of God!

The early Christian community clearly understood the double identity of Jesus as son of David and as Son of God. This is clearly expressed by Paul who begins his letter to the Romans with these words : 'Paul set apart for the Gospel about His Son, descended from David according to the flesh, but established as Son of God in power according to the Spirit of holiness through resurrection from the dead, Jesus Christ, our Lord' (Rom 1:3-4). To be the Messiah (Christ), Jesus had to be of the seed of David. But to be the Savior of the world, Jesus has to be the Son of God. In Jesus, 'the King of kings and the Lord of lords' (Rev 19:16), the promise of God to David to establish an eternal kingdom through Davidic lineage is fulfilled. The early Church proclaimed this message to their Jewish brethren: 'From the descendants of David, God, according to His promise, has brought to Israel, a savior, Jesus' (Acts 13: 23). 'The lion of Judah, the root of David has triumphed' (Rv 5: 5). Jesus is not merely the shepherd king from the house of David, but also the Son of God who has come to feed and save His flock as the good shepherd, leading us to the green pastures of the everlasting life.

I need only six feet of land: A great emperor who ruled over vast territories that he conquered with his mighty army invited a holy man to bless his land and people. He wanted peace and prosperity in his kingdom. He was confident that the holy man's blessings would bring the benedictions from God and thus the land would produce plenty and the people would be prosperous and happy. When the holy man made long prayers and blessed the king, the land and his people, the king was much elated. He wanted to reward the holy man who renounced the worldly things with costly jewels and landed properties. He said, 'O, Man of God! I am pleased with your visit to my kingdom and with your blessings for my subjects. Ask me anything as reward. I will grant you with much pleasure'. The holy man replied, 'Mighty emperor! Grant me only six feet of land, where I would like to live. But command death that it should not enter that six feet of land to seize me'. The message of the holy man was, even if the king possesses all the kingdoms of the earth, still, he is powerless before death. It is our faith that Christ alone, the true and eternal king who conquered death, has the power to lead us from death to life. Jesus, our king, promises everlasting life to us.

Quote: Alexander, Caesar, Charlemagne and I have founded empires. But on what did we rest the creations of our genius? Only upon force! Jesus Christ founded his empire upon love; and at this hour millions of men would die for him - ***Napoleon Bonaparte***

Scripture readings for Day 6:Sir 47:1-12

Prayer for Day 6: O God, you turn all manner of things to the profit of those who love and serve you with a sincere heart. Establish unshakably in our hearts the spirit of your love, so that our desires may spring from your inspiration, and remain unshaken by temptation. Let your grace always precede and follow us and may it make us ever devoted to good deeds of kindness and charity! Amen.

7

SON OF ABRAHAM

*J*esus is called the son of Abraham (Mt 1:1). Abraham's original name was Abram, which meant 'God is exalted'. Abram was the son of Terah. The clan of Terah migrated from Ur of the Chaldeans to go to the land of Canaan. However, when they reached Haran they settled there (Gen 11: 31). After the death of his father Terah, the life of Abraham developed totally under God's free initiative. God said to him, 'Go forth from the land of your kinsfolk and from your father's house to a land that I will show you' (Gn 12:1). He assured him, 'I will make of you a great nation and I will bless you. I will make your name great, so that you will be a blessing. I will bless those who bless you and curse those who curse you. All the communities of the earth shall find blessing in you' (Gn 12: 2-3). In the life of Abraham, we see that it is God who freely chose him out of a family that 'served other gods' (Jos 24:2) and led him into another country that He promised to give him. Trusting in God, Abraham left his home and family and struck out into a future that was unknown. Of course, God promised him remarkable things for that future: a great name, protection, and blessing for both Abraham and the whole earth. However, it was a journey made in absolute faith and total confidence in the promises of God alone. Abraham was 75 years old when he set out into Canaan as the Lord had told him (Gn 12:4). Through the next 25 years the promises of God would unfold in more specific dimensions, as Abraham journeyed with God in total obedience and unwavering faith.

God's countless blessings to Abraham

From the beginning, God's promises outlined a marvelous future for Abraham. The endlessly recurring phrase in the biblical narratives with regard to Abraham is: 'I will give'. God promised to give Abraham the land. When Abraham reached Schechem, God appeared to him and said: 'To your descendants, I will give this land' (Gn 12:7), an area that was occupied by the Canaanites. Abraham responded by building an altar thereby acknowledging Yahweh as the one leading him in his journey. Abraham continued his journey through the land and eventually traversed its full length from north to south. Yet in the middle of all the positive dimension of Abraham's faithful response, we find a note of discord with the observation that there was a famine in the land. In the arid ancient Middle East, famine was a very serious matter. It was not simply an inconvenience, but more a matter of life and death. Famine meant that no one, including the large cattle, had food, so it was not just a matter of trading or buying food from someone else. The only option was to go somewhere where there was no famine in order to survive. Abraham faced tremendous irony here. He had left everything to follow God who promised him the land of Canaan. No sooner had Abraham entered the land that God had so benevolently promised him, he had to leave that very land because it was afflicted by famine and hence was not livable.

Blessing of land and heir

Abraham left his 'promised land' and journeyed on to Egypt. Food was usually plentiful in Egypt because the annual flooding of the Nile watered the Egyptian agricultural land. The journey to Egypt also set the stage for an immediate crisis. As Abraham was about to enter Egypt, he was afraid that Sarah would catch the eye of the powerful ruler and the nobles in Egypt, and they would eliminate him in order to take Sarah. So he said to Sarah: 'Say you are my sister, so that it may go well with me because of you, and that my life may be spared on your account'. When Sarah was taken into the harem of the Pharaoh, God afflicted Pharaoh and his house with great plagues. The Pharaoh saw in a plague of diseases a warning that he had done wrong and released Sarah (Gn 12:10-20). Abraham returned to Canaan. God said to Abraham, 'Look about you and from where you are, gaze to the north and south, east and west. All the land that you see I will give to you and your descendants forever. I will make your descendants like the dust of the earth. Set forth and walk about the land, through its length and breadth, for to you I will give it (Gn 13: 14-17). God returned to Abraham again in a vision and reaffirmed His promise: 'Do not be afraid, Abram! I am your shield and your reward shall be very great'. Abraham's response explains to us his predicament and expectation. 'Lord God! What good will your gifts be if I keep on being childless and have as my heir the steward of my house, Eliezer? Then, God promised Abraham his own offspring: 'This man shall not be your heir; no one but your very own issue shall be your heir'. For the first time God specified that it would be Abraham's own physical descendant that would be the inheritor of the promise. Then, God reiterated the larger promise to Abraham. God brought him outside and said, 'Look now toward heaven, your descendants will be like the stars of the sky' (Gn 15: 1-5). God made a covenant with Abraham and repeated the promise to give him the land (Gn 15: 18).

Renewal of the promise and the covenant

Eleven years went by since the first promise. At the advice of Sarah, Abraham had relationship with Hagar, her maidservant who conceived him a child. Tension emerged as Sarah became jealous of Hagar, and Hagar was forced to flee with her child Ishmael. God took care of Hagar and her child. Another 12 years had gone by. Abraham was 99 years old. It had now been 24 years since God made His promise. After 24 years of living under this promise God came again to Abraham, promised His presence with him, and reaffirmed the promise. God renewed the covenant with Abram saying: 'My covenant with you is this. You are to become the father of a host of nations. No longer shall you be called Abram. Your name shall be Abraham, for I am making you the father of a host of nations. I will render you exceedingly fertile. I will make nations of you. Kings shall stem from you. I will maintain my covenant with you and your descendants after you throughout the ages as an everlasting pact, to be your God and the God of your descendants after you' (Gn 17: 4-7). As the sign of covenant with Abraham and his descendants, God demanded that every male child should be circumcised (Gn 17: 10). God further said to Abraham: 'As for your wife, do not call her Sarai. Her name shall be Sarah. I will bless her, and I will give you a son by her. Him also I will bless. He shall give rise to nations and rulers of peoples shall issue from him' (Gn 17: 15-16). Sarai and Sarah are variant forms of the same name both meaning 'princess'. Then Abraham fell on his face and laughed, and said in his heart, 'Will a child be born to a man one hundred years old? And will Sarah, who is ninety years old, bear a child?' And Abraham said to God, 'Oh that Ishmael might live before you'. But God said, 'No, but Sarah your wife shall bear you a son, and you shall call his name Isaac; and I will establish my covenant with him for an everlasting covenant for his descendants after him (Gn 17:15-19).

The same promise about an offspring is repeated a second time when three men visited Abraham. Then they said to him, 'Where is Sarah your wife?' And he said, 'Behold, in the tent'. And one of them said, 'I will surely return to you at this time next year; and behold, Sarah your wife shall have a son'. And Sarah was listening at the tent door, which was behind him. Now Abraham and Sarah were old, advanced in age; Sarah was past childbearing. And Sarah laughed to herself, saying, 'After I have become old, shall I have pleasure that my lord being old also?' And the Lord said to Abraham, 'Why did Sarah laugh, saying, 'Shall I indeed bear a child, when I am so old?' Is anything too difficult for the Lord? At the appointed time I will return to you, at this time next year, and Sarah shall have a son' (Gn 18:9-14). God promised to do something humanly impossible and that is why when Abraham and Sarah heard about it, they both laughed: Abraham 'fell on his face and laughed' (Gn 17:17) and Sarah 'laughed to herself' (Gn18: 12) because Abraham's reproductive ability was like that of a dead man. And his wife was long past the age of childbearing (Heb 11:11). God could keep His promise in only one way-by performing a miracle, which He did. Sarah bore a son and named him Isaac, which means 'laughter'. What is fascinating here is that both Abraham and Sarah laughed at God and yet God took their laughter and made it part of His promise, by naming the child 'laughter'. Sarah said: 'God has brought laughter for me. Everyone who hears will laugh with me' (Gn 21: 6). God had transformed the laughter that had earlier been a sign of their unbelief into a symbol of promise and blessing in the future.

Abraham was tested and found worthy of blessings

When things were apparently moving happily for Abraham, God asked him to sacrifice Isaac, the son, on whom the promise rested (Gn 22:1). Abraham loved Isaac very dearly, a son of his old age. He had waited for this child in fulfillment of the promise for 24 years. Isaac was unique and irreplaceable for he was the one through whom the covenant promises were to be fulfilled. God told Abraham, 'Take now your son, your only son, whom you love, Isaac, and go to the land of Moriah; and offer him there as a burnt offering on one of the mountains of which I will tell you' (Gn 22:2). Abraham faced a contradiction between the promises of God and the command of God, for the death of Isaac was like the destruction of all the promises of God. However, Abraham refused to see it that way. He had total faith in God and trusted Him to be faithful. How could God be true to His word if Isaac died? Abraham, as a man of faith, held tenaciously to the conviction that what appeared to him to be an insoluble problem was for God no problem at all. Though everything else was obscure, one thing was clear to him, namely, that God, whose word was unshakably true, had a way of resolving the problem. He knew deep down in his heart that God who promised him descendants like the stars of the sky was always good, trustworthy, faithful, omnipotent and omniscient. Abraham 'did not refuse his son, his only son' (Gn 22: 12-16).

The obedience of Abraham resulted in the confirmation of the divine promise. God said: 'I swear by myself. Because you acted as you did in not withholding from me your beloved son, I will bless you abundantly and make your descendants as countless as the stars of the sky and the sands of the seashore. In your descendants, all the nations of the earth shall find blessing, all this because you obeyed my command' (Gn 22: 16-18). Indeed, 'God blessed Abraham in all things' (Gn 24: 1). 'Abraham, father of many peoples, kept his glory without stain. He observed the precepts of the Most High and entered into agreement with Him. In his own flesh he incised the ordinance and when tested he was found loyal. For this reason, God promised him that in his descendants the nations would be blessed, that He would make him numerous as the grains of the dust, and exalt his posterity like the stars' (Sir 44: 19-21). The calling of Abraham was to be a father, by whom all the nations would be blessed. There is a final understated irony at the conclusion of Abraham's inspiring life. Abraham owned no land at all when Sarah died, though God promised him the land of Canaan. He had to go to the Hittites and pay an extravagant amount of money to buy a cave in which to bury Sarah (Gn 23: 1-16). When Abraham died shortly after, he had no great number of descendants, let alone having descendants like the stars of the heaven or the sand of the seashore. So where were the great promises? What had become of all the great things that God had promised Abraham? We know that the extraordinary faith journey of Abraham doesn't end with Abraham's death. Abraham's faith was not for himself because the promise was not for Abraham. The promise was for the children of Abraham. It would be a long time after Abraham, to be more precise almost 800 years before his descendants would ever own the land that he was promised. And it would be some time after that before they would be a great nation, large in numbers.

The promises to Abraham are fulfilled in Jesus

When Matthew calls Jesus 'Son of Abraham', he specifies that Jesus descended from Abraham, the founding father of the chosen people. He presents Jesus as the fulfillment of God's covenant with Abraham. God had promised Abraham: 'in your descendants all the nations of the earth shall find blessing' (Gn 22:18). Jesus, 'the Son of Abraham', will bring that blessing to the whole world, by making disciples of all nations' (Mt 28: 18-20). It is in Jesus Christ, therefore, as the true offspring of Abraham that the divine promises to Abraham are fulfilled. He is the Son of Abraham, who is however greater than him (Jn 8: 53). Among the descendants of the patriarch, only in Jesus, the inheritance of God's promises reaches its plenitude. 'Now the promises were made to Abraham and to his descendant. It does not say, 'and to the descendants', as referring to many persons but as referring to one, 'and to your descendant', who is Christ' (Gal 3: 16). We can infer that Abraham looked forward in faith for that day, when the only 'Son of God' would come to the world to fulfill the promises of God, made to him. Jesus said: 'Abraham, your father, rejoiced to see my day; he saw it and was glad' (Jn 8: 56). However, Jesus concluded the discourse with the assertion that 'before Abraham was born to be, I AM' (Jn 8: 58).

Abraham was a man of faith and therefore he strongly believed in God and loyally served him in exemplary trust and confidence. Consequently those who have faith are blessed along with Abraham who had profound faith (Gal 3: 9). Paul affirms: 'For through faith, you are all children of God in Christ Jesus. If you belong to Christ, then you are Abraham's descendant, heirs according to the promise (Gal 3: 26-29). He further clarifies this theme: 'For this reason, it depends on faith, so that it may be a gift, and the promise may be guaranteed to all his descendants, not to those who only adhere to the law, but to those who follow the faith of Abraham, who is the father of all of us, as it is written, 'I have made you father of many nations. He is our father in the sight of God, in whom he believed, who gives life to the dead and calls into being what does not exist' (Rom 4: 16-17). Faith is being sure of what we hope for and certain of what we do not see (Heb 11:1). Abraham believed even when things looked apparently impossible and was blessed by God for such a strong faith.

Personal reflection- 'Abraham's faith as facing the impossible'

The faith of Abraham can be explained in a single word as totally and perfectly 'trusting' in God because 'for God nothing is impossible' (Lk 1:37). Paul affirms how Abraham trusted in God's promises without wavering: 'with respect to the promise of God, he did not waver in unbelief, but grew strong in faith' (Rom 4:20). By faith Abraham received power to generate an offspring, even though he was past the normal age, and Sarah herself was sterile, for he thought that one who had made the promises was trustworthy. So, it was that there came forth from one man, himself as good as dead, descendants as numerous as the stars in the sky and countless as the sands on the seashore' (Heb 11:11-12). God seemed to have waited until it was humanly impossible for Abraham and Sarah to have children in order to demonstrate His great power as well as His trustworthiness and to show us how great the faith of Abraham was in His sight. To us, it may appear that God often seems to wait until everything seems hopeless in order to show us how He is the master of every situation. At the same time, through difficult circumstances, He enables us to examine how strong our faith is. A man with strong faith believes that God, who is always trustworthy, can do the impossible at any time, according to His holy will. The question before us is whether we have such a strong faith like that of Abraham to fully trust God's fatherly care. God, who tested Abraham, also tests us to reveal to us the depth and strength of our faith. God is omniscient. He knows the level of our faith. Through trials our faith is demonstrated to others and to ourselves. Apart from the trials of Abraham, we would not have known how strong the faith of Abraham was and why God blessed him in the way He did. Today, the wonderful faith of Abraham has become a great example to us, his spiritual children. We can look to him as a true model of faith.

Trusting in God always

As we face trails, we should not be afraid. Rather, we should face them as Abraham did, in total trust, placing our total confidence in the goodness of God, who is our Father. In fact, trials can strengthen our faith in God and deepen our love for Him and thus they may help us to establish a more intimate relationship with Him. 'Abraham believed in God and it was credited to him as righteousness and he was called as 'friend of God' (Jas 2: 23). So God uses trials to strengthen our faith and our relationship to Him, and also, to demonstrate to others and to ourselves the depth and strength of our faith. Abraham passed the test and was justified. He is presented to us as the greatest example of faith: 'He believed, hoping against hope, that he would become 'the father of many nations' according to what was said, 'thus shall your descendants be'. He did not weaken in faith when he considered his own body as already dead for he was almost a hundred years old and the womb of Sarah was also as good as dead' (Rom 4: 18-19). To doubt means to waver in our trust and confidence in God, disputing with oneself, arguing silently in one's mind. Faith never doubts God's intent or ability to keep His promises. Abraham's faith shows us that a strong faith can never have doubts about God's ability to keep His promises. It enables us to accept God's holy will for us and to surrender our entire lives in His loving hands. We all know that life has its ups and downs, periods of bright sunshine and of murky darkness, hours of sweet solace and hours of dismal hardship. There are moments when fortune 'smiles' on us and makes us happy. There are also moments when it frowns on us bringing suffering and pain. We pass through seasons of prosperity and of adversity. We meet with agreeable surprises and also with sad disappointments. In the midst of such vicissitudes of human life, which is our lot as human beings, how do we fashion our daily life in peace and joy? It is only through strong faith like that of Abraham, that we can place all out trust in Him and let Him guide us in His paternal and all-powerful providence. We need not worry about what would happen in the future for us and for our families or how we are going to get over our present hardships and problems. God knows best and His ways are the safest. To our shortsightedness, at times God's ways may appear to be by-ways and blind alleys. But He sees the safe path from on high and guides us by His mighty arm and loving hands. It is our strong faith that offers us the safe anchorage in the stormy ocean of life. It is faith that leads us to place all our trust in His loving care and walk in the journey of life in serenity and peace. Be not afraid!

Give us today our daily bread: When the Second World War was coming to an end, and the German army was losing the battle, the ordinary German people faced the miserable situation of hunger and starvation. The agricultural fields were burnt by the bombardments by the allies and people were unable to engage in any cultivation. The only way people could eat was by buying the essentials in the government regulated shops that were administered by the Nazis. There was a widow with five young children whose husband died in the battlefield a year ago. She sold whatever little possessions the family had to buy regular food for her five young children. Left with nothing, she faced the grim situation of starvation along with her children. Trusting in God, she went to the government shop and asked for bread. Knowing that she had no money, the Nazi officer asked her what she would pay for the bread. She told him that she would pray for him and for the nation. To mock her piety, He asked her to write her prayer in a paper and he weighed it in the balance against loaves of bread. Even when he placed his entire stock of bread in the balance, the little paper would not raise up in the balance. He opened the paper and read the prayer: **'Give us today our daily bread'.**

Quote: I would count a life well spent and the world well lost, if after tasting all its experiences and facing all its problems, I had no more to show at its close or to carry with me to another life than the acquisition of a real, sure, humble and grateful faith in the eternal and the Incarnate Son of God - **P.T. Forsyth**

Scripture reading for Day 7:Heb 11: 8-19

Prayer for Day 7: O, God of light and goodness, in whom there is neither change nor shadow of alteration! Grant us in the midst of vicissitudes of this life ever to abide by our faith like your servant Abraham. We cling in hope to your promises of redemption. May our hearts be always anchored in your love that neither deceives nor fails! Amen.

8.

NEW ADAM

The Hebrew word 'Adam' means man in the sense of 'mankind'. To designate an individual man, the Hebrew term is 'ben adam', which means a member of the human race. This fact is important in the interpretation of the story of the fall of man, in which the inspired author is speaking, not so much about an individual man, as about the whole human race typified by the individual, named as Adam. For this reason, in the story of paradise and fall of man (Gn 2:4- 3: 24), the term 'Adam' is always preceded by the definite article in Hebrew and thus it appears as 'ha-adam', the man. In Gn 2:7, it is implied that man is called 'adam' because God formed him out of the dirt of the 'adama' (ground). The author of Gn 2:4b-3.24 makes skillful use of this derivation: because man (adam) was formed from the ground (adama), after his fall, he is destined to till the ground (Gn 2: 5) in hard labor (Gn 3: 17, 23) and ultimately go back to it in death (Gn 3: 17). The term 'Adam' designates this first man as an individual only in four passages (Gn 4: 1, 25; 5:1, 3; Tb 8:6). In the rest of the usage of the term, clearly the collective sense dominates. In the genealogical list, as found in Gn 4:25-5.5, the first human being is named simply Man, not merely because he was the first man, but also because he was regarded as the 'type' of all mankind: 'God created them male and female. When they were created, He blessed them and named them 'man' (Gen 5:2).

The fall of the first parents

The narrative of creation (Gn 1) reveals that man was created in the image of God. Then, with the help of the genealogies (Gn 5), it shows that all men formed a unity beyond Israel, in the human race. The message conveyed by these narratives is that Adam acted as a representative of the entire human race and stood before God as the head of the entire human race. With the trial that God set before Adam and Eve, He was in fact testing the whole of mankind. Adam was placed in the garden to act not only for himself but also for all of his future descendents. The curse, arising as the result of the disobedience and the fall, affected all his posterity. Not only was Adam destined to make his living by the sweat of his brow, the entire generations had to follow the same destiny. Not only was Eve consigned to have pain in childbirth, but women of all generations were to undergo the same pain. When they were created, Adam and Eve were given dominion over the entire creation. With a father's disposition, God had purposed every conceivable kindness for man, to whom He gave power and authority over His creation: 'You made humans a little less than a god, crowned them with glory and honor. You gave them rule over the works of your hands and put all things under their feet' (Ps 8:6-7). However, misguided by Satan, man endeavored to enlarge his being. He wanted to be like God, his creator and master and thus he stepped out from the simplicity of obedience to God. He thereby forfeited life in the pleasant garden and all the privileges that came to him by being close to God. After the fall, what remained to human race was a life of toil without any reprieve, in the midst of hopeless and often painful struggle with the power of evil and at the end a certain death. As a result of the sin of Adam, not only mankind but also the entire creation suffered. Paul tells us: 'The creation was subjected to futility and entered into bondage and slavery and it groans and labors with birth pangs as it awaits the full redemption of man' (Rom 8:20-22). That we suffer as a result of Adam's sin is explicitly taught in the New Testament. In Romans 5, for example, Paul makes the following observations: 'Through one man sin entered the world and death through sin' (v. 12). 'By one man's offence many died' (v. 15). 'Through one man's offence judgment came to all men, resulting in condemnation' (v.18). 'By one man's disobedience many were made sinners' (v. 19). There is no way to avoid the obvious teaching of Scripture that Adam's sin had dreadful consequences for the entire human race. It is precisely because of the abundance of such biblical statements that virtually every Christian body has composed some doctrine of original sin linked to the fall of Adam. We understand quite clearly that the doctrine of original sin is something very basic to Christian faith.

Original sin

Original sin is both the consequence of Adam's sin and also the punishment for Adam's disobedience. We are born sinners because in Adam, the entire human race failed. Man, created in the image of God, fell from his state of holiness and happiness, through the deceitful wiles of the evil serpent, Satan, the adversary of God and man. By the righteous judgment of God, man was doomed to die: 'Dust you are, and unto dust shall you return' (Gn 3:19). None of the children of Adam have been exempted from this sentence, for 'death passed upon all men, for all have sinned' (Rom 5:12). When our first parents rebelled against the sovereignty of God, who had every right to command them as their creator, they became spiritually dead. The Spirit of God forsook them; the image of God departed from them. Thus forsaken by God, Satan made them his prey, and filled them with all unrighteousness. They were lost to all holy dispositions and to all heavenly joy. They became the willing slaves of sinful attractions and afflictions. In strictest justice, the Almighty might have left the whole human race to perish. He was therefore under no obligation to save any. The prohibition in Paradise about the divine command was clear and the divine sentence definite: 'you shall not eat of it or even touch it, lest you die' (Gn 3: 3). Our first parents did eat and became dead spiritually by losing the friendship of God, their creator and master. Since Adam was the head of the human race as the first parent with his fall, all his posterity fell in him. It had radical repercussions for the entire human race. As a result of Adam's sin, all men are now sinners. Sin is a universal problem. Everyone commits sins, as no one is perfect. Sin is a universal human condition precisely because every person succumbs to his own private temptations. The Bible makes it clear that suffering and death are not 'natural' to man, and they are afflicting humanity as the result of original sin. In creating Adam and Eve in His own image and likeness, God entered into covenant with them by which they would be blessing or curse not only for themselves, but also for their posterity, the entire human race. As the result of their first transgression, all mankind descending from them, sinned in them, and fell with them. Adam being a representative person, while he stood, we stood; when he fell, we fell. 'All of us,' says Augustine, 'sinned in Adam, because we were part of Adam'.

We were as if in Adam's loins. As a child is a branch of the parent, we were part of Adam, our first parent. That is why, when Adam fell, all mankind also fell with him. When he sinned, we all sinned. Not only is the guilt of Adam's sin imputed to us, but the depravity and corruption of his nature is transmitted to us, as poison is carried from the fountain to the cistern. This is that which we call original sin: 'In sin did my mother conceive me' (Ps 51:5). Original sin is a vigorous active principle within us. It does not remain still, but is ever exciting and stirring us up to evil: 'What I hate, that do I' (Rom 7:15). But God, who is not only a righteous judge but also a compassionate creator, does not leave the misery and suffering of mankind unattended. He promised our first parents redemption through their own offspring, a man from the mankind, another Adam, a new Adam. God said to Satan: 'I will put enmity between you and woman, between your offspring and hers; He will strike at your head while you try to strike at his heel (Gn 3:15). Though the first parents disobeyed God, always merciful as He is, He never abandoned human beings to destruction in sin and death. Rather He let them grow in knowledge and civilization through the course of human history. Culture and civilization was given as a gift from God. Humanity progresses in every way, only through the benevolent goodness of God who guides mankind to its destiny. He initiated civilization with His first compassionate act, when He made leather garments and clothed our naked first parents, even though He banished them from His presence and friendship (Gn 3:21). In His appointed time, God fulfilled His promise to redeem humanity through another Adam, His own Son Jesus Christ.

The new Adam, the Son of God

Adam's fall had precipitated the human race into sin and made the redemption necessary. God, in His mercy, desired to raise the fallen mankind and reconcile it with Himself through His own Son, Jesus Christ, whom He promised as the redeemer to the first parents (Gn 3:15). The promise of salvation to Adam and Eve unfolded in history with the covenant made to

Noah after the deluge (Gn 9: 9). It further continued in the covenant with Abraham and his posterity (Gn 17) whereby the patriarch was justified by God because of his faith in the divine promises (Gn 15: 6). The history of salvation reached a definitive stage with the covenant God made with Israel that He concluded through Moses. By giving the Law on Sinai, God added to the obligation of faith and trust in Him, that of observing the Law (Ex 19:6; 24:7-8). Subsequently, through the prophets God announced a new and more perfect covenant which He was to extend to the whole humanity (Jer 31:31-34; Ez 36:26-28, Is 55:3). What we see is an unbroken continuity in God's plan that reaches the climax with the coming of His own Son for the salvation of the entire human race.

The books of the New Testament present Jesus as the new Adam, whom God sent to the world for the redemption of all mankind and the restoration of the entire creation. The synoptic Gospels make an explicit comparison between Jesus and Adam. Matthew recalls Gn 5:1, as he presents 'the book of genealogy of Jesus Christ, the son of David and the son of Abraham' (Mt 1: 1). Mark describes how Jesus dwelt among the wild animals to signify the restoration of the broken relationship between man and creation' (Mk 1:13). For Luke, the one, who had just triumphed over Satan's temptation, unlike the first Adam who failed in the temptation by Satan, is 'the son of Adam' who is also the Son of God (Lk 3: 38). Undoubtedly we can also recognize behind a Pauline hymn (Phil 2: 6-11) the presentation of contrast between the old Adam, who sought to make himself equal to the divine condition, and Jesus, the new Adam, who did not jealously retain it. Paul explicitly presents Jesus as the new Adam in several passages: 'When the fullness of the time had come, God sent forth His Son, made of a woman, made under the law, to redeem those who were under the law, that we might receive the adoption of sons. Because you are sons, God has sent forth the Spirit of his Son into your hearts, crying, Abba, Father' (Gal 4: 4-6). Paul strongly contrasts the old and the new Adam: 'The first man, Adam, became a living being, the last Adam, a life-giving spirit. But the spiritual was not first; rather the natural and then the spiritual. The first man was born from the earth, earthly; the second man, from heaven. As was the earthly one, so also are the earthly, and as is the heavenly one, so also are the heavenly. Just as we have borne the image of the earthly one, we shall also bear the image of the heavenly one' (1 Cor 15: 45-49). He states further: 'For since death came through a human being, the resurrection of the dead came also through a human being. For just as in Adam all die, so too in Christ, shall all be brought to life' (1 Cor 15:21-22).

The theology of the two Adams

It is in the letter to the Romans, that Paul develops the theology of two Adams, the old and the new, in a very remarkable way. He first states how in Adam all sinned and through the failure of the first Adam entered death: 'therefore, just as through one person sin entered the world, and through sin, death, and thus death came to all, inasmuch as all sinned' (Rom 5:12). 'Death reigned from Adam to Moses, even over those who did not sin after the pattern of the trespass of Adam, who is the type of the one who was to come' (Rom 5: 14). Paul goes on to make an important contrast between 'the first, the old, the earthly Adam' of Genesis and the 'new, spiritual heavenly Adam' who is our Lord Jesus Christ and notes the differences in how they impacted the human race. From the first Adam came disobedience, condemnation and death and from Jesus Christ came, obedience, justification and life. Paul states: 'In conclusion, just as through one transgression condemnation came upon all, so through one righteous act acquittal and life came to all' (Rom 5: 18). For Paul, it is Christ who rectifies the damage caused by the disobedience of first Adam: 'for just as through the disobedience of one person the many were made sinners, so through the obedience of one, the many will be made righteous' (Rom 5:19). According to Paul, grace and justification is assured to humanity through the new Adam who obeyed His Father unto death on the cross: 'The law was added so that the trespass might increase but, where sin increased; grace overflowed all the more, so that, as sin reigned in death, grace also might reign through justification for eternal life through Jesus Christ our Lord' (Rom 5:20-21). A Christian is son of Adam by his birth. But he is reborn in Christ Jesus, the new Adam, through his faith. Now, he is caught up in the drama of the two Adams. Paul advises the Christians to 'strip off the old Adam and his deeds and put on the new Adam, so that he may be renewed unto perfect knowledge according to the image of his Creator' (Col 3: 9-10). 'You must quit now of the old self, whose way of life you remember, the self that wasted its aim on false dreams. There must be a renewal in the inner life of your minds. You must be clothed in the new self, which is created in God's image, justified and sanctified through the truth' (Eph 4: 22-24).

When Paul speaks about death, it is not only the bodily death, but also the spiritual death as well as the eternal death that comes as the result of the spiritual death that comes with the sin. Death understood in this multiple sense touches all men as all have sinned. The power of sin entered into the world as the moral disease and it shows its effect on human beings through their personal sins. Jesus came to repair the consequences of the first transgression, the original sin and to wash us clean from all our sins. In old Adam, Man who had come forth from the hands of his Creator innocent and pure had become the slave of sin. The divine gift of grace and justification came through Jesus Christ who brings deliverance from sin and death. Through justification, man receives a new self in Jesus Christ whom we put on in baptism (Gal 3:27), in an act of complete submission to his divine influence. The change resulting from union with Christ is so radical as to result in a new creation in Christ Jesus (Eph 2:10), in other words a new creature (Gal 6:15). There has been a new generation, a renewal of our nature in the Holy Spirit. Those who believe in Christ have turned away from idolatry to the worship of the one living God, and thus from darkness to light, from sin and death to that of the spirit of life, from the service of the law to grace, from the bondage of pride to love. The ultimate effect of conforming to the new Adam will become clear on the day of resurrection (Rom 8:11). In the new state of being with the new Adam, who conquered sin and death, mankind is forgiven and reconciled with God. For man has been ransomed, at a great price, by the outpouring of the blood of Jesus. He has been sanctified and reconciled to God and no judgment now stands against him. From being God's enemy, man has become a son of adoption. Thus man is justified and this justification puts an end to the state of sinfulness and brings sanctification. Justification, then, is the destruction of sin and death brought by old Adam and the communication of new life by the new Adam.

Personal reflection – 'Jesus, the new Adam'

Paul introduced the title the 'new Adam' in his theological discourse to contrast Jesus with the old Adam. We can make a clear contrast between the two Adams. The first Adam was tempted and failed the test, and in him, we all continue to sin and die. The Last Adam was tempted as was the first, but remained sinless, and lived a perfect life of righteousness. Jesus Christ is 'One who has been tempted in all things as we are, yet without sin' (Heb 4: 15). The first Adam began with everything provided for him in the Garden of Eden and he lost everything. The Last Adam began with nothing in a stable and ended with everything: 'For you know the grace of our Lord Jesus Christ, that though He was rich, yet for your sake He became poor, so that you through His poverty might become rich' (2 Cor 8:9). The first Adam was commissioned to 'be fruitful' and to replenish the earth. The Last Adam came to 'bring many sons to glory' and to fill the heaven with His redeemed people. The first Adam lived a long and fruitful life to accomplish his destiny. The Last Adam was born to die on the cross to accomplish God's eternal purpose. The first Adam was given a bride as a helpmate. The Last Adam had to purchase His Bride, at the cost of His very life. The bride of the first Adam was painless since he was placed in a deep sleep. However, the bride of the Last Adam was purchased through the deep sleep of His death on the cross of Calvary. The first Adam lost his bride through age, disease and death. The Last Adam will never be separated from His bride. Through the first Adam's disobedience the whole mankind became sinners. However, through obedience the Last Adam 'many were made righteous' through His obedience (Rom 5:19). That righteousness that we have received as believers is His gift to us. It is not because we merited it, or earned it. It is ours because Jesus has adopted us and placed us into His family. He is now the head of our family, not the old Adam, our first parent. Before the fall, Adam and Eve enjoyed the Garden of Eden, a perfect paradise, from which they were banished. As God's redeemed children, we shall sit with Christ in heavenly places forever.

To all who believe in the new Adam, He is their All. They receive Him as their Prophet, Priest, and King. They trust in Him as their Atonement, Righteousness, and Advocate with the Father. They receive the gift of the Spirit through His intercession, to renew them after the divine image. He gives them the persevering grace in order to make them conquerors over sin and Satan. He brings them in triumph into the realms of glory and presents them before the throne of the Eternal Almighty. His grace alone can counteract the evil, and produce a new creation in the human being. Now, the believers can sing: 'I choose Him as my portion because He has first chosen me. I love Him because He has first loved me. I happily give my heart to Him because He first loved me and gave Himself for me. I desire to be united to Him always because He draws me with the cords of love and clothes me in His grace'. Indeed, such is the power and grace of the new Adam, Jesus Christ'.

He redeemed his father: There was a rich man who had a lot of parcels of farm land in a small village withithin the territory of my Parish. He paid his workers well, thereby helping them to lead a good life. He was very happy, healthy and content. During one of his visits to a nearby town he became acquainted with a man who became his good friend. This man led him to evil ways. He taught him gambling, drinking and other notorious habits. Unable to pay for his bad habits, the rich man sold most of his cultivable land and became a poor, sick old man. When his only son reached his adulthood, he saw the miserable situation, to which the family had come to as the result of the bad habits of his father. With the remaining lands, he started working hard and slowly bought back all the cultivable lands that his father had lost. He could give work to his villagers once again. Above all, he took his father for treatment and restored him to his former self. The villagers praise him even today as the redeemer of his father. Jesus, the Son of God, became man and redeemed not only Adam but also the entire human race.

Quote: Adam, ambitious, desires to be wise, casts out obedience, then lusts with his eyes; grasps his sweet fruit: 'As God I shall be'! Lord, forgive Adam, for Adam is me- *Richard G. Jones*

We think that Paradise and Calvary, Christ's cross, and Adam's tree, stood in one place; Look Lord, and find both Adams met in me; As the first Adam's sweat surrounds my face, may the last Adam's blood my soul embrace- *John Donne*

Scripture reading for Day 8: Gn 3:1-24

Prayer for Day 8: Almighty and merciful God, you show your power over evil chiefly by pardoning sin and sparing the sinner! Grant us, we beseech you, light and strength, so that, following the example of your only Son, the new Adam and with the help of your abundant grace, we may overcome evil by good. Help us to abide in your love and grace so that we may do what is good and avoid what is evil! Amen.

9

NAZARENE

N azarene is a title by which Jesus was referred to as 'Iesou Nazarene' in all the Gospels. Matthew writes: 'Joseph went and lived in a town called Nazareth. So was fulfilled what was said through the prophets: 'He will be called a Nazarene' (Mt 2:23). Mark states: 'At that time, Jesus came from Nazareth in Galilee and was baptized by John in the Jordan'. (Mk 1:9). A man cried out, 'what have you to do with us, Jesus of Nazareth? Have you come to destroy us? I know who you are - the Holy one of God' (Mk 1:24). The unclean spirit cried out in a loud voice, 'Ha! What have you to do with us, Jesus of Nazareth? (Lk 4:34). The blind man, on hearing that it was Jesus of Nazareth, began to cry out and say, 'Jesus, son of David, have pity on me' (Mk 10: 47). As Peter went out to the gate, another girl saw him and said to those who were there, 'This man was with Jesus of Nazareth' (Mt 26:71). The High Priest's maid seeing Peter warming himself, looked intently at him and said, 'you too were with the Nazarene, Jesus' (Mk 14:67). Pilate had a notice prepared and fastened on the cross. It read: 'Jesus of Nazareth, the king of the Jews' (Jn 19: 19). Peter declared,' Men of Israel! Hear these words. Jesus of Nazareth was a man commended to you by God with mighty deeds, wonders, and signs, which God worked through him in your midst, as you yourselves know' (Acts 2:22). Paul narrating his conversion mentions: 'I asked 'who are you, sir?' And He said to me, 'I am Jesus of Nazareth, whom you are persecuting' (Acts 22: 8). Jesus was indeed known as Nazarene.

Jesus, the Nazarene (of Nazareth)

It is important for us to recall that 'Christian' was not the earliest term that was in regular use to designate the followers of Jesus. Acts 11:26 reports that the term 'Christian' was first used in Antioch, a place far from Palestine and at least 10 or possibly 20 years after the death and resurrection of Jesus. 'Nazarene', a term that was used to refer to Jesus Himself in Palestine, became the early dominant term to designate also those who followed Jesus. It appears that as Christians became more numerous outside Palestine, the term 'Christian' came to be used and became a regular term of reference among the Gentile converts in the Roman Empire. That 'Nazarene' was the first term in use to refer to the followers of Jesus is supported by much evidence. For example we see in Acts 24: 5, where Paul is accused of being 'a ring leader of the Nazarene sect'. The name 'Nazarene' seems to have been derived from the name of the viallge 'Nazareth' assumed to be the place where Jesus grew up from His infancy to manhood.

Some scholars argue that Iesou Nazarene was derived not 'from Nazareth', but rather from the word 'nazir', meaning separated. There are a number of references to Nazirites in the Old Testament (Nm 6: 1-4; Jgs 13: 5-7). A Nazirite was a Jew who had taken special vows of dedication to the Lord whereby he abstained from alcohol and grape-products, from cutting his hair and from approaching corpses for a specified period of time. At the end of the period he was required to immerse himself in water. Luke 1:15 describes John the Baptist as a Nazirite. Early Christian writers describe James the Just, as a Nazirite. However, we know that Jesus was not an ascetic and hence a reference to him as Nazirite is unwarranted: 'For John the Baptist came neither eating bread nor drinking wine and you say, 'He has a demon'. The son of Man came eating and drinking and you say, 'Here is a glutton and a drunkard' (Lk 7: 33-34). Jesus was called Nazarene for the simple reason that He was from Nazareth. However, Matthew's declaration that 'so was fulfilled what was said through the prophets: 'He will be called a Nazarene' (Mt 2:23) poses problems as no convincing identification of the prophecy has been found, either in the canonical books of the Old Testament or in the Midrash traditions. Many conjectures have been made as to which prophetic word Matthew was referring.

The great Church father, Jerome (349-419 A.D), who had an excellent knowledge of Hebrew, suggests a very plausible solution. He mentions in his Commentary that this word 'Nazarene' referred to the prophecy of Isaiah 11:1: 'A shoot shall sprout from the stump of Jesse'. We know that stump of Jesse refers to Davidic lineage as Jesse was the father of king David (1 Sm 17: 12). The Hebrew word for 'shoot' is 'netzer'. Then, the title 'Nazarene' actually emerges from the word 'Netzer' and refers to the Davidic descent of Jesus. The blind beggar Bartimaeus sitting by the roadside in Jericho and hearing that Jesus of Nazareth was passing by, understood it in this way, when he cried out, 'Jesus, Son of David, have mercy on me' (Mk 10: 47; Lk 18:37). Till recently, rarely anybody assumed that the prophecy of Isaiah (11:1) had something to say about that insignificant hamlet in Galilee, 'Nazareth', a small village nowhere ever mentioned except in the New Testament. However, the results of excavations in Palestine seem to confirm that indeed Matthew was correct and justified in referring to the prophecy of Isaiah. During excavations in Caesarea in 1962 a fragment of a marble plaque was discovered with Hebrew inscriptions, which contained a list of priestly families, who had settled in Galilee during the late Roman era. Among them is mentioned a family in Nazareth. The inscription dates back to 3rd or 4th century AD and is the earliest reference to Nazareth in the Jewish epigraphy. It was an important discovery, since it settled an old point of controversy. The Hebrew inscription solved the problem in favor of 'netzer' which means 'shoot'. It also eliminated the supposition that the appellation Nazarene was linked to the name Nazirite, a person consecrated to God. So, the designation of Jesus as 'Nazarene' means in the first place that He was of Davidic lineage. Matthew's declaration, 'He shall be called a Nazarean' (2:23) that fulfilled the prophecy of the prophet Isaiah 11:1

should be taken to refer to Jesus as the descendant of king David. This designation arises from the term 'netzer' which means 'shoot'. Jesus is the shoot that has sprout from the stump of Jesse, the father of David.

Nazareth as the place of the Davidic clan

The excavations during recent decades in Nazareth have shown that the population of Nazareth at the time of Jesus could hardly have numbered more than 200 people. It is most likely that this hamlet in the hills of Galilee belonged to the larger village Japhia, just about a mile away, which was a strongly fortified place. It played an important role in the Great War against the Romans in 66-70 A.D. What the original name of this location of the tribe of Zebulon may have been is unknown to us. The old settlement reaching back into the Bronze Age was apparently deserted in the year 733 B.C. after Tiglath-pileser III, the Assyrian emperor, took most of the Israelites into exile and replaced the territory with people from other conquered territories. As a result, Galilee became a country of Gentiles. That is why, the prophet Isaiah calls it the 'Galilee of the Gentiles' (Is 9: 1). The findings of excavations in Nazareth point out that Nazareth was uninhabited after exile, during the period, 8th to 2nd century BC. During the Maccabean era, of the second century B.C., a strong immigration of Diaspora Jews from Babylon and Persia took place. We may conclude that a group of the Davidic 'Nazarene' clan settled in the deserted village and it is this clan that would have given the name to their new settlement as Nazara 'village of the shoot'. Most of the inhabitants of Nazareth would have belonged to the same extended family, the clan of Nazarene. We can safely conclude that Nazareth assumed its name from the Davidic clan that presumably came from Babylon around the year 100 B.C. and settled in the present location of Nazareth. After the death and resurrection of Jesus, the designation 'Nazarenes' was applied to the early Jewish believers who gathered around apostyle James, known also as the brother of the Lord in Jerusalem. Later, this term would have been applied to all who belonged to this new religious movement especially in Palestine, as evidenced in Acts 24: 5, where Paul was accused of being the ring leader of the Nazarene sect. Even today the Hebrew word for Christians is 'Notzrim' and the popular expression for the Christians among the Arabs is Nassara. No doubt, Christians derived their first name from Jesus, the 'Nazarene', who in turn received His name from the place, where His Davidic clan settled down, about a century earlier.

A brief history of Nazareth

The village Nazareth is not mentioned in the Old Testament nor in the writings of Jewish historian Josephus nor in the Talmud and there are no indications that it was settled during the prehistoric times. Nazareth is in the area that was allotted to the Israelite tribe of Zebulun during the Old Testament period, although it is not mentioned by name. While the site was settled during the period 900 - 600 BC, it was too small to be included in the list of settlements of the tribe of Zebulon (Jos 19:10-16) which mentions twelve towns and six villages. Nazareth is not included among the 45 cities of Galilee that were mentioned by Josephus and its name is missing from the 63 towns in Galilee mentioned in the Talmud. Though insignificant, Nazareth has an ancient past. Many Jewish tombs and caves have been found near Nazareth, indicating that the site was indeed inhabited as early as in the Bronze Age. Along with silos, cisterns and other agricultural equipment that were discovered in archeological excavations, there is also other evidence that confirms that Nazareth was occupied from the early days of the Israelite occupation of the 12th century BC. The pottery remains attest to a continuous settlement during the period 900-700 BC. After those years, there was a break in settlement until the year 200 BC. As we have described earlier, in the Maccabean time, a Davidic clan returning from Exile established a settlement there and named it as 'Nazareth'.

Nazareth is situated in the most southerly hills of the Lebanon range, just before it drops abruptly down to the Plain of Esdraelon. It lies in a hollow plateau about 1200 feet above the level of the Mediterranean, between hills that rise to an altitude of 1610 feet. Mount Tabor is prominent 5 miles to the east, with an altitude of 1930 feet. Numerous Jewish tombs that have been discovered on the slope of Jebel es Likh mark its northwestern boundary. The southeastern limit is the small valley that descends from the beautiful spring presently called as Mary's well. Nazareth is located in Galilee about 65 miles north of Jerusalem nearly half-way between the Mediterranean Sea and the Sea of Galilee. Nazareth has little history, neither before nor after the birth of Jesus. Always a small town, it was neither on a major route nor it had any specific export. A little settlement, able to subsist alone for the most part, there existed little opportunity to draw traders up from the caravan route that went down the hillside. Therefore, Nazareth was a small and insignificant village during the time of Jesus. We have to only remember the famous words of Nathanael who asks Philip: 'Can anything good come from Nazareth'? (Jn 1: 45-46). During the time Jesus spent in Nazareth, prior to His ministry, He would have walked many times on the mountain ranges and in the valley of Jezreel, a place of great battles in Jewish history. This fact must have influenced His assertion that all the holders of swords shall fall by the sword (Mt 26: 52). The people of Nazareth did not welcome their native prophet in their midst, as they said: 'Isn't this the carpenter? Isn't this Mary's son?. They took offense at Him. He was amazed at their lack of faith' (Mk 6:3-6). Luke describes with great drama how the people of Nazareth rejected Jesus. After His sermon in the synagogue aroused their anger, the people took Him 'and brought Him to the precipice of the mountain that their city was built upon, to throw Him down' (Lk 4: 28-30). He moved away to Capernaum where He established the base for His ministry. Although Nazareth was a staunch Jewish village, it seems that it did not have a good reputation for following Jewish law faithfully. The inhabitants were lax in their devotions as determined by the local authorities in Jerusalem. This laxity was to be one of the objections raised against Jesus as the possible savior of the Jews.

Nazareth after Jesus

During the Jewish War, Galilee was the center of resistance to Roman authority. As the result of the aid given to the Jewish rebels, Nazareth and Japhia were both destroyed in 67 AD by the Roman general Titus. In the 2nd century AD, the priestly family of Haspises lived in Nazareth. An inscription discovered in Caesarea mentions Nazareth as one of the places in Galilee where priests of Judea migrated after the war of Hadrian in 135 AD. This was assuredly because this town was all Jewish while other towns of Palestine were hellenized by people who settled there after the Jewish war. Epiphanius, who died in 402 AD, writes that until the time of Constantine (4th century), only Jews inhabited Nazareth. From the 6th century onwards, legends about Mary began to spark the interest of the Christian pilgrims who visited the site, including the supposed house of Joseph and Mary. This led to the construction of the Church of the Annunciation and to the association of a well there with Mary, the mother of Jesus. In the last fifty years, the population of Nazareth has increased rapidly. The modern houses, white and clean, run up all along the hillsides, especially on the north. Spread out in the shape of an amphitheater, set in a green framework of vegetation, modern Nazareth offers to the visitors a very attractive picture. The present city lies lower down upon the hill than the ancient one. It has a population of 60,000. The majority of Nazarenes are Israeli Arabs about 35-40% of which are Christians and the rest are Muslims. The Israeli government built a new city since the 1950s at the upper end, and named it 'Natzrat Illit 'Upper Nazareth' and populated it with a Jewish majority. Even today, Nazareth's singular fame is its association with the Savior of the world, whom ironically it rejected.

Personal reflection – 'Jesus of Nazareth, the Son of God'

Nazareth has the honor of being known as the 'home town' of Jesus Christ and that is why Christian people often refer to their Lord and Savior as 'Jesus of Nazareth'. It was in Nazareth that the angel Gabriel appeared to Mary to announce the coming birth of Christ. Joseph and Mary lived there after their marriage, and it was from there, as the well-known account goes, they went down south to Bethlehem to register for the census that had been ordered by the Roman rulers. It was during that trip that Jesus was born, in Bethlehem. Jesus did not however get to see Nazareth for some time. After being warned by an angel Joseph and Mary fled to Egypt with the newborn Jesus to save His life from Herod. There they remained for a time until after the tyrant's death. Jesus grew up to be a young man in Nazareth. He would have worked hard with Joseph (who is very likely buried somewhere around Nazareth) in the family construction business. When the time came He set out on His ministry. Jesus' activity was located largely in Galilee, and indeed in the more obscure quarters of this 'up country' province. It is to be remembered that Jesus made the unexpected, indeed, scandalous choice of opting for the religious outcast (Galilee), rather than for the religiously respectable (Jerusalem) for His public ministry. Even in Galilee, neither Sepphoris, nor Tiberias, capital cities of Galilee, are mentioned in the Gospels as places where Jesus preached. Instead, He seems to have lived out His life in hamlets like Nazareth, mentioned only in the New Testament, in fishing villages like Bethsaida and in small townships like Capernaum, which seems to have been the center of His missionary operations in Galilee. Given Jesus' well attested and explicitly affirmed preferential option for the poor and the lowly, it is likely that this was not just an accident of history, but a willed choice on His part. For Him, salvation was to be proclaimed and realized not among the rich, the powerful and the cultivated population of the urbanized cities, but among the 'poorest', the lowliest and the lost. He learnt much from the simple folk among whom He lived and in the midst of whom He was brought up before, at the appointed time, He preached them the good news of salvation and called them to conversion.

Jesus, the tekton

Was Jesus a farmer? Was He not rather a 'tekton', a carpenter, as testified in Mark 6:3. A surprising element of Jesus' language is that it seems to reveal a type of imagination closer to the farmer's life than to the artisan's. There is no parable dealing with timber, paring and planning, hammer, nails, furniture, yokes, and plows. The only two logia (sayings) of Jesus referring to wood material are the sayings on the 'easy yoke' (Mt 11:30) and the 'beam in the eye' (Mt 7:5), sayings that hardly evoke any specialized qualification in woodwork. A 'good tree' giving 'good fruits' is the viewpoint of an agriculturist; for a woodworker, the 'good tree' would give good timber. The setting of the parables is more the open field than the workshop. In fact, the Greek word 'tekton' does not mean exactly 'carpenter' but rather 'house builder'. Actually quite a few words of Jesus refer to building techniques: the 'house built on rock' (Mt 7:24-27), the church built on 'Kepha', the Stone (Mt 16:18), the corner stone (Mt 21:42-44), the tower in the vineyard (Mk 12:1), the tower of Siloe (Lk 13:4) and the tower builder (Lk 14:28). Jesus' work in His rural setting must have been rather that of a house builder. The woodwork of those humble mud-wall huts (Mt. 6:19) would have been restricted to narrow windows and a light support of rough rafters with branches laid across for the flat mud roof. This kind of work did not give the expertise to go to Sepphoris as a cabinetmaker for the Roman headquarters and the high officials. More significantly, such an occupation, confined to the limited range of the small village of Nazareth could hardly have fed a man and his family. We may presume that a little plot of land would have added its contribution to the maintenance of the holy family of Nazareth. Or else a landless Jesus could have lent His services as a casual farm-worker at the time of plowing, sowing, or harvesting and at the time of grape or olive picking, thus adding an occasional shekel or two to the meager income of his 'tectonic' employment.

Respecting the local cultural traditions in Mission engagements

Of particular significance is the fact that none of the main Galilean centers like the cities appears on Jesus' itineraries. A map of the main cities of Galilee, as reconstituted, for instance, on the basis of Josephus's account of the Roman reoccupation of Galilee (Jotapata, Gischala, Sepphoris, Tarichaea and Tiberias), would be exactly the map of the places where Jesus did not go. Tiberias was a new city, recently built on the Sea of Galilee, a beehive of activity with the royal court and its hot-water springs frequented by the aristocracy of the Syrian world. Tarichaea was still closer to the northern shore of the lake where Jesus exercised His ministry, just a few miles south of the traditional site of the multiplication of the loaves and of the mount of the Beatitudes. It was the main fishing center on the shores of the lake. According to Josephus, it had a population of forty thousand souls and counted 230 fishing boats. It was famous for its pickled fish (it is the meaning of 'taricheia' in Greek), which were exported far away. Yet it is mentioned only indirectly in the Gospels under its Aramaic name of Magdala. A certain Mary left the town of Magdala to join the group of Jesus' disciples, but there is no report of Jesus having exercised a ministry in this city. The Gospel data do not present an 'urban portrait of Jesus'. Jesus maintained His distance from the 'cities' despite His geographic proximity to them. In a Galilee that experienced the influence of surrounding city-states from outside and the pull of a growing urbanization from inside, the subculture of Jesus remained attached to His rural roots and to a peasant ethos. It is through rural language and its subculture or little tradition that Jesus expressed His experience of God to the ordinary folk that gathered around Him to hear His parables and to experience His healings, as He preached to them, day after day, about the great mystery, the kingdom of God. For the Churches and the believers, who seek to proclaim the Gospel of Christ, the public ministry of Jesus has a very important lesson. They should respect and honor the cultural traditions of the peoples to whom they preach the good news, upholding whatever is good and noble and purifying, by the power of the gospel, whatever is corrupted in their religio-cultural traditions. The good news of the Gospel should be communicated in such a way that it may be able to penetrate the minds and hearts of the peoples and bring forth abundant fruit in their lives.

The flower from Nazareth: A twelve year old boy who came with His parents from Nazareth in Galilee to the Jerusalem temple brought a little branch, full of flowers from His native village to offer to God, whom He called His beloved Father. The parents lost Him for three days when He was in the company of the wise scribes discussing difficult questions about the God of Israel. When He left the temple He left the branch outside the wall of the temple where it weathered. Yet it held on to life to see His glory. After eighteen years, it saw Him again, when people held fresh olive branches and flowers to welcome Him as the Son of David. It rejoiced for its native son. Alas, after five days, there He was, walking as the suffering servant carrying a heavy cross. This time, it cried in sorrow out of love for Him. But it persevered in hope. Forty-three days passed since that sad event. A crowd gathered where the branch was lying on the ground. There He was again blessing the crowd as He ascended into heaven. In joy the shoot bloomed again and shone with beautiful flowers in honor of the man from Nazareth, whom it recognized as the Son of God.

Quote: In the days of His earthly ministry, only those could speak to Him who came where He was. If He was in Galilee, men could not find Him in Jerusalem. If He was in Jerusalem, men could not find Him in Galilee. But His Ascension means He is perfectly united with God. We are in Him wherever we are present to God and this is everywhere and always - *William Temple*

Scripture reading for Day 9:Lk 4:14-30

Prayer for Day 9: O Jesus of Nazareth, our Lord and Savior! We beg you to solidly establish our families in your love, joy, peace, prosperity and above all in your grace. Be with us, protect us from every harm and danger and guide us in the ways of your heavenly Kingdom. Be pleased to give us strength and courage to remain faithful to you all the days of our life on earth! Amen.

10

RABBI - TEACHER

A s Jesus went about preaching the Kingdom of God in Galilee, He was known as Rabbi, along with the related title, Rabbouni, a term ranging in meanings from respectful 'Sir' to a more formal term of 'teacher/role model'. The New Testament calls Jesus 'rabbi' about 13 times. Here are three examples: Then Peter said to Jesus, 'Rabbi, it is good for us to be here; let us make three dwellings, one for you, one for Moses, and one for Elijah' (Mk 9: 5-6). Nathanael asked Him, 'Where did you get to know me?' Jesus answered, 'I saw you under the fig tree before Philip called you'. Nathanael replied, 'Rabbi, you are the Son of God! You are the King of Israel!' (Jn 1:48-50). The disciples were urging Jesus: 'Rabbi, eat something'. He said to them, 'I have food to eat that you do not know about. My food is to do the will of Him who sent me and to complete His work' (Jn 4:31-34). The word 'Rabbi' is derived from the Hebrew root-word 'RaV', which in biblical Hebrew means 'great' or 'distinguished'. Rabbi is a Hebrew term used as a title for those erudite scholars who were distinguished for their learning. They were the authoritative teachers of the Law or the appointed religious leaders of their community. Today rabbis are still responsible for teaching on matters of Jewish religion in general and of the Law in particular. They are qualified to determine the applicability of Jewish law. The Aramaic term was 'rabban and the Hebrew is 'rabbon' and the latter with the suffix 'i' (my) is 'rabbi' or rabboni, literally meaning 'my teacher'. Rabbi was the title normally given by a student of the scribes to his teacher and thus in Greek it is translated as 'didaskale' which means 'teacher'. Rabbi as a title is not found in the Old Testament. However, during the time of Jesus, it was a commonly used title. As per Jewish tradition, Moses was the first rabbi of the children of Israel. To this day he is known to most Jews as Moshe Rabbeinu, 'Moses our Teacher'. Moses is honored as the first and the greatest teacher in the Old Testament. Moses passed his leadership on to Joshua as commanded by God in the Book of Numbers where the subject of semicha (laying of hands or ordination) is first mentioned (Nm 27:15-23). Jewish tradition says that the authority granted through semicha by Moses to Joshua has been passed from rabbi to rabbi to the present day. In the New Testament and in other Christian writings, Jesus is portrayed as the Rabbi in whom the teaching of Moses was fulfilled and yet superseded, the one Rabbi who both satisfied the law of Moses and transcended it: 'The law was given through Moses; grace and truth came through Jesus Christ' (Jn 1:17). Jesus is the Teacher of all the teachers, the Rabbi par excellence.

Jesus, the Rabbi

In the Gospels, Jesus is addressed as rabbi or teacher, a title more often used than any other title except 'Lord'. In Mark, He is called rabbi or teacher 16 times which is more than the title 'Lord' is used in that Gospel. Even the Gospel according to John that elevates Jesus to otherworldly status, more than any other Gospel, has the occasional 'rabbi' (Jn 1:38, 49; 3:2; 4:31; 6:25; 9:2; 11:8) or the Aramaic 'rabboni' (Jn 20:16). Totally, the New Testament calls Jesus 'teacher' about 47 times. On the first day of Unleavened Bread, the disciples came to Jesus, saying, 'Where do you want us to make the preparations for you to eat the Passover?' He said, 'Go into the city to a certain man, and say to him, 'The Teacher says, 'My time is near; I will keep the Passover at your house with my disciples' (Mt 26:17-19). We notice that in this passage Jesus is referring to Himself as a teacher and it is evident that that is how ordinary people recognized Him during His public ministry. John states that Rabbi means 'Teacher' (Jn 1:38). Behind the disputes and confrontations between Jesus, the Rabbi and other Rabbis, the representatives of the rabbinical tradition, the affinities are nevertheless discernible in some forms. One of the most familiar teaching methodology of the Rabbis was the question and answer method, where the question was often phrased as a teaser. Like other Rabbis, Jesus made use of this teaching method: A woman had seven husbands (in series, not in parallel): whose wife will she be in the life to come? (Mt 22: 23-33). Is it lawful for a devout Jew to pay taxes to the Roman authorities? (Mt 22: 15-22). What must I do to inherit eternal life? (Mk 10:17-22). Who is the greatest in the kingdom of heaven? (Mt 18:1-6). The one who put the question acted as a straight man, setting up the opportunity for Rabbi Jesus to drive home the point as response. However, the Gospels in general seem to accentuate the differences between Jesus and other rabbis and the teachers of the Jewish sects, rather than the similarities.

Rabbi Jesus and the Jewish groups of His time

There were many religious groups that the Rabbi Jesus had to encounter during His public ministry. We present only the very important groups and how Jesus differed from them both in His message and in His vision. The groups are: The Sadducees, the Essenes, the Zealots and above all the Pharisees and the Scribes. Sadducees formed the priestly group who held a monopoly over the high priesthood of the Jerusalem temple. Jesus, born to a family that claimed Davidic ancestry in the tribe of Judah, did not belong to the priestly tribe of Levi and had no ancestral tie with the Sadducees. Living and preaching in Galilee, He had hardly any contact with them. When He met them in Jerusalem, Jesus did not feel comfortable with the Sadducee outlook and neither would they have felt comfortable with His. It all ended with the tragedy of the trial, crucifixion death in Jerusalem, the stronghold of the Sadducees. The Essenes and the Jesus movement shared a vivid eschatological expectation and awaited the rule of God. However, the differences are quite obvious. The Essenes were obsessed with rules of purity and other ceremonial practices. Jesus preached His message of God's unconditional love, in a typical rural language as seen in his parables: sowing and harvesting, fishing and building, stitching and kneading the dough, feeding and feasting and settling the accounts for daily workers or for debtors. The mental horizon of these two movements is poles apart. For Jesus, the poor are the blind, the lame, the lepers and all the sundry humble folk found on the Galilean byways (Mt 11:5; Lk 14:21). At Qumran, the seat of Essenes, the poor are the members of the sect, rejected from their rightful place in the Jerusalem temple and persecuted. We know of the Zealots particularly in the context of the Jewish War. They became the soul of the resistance to the Roman legions during the war. Their last stand on the rock of Masada paints a tragic and glorious picture of their fierce commitment to freedom and readiness to die rather than surrender. There remains a vast difference between the outlook of Rabbi Jesus and the Zealots. For the Zealots, the sword and the inevitable violence was the way to the advent of the kingdom. For Jesus, it was love, compassion and forgiveness that lead to God's kingdom. Jesus could not approve of the violent ways of the Zealots.

The life of the Pharisees was that of ordinary lay people sharing in the various avocations and concrete problems of the common folk. But it was also a life inspired by a fierce attachment to God and to the demands of the Covenant. They paid great attention to the ritual of the temple and its laws of purity that came down to matters of kitchen, food, clothing and the Sabbath. The culture of the Pharisees was so deeply rooted in the Jewish tradition that it was the only current that survived the disaster of 70 AD. It became the solid basis on which shattered Judaism could be reconstructed after the debacle of the Jewish War. Like the Pharisees, Jesus lived among the common folk. However, unlike the Pharisees, He was not very much obsessed with the ritual regulations of purity. He sympathized with the forlorn situation of the ordinary people and had much compassion for them. The ordinary people, called the 'am ha-'arets or the 'people of the land' did not belong to any of the Jewish groups. A mixed lot of simple honest souls and of professed sinners, of poor people struggling to make both ends meet and of corrupt publicans, they had this in common that they were more concerned with the cares of daily life than with theological issues. Jesus reached out to these people to impress on them the power of God's love and compassion and to call them to conversion and renewal.

Jesus the Rabbi and the Rabbis, the teachers of the Law

In the time of Jesus, the teachers of the law received the title as Rabbi. They are scholars in law which they regarded as the sum of wisdom and true learning. The position of a teacher of the law in the Jewish community was a respected position of leadership. The scribes as such did not belong to any particular religious group, but most of them were Pharisees, adhering to the strict interpretation of the law. Jesus had to endure the hostility of the scribes or the teachers of the law throughout His public ministry and they too joined the conspiracy of the Jewish religious authorities to eliminate Jesus. The scribes loved the signs of respect and honor bestowed on them. Jesus says this about them: 'They love to be greeted in the market places and to have men call them Rabbi' (Mt 23:7). 'They like to walk around in flowing robes and love to be greeted in the market places and have the most important seats in the synagogues and the places of honor at banquets' (Lk 20: 45-46). Jesus, though addressed as Rabbi, was quite different from those Rabbis, a fact which people could easily observe. We surmise all the differences between Rabbi Jesus and others Rabbis or the teachers of the law under three headings: His message, His methodology and His manner of teaching.

The Message of Jesus - the Kingdom of God

The Kingdom of God is the central theme of the preaching of Rabbi Jesus, the referent of most of His parables and the subject of a large number of sayings. It is also the content of the symbolic actions that form so large a part of His ministry: His table-fellowship with tax-collectors and sinners and His healings and exorcisms. To the listeners of Jesus' preaching, kingdom of God would have indicated not so much a place ruled over by God, which is what the English word 'Kingdom' suggests, but the activity through which God reveals Himself as King. Kingdom of God is synonymous with 'God reigns'. God shows Himself to be King by creating the universe, and by liberating His people through His mighty deeds in history. For Jesus, the realization of the kingdom of God which is the kingdom of love, justice, fellowship and freedom is the very purpose of creation and the goal of salvation history. While the Rabbis spent time teaching and explaining the Law, the Rabbi Jesus proclaimed a distinct and unique message of the Kingdom of God. Jesus announced that the kingdom of God has come in His person and in His ministry. With its coming, the domination of Satan and his evil effects on the world, sin and death, will be ended by the manifestation of God's power. He invited the people to understand and receive God's power and respond to Him by repentance and renewal. Drawing from His own experience of God as 'abba', the dear Father, He proclaimed God's power as His unconditional love for mankind. It is God's gracious gift offered so lovingly and so generously in the person of His only Son. When people encounter this love and respond to it appropriately in trusting surrender, they can experience true freedom, happiness and peace as individuals and in community, by being freed from the clutches of Satan, sin and death. God is approaching humanity through His Son, because He loves mankind with an unconditional and gracious love. Thus, the infinite and unconditional love of Father, witnessed by men in the sending of His only Son, is the great revelation that Jesus taught under the message of the kingdom of God. As the sign of the arrival of the kingdom, Jesus forgave the sins, cast out the demons and healed the sick, in order to reveal that in His person, the saving power of God is operative in the world to redeem mankind and is offered to every person as grace and blessing. He proposed loving surrender to God as the appropriate response.

The methodology of Jesus - the parables

Jesus taught the people and explained to them the mystery and reality of the kingdom of God, using a distinct methodology known as the Parables. In this way, Jesus made a new departure as a teacher. He was not teaching in the synagogues alone. Rather, He was teaching by the lakeside and in the open fields. He was willing to take His teaching out of the conventional setting of the synagogues to the open air and among the crowds of ordinary men and women. In parables, Jesus told earthly stories to convey heavenly truths. Jesus used the parabolic method, first of all, to make people listen. His listeners were ordinary people whose interest He sought to awaken by telling stories related to the ordinary things of their daily life. The parables were the vehicles by which He made abstract ideas concrete and understandable. However, the parables compel the listeners to think for themselves. They were forced to make their own deductions from the stories and discover the truth for themselves. Jesus presented His message of the Kingdom of God mostly through His parables. It was for the listeners to make the right effort in the right frame of mind and heart to understand them and draw their conclusions for their salvation. Eight major themes occur in the parables: the assurance of the approach of the reign of God, the present arrival of the new age, the mercy of God for sinners, the imminence of judgment, the necessity of an immediate personal response, the conditions of discipleship, the passion and the end of the age as consummation.

The message of the kingdom is a clear invitation for repentance and obliged a person to reflect on the message, seek its meaning and apply it for reforming one's life. Jesus taught in two stages, which is well brought out by Mk 4: 33-34: The first is the public teaching making use of classical themes such as king, feast, vine, shepherd and sowing that set the whole audience on reflection. The second is the private teaching and explanation to the disciples that developed at a deeper level what Jesus preached to the villagers who came to listen to Him. Jesus illustrated His message through the happenings of the daily lives of people and their experiences with nature and its rhythm. He pointed to the lilies of the field as He taught the people about avoiding anxieties and worries (Mt 6:28-30). He spoke about the shepherd and his sheep to emphasize that He is the door of the sheep as well as the good Shepherd (Jn 10:1-18). He used the vineyard to teach that He is the vine and His disciples are the branches (Jn 15:1-8). He taught about a plentiful harvest to insist that more laborers are needed (Mt 9:37-38). He spoke about the salt and the light to show the importance of having a positive influence (Mt 5:13-16). This Teacher of all teachers taught about two roads or ways-one is narrow and the other one wide, to show the free choice of humanity regarding its destiny (Mt 7:13-14). Jesus described to them the success of a planning farmer who wanted to build new barns, to show that death can come at any time and that everything will be lost if God does not will it (Lk 12:13-21). He spoke of a sower who sowed seed in different kinds of soils, to illustrate how the word of God is received by different kinds of hearts (Mt 13:3-9, 18-23). He gave the example of the tiny mustard seed to show the power of faith and the growth of the kingdom of God (Mt 13:31; Lk 13:19). In this way, He began with things that were familiar to the ordinary people such as mustard seed and moved into the unknown, transcendent and divine message such as the caring and forgiving love of God for mankind. In His parables, He first told a familiar story and then placed beside it the spiritual lessons. Today, as we reflect on His teachings, especially on His parables, how can we not exclaim that indeed Jesus is the Teacher of all teachers?

The teaching manners of Jesus - with authority and power

The Teacher of all teachers, Jesus 'taught them as one having authority and not as the scribes' (Mt 7:29) who used to hide behind the authority of the elders, without proposing anything as their own teaching. On the contrary, whenever Jesus preached, He spoke on His own authority that amazed the people: 'The people were all so amazed that they asked each other, 'what is this? A new teaching- and with authority! He even gives orders to the evil spirits and they obey Him'. News about Him spread quickly over the whole region of Galilee' (Mk 1: 27-28). Even in His hometown of Nazareth, people marveled at the gracious words that proceeded out of His mouth. And they asked each other, 'Is this not Joseph's son?' (Lk 4:22). In the Temple of Jerusalem, on listening to His teaching, the people were amazed and asked, 'How did this man get such learning without having studied?'(Jn 7:15). Jesus made it clear that the message that He preached is not His own but what He received from the Father: 'My teaching is not my own. It comes from Him who sent me. If anyone chooses to do God's will, he will find out whether my teaching comes from God or whether I speak on my own' (Jn 7: 16-17). 'I speak just what the Father has taught me' (Jn 8: 28). To receive the message of His teaching, a person has to open his heart and mind in docility to God Himself, who speaks through Jesus. In this way the parables are seen as a necessary means of opening up the minds and hearts to receive the good news. The more the listener opens his heart to God and let the revealed mystery penetrate his being, the more he will understand the parables; and, conversely, the more a man fails to open his heart to God and refuses Jesus' message, the more difficult he will find it to understand the parables of the kingdom. The paradox is that 'the blind will see and those who see become blind' (Jn 9:39).

The meaning is unless people surrender themselves totally to the love of God and open their hearts to God in docility, they will neither be able to receive the good news that Jesus preached on behalf of God nor see in Jesus the Son of God, who has come to redeem the world. This fact is underlined in the words of Mark: 'They may be ever seeing but never perceiving, and ever hearing but never understanding; otherwise they might turn and be forgiven' (Mk 4:12). When, struck by the hardness of heart shown by many listeners toward the Gospel, Jesus remarked to His disciples with a quotation from Isaiah 6: 9-10: 'For this people's heart has become calloused; they hardly hear with their ears, and they have closed their eyes' (Mt 13:10-15). To those people, who closed their hearts like the scribes and the Pharisees and refused to believe in Jesus, the message of the parables became unintelligible. The parables brought to focus the blindness and deafness of those who deliberately refused to open themselves to God's grace and hence rejected Christ's message. While the proud and the powerful closed their hearts, the ordinary simple people found comfort and consolation in the message of Jesus. It is exactly in this context that we should understand the prayer of Jesus: 'I praise you, Father, Lord of heaven and earth, because you have hidden these things, and revealed them to little children. Yes, Father, for this was your good pleasure' (Mt 11: 25-26).

Personal reflection – 'Jesus, the Teacher of the teachers'

In those times, Rabbis were the community celebrities and most young men wanted to study under a famous rabbi to get a good education and later to establish a name for themselves as teachers. The Apostle Paul studied under a very famous Rabbi named Gamaliel (Acts 22: 3). Men would approach a renowned rabbi and attempt to gain his attention, his favor in order to be accepted and be trained. Jesus was not concerned about getting the best men as His disciples. Over and over again in the Gospels we see Jesus making Himself accessible to everyone and anyone! He was a Rabbi for all times and for all seasons: a Rabbi who relates to anyone, anytime, anywhere! He chose ordinary men as His apostles. He should have had a great attractive personality that drew people so passionately to Him. We wonder why Simon and Andrew immediately 'left their nets of livelihood and followed Him! In the same way after being called, James and John followed Him immediately. What made those men leave so abruptly and with such decisiveness? We conclude that Jesus must have been a special Rabbi, with a magnetic personality! Great multitudes followed Him, wherever He went. He was comfortable with people of all kinds, was compassionate toward the learners, established a relationship with the listeners and stimulated and maintained interest as He taught. Jesus, above all, loved the people, unlike the other Rabbis or teachers of the law who harassed the people, by heaping heavy burdens in the name of law. Jesus Himself says this about them: 'They tie up heavy loads and put them on men's shoulders, but they themselves are not willing to lift a finger to move them' (Mt 23: 4) and 'They devour widow's houses' (Lk 20: 47). On the contrary, Jesus proposed only the commandment of love as the ethics of the kingdom of God and gave the light yoke and easy burden (Mt 11: 30) of loving God and loving neighbor as the greatest commandment (Mt 22: 36-40) and as His new commandment

(Jn 13: 34). Jesus Himself became the best model for loving God and loving others in His entire life, leading Him to sacrifice His life on the cross. The leading force that motivated Jesus to daily climb the hills and mountains of Palestine and to walk through valleys and to travel across the lake to meet people in different villages and preach the good news to them for long hours was His profound love for the Father as well as His deep compassion for the people. Matthew has this to say about the wonderful love of Jesus, the Rabbi: 'Jesus went through all the towns and villages, preaching the good news of the kingdom and healing every disease and sickness. When He saw the crowds, He had compassion on them, because they were harassed and helpless, like sheep without a shepherd' (Mt 9: 35-36).

A Parable of the Body and the Soul: Antoninus, the Roman Emperor, asked Rabbi Judah the prince (190 AD), how there could be punishment in the world beyond. Since body and soul after their separation could not have committed sin, they could blame each other for the sins committed upon earth. The Rabbi answered in a parable: A certain king had a beautiful garden in which were excellent fruits; and over it he appointed two watchmen, one blind and one lame. The lame man said to the blind man, 'I see tasty fruits in the garden. Carry me thither that I may get them and we will eat them together'. The blind man consented and both ate of the fruits. After some days the Lord of the garden came and asked the watchmen concerning the fruits. Then the lame man said, 'As I have no legs I could not go to it, so it is not my fault'. And the blind man said, 'I could not even see it so it is not my fault'. What did the Lord of the garden do? He made the blind man carry the lame and thus passed judgment on them both. So God will replace the souls in their bodies and will punish both together for their sins.

Quote: I am trying here to prevent anyone saying the really foolish thing that people often say about Him: 'I'm ready to accept Jesus as a great moral teacher but I don't accept His claim to be God'. That is the one thing we must not say. A man who was merely a man and said the sort of things Jesus said would not be a great moral teacher. He would either be a lunatic-or else he would be the Devil of Hell. You must make your choice. *-C. S. Lewis*

Scripture reading for Day 10:Mk 4: 1-20

Prayer for Day 10: Lord Jesus, you revealed yourself and the secret of your Father's kingdom to the little ones. Grant that through our intimacy with you we may become like those little ones. Give us a share in the treasures of wisdom and knowledge of your Divine Heart! Make our wills be ever devoted to you and our hearts ever eager to serve your divine majesty! Amen.

11

PROPHET

*A*s the public ministry of Jesus was nearing its end, the Jewish multitude oscillated between describing the role of Jesus as Rabbi and attributing to Him an authority as a Prophet. In the beginning of His ministry, they were convinced that He was a Rabbi, a teacher of the law, though somewhat different from other Rabbis. However, during the course of His ministry, they saw that He had also the attributes of a prophet. That is best seen on Palm Sunday, when they acclaimed: 'This is the prophet Jesus from Nazareth of Galilee' (Mt 21:11). Jesus was at times hailed as a prophet during the public ministry: 'He is a prophet, like one of the prophets of long ago' (Mk 6:15). When Jesus raised the widow's dead son back to life at Nain, the people exclaimed: 'A great prophet has appeared among us' (Lk 7:16). Acknowledging Jesus as a prophet might come short of a true discipleship since it failed to recognize the divinity of Jesus. But the people were at least far in advance of the Pharisees, the Scribes and the Sadducees, who came to Him in a tempting mood to ask for a sign from heaven. No sign, whether in heaven or on earth, would convince them as they saw in Jesus a Samaritan, blasphemer, glutton and drunkard, and the companion of publicans and sinners (Mt 11:19). However, as for the ordinary people, Jesus appeared to be a great prophet sent by God.

When Jesus asked His disciples, 'Who do people say the Son of Man is?' they replied: 'Some say John the Baptist; others say Elijah; and still others, Jeremiah or one of the prophets' (Mt 16: 13-14). Among the ordinary people many seemed to have agreed in regarding Him as a prophet of the highest rank, differing only as to which of the great prophets of Israel He most nearly resembled or personated. These opinions are explained in part by an expectation then commonly entertained, that the advent of the Messiah would be preceded by the return of one of the prophets. For the disciples, Jesus Christ was the 'prophet', predicted in Deuteronomy by Moses: 'The Lord your God will raise up unto you a Prophet from your midst, of your brethren, like unto me; unto him you shall hearken' (Dt 18:15). God also made this promise to Moses: 'I will raise them up a Prophet from among their brethren, like unto you, and will put my words in his mouth; and he shall speak unto them all that I shall command him. And it shall come to pass, that whosoever will not hearken unto my words which He shall speak in my name, I will require it of him' (Dt 18:18-19). That is why Jesus said to the Jews: 'For had you believed Moses, you would have believed me: for he wrote of me' (Jn 5: 46). For us, the believers, Jesus Christ is the Son of God, and when He speaks, God is speaking to us and hence Jesus Christ is the 'prophet' of God par excellence.

We, the believers, share in His prophetic function through our baptism and thus we proclaim His good news, just as the prophets in the Old Testament were sent by God and spoke in His holy name.

Prophetism in the Old Testament

The English word 'prophet' is derived from the Greek 'prophetes', a term that always denotes one who communicates divine revelation. In the LXX or the Greek Old Testament, the Greek term 'prophetes' translated the Hebrew 'nabi', the usual word for a prophet. Hebrew prophetism is generally recognized as a uniquely distinctive Hebrew phenomenon. Parallels that can be adduced from other ancient Near Eastern sources are superficial. A remarkable example of prophecy from the Near East comes from the archives of the upper Mesopotamian town of Mari in the time of Hammurabi, King of Babylon (1728-1686 BC). In the letters of Mari there appears a priest called the 'muhhu' who delivers oracles of the god 'Hadad' to king Zimri-lim. These oracles resemble the utterances of the prophets of the Old Testament in their introductory formula and in their form and style. In their content, they refer to the relation of the king with his god in terms that are not dissimilar to the dynastic oracle of David. However, the resemblance, quite superficial, between these phenomena and Israelite prophecy stops at the form and style. The ethical and religious content of Israelite prophecy has no parallel whatever in the ancient world and as such it manifests unique characteristics.

The origins of Jewish Prophetism

The origins and early development of Hebrew prophecy are somewhat obscure. Moses is identified as the head of all the prophets and greater than any one. He is the supreme example of one who receives the word of Yahweh and speaks it to Israel thereby leading Israel to the affirmation of basic and foundational Israelite beliefs. Along with him, the patriarchs like Abraham are also called prophets, but these are only later additional titles to the great leaders of the Jewish people. Prophetism as such seemed to have appeared in Israel at the end of the period of the Judges. Shortly before the establishment of the early monarchy there appeared groups called 'the sons of the prophets'. As they are described in 1 Samuel 10:5-12 and 19:20-24, it seems that they were groups organized for worship in cultic song and dance. Of these prophets, the first who can be discerned with any degree of clarity is Samuel. In 1 Samuel, prophetism is presented rather suddenly as an established institution, and it played a role of some importance in the events leading to the institution of the Israelite monarchy. It was Samuel who anointed Saul as the first king of Israel. At that time, a number of different names were given to the prophets. He could be called 'is-elohim (a man of God: 1 Sm 9:6) and ro eh (a seer: 1 Sm 9:9), as well as nabi (prophet: 1 Sm 10:10). The last term 'nabi' eventually came to be the standard designation of the prophet. It is an ancient term as the people of Ebla (north Syria) already used the term 'nabi' in the 23rd Century BC. Most likely 'nabi' is a passive form that designates 'someone' who has been called and sent. In Jewish prophecy, the one who was calling and sending was always God. The prophets were men called by God and were sent to bring His words to others. The prophet was thus delegated to speak for Yahweh (Is:8-9; Jer 1:9). The prophetic vocation was compelling even though the prophet might be reluctant or untalented (Am 3:7-8: Jer 1:7-8); God communicated His word to prophet (Is 6:9; Jer 1:7-9; Ez 2:8-3.3) and this communication involved visions and auditions, states analogous to those known in later mystics. The same Spirit of God animated all the prophets of the Old Testament.

Functions of the prophets

The prophet speaks not for himself but for God. The prophetic form of utterance is introduced by the set formulae, 'Thus speaks Yahweh' and often concludes with the phrase, 'the oracle of Yahweh'. The prophetic message might contain threat or warning, promise, reproach and admonition, lamentation, taunt-song, drinking song, love song, wise saying, priestly response, legal plea and dialogue. The use of these popular forms added much to the power and appeal of the prophetic discourse, which is far removed from what is conventionally conceived as 'preaching'. Sometimes the prophetic discourses included symbolic actions. In the lives of the prophets, the message of God was lived out before the people of Israel. For example, purchase of a field (Jer 32), illness and mental anguish (Ez 3:25; 4:4-8) and even marriage (Hos 1:2-3) and celibacy (Jer 16:1-9) and the widower status (Ez 24: 15-27) are presented as symbols. For a considerable period of history, kings, priests, and prophets were the three pillars of the society of Israel, sufficiently distinguished so, as to be occasionally antagonistic to one another. Normally they were linked in a necessary interdependence. The prophets were on hand to counsel the kings: Nathan, Gad, Elisha, Isaiah and Jeremiah are good examples. It was their prerogative to declare whether the action undertaken was such as God wished, whether such a policy clearly fitted into God's will. Though related to them by interdependence, the prophetical office in the strict sense of the word was not an institution like the kingship and the priesthood. Israel on its own initiative could make a king or even a priest (Dt 17: 14), but it should not create a prophet. The latter is a pure gift of God, object indeed of His promise (Dt 18: 14-19), yet freely given. The prophet has a place in the community, but it is the divine call that constitutes him a prophet.

The prophets of the Old Testament are divided into four Major Prophets (Isaiah, Jeremiah, Ezekiel, and Daniel) and 12 Minor Prophets (Hosea, Joel, Amos, Obadiah, Jonah, Micah, Nahum, Habakkuk, Zephaniah, Haggai, Zechariah, and Malachi). The terms major and minor have nothing to do with the relative importance of these men and their message. They simply refer to the respective extent or size of the prophetic books of the Old Testament. It must be remembered also that in the Old Testament, the prophetic name and office were not confined to the 16 canonical prophets of the modern Bible, the so-called writing prophets. There are other men who appear in Israel's history, men such as Elijah and Elisha, who were equally inspired bearers of God's word, although few of their words have been preserved in writing. We should remember that even the so-called writing prophets did not write their books. Their words were preserved in oral tradition and later, inspired writers recorded and arranged their traditional words. Thus, it is the prophetic word as edited, arranged and even added to by these writers that the Church now possesses in the inspired text of the Holy Bible. In Judaism, all the books of the Hebrew Bible and of Jewish versions derived from it are divided into three main groups: the Torah, the Prophets and the writings. The prophets are divided into the First Prophets including Joshua, Judges, Samuel, and Kings, which were believed to have been written by prophets, and the later Prophets including Isaiah, Jeremiah, Ezekiel, and the 12 Minor Prophets. The Hebrew Bible puts Lamentations and Daniel among the Writings, and it does not have Baruch at all. Already in the second century BC the prophetic books had begun to become classical and canonical, as prophetism ended in Israel.

Jesus, the Prophet

In the Sermon on the Mount, Jesus is quoted as asserting 'Think not that I have come to abolish the law and the prophets; I have come not to abolish them but to fulfill them. For truly I say to you, till heaven and earth pass away, not an iota, not a dot, will pass from the law until all is accomplished' (Mt 5:17-18). The affirmation of the permanent validity of the law of Moses is followed by a series of specific quotations from the law. Each is introduced with the formula: 'You have heard that it was said to the men of old'. Each quotation is then followed by a commentary opening with the magisterial formula, 'But I say to you' (Mt 5:21-48), that proposes something different. The commentary seems to be an intensification of the commandment, to include not only its outward observance but the inward spirit and motivation of the heart. All these commentaries are an elaboration of the warning that the righteousness of the followers of Jesus must exceed that of those who followed other teachers of the law (Mt 5:20). The entire Sermon on the Mount confirms the special status of Jesus as a teacher or Rabbi and as a Prophet. He not only taught about the kingdom of God as a teacher but also performed accompanying signs as a prophet sent by God. Jesus exercised both a prophetic role and a teaching role. In this way, Jesus differed from the Rabbis, who only interpreted the law and hid behind the authority of the law for explanation. Unlike Jesus, these teachers of the law neither spoke with any originality nor performed any accompanying signs.

Denunciation and prediction

The prophets spoke in the name of God, which involved at times the unpleasant task of denunciation, condemnation and also prediction of destruction. The prophetic role of Jesus is seen in His denunciations of the unrepentant cities, where most of His miracles were performed: 'Woe to you, Korazin! Woe to you, Bethsaida! If the miracles that were performed in you had been performed in Tyre and Sidon, they would have repented long ago, in sackcloth and ashes. But I tell you, it will be more bearable for Tyre and Sidon on the day of judgment than for you. And you, Capernaum, will you be lifted up to the skies? No, you will go down to the depths. If the miracles that were performed in you had been performed in Sodom, it would have remained to this day. But I tell you that it will be more bearable for Sodom on the day of judgment than for you' (Mt 11: 20-24). He also condemned the teachers of the law and the Pharisees:' Woe to you, teachers of the law and Pharisees, you hypocrites! You shut the kingdom of heaven in men's faces. You yourselves do not enter, nor will you let those enter who are trying to' (Mt 23:13). Jesus predicted of the consequences for Jerusalem, the holy city, for rejecting Him. Forty years after Jesus was crucified, the Romans came and fulfilled His prophecy. A great judgment came upon that generation. It is amazing how each detail was fulfilled exactly. Jesus made the following predictions: Jerusalem and the temple would be destroyed (Lk 21:20; Mt 24:2). Jerusalem was to be encompassed with armies (Lk 21:20). Jerusalem was to be besieged and a trench dug around it (Lk 19:43). Great tribulation and woes were to accompany the siege and the destruction of Jerusalem (Mt 23:35-36; Lk 21:20-23). Jerusalem was to be leveled and not a stone of the Temple was to be left standing upon another (Lk 19:43-44; Mk 13:2). The Jews would be slain or led away into captivity (Lk 21:24). Those that were not killed were placed on the slave market and carried away to other nations. Jesus is never wrong. In fact we have just barely touched upon the prophecies of Jesus Christ. Jesus Christ is the greatest of the prophets who establishes His believers as the prophets to proclaim the word of God, in words and deeds, above all by their dedicated lives.

The symbolic actions of Jesus, the prophet

The New Testament does not attribute the power of performing miracles only to Jesus and His followers (Mt 12:27), but it does cite the miracles as substantiation of His standing as the great Prophet. The numerous miracles as signs and wonders affirmed His continuity with the prophets of Israel and asserted His superiority to them as the Prophet whose coming they had predicted. We can better understand the kind of prophet Jesus was, and how He attracted crowds and followers, if we focus on His miracles. People flocked to Him seeking to be healed (Mk 1:32-34). Neither He nor others thought that His miracles showed that He was a supernatural being. According to Jesus, the miracles were evidence that the Spirit of God was on Him. The people, at the time of Jesus, believed in spiritual powers, some demonic, and they attributed many illnesses as well as antisocial behavior, to them. For example, in Mark 5:1-13, we see Jesus sending the evil spirit that inhabited a demoniac into 2,000 swine, which rushed into the Sea of Galilee and drowned. They also believed that God sent sickness and death as punishment for sins; this is reflected in the story of Jesus healing a man by telling him that his sins were forgiven (Mk 2:1-12; Mt 9:1-8). However, Jesus presented Himself as the author of life and brought healing to numerous people through His miracles. Jesus' followers and possibly Jesus Himself, besides, saw the miracles as proof that He had the Spirit of God and was imbued with the power from above, as God's Chosen One. When John the Baptist sent a message to Jesus, asking, 'Are you he who is to come?' Jesus appealed to the miracles: 'Go and tell John what you hear and see. The blind receive their sight and the lame walk, lepers are cleansed and the deaf hear and the dead are raised up and the poor have good news preached to them' (Mt 11: 4-5).

Signs and wonders

In the four Gospels, so many miracles are reported. In Mark, for example, out of that Gospel of 661 verses, as many as 209 narrate the miracles. Matthew and Luke carry the same tendency still further. In addition to the familiar collections of sayings, the Synoptics repeatedly retold the tales of Jesus' prophetic acts of power, His healings and exorcisms. John omits the vast majority of Jesus' reported miracles, retaining only seven, of a particularly stupendous character. However, the last chapter of that Gospel offers the comment that Jesus, with His followers as witnesses, performed many other actions as well, 'which are not recorded in this book' (Jn 21: 25). Many of those actions, indeed, were miraculous, described by the word 'sign' (semeion) which appears no less than seventeen times in John's Gospel. The miracles attributed to Jesus in the four Gospels amount to nearly forty and a good many more can be added from non-canonical writings. Even Jews who maintained a profound hostility to Jesus believed that He possessed gifts as a sorcerer and worker of wonders. As we have seen, John refers with particular emphasis to these signs, and it seems that the writer of that Gospel, and others, believed that Jesus regarded His apparently miraculous actions as possessing a symbolic character. The miracles act out, and symbolize, the present coming of the Kingdom of God, and its complete realization in Jesus Christ. These miraculous happenings are signs that the Deliverer has come. They are also signs of the greatness of His power. When Jesus walks on the water, He is demonstrating a triumph over satanic evil forces that He is reducing to subjection. At the same time He displays the power of the true faith. The reference to waters appears again when Jesus calmed the storm that made them turbulent. In the Jewish thought, in which winds and sea were anthropomorphized, this kind of turbulence stood for the worldly troubles that the Kingdom of God is bring to an end. Jesus is accomplishing two things at one and the same time through the miracle: He is symbolizing the transformation that is happening in the world by the arrival of the rule of God in His person. Simultaneously He is also bringing God's kingdom to the world.

Personal reflection – 'The Gospel in deeds'

Jesus' miracles are the gospel proclaimed in deeds. Jesus proclaims the Good News to the poor not only in words, but in deeds, as well. The prophet Isaiah assured that 'glad tidings are to be proclaimed to the lowly' (Is 61:1), a prophecy that found fulfillment in Jesus' public ministry. Jesus loved the Poor, the blind, the lame, the lepers, the impure, the sinners and all of those that were marginalized by the Palestinian society and brought them comfort in words and deeds. Jesus' activities on behalf of the poor are presented as the evidence that He is the evangelizer foretold by Isaiah. Jesus works are part of God's campaign of liberation from the alienation of disease and death. The exorcisms demonstrate that the reign of God has arrived (Mt 12:25-27; Lk 11:17-22; Mk 3:24-27). These deeds of (divine) power (dunameis), as they are named in the Synoptics, constitute more than a simple apologetical confirmation of the validity of the Prophet Jesus and His ministry. They are not a mere attempt to prepare people's minds to receive the Good News. They have as much evangelical value as the Sermon on the Mount, the Beatitudes, or the Parables. Like symbolic actions of a prophet, the miracles performed on behalf of the lowly of Galilee speak the messianic Good News to the poor. Like the Old Testament prophets, Jesus proclaims His message by symbolic deeds as much as by words. Thus His entry into Jerusalem seated upon a donkey and the purification of the Temple, His meals taken with tax collectors and the welcome He offers to the sinners, have the value of evangelical signs. In Jesus, the Word of God had 'emerged' from the Temple to journey in Galilee, on the periphery of the Promised Land, there to encounter not sages and scholars, but the weak and the humble (Mt 11:25).

What so many prophets and righteous would have wished to see and hear but could not, was now manifested to the marginal population of far-off Galilee (Mt 13:16-17; Lk 10:23-24). As did many prophets before Him, Jesus communicated by symbolic acts as well as by words. He called 12 disciples, apparently to represent the coming restoration of the 12 tribes of Israel. He ate with sinners, in order to indicate that they would be included in the kingdom of God. He entered Jerusalem on a donkey perhaps to remind His followers of Zechariah 9:9 (cited at Matthew 21:5: 'Your king is coming to you, humble and mounted on an ass'). When He overturned tables and stalls in the Temple area, He was also acting symbolically, indicating that the Temple and its cult would be renewed in His person. His last meal with the disciples seems also to have been a symbol, one that pointed toward the coming of the kingdom that would be like a banquet (Mt 22:1-14). Today, Jesus grants us a share in His prophetic role through our Baptism to proclaim the Gospel message not only in our words but also in our deeds, especially by our exemplary and witnessing lives in this world.

He became a prophet in his death: There lived a monk called Telemachus, late in the 4th century. By this time, Rome was officially Christian but one thing had lingered on in the now Christian Rome: there still existed an arena. There were still gladiatorial games. Of course, Christians were no longer thrown to the wild beasts. But still those who were captured in the war had to fight and kill each other during the Roman Holidays. Men still shed blood and lost their lives in violence promoted as gladiator fight. Telemachus who came to see Rome entered the arena. He was shocked by what he saw in the arena, as the bloodthirsty crowd consisted of the Christians who promoted the killing by violence as sports. He crossed the barrier and ran to the center of the arena and stood between the gladiators. The crowd shouted and threw stones at him and asked him to get out. People shouted to the gladiators: 'Kill him! Let the games go on'. The organizer of the game gave the order to kill the monk and one of the gladiators killed him with his sword. As Telemachus lay dead, the crowd realized that the gladiaitor had killed a holy monk. They felt guilty and were ashamed. The game ended that day abruptly, never to start again. Telemachus became a prophet in his death.

Quote: 'I am no prophet', Amos replied to Amaziah, 'nor am I a prophet's son; I am a herdsman and a dresser of sycomore figs. But the Lord took me as I followed the flock and said to me, 'Go and prophesy to my people Israel'- *Amos 7:14-15*

Scripture reading for Day 11:Lk 4: 14-30

Prayer for Day 11: Lord Jesus, grant us the grace ever to live and labor for you alone, with a pure intention of a prophet and not to wonder or to be disheartened when we suffer opposition and fail in our efforts. Whisper into our ears those words of yours: 'Have confidence, I have overcome the world'. O Lord God, take from me whatever keeps me from you and give me whatever brings me closer to you. Take me from myself and give me to yourself! Amen.

12

MASTER

*T*he disciples of Jesus called Him, the 'Master'. While for the crowd He was a Rabbi or possibly a Prophet, to those who believed in Him and followed Him, Jesus was 'the Master'(Lk 9: 49) and they were His disciples. The term disciple, in Greek 'mathetes' occurs about 250 times in the New Testament and most of these occurrences refer to the disciples of Jesus. In Latin, the word is 'discipulus'. Both the Greek and the Latin signify 'learner' and thus a disciple is a person who 'learns' from his master by being with him. The relation of Jesus and His disciples was in some respects similar to the relation of the Jewish Rabbi and his disciples, who gathered disciples around them and transmitted their teachings. We have seen how Jesus Himself was addressed as Rabbi. However, in many respects the relation between Jesus and His disciples was also different from that of the Rabbis and their disciples. Jesus demanded a more complete personal surrender to Himself than did the Rabbis. His disciples must be willing to abandon father and mother, son and daughter, and to take up the cross and even lose his life in following Jesus (Mt 10: 37-38). Jesus demanded a more radical loyalty and fidelity from his disciples. The disciples of Jesus differed from the disciples of the Rabbis also in the sense that they could not hope to attain His dignity. Their entire life was to be spent in His discipleship, following Him and serving Him, whereas the disciples of Rabbis often left their masters and began gathering their own disciples. Also, the attitude of the disciples of Jesus toward tradition was not that of the Jewish disciples. The disciples of the Rabbis strove to preserve the exact teaching of their Rabbis word for word to the best of their ability and the most successful disciple was the one who could best repeat by memory what he had heard. The disciples of Jesus were not merely channels of verbal tradition. They were called to be the 'privileged' witnesses to the Master, to His life and divinity, to His public ministry of teaching and healing and above all to His passion, death and resurrection and proclaim their salvific significance to all the nations and the peoples.

The Disciples of Jesus

The term 'disciples' is used in the New Testament, in the broad sense, in a more specialized sense and finally in a strictly technical sense. During the public ministry of Jesus, many persons believed in Him and accepted His teachings. In the broad sense, it is used 230 times in the Gospels and 22 times in the Acts to refer to all those who believed in Him. Among these many followers, Jesus, the Master, chose some to follow Him more closely and get involved more actively in His public ministry. In a more specialized sense, the term 'disciple' refers to those close followers. In this specialized sense, the term is applied to the 70 or 72 who followed Jesus more closely than the average believer but not as closely as the twelve apostles. It seems that the disciples of Jesus were gathered in concentric circles, of which the Twelve were the innermost group and they were called the specific term, the 'Apostles'. Along with the Twelve, a larger number of eligible men and some women were found in the circle of the disciples of Jesus. That is how, we find two missions in the Gospel according to Luke. First, 'Jesus sent the twelve to preach the kingdom of God and to heal the sick' (Lk 9: 2). Later, 'He appointed seventy-two others and sent them two by two ahead of Him to every town and place where He was about to go' (Lk 10: 1). We may also remember that the disciples of Emmaus did not belong to the group of the Twelve apostles (Lk 24:33). Some women too followed Jesus: 'Some women who had been cured of evil spirits and diseases were with Him. Mary called Magdalene, from whom seven demons had come out; Joanna, the wife of Cuza, the manager of Herod's household; Susanna; and many others. Those women were helping to support them out of their own means' (Lk 8:2-3).

There was, however, a clear differentiation between the Twelve and the rest of the disciples, including the 70 or 72 who were authorized to preach and to confirm His teachings with miracles: 'Many of His disciples turned back and no longer followed Him. Jesus asked the Twelve, 'You do not want to leave too, do you?' and Simon Peter answered Him: 'Lord to whom we shall go! You have the words of eternal life. We believe and know that you are the Holy one of God'. Then, Jesus replied: 'Have I not chosen you, the Twelve? (Jn 6: 66-70). In its strictly technical sense, the term 'disciple' is synonymous with the Twelve or with one or more of their members (Lk 9: 54; Jn 6:8; 12:4; 20: 24-25). It is found more commonly in the gospel according to Matthew than in the other gospels. Matthew introduces a certain limitation to the term 'disciple' and the pivotal text that makes the meaning quite definitive is 10: 1-4. In the opening verse, Matthew identifies the twelve disciples by listing the twelve apostles: 'He called his twelve disciples to Him and gave them authority to drive out evil spirits and to heal every disease and sickness (Mt 10:1). Up to this time, his use of the term 'disciple' is indefinite, but beginning with chapter 10, his reference to the disciples means only the Twelve.

The Twelve as the privileged disciples of Jesus

We know from Christ's own words that the number twelve was designed to bear a mystic meaning. Describing the rewards awaiting them in the kingdom for their services and sacrifices, Jesus said: 'Truly I tell you. At the renewal of all things, when the Son of Man sits on His glorious throne, you who have followed me will also sit on twelve thrones, judging the twelve tribes of Israel (Mt 19:28). The Greek word 'apostle' conveys to us the meaning of messenger, delegate, envoy or collector of tribute paid to the temple service. In the Gospels the Twelve were simply to be Christ's envoys. As Jesus was sent by His Father so the Apostles were sent by Jesus. It is Jesus Christ who gave the title 'Apostle' to the Twelve: 'When morning came, He called His disciples to Him and chose the twelve of them, whom He also designated as apostles' (Lk 6:13). 'He appointed twelve, designating them apostles, that they might be with Him and that He might send them out to preach and to have authority to drive out the demons' (Mk 3:14-15). The term 'apostle' (apostolos in Greek- a derivative from 'apostellein', meaning to send) signifies a special mission. The Apostle not only transmits a message, but also guides the recipients to apply the transmitted message in their lives. In short, an Apostle is a spiritual leader and a guide to the community gathered in the name of Jesus.

The number twelve

The number twelve was the choice for obvious symbolic reasons. It happily expressed in figures what Jesus claimed to be, and what He had come to do. It significantly hinted that Jesus was the divine Messianic King of Israel. He has come to set up the kingdom whose advent was foretold by prophets in glowing language, as the kingdom of the New Covenant, made with the renewed Israel. Choosing the twelve was one of the most crucial moments of the destiny of His mission. Jesus spent the entire night in praying to His Father for the right choice (Lk. 6:12). And when it was day, He called unto Him His disciples, and of them, He chose twelve, whom also He named apostles. They were, 'Simon (whom he also named Peter) and Andrew, his brother; James and John, Phillip and Bartholomew, Matthew and Thomas, James the son of Alphaeus, Simon called Zealot, Judas the brother of James and Judas Iscariot, who became the traitor (Lk. 6:12-16). Jesus saw in the twelve His church in miniature or germ that consisted of people as diverse as fishermen, tax collector, and even zealot. We recall how Jesus chose these men of diverse background and His was a conscious and deliberate choice to constitute a definite diversity among the twelve. First, walking along the shore of the 'sea of Galilee', Jesus met two brothers, Simon and Andrew, who were casting their nets. He commanded them to follow Him and become fishers of men. At the same time and place Jesus found James and his brother John, fishers at the shore of the sea of Galilee. He called them to follow Him. All obeyed instantly (Mk 1:16-20). Jesus called Matthew, Levi, in the same way (Mk 2:16; Mt 9:9) in Capernaum. He was a collector of taxes, probably of the custom house of this city. Matthew left this position, bade farewell to his fellow officials and followed the Lord. Jesus showed that, as among them distinctions such as fishermen, publican and zealot were unknown, so in the church of the future, there should be neither Greek nor Jew, circumcised nor uncircumcised, bond nor free, but all constitute one family of Jesus Christ, the beloved Master- all to each and each for all.

The training of the Twelve

The Apostles were God-fearing people. Their faith and devotion bound them to Jesus. Their integrity, justice and mercy cannot be denied. They were diligent, honest and pious people, and above all dedicated to the Lord and to His command. They were not men of higher education, but neither were they illiterate. Most of them spoke Aramaic and Greek. The Gospels do not present them as men of genius, or original thinkers. They were men of different background, temperament, habits and expectations. They came together under the same roof to learn from their Master and to obey Him always. They accompanied the Master from place to place. They heard all His preaching and admonitions and even His private conversations. They witnessed the healing of people and learned the causes of sickness and understood the power of the evil spirits. The Twelve formed a family of which Jesus Christ was the head. They had a common purse and one was appointed treasurer. They were together with the Master who trained them for their future mission.. He called them 'that they might be with Him' (Mk. 3:14) to be trained and educated, and then 'that He might send them forth to preach' the Gospel and minister unto the people. First of all they were learning from the personality of Jesus. His presence was an education in itself. His acts and words in everyday life, His compassionate dealing with the depressed, the lowly and the humble, His forgiveness of sinners, His concern for the underprivileged and the downtrodden were an education to them. They saw Him preaching and praying, healing infirmities and sicknesses and restoring broken hearts. They understood the Master's revolting attitude towards dry and meaningless customs and witnessed His stand against the Pharisees, regarding Sabbath, circumcision, foods and practices of prayer. They learned much from the Sermon on the Mount, from the parables and the statements of profound implications, such as, 'God is spirit and those who worship Him must worship in spirit and truth' (Jn 4:24).

Functions of the Apostles

Jesus prayed for them and their future, even up to a few moments before His arrest and John, one of His Apostles, recorded this beautiful prayer: 'I have revealed you to those you gave me out of the world. They were yours; you gave them to me and they have obeyed your word. I pray for them (Jn 17: 6-9). After His resurrection, Jesus empowered them with the Holy Spirit on the day of the Pentecost, 'He breathed on them and said: 'Receive the Holy Spirit' (Jn 20:22). The mighty Spirit as 'tongues of fire' descended on the Apostles and transfigured their doubts and fears and attitudes in such a marvelous way that they became heralds of the new mission. Their chief duty was to bear witness to the Savior Jesus Christ, His life, teaching, and atoning work, and especially to bear witness to Christ's resurrection. And with great power the Apostles gave their testimony to the resurrection of the Lord Jesus (Acts 1:22; 4:2, 33). The influence of their witness and testimony was enormous. They simply stated what they knew. There was no doubt in their minds as to the certainty of their knowledge. John explains the entire process of learning and formation by the twelve under the Master Jesus: 'That which was from the beginning, which we have heard, which we have looked upon and our hands have touched, of the Word of life ... that which we have seen and heard we declare unto you, that you also may have fellowship with us; and truly our fellowship is with the Father, and with His Son, Jesus Christ' (1 Jn 1:1-3).

The Apostles had much to learn before they could satisfy the high requirements. The time of their apprenticeship for their apostolic work, even reckoning it from the very commencement of Christ's ministry, seems all too short. They were indeed godly men, who had already shown the sincerity of their piety by forsaking all for their Master's sake. But, at the time of their call, they were exceedingly ignorant, narrow-minded, and superstitious and carried with them their traditional prejudices, misconceptions and animosities. They had much to unlearn of what was bad, as well as much to learn of what was good, and they were slow both to learn and to unlearn. Old beliefs already in possession of their minds made the communication of new religious ideas a difficult task. Men of good honest heart, the soil of their spiritual nature was fitted to produce an abundant harvest; but it was stiff and needed much laborious tillage before it would yield its fruit. Then, they were mostly poor men, of humble birth, low station and lowly occupations who had never felt the stimulating influence of a higher education or of social proximity with persons of cultivated minds. They were enthusiasts: their hearts were fired, and, as an unbelieving world might say, their heads were turned by a dream about a divine kingdom to be set up in Israel, with Jesus of Nazareth for its king. That dream possessed them and imperiously ruled over their minds and shaped their destinies, compelling them, like Abraham, to leave their kindred and their country and to go forth. The fishermen of Galilee did become fishers of men on an extensive scale and by the help of God, gathered many souls into the church. In a sense they were casting their nets into the sea of the world and by their testimony to their Master, Jesus Christ, brought multitudes to become disciples of Him who chose them as His first followers and named them as the foundation of His new Temple, the Church.

Personal reflection - 'Take up your Cross'

It is Jesus who takes the initiative to call the disciples. They are to be the witnesses to the Gospel. The duty of a disciple is to walk in the footsteps of the master and the clearest sign of an authentic discipleship is following Jesus, the Master, with total devotion and absolute dedication. This path is a walk through suffering and trials, in imitation of the passion and death of Jesus. However, in the end, the way of the cross culminates in glory. According to Mark, one cannot think of a discipleship that is separated from suffering. However, the twelve disciples, whom Jesus chose in a very special manner, could not grasp the meaning of the cross. They envisaged the Messiah as a King and could not understand the significance of a suffering Messiah for the salvation of mankind. Peter vehemently opposed a path of suffering

(Mk 8:32). Jesus spoke strongly against this temptation of Peter: 'Get behind me, Satan! For you are setting your mind not on divine things but on human things' (Mk 8:33). Jesus then called the crowd along with the disciples and explained the path of discipleship. This way of the cross is applicable to all who follow Him. 'If any want to become my followers, let them deny themselves and take up their cross and follow me' (Mk 8:34). From us, His disciples, Jesus demands, first of all, self-renunciation: Jesus asks us to deny ourselves which means that we must renounce our own self-interests. The disciple must be one who has thrown away the outer shell of the ego. He must run away from the worship of the idol that is self. Both Luke (14:26) and John (12:25) insist in their Gospels that Jesus asks us to deny ourselves. This self-denial is the refusal to indulge in selfish interests and desires and to accept God's will in all things. We should understand the meaning of the injunction 'take up your cross' against the then prevalent practice. Those condemned to die had to bear their crosses and walk to the place of execution. That the disciple should take up the cross means, that he should be always ready to suffer for Jesus' sake. Scholars affirm that following this exhortation of Jesus, Christians in the community of Mark used to literally carry the cross to remind themselves of the injunction of the Master.

Follow me

To His disciples Jesus says: 'Follow me!. What is meant here is not a following for some days. The meaning of 'following' denotes a continuous association and relationship with Jesus. Jesus is journeying to Jerusalem. It is in Jerusalem that Jesus Christ suffers his passion. It is there that he dies. He also rises in glory in Jerusalem. In other words, the disciple of Jesus must constantly walk along the path of suffering and then accept the crown of glory. Therefore, to follow Jesus, eschewing suffering from one's life is not possible. The path of suffering is inevitable for a disciple of Jesus. He should not abhor suffering. As soon as suffering enters our life, we must be aware that we are walking along the path of Jesus' passion. In the modern world that is steeped in the consumerist culture, man is not able to grasp or accept the meaning, significance and the corrective and purificative value of suffering. He is hungering and yearning for comfort and luxury. He turns his face away from suffering and the cross. He is ready to follow Jesus, but not ready to bear the cross. If we think we can follow the crucified Lord without bearing the cross, it is an illusion: 'Whoever does not carry the cross and follow me cannot be my disciple'(Lk 14: 27). Instead of taking us closer to the experience of God and increasing our faith in Him, today suffering is taking many of us away from faith in God; the reason is the refusal to accept the cross. Why did this happen to me? Why this sickness only for me? Why this sorrow only in my family? Such are the questions that rise up at least once in a while in our minds.

A disciple of Christ is not the one who collapses under pain or lives in despair cursing the day he was born. We must be able to see the resurrection behind the cross, the glory behind the suffering. Only those, who follow the suffering Jesus in the reality of the cross, can grasp the true meaning of discipleship. Let us, who have been called to the discipleship of Christ, understand the meaning of the cross that Jesus bore. Let us walk along the path of suffering and attain glory. Christ made the conditions of discipleship unmistakably clear. The disciples had to abandon all hope of a political Messiah and be prepared to follow His example by renunciation of self-interest and by the readiness to suffer all things (Mt 16.24). Their love of Him must prevail over love of material possessions (Lk 5.27-28), love of family, of self, and even of life (Lk 14.26-27). Freed from attention to extraneous things they could spend themselves and be spent for the kingdom of God.

In God's garden, we have flowers of all colors: Some years ago, I employed a professional painter who was a member of my parish. I asked him to paint the scene of the ascension of Christ to Heaven, with the disciples standing at the feet of the ascending Jesus. The artist completed the picture of Jesus and began painting the figures of the disciples. He painted all the disciples as white people since historically they were all Jews. The next morning he came to me and told me about his dream he had the previous night. He saw Jesus painting the figures of the disciples and some He drew white, some black, some brown and some yellow. He told me that he understood the message. The Lord of the world, Jesus Christ, is master not only of the white people or the black people but of all the people of the world, people of all colors and races. The master invites people of every race and tongue and nation into His community as His disciples. Nobody is excluded from the community of the master unless the person separates himself/herself from the master. The painter decided to follow the example of Jesus and painted the figure of the disciples as white, brown, black and yellow. When he completed the scene, it looked not only excellent but also very meaningful. I realized, in God's garden, we have flowers of many colors.

Quote: The first mark of a Christian is a deep reverence for persons as destined for eternity with God. The second is a kind of heavenly serenity which is able to draw the sting of suffering. And the third is the humility of a man or woman who has known authentically the presence of God- *Archbishop A. M. Ramsey*

Scripture reading for Day 12: Mt 10: 24-42

Prayer for Day 12: O God, whose mercies are without number, and the treasure of whose goodness is infinite! We render thanks to your Most Gracious Majesty for the gifts you have bestowed upon us especially for choosing us to be the disciples of your Son! We evermore beseech your strength and guidance to take up our cross and follow your Son faithfully all the days of our earthly life! Amen.

13

SON OF MAN

*T*he title 'Son of Man' is of special interest because it was the preferred title that Jesus employed to designate Himself and His mission. The phrase 'son of man' is a literal rendering of the Hebrew 'ben-adam', and Aramaic 'bar-enos', an expression that more exactly means 'a man', or 'human individual'. Jesus made the title 'Son of man' His most characteristic way of referring to Himself, as the One in whom and through whom the salvation of the entire mankind would come to be realized. Though the saying was so frequently employed by Christ it is employed neither by the Apostles and the Evangelists nor by the early Christian writers. We do not find it also in the writings of Paul or in other Epistles. The expression seems to be uniquely Christ's. The writers of the Gospel neither invented it nor used it for Christ. It is also true that while Jesus avoided the title Messiah until the very end of His public ministry, He freely used the title 'Son of Man'. He applied the title to Himself, a title that He preferred above all others. He used it almost exclusively to refer to His mission of suffering and dying as the Servant of God, for the salvation of the world, to His glorification as the Risen Lord and to His second-coming as the Judge to judge the living and the dead.

Son of Man in the Old Testament

In the Old Testament 'son of man' is always translated in the Greek Septuagint without the article as 'anthropou'. It is not the common expression for man. It is however employed as a poetical synonym for the ideal man as in 'God is not as a man that he should lie nor as a son of man that he should be changed' (Nm 23:19). It is again used as poetic parallelism as seen in Is 56:2: 'Happy is the man who does this, the son of man who holds to it; who keeps the sabbath free from profanation, and his hand from any evildoing'. We find similar notion in 'Let thy hand be upon the man of thy right hand: and upon the son of man whom thou hast confirmed for thyself'' (Ps 79:18). The prophet Ezekiel is addressed by God frequently, almost 93 times, by the title, 'son of man' a usage intended to accentuate man's lowliness before the majesty of God. The term contrasts human beings to God or angels. It also highlights the prophet's role as a special representative of the people: 'The Lord God said to me: Son of man, eat what is before you; eat this scroll, then go, speak to the house of Israel' (Ez 3: 1). It is interesting and remarkable to note that the term 'son of man' is found 93 times in the book of Ezekiel and only 13 times in the rest of the entire Old Testament. In Daniel 7:13, this phrase describes a heavenly figure nearly equivalent to God in power and authority. Thus we can affirm that the most important Old Testament occurrence of the expression 'son of man' is found in Dn 7.13: 'As the visions during the night continued, I saw One like a son of Man coming on the clouds of heaven. When He reached the Ancient One and was presented before Him, He received dominion, glory, and kingship; nations and peoples of every language serve Him. His dominion is an everlasting dominion that shall not be taken away, His kingship shall not be destroyed'. The interpretation of the apocalyptic vision of Daniel in chapter 7 is fairly clear. Four immense beasts emerged from the sea, each different from others. The first was like a lion. The second was like a bear. The third was like a leopard and the fourth was different from all the others, terrifying, horrible and of extraordinary strength' (Dn 7:1-13). The four beasts represented the succession of world empires as Babylonian, Median, Persian, and Greek. While the judgment passed upon them represents the negative element of God's saving intervention in the history of the world, the positive element is seen in the establishment of God's rule, the messianic kingdom, represented by the investiture of 'one like a son of man' with dominion, glory, and kingship. In contrast to the worldly kingdoms opposed to God, which appear as beasts, the glorified people of God that will constitute His kingdom on earth is represented in human form. The human figure represents a collectivity, 'the Holy ones of the Most High' (Dn 7:18, 27). Just as the beasts were apt for symbolizing the pagan empires, so a human figure was apt for symbolizing God's kingdom. But the human figure may have been intended also to represent an individual.

In apocalyptic literature

In later Jewish apocalyptic literature, the 'son of man' is an individual figure of divine judgment. In the parables of Enoch (1st century B.C), the 'son of man' clearly emerges as an individual rather than as a symbol for a collectivity, as the Danielic figure was, although intimately united to the community of the Elect. He is preexistent (48: 2-3), will appear at the end of the world (62: 4-5) to sit upon the throne of God (51:3) and exercise the judgment (62:1). He is identified with the Messiah (48:10; 52:2) and in many passages is referred to as 'the Elect One'. The same concept appears in 4 Esdras, in which 'as it were the form of a man' arises from the sea and travels with the clouds of heaven (13:3), destroys the wicked with his breath (13:10-11, 27), and gathers together the lost 10 tribes (13:12-13, 39-42). Like the son of Man in Enoch, he has been kept by God for many ages to deliver creation (13:26) and is identified with the Messiah (13:32, 37, 52), who is referred to as son of God. The question arises as to whether the 'Son of Man' of Enoch and the 'Form of Man' of Esdras can be explained simply as an evolution from the figure in Daniel, or whether non-biblical ideas have entered into Jewish thinking. Perhaps, some non-biblical traditions might have used the term 'son of man' to refer to human collectivity as in the Chaldean tradition. What is important to us is that before the time of Jesus, there existed in some circles of Judaism, belief in a transcendent Messiah who could be referred by the title 'Son of Man', as demonstrated very clearly by the parables of Enoch. Without hesitation, we may assert that the Christian community did not invent the title Son of Man and applied it to Jesus.

Jesus, the Son of Man

There is no doubt that the term 'Son of Man' was considered a Messianic title in at least some circles during the time of Jesus. However, it has to be added that in the time of Christ it was not very widely known as a Messianic title among the people. For this reason, the employment of the expression 'son of man' in the Gospels is quite remarkable. In the New Testament, it is used 85 times, mostly in the four Gospels always by Jesus who referred to Himself. However, in the discourses of Jesus, this title conveyed various meanings. Some 'Son of Man' sayings refer to the human activity of Jesus (as in Ezekiel), while others refer to His future role in divine judgment (as in Daniel 7). Quite new is Jesus' use of 'Son of Man' when He is telling His disciples about His upcoming suffering and death, especially in Mark 8:31, 9:31, 10:33. In the Gospels, it is used to designate Jesus Christ no fewer than eighty-one times, thirty times in Matthew, fourteen times in Mark, twenty-five times in Luke and twelve times in John. Contrary to how it appears in the Septuagint Old Testament, it appears everywhere with the article, as 'ho huios tou anthropou' in the New Testament. Greek scholars agree that the correct translation of this is 'the son of man', not 'the son of the man'. The most remarkable fact connected with 'the Son of Man' is that it is found only in the mouth of Christ. The rare exceptions can hardly be called true exceptions: 'So the crowd answered Him, 'we have heard from the law that the Messiah remains forever. Then how can you say that the Son of Man must be lifted up? Who is this Son of Man?' (Jn 12: 34). In the book of Acts, Stephen said, 'Behold, I see the heavens opened and the Son of Man standing at the right hand of God' (Acts 7: 56). It also appears in the Book of Revelation 1:12-18, again used as a title of Jesus and with an accompanying description that seems to emphasize his divinity: 'Among the lampstands was someone 'like a son of man' dressed in a robe reaching down to his feet and with a golden sash around His chest' (Rv 1:13).

The implications of the title 'Son of Man'

Citing all 81 incidences of this term, as used by Jesus in the gospels, would take up an inordinate amount of space and hence it is not attempted in this book. Taken together, those passages are indisputable evidence that Jesus proclaimed His divinity and humanity through the title 'Son of Man'. Let us examine the meaning of the term 'Son of Man' in the light of the teaching and ministry of Jesus. We distinguish two series of Son of Man sayings: those in which the title refers to the glory and power of Jesus, hidden during His earthly ministry, but to be revealed at His Parousia or second coming. The first series of sayings builds in part upon the figure of Dn 7: 13 (glory, power, clouds of heaven), but also goes beyond it (the 'Son of Man' sits upon the throne of glory and judges), perhaps building upon the usage of the 'Son of Man' in Enoch. The second series of texts finds no parallels in earlier literature mentioning the Son of Man. However, the basic expression was apt for expressing the condition of human weakness (as it is used in Ezekiel) in which the Savior had come, as well as the suffering He would endure in the absolute obedience to the Holy will of His Father, by which He redeemed mankind. Jesus brought a whole new content to the term 'Son of Man' by applying to Himself under this title, what had been said of the suffering Servant of the Lord. For the expressions of the glorified Messiah we present numerous examples: 'But that you may know that the 'Son of Man' has authority to forgive sins on earth' (Mk 2:10). 'Whoever is ashamed of me and of my words in this faithless and sinful generation, the son of Man will be ashamed of when he comes in his Father's glory with the holy angels' (Mk 8:38). 'And then they will see 'the 'Son of Man' coming in the clouds' with great power and glory' (Mk 13:26-27). Jesus answered "I am; and 'you will see the Son of Man seated at the right hand of the Mighty One and coming on the clouds of heaven' (Mk 14: 62). 'When they persecute you in one town, flee to another. Amen, I say to you, you will not finish the towns of Israel before the 'Son of Man' comes' (Mt 10.23). 'For the Son of Man will come with His angels in His Father's glory, and then He will repay everyone according to His conduct' (Mt 16:27). Jesus said to them, 'Amen, I say to you that You who followed me, in the new age, when the Son of Man is seated on his throne of glory, will yourselves sit on twelve thrones, judging the twelve tribes of Israel' (Mt 19:28). 'When the Son of Man comes in His glory, and all the angels with Him, He will sit upon his glorious throne' (Mt 25:31). 'If anyone is ashamed of me and my words, the Son of Man will be ashamed of Him when He comes in glory and in the glory of the Father and of the Holy Angels' (Lk 9:26). 'At that time, they will see the Son of Man coming in a cloud with power and great glory' (Lk 21:27). The Son of Man will be seated at the right hand of the mighty God' (Lk 22:69).

Passion and Resurrection

There are also sayings in which the title recalls the humble circumstances of His coming, ministry, and Passion: 'He began to teach them that the Son of Man must suffer greatly and be rejected by the elders, the chief priests, and the scribes, and be killed, and rise after three days' (Mk 8.31). 'It is written regarding the Son of Man that he must suffer greatly and be treated with contempt' (Mk9: 11). 'Behold, we are going up to Jerusalem, and the Son of Man will be handed over to the chief priests and the scribes, and they will condemn him to death and hand him over to the Gentiles' (Mk10: 33). 'Jesus answered, 'Foxes have dens and birds of the sky have nests, but the Son of Man has nowhere to rest his head' (Mt 8: 20). 'The Son of Man came eating and drinking and they said, 'Look, he is a glutton and drunkard, a friend of tax collectors and sinners' (Mt 11:19). 'So also the Son of Man is going to suffer at their hands' (Mt 17: 12). 'Behold, we are going up to Jerusalem and all things that are written by the prophets concerning the Son of Man will be accomplished. For, He will be delivered to the Gentiles and will be mocked and insulted and spit upon. They will scourge Him and kill Him. And the third day He will rise again'. (Lk 18:31-33). 'The Son of Man is going to be betrayed into the hands of men' (Lk 9: 44). 'The Son of Man will be handed over to the Gentiles. They will mock him, insult him, spit on him, flog him, and kill him' (Lk 18: 32). At the Last Supper Jesus said, 'the Son of Man indeed goes his way, as it is written of him' (Mk 14:21). The Scripture referred is certainly Is 53:1-12. The sayings that combine predictions of the passion and the resurrection find their natural source in the oracles of the prophet Isaiah regarding the Servant of God. Jesus combined two currents of thought regarding His mission - suffering and glorification, within a single title, 'Son of Man'. Thus, Jesus immeasurably clarified and enriched both the perspectives of the Old Testament, 'the divinity and the humanity' of the 'Son of Man'. The Servant of the Lord, who by His obedient suffering and death on the cross would redeem Israel and the entire human race from sin and evil, is also the Son of Man who would one day be revealed in glory as God's Son and judge of all men.

Personal reflection – 'Perfectly God and perfectly man'

After the ending of the Davidic lineage of kingship with the destruction of Jerusalem and Babylonian exile (598-586 BC), the Jewish people began to dream of an ideal king who would someday restore the throne of David and who would inaugurate the lasting kingdom of Israel. In time this expected messianic figure became transformed in Jewish expectations and in Jewish prayers to a divine and even to a preexistent figure. From the writing of Daniel (ca. 165 BC) on, the Messiah was identified as the Son of Man, who sat at God's right hand and who rode on the clouds of heavens (Dn 7:13-14). This apparently supernatural figure would, at the end of time, be God's agent in establishing the new heaven and the new earth. The odd definite article 'the' at the beginning of the Greek phrase for 'Son of Man' may be a pointer that Jesus is presenting Himself to the well-known 'Son of Man' in the book of Daniel (Mk 8:38; Mt 16:27). The first connection in the New Testament with Daniel 7:13 can be found in Paul's assurance: 'Then we which are alive and remain shall be caught up together with them in the clouds, to meet the Lord in the air: and so shall we ever be with the Lord' (1 Thes 4:17). We have seen that an examination of Scripture reveals that the phrase 'Son of Man' carries broad significance. First of all, even if the phrase 'Son of Man' is a reference to Jesus' humanity it is not a denial of His divinity. By becoming a man, Jesus did not cease being God. The incarnation of Christ did not involve the subtraction of deity, but the addition of humanity to His divinity. Jesus clearly claimed to be God on many occasions (Mt 16:16-17; Jn 8: 58, 10:30). But in addition to being divine, He was also human and the hymn in the letter to the Philippians 2:6-8 portrays beautifully the union of divinity and humanity in Jesus. He had two natures (divine and human) conjoined in one person. Further, Scripture indicates that Jesus was not denying His deity by referring to Himself as the Son of Man. In fact, it is highly revealing that the term 'Son of Man' is used in Scripture in contexts of Christ's divinity. For example, the Bible says that only God can forgive sins. 'It is I, I alone who wipe out for my own sake your offenses. Your sins I remember no more' (Is 43:25). 'Why does this fellow talk like that? He is blaspheming! Who can forgive sins but God alone? (Mk 2:7). But as the 'Son of Man', Jesus had the power to forgive sins (Mk 2:10). Likewise, Christ will return to earth as the 'Son of Man' in clouds of glory to reign on earth (Mt 26: 63-64). In this passage, Jesus is explicitly citing Daniel 7:13 where the Messiah is described in terms that indicate His divinity (Dn 7: 14). Further, when Jesus was asked by the high priest whether He was the 'Son of God', He responded affirmatively, declaring that He was the 'Son of Man' who would come in power and great glory (Mt 26: 63-64). This indicated that Jesus Himself used the phrase 'Son of Man' to indicate His divinity as the Son of God.

The perfect mediator

For us, the phrase 'Son of Man' also emphasizes who Jesus is in relation to His incarnation and His work of salvation. In the Old Testament the next kin, persons related by blood, always functioned as the 'kinsman-redeemer of a family member who needed redemption from poverty or jail: 'When one of your country men is reduced to poverty and has to sell some of his property, his close relative who has the right to redeem it, may go and buy back what his kinsman has sold (Levi 25: 25-26 48-49). Jesus became related to us 'by blood' by becoming a man, so that He could function as our Kinsman-Redeemer and rescue us from sin. We lost our right to be the children of God and the heirs to His kingdom by the original sin of our first parents. Jesus became one with us as a member of our human race and paid the price of His life to His Heavenly Father and restored to us our dignity as the Children of God and made us the heirs of the Kingdom. The only rightful heir, the 'Son of God' became 'Son of Man' and brought us redemption. 'Son of Man' is essentially the same person who is also the 'Son of God'. When Jesus used the phrase consistent with its original meaning, it is a powerful and clear claim to deity. A considerable factor in Jesus' words is His comment that the Son of Man will be seated at the right hand of God. The right hand reference, which in Jewish culture means that Jesus is claiming to be seated by God in order to the highest honor with Him. The 'right hand of God' is the place where the splendor and majesty of God comes from and the righteous are honored by being allowed to stand (not sit!) at the right hand of God. In short, Jesus claims the prerogatives of God with the combined honor of being seated at the right hand of God, and therefore asserts His divine identity. At the same time, by always calling Himself as the 'Son of Man', Jesus affirmed His proximity to the human beings. As both Son of God and Son of Man, Jesus stands between God and man as Mediator. Jesus is on the one hand the perfect heavenly God and on the other hand a sinless perfect human being. In this sense, 'Son of Man' and 'Son of God' is the same identical person. The title 'Son of Man' conveys an intentional ambiguity, reflecting both Jesus' mortal and immortal parentage.

The Most Beautiful Hands - Once there were four young girls seated and talking by the riverside. They were good friends. One of them was boasting about the beauty of her hands. At that time, an old woman was passing by them. She was returning from the church after her evening prayer to her house. The proud girl asked the old woman to select the most beautiful hands among the hands of the four girls. She first showed her own soft, white hands. She had never done any manual work and kept her hands always clean and that is why they were soft and white. The next girl showed her hands to the old woman. They were pink and soft, for she was also hardly doing any manual work at home. The third girl showed her hands to the old woman. They were soft and white too even though they were slightly harder since she occasionally helped her mother in the various tasks of the household. The fourth girl would not even lift her hands up because they were quite hard from the toils of hard labor. She used to help her widowed mother in the garden and in the fields. She used to cook the meals and sweep the floor at home. The old lady, looking at the hard hands exclaimed, 'Oh, these are the most beautiful hands that help the poor widowed mother by sharing the toil at home bringing comfort and help to all the members of the family'. The old lady took a precious ring from one of her fingers and gave it to the fourth girl. The crucified and pierced hands of the most blessed Savior are the most beautiful hands for us.

Quote: Christ is the world's Redeemer, the lover of the pure, the fount of heavenly wisdom, our trust and hope secure; the armor of His soldiers, the Lord of earth and sky; our health while we are living, our life when we shall die- *St. Columba*

Scripture reading for Day 13:Mt 24: 1-35

Prayer for Day 13: O Lord Jesus, before whom every heart lies bare and every will is an open book, and to whom no secret is hidden! In your ineffable goodness you have called us, knowing all about us when you invited us to become yours in a special manner. Grant us the grace everyday to cling more closely to you, that we may faithfully follow wherever it pleases you to lead us! Amen.

14

LAMB OF GOD

*J*esus is called the 'Lamb of God' who takes away the sin of the world'. It is John the Baptist who gave this title to Jesus. The incident is mentioned in the Gospel according to John: 'The next day, John saw Jesus coming towards him and said: 'Look, the Lamb of God, who takes away the sin of the world'. This is the one I meant when I said, 'A man who comes after me has surpassed me because he was before me' (Jn 1: 29-30). For us, the key to understand the significance of the term 'Lamb of God' is the context of the Baptism of Jesus, after which John the Baptist makes this description about Jesus: 'I saw the Spirit come down from heaven as a dove and remain on him' (Jn 1: 32). The entire account of the baptism of Christ, within the framework of which John places the proclamation by the Baptist that Jesus is the Lamb of God, directs our attention to the Servant of Yahweh, described by the prophet Isaiah, who states: 'Here is my servant whom I uphold, my chosen one with whom I am pleased, upon whom I have put my spirit' (Is 42:1). The divine revelation, 'This is my beloved Son, in whom I am well pleased' and the descent of the Spirit during the Baptism of Jesus as described in Mt 3.16-17 and parallels in the other synoptic gospels recall clearly the prophecy of the prophet Isaiah about the Servant of Yahweh. The title 'the Lamb of God' finds clarification in the songs of Isaiah about the Servant of Yahweh. In fact, the prophet compares the suffering servant of Yahweh to a lamb: 'Like a lamb led to the slaughter or a sheep before the shearers, he was silent and opened not his mouth' (Is 53:7). Philip when explaining this passage to the Eunuch, applies this text explicitly to Christ and tells him that this prophecy was fulfilled in Jesus Christ (Acts 8: 32-34). When we honor Jesus as the 'Lamb of God', we can not but think about His supreme sacrifice on the cross as the suffering servant of Yahweh. That is why we begin our reflection with a presentation on the meaning and the significance of the sacrifices.

Sacrifices as a religious practice in Israel

The offering to a divinity, often an animal, vegetable, food, drink and incense belong to the very essence of the religious practice of worship and surrender to God. It is found in the earliest known forms of worship and in all parts of the world. In a sacrifice, a circuit of power goes from human gift to the god and returns to the man. Often, through a sacrifice, a meal is offered to the god in which, man participates and establishes a kind of communion with the deity. In all the religions, there are bloody and also non-bloody sacrifices. In the bloody sacrifices, the usual victims are bull, sheep, female or male goats and even pigs, as well as fowls. Sacrifice, like prayer, was so essential that often its suppression can even destroy the very fabric of religion. Accordingly the philosophers, who critique religions, are not against the sacrifices as such as against the abuses and meaningless rituals. Plato says in the Laws (4. 716D): 'to sacrifice to the gods and to be continually in communion with them by prayers and offerings and every form of divine worship is for the good of man. It is most noble and good and helpful toward the happy life of human beings'. Israel came before the Lord to worship Him and praise Him and thank Him, to petition His aid and asks His forgiveness. It did so through its sacrificial rites. The people of Israel used the same basic rites as their Canaanite neighbors. However Israel's sacrifice had its own distinctive character. The sacrificial rites were sacred: a specific place was set aside for sacrifice, first various sanctuaries and finally the temple of Jerusalem. Holy objects like the altars were employed. The rites were performed under the leadership of holy men like the priests who were explicitly set apart by the society for this purpose. In addition, ritual practices, fixed holidays and seasons were established along with regular religious festivals and feasts. Public sacrifices were offered for the community as a whole. Private sacrifices were offered on the behalf of individuals. In the category of private sacrifices, there were sin offerings and guilt offerings. The predominant objects of the sacrifice were things on which daily life most depended. They were the products of herd, flock and the field. The sacrificial gifts were things that the people needed for their sustenance. By offering as sacrifice the things of their daily need, the people consecrate their very lives to God as they sought His protection and blessings. When the prophets made critique of the sacrificial system of Israel, their condemnations were not directed at the institution of the sacrifice itself. Rather, the prophets condemned the hypocritical ritualism where the fitting interior disposition was missing. They attacked the formalistic mechanical performance of the sacrificial rites. They stressed obedience to the Lord's word, moral goodness and justice.

The Paschal Lamb in the Old Testament

One important aspect of the Jewish sacrifices was the immolation of the lambs. When God had decided to deliver His captive people from the Egyptians, He ordered each family of Hebrews to immolate a lamb 'without blemish, male, and one year old' (Ex 12: 5), to eat it at night and to mark with its blood the lintels over their doors. Thanks to this 'sign' the exterminating angel coming to strike at the first-born of the Egyptians would spare them. Enriching the primitive theme, Jewish tradition later on gave a redemptive value to the blood of the lamb. A Jewish commentary on Ex 12, makes this observation: 'Because of the blood of the covenant of circumcision, and because of the blood of the Paschal lamb, I have delivered you from Egypt'. Understood that way, it appears that it is in the context of the blood of the paschal lamb that the Hebrews were freed from the slavery of Egypt and that thereafter they were able to become a 'consecrated nation', 'a kingdom of priests' (Ex 19:6), bound to God by a covenant and governed by the Law. Two lambs were offered, one every morning and one every evening in the Temple of Jerusalem for the sins of the world: 'Now this is what you shall offer on the altar: two yearling lambs as the sacrifice established for each day; one lamb in the morning and the other lamb at the evening twilight. With the first lamb there shall be a tenth of an ephah of fine flour mixed with a fourth of a hin of oil of crushed olives and as its libation, a fourth of a hin of wine. The other lamb you shall offer at the evening twilight, with the same cereal offering as in the morning. You shall offer this as a sweet-smelling oblation to the Lord. Throughout your generations this established holocaust will be offered before the Lord' (Ex 29: 38-42). So long as the Temple was there, this daily sacrifice was offered. This tradition was so faithfully kept that even when the people were starving in war and in siege they never omitted to offer the lambs until the Temple was destroyed by the Romans in 70 AD. A further reference to the lamb is found in the book of Jeremiah. Persecuted by his enemies, the prophet Jeremiah compared himself to a 'lamb which one leads to the slaughter' (Jer 11: 19). Subsequently this image was applied to Servant of Yahweh who appeared 'as a lamb led to the slaughter, like a sheep before the shearers, silent and not opening its mouth" (Is 53: 7). There it is said that the Servant of Yahweh bears our sins. 'The Lord laid upon him the guilt of us all' (Is 53:6) and 'through his suffering, my servant shall justify many and their guilt he shall bear. He shall take away the sins of many and win pardon for their offenses' (Is 53: 11-12).

Jesus fulfills all the sacrifices

The New Testament acknowledges that God was the initiator of the sacrifices of the Old Covenant. However, it insists that the sacrifices of the Old Testament were only foreshadowing and pointing to the unique sacrifice of Christ on Calvary. All of the sacrifices were temporary and thus the holocausts, the covenant sacrifices, the sin offerings and the sacrifices of atonement have been replaced and brought to completion by the unique, efficacious and eternal sacrifice of Jesus Christ on the Cross. Jesus expiated the sins of the entire human race once and for all. The blood of Jesus Christ had replaced the blood of the goats, the sheep and the calves. He had once for all destroyed sin of the world by His supreme and final sacrifice. The entire earthly life of Jesus is viewed as an expression of His inner self-offering to the Father. Very often, when we discuss about the sacrifice of Jesus, our discussion is focused on the unique event of the Passover sacrifice on the cross. But the New Testament presents the entire life of Jesus as the sacrifice ever pleasing to God, His Father. The scene of Baptism at the Jordan reveals how Jesus dedicated His entire public ministry to the redemption of the human race and thereby glorified His father. The one and only sacrifice of the entire public life of Jesus comes to a climax in the singular Last Supper-Calvary-Easter event. The account of the Last Supper and institution of the Eucharist clearly shows that Jesus intended His own sacrifice on the cross to be a parallel to the sacrificial establishment of the

Covenant at Mount Sinai. His blood poured out for humanity is the blood of the New Covenant. It fulfilled the old covenant and its Passover. At the moment of Christ's death, the temple veil was torn (Lk 23: 45). It signifies that the passion and death of Jesus replaces all the sacrifices of the temple. John connects Christ's death on Calvary with the slaying of the Paschal lambs at the temple (Jn 19: 14-36)

From His public identification by John the Baptist as the 'Lamb of God', until His final solemnization of the Paschal meal (Lk 22:14-20), Jesus progressively revealed Himself as a victim-messiah, the true Lamb of God. He is 'the immolated lamb without blemish or defect (1Pt 1: 19). He expiates men's sins by becoming the victim: 'God presented Him as a sacrifice of atonement' (Rom 3:25). The oblation of the Lamb of God, Jesus Christ, was the consummation of all the sacrifices that were established at the command of God Himself (Heb 9: 1-14). In consummating His sacrifice on the cross, Jesus Christ, in one perfect gesture of devotion, fulfilled all the moral, ceremonial and juridical requirements of the Old Testament. The precious blood of Jesus Christ as the Lamb of God redeemed the entire human race: 'God forgave us all our sins, since Jesus took them away and nailed them to the cross' (Col 2:14). The cross assures all men that the whole universe has been redeemed by the power of the crucified, the Lord of all creation.

The Lamb of God in the New Testament

For John, the title of Lamb of God is of great theological importance. The whole Gospel seems to be an account that is enclosed between two proclamations about Jesus as the Lamb of God. The first is the direct proclamation by the Baptist as in Jn 1:29. The second is in Jn 19.36, where the Evangelist attests that 'these things happened so that the scripture would be fulfilled: 'Not one of his bones will be broken'. John makes additional observations that confirm the conclusion that for John, the paschal lamb was a privileged image to express the mystery of the passion and death of Christ: 'Then the Jews led Jesus from Caiphas to the palace of the Roman Governor. By now it was early morning and to avoid ceremonial impurity the Jews did not enter the palace; they wanted to be able to eat the Passover'(Jn 18:28). 'It was the day of Preparation of Passover Week, about the sixth hour, when Jesus was brought before Pilate and was handed over to be crucified' (Jn 19:14). 'Now it was the day of Preparation and the next day was to be a special sabbath' (Jn 19: 31). John emphasizes the analogy between the immolation of the paschal lamb and the sacrifice of Jesus, at the Hour, when His destiny is accomplished on the cross. The whole identity and glory of Jesus as the Son of God was revealed when Jesus was lifted up on the cross. 'When you have lifted up the Son of Man, then you will know that I am the one I claim to be' (Jn 8:28). Jesus further states, 'When I am lifted up from the earth, I will draw all men to myself' (Jn 12:32). Jesus sacrificed His life at the very hour when, according to the prescriptions of the Law, the lambs were being immolated in the temple. After His death, they did not break His legs, as they did to the other condemned men (Jn 19:33). The evangelist sees in this fact the realization of the ritual prescription concerning the paschal lamb (Jn 19:36). John makes sure to call Jesus the Lamb of God from the beginning of the Gospel, because for him, the entire life of Jesus is a sacrifice for taking away the sin of the world. From the beginning there is in Him the sacrificial consecration (Jn 10:36), and it reaches its plentitude in His death. By His sacrifice, the Lamb of God takes away the sin of the world: 'The blood of Jesus purifies us from all sin' (1Jn 1:7). 'He is the atoning sacrifice for our sins, not only for our sins but also for the sins of the whole world' (1Jn 2:2). 'This is love: not that we loved God, but that He loved us and sent His Son as an atoning sacrifice for our sins' (1Jn 4:10).

In the book of Revelation, the name 'the Lamb' is used no less than twenty-eight times and was always applied to Jesus. The author presents a striking contrast between the powerlessness and meekness of the immolated Lamb and the power which His exaltation and glorification confers on Him. A lamb in His redemptive death, Christ is at the same time a lion whose victory has liberated the people of God who were captives of the powers of evil (Rv 5: 5). Enthroned now on the throne of God (Rv 22:1-3), receiving with Him the adoration of the celestial beings (Rv 5: 9-13), Jesus is now invested with divine power. It is He who executes the decrees of God against the impious and His wrath plunges them into terror. It is He who leads the eschatological war against the united powers of evil, and His victory will consecrate Him as the 'King of kings and Lord of lords (Rv 17: 14). The faithful are made clean by the sanctity of the blood of Christ through communion with Him: 'The faithful washed their garments and made them white in the blood of the Lamb' (Rv 7:14). Paul exhorts the faithful of Corinth to live 'in sincerity and truth', because 'Christ, our Passover Lamb has been immolated' (1 Cor 5: 7) for taking away our sins.

Personal reflection- 'Behold the Lamb of God'

To understand what the title 'Lamb of God' means, we should remember what God promised our first parents Adam and Eve after they had sinned. He spoke of their own 'seed' (Gen 3:15), who would be the savior of the world. The punishment for the sin of our first parents was toil, suffering and death. Adam and Eve's second son, Abel, slaughtered a lamb and offered it to God on an altar as a sacrifice to cover his sin. When God saw the blood of the lamb, He judged him as righteous. Nevertheless, the blood of a lamb could not be accepted as a sufficient payment for sin forever, because the value of an animal and the value of a man are not equal. The lamb was only a shadow and an illustration of the holy Redeemer who was to come into the world and shed His blood to deliver sinners from God's righteous judgment. Seven hundred years before the birth of Jesus, the prophet Isaiah wrote how the Messiah would be 'led like a lamb to the slaughter' as a sacrifice to take away our sins (Is 53:7). Thus, between the time of Abel and the time of the Messiah, all who believed in God participated in the sacrifices of lambs. Thus we see that Noah, Abraham, Moses, David, Solomon and all the prophets and the entire community of the chosen people of Israel presented to God sacrifices of spotless lambs. In this way they were all looking ahead to the day when God would send down His own Son, the Servant of God and the holy Redeemer, who would shed His precious blood as a sacrifice in order to take away the sin of the world forever. When John the Baptist saw Jesus, he recognized Him to be the redeemer of the world, the suffering servant and said to his disciples: 'Look, the Lamb of God, who takes away the sin of the world' (Jn 1:29). He made known to his disciples that this Jesus standing before them was the Messiah, 'the Lamb' that God sent down from heaven, the Perfect Sacrifice of which the prophets foretold especially in the passages of the Servant of Yahweh. Incidentally the word in Aramaic for both the 'lamb and the servant' is the same - 'Talya'. Jesus is the holy sacrifice who came into the world to suffer and die for the children of Adam so that God may forgive us our sins forever! It was part of God's salvific plan all along that His Son would become the perfect sacrifice for our sins.

The redemptive sacrifice of Jesus

Jesus was betrayed by one of His disciples and condemned to death by the Council of the religious leaders who asked the pagan Roman governor to have Jesus crucified. All through the proceedings not one word was uttered in His defense, not one testimony was borne in His favor. His own disciples abandoned Him and fled in fear. Without realizing, all of these men were playing a part in God's plan. The New Testament tells us that Jesus, as the 'Lamb of God' cleansed away our sins through His perfect and unique sacrifice on the cross. The use of the name 'the Lamb of God' conveys to us the message that Jesus came to the world as the redemptive sacrifice. He is the Lamb that was slain and through His death and resurrection, has delivered us from death and has given us a new life. He was led forth like a lamb; he was slaughtered like a sheep. Through His immolation, He brought us out of slavery into freedom, out of darkness into light, out of death into life, out of tyranny into an eternal kingdom. He made us a new priesthood, a people chosen to be His own forever (1 Pt 2:5). He is the Passover that is our salvation. He was the suffering servant of Yahweh who endured every kind of suffering for our sins. 'God made Him who had no sin to be sin so that in Him we might become the righteousness of God' (2 Cor 5: 21). On the tree of the cross, no bone of His was broken; in the earth His body knew no decay. He is the One who rose from the dead on the third day, and now, seated at the right hand of God, He assures eternal life to all those who believe in Him.

God is pleased only with a kind and good heart: Once three holy men went on a pilgrimage in fulfillment of their vows. They made their journey by horse driven carts. As the sanctuary was situated far away, they had to travel several days. The festival was fixed on a particular day and hence they decided to waste no time in order to be present for the festival. The practice in the sanctuary was each pilgrim would go into the inner sanctuary, which is a very small narrow place and offer worship to the deity with flowers and other offerings for a minute or two. On their way to the sanctuary, they met a villager who begged them for help. His wife was having the pangs of childbirth and as her condition was quite complicated, she needed to be rushed to the only doctor in the nearby town. Because the three holy men did not want to miss the festival and the privileged worship of the deity, they declined to help and proceeded on their journey. On the day of the festival, when they entered the inner sanctuary, they did not find the statue of the Lord. They were shocked and also pained. That night in their sleep, the Lord told them that since they refused to help a woman in her desperate need, He was not pleased with their offerings and hence disappeared from them.

Quote: A dreadful matter is sin, and disorder of life is the soul's worst sickness. Sin is evil of man's own choosing, springing from free-will- *Cyril of Jerusaelm*

Scripture reading for Day 14:Is 53:1-12

Prayer for Day 14: Almighty and eternal God, who, in order that all mankind might have His example of humility for their imitation, did cause our Savior to become man and to suffer on the cross. Mercifully grant that we may both keep in mind the lessons of His patience and be made partakers of His resurrection! Amen.

15

TEMPLE

*T*he evangelist John states a mysterious utterance of Jesus wherein Jesus emphatically declares that He is the new 'Temple'. The context was the cleansing of the Jerusalem Temple (Jn 2: 13-17). The Jews demanded Jesus, 'What miraculous sign can you show us to prove your authority to do all this? Jesus answered them, 'Destroy this temple and I will raise it again in three days. The Jews replied, 'It has taken forty-six years to build this temple and you are going to raise it in three days? But the temple He had spoken of was His own body. After He was raised from the dead, His disciples recalled what He had said (Jn 2: 19-22). The three Synoptic Gospels relate that Jesus foretold the complete destruction of the temple of Jerusalem, which included the destruction of the actual sanctuary, called in Greek the naos: 'I tell you the truth, not one stone here will be left on another; everyone will be thrown down' (Mt 24: 2). In Mark and Luke, we find identical words (Mk 13: 2; Lk 21:6). In John, Jesus speaks about not only the destruction, but also a new reconstruction in three days. The allusion to the Resurrection of Jesus is obvious. The implication is the 'Risen Jesus' became the new Temple of God.

Jerusalem Temple as the dwelling place of God

In all religions, the temple is the sacred place where the divinity is thought to be present to men to receive their worship. Thus it is first of all the residence of god and consequently a cultic center of rituals and worship. In the temple, an image or a symbol in a special place that is architecturally secluded from other areas represents the deity. The Hebrews of the patriarchal period did not have a temple, although they had sacred places, where they called upon the name of Yahweh. 'Abraham built an altar to the Lord at Bethel and invoked the Lord by name' (Gn12: 8). At Bethel, Jacob cried out, 'This is nothing else but an abode of God and that is the gateway to heaven' (Gn 28: 17). 'Isaac built an altar at Beer-sheba and invoked the Lord by name' (Gn 26: 25). Jacob set up a memorial stone at Shechem and invoked El, the God of Israel (Gn 33: 18). At Horeb, the mountain of God, the Lord appeared to Moses in fire flaming out of a bush (Ex 3:3). 'When the Lord came down to the top of Mount Sinai, He summoned Moses to the top of the mountain, and Moses went up to Him' (Ex 19:20). The tabernacle or the meeting tent at Mount Sinai of which Exodus 26-27 gives a description is the place where the people encountered God (Nm 1:1). 'I will meet you on the ark of the commandments' (Ex 25:22). 'After the establishment of the confederation in Canaan, the common sanctuary for the tribes is successively located at Mount Ebal at Gilgal (Jos 8: 30-35), at Shechem (Jos 24: 1-28) and at Shiloh (1Sm 1-4).

It is this sanctuary of the confederation which David places at Jerusalem after having freed the ark from the hands of the Philistines (2 Sam 6). The political capital, Jerusalem that he has just conquered will also be the religious center of the people of Yahweh. After having built himself a palace, he thinks of building a Temple to Yahweh (2 Sm 7: 1-4). However, it was given to his son Solomon to build the Temple (1 Kgs 5:15-7:51). In the Temple, the ark of the covenant, which contained the two stone tablets which Moses had put there at Horeb when the Lord made a covenant with the Israelites, was its center (1 Kgs 8:1-9). Thus, the sanctuary of Jerusalem continued the ancient place of central worship for all the tribes. Further, by manifesting His glory in the midst of cloud God visibly indicated that He had accepted the Temple as His dwelling place (1 Kgs 8: 11). Henceforth, the Temple of Jerusalem became the center of the worship of Yahweh and the central symbol of Judaism. People came there, as pilgrims, from every land in order to look upon the face of God (Ps 42:3).However, even though God resided in the Temple of Jerusalem, the people of Israel were fully conscious that the heavens and the highest heavens could not contain Him (1Kgs 8: 27). For more than 1, 000 years (c. 950 BC to 70 AD, except from 587 until 514 when the temple was in ruins), Jerusalem's Temple was the most important sanctuary in Israel. Actually there were three Temples, Solomon's, Zorobabel's and Herod's, in the same place at Jerusalem. Solomon's temple was destroyed by the Babylonians in 587 BC. After the exile, a more modest Temple was built according to the pattern and on the site of the former temple (Ezr 1-3). The rebuilding was authorized in 538 BC, by Cyrus, the Persian emperor and was completed under the leadership of Zorobabel, after many hurdles in 515 BC. Although Zorobabel's Temple was not as richly decorated and elaborate as Solomon's, it was probably the same in size and general plan. In 20-19 BC, Herod the Great undertook to reconstruct the Temple and its surrounding courts and buildings. The essential reconstruction was completed in about 10 years, but the work on the annexes and courts continued until well after Our Lord's public ministry. The entire Temple area was destroyed by the Romans in 70 AD, and its treasures and furnishings were carried off to Rome as trophies by Titus.

The Critique by the Prophets

Despite the profound attachment of the Israelites to the Temple, there arose a current of thought in Judaism with the focus on a more spiritual worship corresponding to the demands of religion of the heart (Dt 6:5). Jeremiah spoke of the destruction of the Temple: 'I will do to this house, named after me, that you trust, just as I did to Shiloh' (Jer 7: 14). The sanctuary at Shiloh was destroyed by the Philistines (1 Sm 1:9). Put not your trust in the deceitful words: This is the temple of the Lord! The temple of the Lord! The temple of the Lord: Only if you thoroughly reform your ways and your deeds, if each of you deals justly with his neighbor; if you no longer oppress the resident alien, the orphan, and the widow; if you no longer shed innocent blood in this place or follow strange gods to your harm, will I remain with you in this place' (Jer 7: 4-7). While condemning the sacrifices that were performed without an appropriate spiritual disposition, the prophets called for the reform of the hearts: 'the heavens are my throne and the earth is my footstool. What kind of house can you build for me; what is to be my resting place?; My hand made all things when all of them came to be. This is the one whom I approve: the lowly and afflicted man who trembles at my word' (Is 66: 1-2). Yahweh dwells in heaven and hears from there the prayers of His faithful ones in whatever place they are uttered (Tb 3:16) as He is not constrained by the Temple of stone. The existence of such a current of thought explains why, a little before the coming of Christ, the Essene sect could break with the worship of a temple which it considered defiled by an illegitimate priesthood. The sect considered itself the spiritual temple where God received adoration worthy of Him.

Temple in the time of Jesus

During the time of Jesus, the Temple was the central and dominant symbol of Israel's culture, religion, and politics. There are many ways by which the Jews manifested their overwhelmingly powerful attachment to the Temple of Jerusalem. Chief among them was that each year they sent the temple tax to Jerusalem. Cicero states in Pro Flacco, that every year this gold was taken to Jerusalem from Italy and all the provinces. Philo of Alexandria, in 'On the Embassy to Gaius', written in the late 40s AD describes how Augustus showed his approval of the religious practices of Jews. Included in the emperor's acts of benevolence towards Jews was that he approved of the collection of sacred money from their first-fruits which they sent to Jerusalem by the hand of envoys who would offer sacrifices. There existed also spiritual relationship between those in the diaspora and the temple in Jerusalem. For example, prayer meetings were held in the synagogues on the days when feasts were occurring in the temple and the worshipers in the synagogues offered their prayers facing Jerusalem. In some cases, the synagogues were constructed oriented toward Jerusalem. In this way, the diaspora synagogues provided a means for Jews to be connected to the central sanctuary while still residing in distant cities throughout the Greco-Roman world. In a revealing statement, Philo notes that while diaspora Jews counted their adopted countries as their 'fatherland', they held the holy city where stands the Temple of the Most High to be their 'mother city'.

Also thousands of pilgrims from around the Mediterranean traveled to Jerusalem for the great feasts, especially the Passover. Within the compass of Jerusalem dwelt a population of 600,000. At the time of the Passover the crowd swelled to between two and three millions. The temple treasury defrayed whatever funds necessary for the services of the sanctuary, all temple repairs and the salaries of a large staff of regular officials. These included those who saw to the correctness of the copies of the law used in the synagogues, those who examined the Levitical fitness of sacrifices, those who instructed the priests in their various duties and those who made the necessary articles such as curtains. The fees of the Rabbis, according to their own testimony, were also included in the expenditure of the temple. After all this lavish expenditure, there was not only enough to pay for the repairs of the city-walls, the roads, and public buildings of Jerusalem, but sufficient to accumulate immense wealth in the treasury. At the time of Jesus, the Temple was the supreme religious and political institution for the Jews. It overshadowed Jerusalem and dominated life in the city. Eighty percent of employment in Jerusalem depended on the Temple, not only on its day to day ritual needs, but also on the periodic pilgrim festivals and the ongoing building project which it constituted.

The priests and the sacrifices

Every day, priests offered public and private sacrifices for the good of society. At the time of Jesus, at the core of Judaism, there was an overwhelming concern for purity and the purification from impurity was carried out through the Temple-based rituals, making the Temple the very center of cult and rituals. The twice-daily official sacrifices on the vast ever-burning altar consumed animals and forests of wood. There were cattle pens on the north side and sometimes the water of the Kidron stream where the blood was flushed became so thick that it was sold to farmers as fertilizer. Over it all hung a pall of smoke from burning flesh, and when the great pilgrim festivals, like Passover, were in full swing, the Temple was like a 'slaughter house'. The priests stood in blood sacrificing the victims of private offerings. Enormous amounts of animal blood spilled around the altar everyday and splashed upon the priests as they worked. Nine thousand priests and Levites worked there, although not at the same time, operating what was in fact a giant 'abbatoir'. Jews were expected to make the pilgrimage to the temple three times a year, twice in the spring - at Passover and Pentecost - and once in the fall, at Succoth. Therefore Jerusalem thrived on what today would be called the convention business. The high priests were in league with the Roman power to preserve their office and their landed interests.

The separating purity system

There was a clear perception by Jews, of what it means to be an observant Israelite, which was symbolized in the social importance of certain customs, rituals, places, and persons. The temple purity system established and controlled the social identity, social classifications, and social boundaries of the Jewish people as the holy people of God. This system established the structure and social stratification of the Jewish community, the norms of public and private behavior, and the lines of demarcation between holy Israelites and those at or beyond the margins of God's holy people. The structure of the Temple itself revealed the concern of Judaism for purity regulations. The Court of Gentiles, about thirty-five acres, was for Gentiles, and the actual Temple was separated from this court, in order to receive only the

Jewish population. The Temple itself was divided into three basic areas - open to men and women, only men, and only to priests. The priestly area was further divided into three areas - the first was the place of sacrifices. The second was the holy place, where stood a golden table for the Bread of the Presence, a golden lamp stand with seven branches and a golden incense stand. The last was the holiest of the places, the inner room, called 'the Holy of Holies', a dark completely empty room thirty feet square, where only the high priest entered. The organization of society along purity lines called for a careful avoidance of contact with all those that were judged impure or unholy (sinners, lepers, blind, lame, menstruants, corpses, toll collectors, Samaritans and Gentiles) and proper respect for the holy places (temple, synagogue) and the holy persons (temple personnel). It required acts of purification (hand washing before meals) and holy times (Sabbath, festivals). In a society already conditioned by economic and social stratification, this system advocated and legitimized hierarchy in the Jewish society based on purity classifications. What we see is a definite hierarchy: the rich were ranked above the poor, the clergy above the laity, the urban dwellers (especially in Jerusalem) above the rural peasantry (especially in distant Galilee), men above women, married above unmarried, the healthy above the ill, and the conforming above the deviants.

Jesus and the temple of Jerusalem

Jesus had devotion to the Temple. He tells the cleansed leper to 'Go, show yourself to the priest, and offer for your cleansing what Moses commanded' (Mk 1.44; Luke 17:14). It was there that His parents presented Him to God when He was a child (Lk 2: 22-39). He went up there for the solemnities (Lk 2: 41-50). The Temple for Him was a house of God, a house of prayer and the house of His Father. However, Jesus condemned the sacrificial system of the Temple especially when it became a place of trade. As a result He drove out the 'money-changers' (Mk 11:15-19). It was an act of prophetic symbolism that declared the end of the sacrificial system. The attack on the traders in the temple and the cursing of the barren fig tree are conceptually related, in the sense that the attack on the traders is placed within the context of the cursing of the fig tree (Mk 11:12-14). Jesus' cursing of the fig-tree was a clue given privately to His disciples to explain His enigmatic public action in the temple. What Jesus had done in miniature for the fig-tree, God would do for the temple. Jesus pointed out that the temple had become barren and failed to produce the expected fruit. This composition warrants our seeing the tree as a symbol of the sacrificial system whose time is now passed: 'It was not the season for figs' (Mk 11:13). The command, 'may no one eat fruit of you ever again' (11:14), is interpreted by the expulsion of the 'money-changers' (11:15-16) from the Temple, to mean that the sacrificial system must come to an end. The 'money-changers' were essential to the operation of the sacrificial system. They provided the currency and the victims necessary for the offering of individual sacrifices. In attacking them, Jesus attacked the whole sacrificial system, because it did not bear fruit, and was barren.

Jesus' unconditional forgiveness of sinners was one of the most shocking dimensions of his ministry. We see that forgiving sins was a regular feature of His public ministry (Mk 3:28; Lk 7:47-49). In Judaism, the sacrificial system, particularly the sin-offerings and rituals of the Day of Atonement, were designed precisely to provide forgiveness. In Leviticus 4-5, where the legislation governing sin-offerings and guilt-offerings are explained, the following verse occurs repeatedly at the end of the instructions as : 'so the priest shall make atonement for him for his sins, and he shall be forgiven' (4:26, 31, 35; 5:10, 16, 18). We note wide range of sins against God and neighbor covered by such provision (Lv 6:1-7). When Jesus pronounced that the sins were forgiven outside the cult of sacrifice and without any reference (even by implication) to the cult, He operated outside the structures of the Temple, the priesthood and the sacrifice. To hinder or prevent the provision of pure animals for sacrifice by ousting them was tantamount to prophesying the end of the whole sacrificial system. The accusation against Jesus of having spoken against the Temple was widely known in Jerusalem (Mk 15: 29/Mt 27:39-40). All three Synoptic evangelists report the prediction of Jesus regarding the destruction of the Temple of Jerusalem. John 2:19 reports his equivalent to the accusation on the lips of Jesus himself: 'Destroy this temple, and in three days I will raise it up'. We should also note that the accusation against Stephen in Acts 6:14 echoes the same charge: 'We have heard him (Stephen) say that this Jesus of Nazareth will destroy this place'. The prediction of the destruction of the Temple found fulfillment in the events of 70 AD.

Jesus, the new Temple of God

The messianic character of Jesus' words 'destroy this temple and in three days I will raise it up (Jn 2:19) may have been apparent to people familiar with Jewish traditions. According to the expectations as found in the Jewish religious literature, a new and glorious temple would be erected in Jerusalem in the new age of salvation. Some texts do not identify the builders of the temple, and others anticipated that God would establish it. Still other texts expected the Messiah to raise the new structures. According to 2 Samuel 7:12-13, the heir to David's throne would build Israel's house of worship: 'I will raise up your heir after you. It is he who shall build a house for my name' (2 Sm 7: 13). There is the evidence that people expected Israel's worship to be purified by someone sent by God. We see how God assured the people through Prophet Ezekiel: 'I will put my sanctuary among them forever. My dwelling place will be with them. I will be their God and they shall be my people. Thus all the nations shall know that it is I, the Lord who make Israel holy, when my sanctuary will be set up among them forever' (Ez 37: 27-28). 'I saw that the Temple was filled with the glory of the Lord. The voice said: This is where my throne will be. Here, I will dwell among the Israelites forever' (Ez 43: 2-7). The prophet Zechariah said that the Davidic Branch, a descendant of David would build the new Temple.'He shall build the Temple of the Lord and taking up the royal insignia, He shall sit as ruler upon His throne' (Zec 6: 12-13). Zechariah further stated that when the anointed of God would come to rule over all the earth, worship would be pure and holy, all nations would worship in Jerusalem, and there would no longer be a trader in the house of the Lord (Zec 14:20). The prophet Malachi, said that God would send a messenger who would come suddenly into the temple to purify the priesthood and its offerings (Mal 3:10). Jesus became the fulfillment of the prophetic longings for the days when God would miraculously reestablish His Temple and would once again dwell among His people.

Personal Reflection- 'Jesus, the Temple of God'

What do we understand when Jesus states that He is the new Temple of God? The Temple in Jerusalem was the place where God made His name or glory to dwell. Although God's presence was not confined to the Temple, it was generally understood that the sanctuary was, in some sense, God's dwelling place. With the arrival of the Son of God, God's glory would be manifested, not in a building, but in the person of Jesus. The crucified and risen Jesus would be a unifying symbol for God's people of the New Covenant, as the Temple had been for the people of the old covenant. In Him the divinity resides as with the Temple. Jesus is the new and definitive temple of God, that is not made by the hands of men, the Temple in which the Son of God establishes His dwelling place among men (Jn 1: 14). In earlier times, God established His dwelling place in the tabernacle of Israel and later in the Temple of Jerusalem. The Body of Jesus was broken on the cross. But after three days, as He promised to do, He built it again in glory. After the resurrection, the glorified and transfigured Body of Christ makes itself present in all places and at all times, in order to enable the people of all the nations and all the ages to encounter God in Him, as the new and everlasting Temple. Now, His glorified humanity, entirely imbued with the Holy Spirit, gives to those who are united to Him the opportunity to be transformed by the Spirit in such a way that they become the House of God. Paul states: 'In the Lord you yourselves are also built together into a dwelling of God in the Spirit' (Eph 2: 22).

Since it is at the same time the Temple of God as well as the living Community of Believers, the Spiritual house appears as the perfect realization of the New Covenant, under its two inseparable aspects: communion with God and communion among human beings. The believers, when united to Christ, become a 'spiritual house, the holy priesthood (1 Pt 2:5) and the temple of the Holy Spirit' (Rom 8:11; 1 Cor 6:19). The ancient Temple of Jerusalem was a figure or prototype, imperfect and provisional and it was superceded by the definitive Temple, not made by the hands of men. It is the Church, the Body of Christ, the place of authentic encounter between God and men, the sign of the divine presence here below. Indeed, the Christian community has a much better claim than any material building to be called God's dwelling. The house of God constructed by Christ is not a material building like Solomon's Temple. It is the believers who become 'the sanctuary of God' in Jesus (Heb 3: 6). In this sanctuary on earth, the faithful worship God in Spirit and Truth (Jn 4:23), by offering their lives of goodness and charity as a pleasing offering to God. The Church prefigures and stands for the Heavenly Temple where the immolated Lamb of God, Jesus Christ, is enthroned and where a liturgy of prayer and praise is celebrated (Rv 5: 6-14). When the heavenly Jerusalem will descend here below, there will no longer be any need of the Temple in it. Its Temple will be God Himself and the Lamb: 'I did not see a Temple in the city, because the Lord God almighty and the Lamb are its Temple' (Rv 21:22). The faithful will see God and the Lamb face to face and share with them the everlasting life that God has reserved for His holy people from all eternity through His son, Jesus Christ, in the Holy Spirit.

How wonderful it is for brothers to live in unity and brotherhood: In the day of King Solomon there lived two brothers who reaped wheat in the fields of Zion. One night, in the dark of the moon, the elder brother gathered several sheaves of his harvest and left it in his brother's field, saying to himself: 'my brother has seven children. With so many mouths to feed, he could use some of my bounty'. And he went home. A short time later, the younger brother slipped out of his house, gathered several sheaves of his wheat, and carried it into his brother's field saying to himself 'my brother is all alone, with no one to help him to harvest. So I will share some of my wheat with him'. When the sun rose, each brother was amazed to find he had just as much wheat as before. The next night they paid each other the same kindness, and still woke to find their stores undiminished. But on the third night, they met each other as they carried their gifts into each other's fields. Shedding tears of joy for their mutual goodness and compassion, they threw their arms around each other. When King Solomon heard of their authentic fraternal love, he built the temple of Israel there on the place of authentic brotherhood. Where there is true love, there abides God and His divine presence is assured to the man. Jesus, the revelation of the love of God is the 'new Temple'.

Quote: Anything else one may doubt but that he who desires only the divine shall reach the divine is certitude and more certain than two and two make four- *Aurobindo*

Scripture reading for Day 15:Rev 21: 1-27

Prayer for the Day 15: Almighty and everlasting Father! You sent your only Son, our Lord Jesus Christ, to live in our hearts and to make us the Temple of the Holy Spirit. Help us, we beseech you, to preserve our hearts from all stain so that we may always remain worthy as the dwelling place of your Holy Spirit and the sacred temple of your Son, who together live and reign with you as one God, for ever and ever! Amen.

16

WITNESS

*J*esus presents Himself as the 'witness' of His Father to the world. The expression witness and its verb 'to bear witness' and the related words 'testimony' and 'to testify' are the terms used in the New Testament to describe the role of Jesus as the 'witness' of His Father. The word for witness in Greek is 'Martus'. It occurs 34 times in the New Testament. Its verb 'Marturein' translated in English as 'to bear witness' is found 76 times. Another word, 'Marturia' which means 'testimony' is employed 37 times. Another Greek word for testimony 'Marturion' is found 20 times. Witness is personal testimony and involves the commitment of a person to a fact, or to a truth, or to another person. It may be made by words, by deeds or even by dying. To bear witness is to attest to the reality of an event or a fact by giving to the affirmation of it with all the solemnity that the circumstances require. Jesus came to witness to the eternal love of the Father as 'the truth' and in affirmation of this truth He even gave up His life on the cross, which became the supreme testimony to the love of His Father before the world: 'God so loved the world that He gave His one and only Son' (Jn 3: 16). Jesus is also the witness to what He has seen and heard in the presence of His Father. Jesus declares 'I tell you the truth. We speak of what we know, and we testify to what we have seen' (Jn 3: 11).

Witness in Old Testament

In classical Greek, the word 'witness' is derived from the law court and is used in legal terms in the LXX , the Greek Old Testament. It designates a person who has observed an event and can give account of it. It was in regular usage in courts to establish where liability does or does not lie, by way of proof: 'If any person refuses to give the information which, as a witness of something he has seen or learned, he has been adjured to give and thus commits a sin and has a guilt to bear' (Lv 5: 1). 'The testimony of two or three witnesses is required for putting a person to death; no one will be put to death on the testimony of only one witness (Dt 17: 6). In this way, the law regulates its use: there is no condemnation possible without the evidence of witnesses (Nm 5: 13) and to prevent error or ill will, there must be at least two of them (Nm 35:30; Dt 17:6; 19:15; Mt 18:16). In capital cases, involving the responsibility for condemnation, they must be the first to execute the sentence (Dt 17: 7; Acts 7: 58). But a lie can slip into that act by which a man pledges his word: the psalmists complain of false witnesses who overwhelm them (Ps 27:12; 35:11), and there are instances of tragic trials where they have played an essential part (1 Kgs 21: 10-13; Dn 13: 34-41). From the time of the Decalogue, false witness is strictly forbidden (Dt 19:16-20).

Along with its usage in the law courts, there are references about being a witness to a fact. It is designated as the 'witness' to truth. It designates a man who testifies something to be true. The witness is a man who proclaims truth, stands for his conviction, expresses his points of view and gives reasons for them. In this sense, the word 'witness' meaning testimony to the truth is found only in a few passages in the Old Testament. A clear example is the role of 'witness' of the entire people of Israel before all the nations to testify that Yahweh alone is God as opposed to the idols which cannot produce witnesses on their own behalf: 'You are my witness' says the Lord, my servants whom I have chosen. Before me no god was formed and after me there shall be none. You are my witness, says the Lord. I am God, yes, from eternity I am He' (Is 43: 9-13). 'You are my witness! Is there a God or any Rock besides me?' (Is 44: 7-11). Israel has been chosen to testify to all the nations that Yahweh alone is God, and there is no other. Only by being faithful to the Law, which God gave to Israel as the mark of the Covenant, can Israel bear witness to the one true God. When Israel was engaging in idolatry, as it happened during the time of several kings, Israel was failing in its primary role to be the 'witness' to the one and only God. God chastised Israel for not being His faithful 'witness'.

The witness of God in the Old Testament

Beyond the witness of men, there is that of God, which no one can contradict. At the time of marriage God is witness between a man and the woman of his youth: 'The Lord is witness between you and the wife of your youth, she is your companion, your betrothed wife (Mt 2: 14). In the same way, He is the guarantor of human contracts made before Him (Gn 31: 53; Jer 42: 5). He can be taken as a witness in a solemn affirmation (1 Sm 12:5; 20:12). He is the supreme witness to whom appeal can be made to refute the false testimony of men (Jb 16: 7). The witness of God can be understood in another meaning, closely connected with His own word. In the first place God bears witness of Himself, when He reveals to Moses the meaning of His Name (Ex 3: 14) or when He declares that He is the only God (Ex 20:2). This witness is made under oath (Is 45: 21-24) and forms the basis of the monotheism of Israel. But God also gives witness through the commandments contained in the Law (2 Kgs 17: 13; Ps 19: 8). For this reason, the tables of the Law have been called the witness (Ex 25: 16). Placed in the Ark of the Covenant, they make it the ark of witness, and the tabernacle becomes the dwelling of witness (Ex 38: 21; Nm 1: 50-53). There is finally a divine witness that the prophets bear. This is a matter of a solemn affirmation set in the context of the legal action brought by God against His unfaithful people (Ps 50: 7). A witness from whom nothing can escape, God denounces all the sins of Israel (Jer 29: 23); He becomes an accusing witness in order to obtain the conversion of sinners.

The witness of Jesus

Jesus is the prime and sublime witness of the Father to the world, especially of what He has seen and heard in the presence of the Father: 'Amen, I say to you, we speak of what we know and we testify to what we have seen, but you people do not accept the testimony. If I tell you about earthly things and you do not believe, how will you believe if I tell you about heavenly things? (Jn 3: 11-12). The calling to be a 'witness' to the one and only God, as demanded in the Law and in the preaching of the prophets centers now around Jesus, who is the faithful witness par excellence: 'Jesus Christ is the faithful witness, the firstborn from the dead, and the ruler of the kings of the earth' (Rv 1:5). Jesus is the faithful and true witness, the ruler of God's creation' (Rv 3: 14). Jesus has come into the world to bear witness to the truth. So, Pilate said to Him, 'Then you are a king?' Jesus answered, 'You say I am a king. For this I was born and for this I came into the world, to testify to the truth. Everyone who belongs to the truth listens to my voice' (Jn 18: 37). He bears witness to the truth what He has seen and heard in the presence of the Father (Jn 3: 11, 32). He bears witness against the evil world: 'The world cannot hate you, but it hates me, because I testify to it that its works are evil' (Jn 7: 7). Jesus also bears witness of what He Himself is: 'The Pharisees said to Him, 'You testify on your behalf so your testimony cannot be verified' (Jn 8: 13). His confession before Pilate is a supreme testimony: 'I charge you before God, who gives life to all things, and before Christ Jesus, who gave good testimony under Pontius Pilate' (1 Tim 6: 13). His death becomes the supreme testimony: 'Christ Jesus gave Himself as a ransom for all men, the testimony given in its proper time' (1 Tim 2: 6). Witness is not an impersonal marshalling of facts, but always remains a personal attestation. It is in this sense that Jesus is the 'witness' who came to make a personal attestation about the everlasting love of His Father to the world that He revealed through His proclamation of the Gospel and by performing the works of healing. Both His words and deeds witnessed to His Father's love and He made the ultimate test of 'witnessing' by laying down His life.

The witnesses who attest to Jesus

The witnessing of Jesus, though contested by the unbelieving world, possesses juridical and uncontestable value because other evidences support it. The witness of John the Baptist summarizes the whole mission of Jesus (Lk 7: 21-22). Jesus states, 'You sent Emissaries to John and he testified to the truth. I do not accept testimony from a human being but I mention it so that you may be saved. He was a burning and shining lamp, and for a while you were content to rejoice in his light. But I have testimony greater than that of John (Jn 5:33-35). Jesus refers to the miracles as signs or works that He accomplished at the command of His Father who has given Him power to perform them. Jesus calls them of greater value than the human testimony: 'The works that the Father gave me to accomplish, these works that I perform testify on my behalf that the Father has sent me' (Jn 5: 36). 'The miracles I do in my Father's name speak for me (Jn 10:25). They are the works of the Father Himself, who lives in Jesus as Jesus lives in Him: 'Even if you do not believe me, believe the miracles, that you may know and understand that the Father is in me and I in the Father' (Jn 10:38).

There is also the witness of the Scriptures that reveal the testimony of the Father Himself: 'You search the Scriptures, because you think you have eternal life through them; even they testify on my behalf' (Jn 5:39). All the prophets bear witness to Him as seen in the Scriptures: 'To him all the prophets bear witness, that everyone who believes in Him will receive forgiveness of sins through His name' (Acts 10:43). Along with the Scriptural testimony, Jesus insists that the Father and the Holy Spirit bear witness to Jesus and to His role as the 'witness' of the Father: 'If I testified on my own behalf, my testimony cannot be verified. The Father who sent me has Himself testified concerning me' (Jn 5: 31-37). A voice came form heaven: 'You are my beloved Son, whom I love; with you I am well pleased' (Lk 3: 22). In this way, God, the Father, witnessed to the Son. God's testimony has much more value than the human testimony. John states: 'we accept man's testimony. God's testimony is greater because it is the testimony of God, which He has given about His Son. Anyone who believes in the Son of God has this testimony in his heart. Anyone who does not believe God has made Him to be a liar, because he has not believed the testimony God has given about His Son. And this is the testimony: God has given us eternal life and this life is in His Son. He who has the Son has life. He who does not have the Son of God does not have life' (1 Jn 5:9-12). The Holy Spirit gives witness to Jesus: 'When the advocate comes whom I will send you from the Father, the Spirit of truth that proceeds from the Father, He will testify to me' (Jn 15: 26). The Holy Spirit descended upon Him in bodily form like a dove during His Baptism and, in this way, testified that Jesus is the beloved Son of God. Before ascending into heaven, Jesus promised to send the Holy Spirit who would be the principle witness to Him, as He guides the disciples of Jesus: 'You will receive power when the Holy Spirit comes upon you, and you will be my witnesses in Jerusalem, throughout Judea and Samaria, and to the ends of the earth' (Acts 1: 8).

The threefold witness to Jesus

To this testimony of the Father about His only son, and the testimony of the Holy Spirit is added the Christian experience of the witness of the baptismal water and of the blood of the Eucharist. They attest in their symbolic language that Jesus is indeed the Son of God, who gives life to the world. Jesus Christ has come 'by water and blood', that is in the baptism at the Jordan and through death on the Cross. There is also another reference to the 'water and blood' which flowed from Jesus side' (Jn 19: 34). Behind the visible experience of water and blood, there lies the invisible presence of the Son of God who by His saving act brings life to believers through the sacraments of Baptism and Eucharist. Along with the testimony of Baptism and Eucharist, John adds the testimony of the Holy Spirit who, through those sacraments, brings new life to those who believe in Jesus Christ. The Holy Spirit testifies to the reality and the presence of the Son of God in baptism and the Eucharist. John explains this threefold witness: 'This is the one who came by water and blood - Jesus Christ. He did not come by water only, but by water and blood. And it is the Spirit who testifies, because the Spirit is the truth. For there are three that testify: the Spirit, the water and the blood' (1 Jn 5: 6-8). Thus to the historical witness of water and blood, John adds a third witness, namely, the Spirit. The threefold witness becomes the witness of the Father who combines all three witnesses, of the Spirit, of the Baptism and of the Eucharist, and makes His own testimony regarding His Son: 'This is the testimony of God that He has given about His Son and this is the testimony; God has given us eternal life and this life is in His Son' (1 Jn 5: 10-11). What we see is a cluster of the witnesses, human, divine and sacramental, which strengthen the witness of Jesus. In accepting the witness of Jesus, a man enters into the life of faith. It is Jesus Christ who constitutes the focal point of faith. Those who accept His witness receive life, because the Father has so constituted Him, as the savior of the world through His death and resurrection: 'He who has the Son has life; he who does not have the Son of God does not have life' (1 Jn 5: 12).

The apostolic witness

The apostles are first and foremost the eye and ear-witnesses of the risen Lord (1Jn 1: 1-3) who proclaim what they have seen and heard. In the course of choosing a successor in place of Judas, Peter outlines the primary responsibility of apostle: 'It is necessary to choose one of the men who have accompanied us during all the time that the Lord Jesus went in and out among us, beginning from the baptism of John until the day when he was taken up from us - one of these men must become with us a witness to His resurrection' (Acts 1:21). With inspiration and 'with great power', the apostles gave testimony to the resurrection of the Lord Jesus (Acts 4: 33). Luke, however, draws a subtle distinction by which Paul is primarily 'a minister of the word' and only secondarily a 'witness' to the glorified Lord (Acts 26:16), whereas the converse is true of the eleven, namely that they were primarily 'eye-witnesses', and only secondarily 'ministers of the word' (Lk 1:2). The facts to which the apostles are to bear witness comprise not merely the resurrection and exaltation of Jesus, but also His life: baptism, miracles, healing, casting out the demons and preaching of the joyful message of the Gospel. Peter declares: 'We are witnesses of everything He did in the country of the Jews and in Jerusalem' (Acts 10: 39). In order to reach all men, their witness must take a concrete form of the preaching of the Gospel (Mt 24: 14). The mission of Paul is defined in the same terms. As he powerfully attested to the resurrection of Jesus, Paul has been constituted a witness of Christ before all men and in pagan lands (1 Cor 15:15). The powerful witnessing of the Apostles brought into existence the primitive Church that became the community of believers who bore testimony to the Lord Jesus through their worship and through their exemplary sharing and caring for one another (Acts 2: 42-47).

Personal reflection: 'Jesus, the witness to the love of the Father'

Jesus by His life and mainly by His death and resurrection had testified to the Trinity's everlasting love for the human family. That witness of Jesus continues on, witnessed, in turn, by the Church. In its very being the Church is the witness. Each sacrament administered or received, each word preached, each sick person tended, each poor person helped is a continuing witness to the first and the prime witness, the witness par excellence, Jesus Christ. Jesus, the primary witness, constituted His Apostles and His disciples in every age, as His witnesses. The Apostles were the eye-and ear witnesses of the Lord, in the sense that they lived with Jesus during His public ministry and later saw Him after His resurrection. They bore a threefold witness to the Lord. First of all, as the ministers of the word, they proclaimed the good news of the risen and glorified Lord to all the nations (Mt 28: 19-20). They boldly said: 'God has raised the author of life from the dead. To this we are witnesses' (Acts 3:15; 5:32). Though, 'unlettered and uneducated' (Acts 4:13), the apostles bore a powerful witness for Christ with the power of the Holy Spirit (Acts 2: 4). The Holy Spirit filled the apostles with power as He had formerly filled the prophets, so that in spite of all difficulties and dangers, all persecutions, they proclaimed the gospel tidings without any fear (Acts 4:20). Secondly, like their divine master, the apostles reinforced their preaching, as the witnesses of the word, with 'signs', acts of miraculous power. Many wonders and signs were performed by the apostles that attested to the fact that God's power was with them (Acts 2:43; 5:12). Finally, the apostles bore witness to Jesus by facing persecutions and sufferings, without any fear and testified before the authorities and the tribunals to the Lordship of Jesus. Indeed, the power from on High had turned timid men into heroes who were ready even for the ultimate test, to seal their witness to the master with their blood (Mt 10: 17-31, Acts 5: 40-41). Martyrdom is witness to the faith consecrated by the testimony of blood. Stephen was the first to seal his witness with the outpouring out of his blood (Acts 7: 60). Throughout the history of the Church, thousands of courageous believers shed their blood and became the witnesses of the Gospel. So many were slain as they bore witness to Jesus and to His word (Rv 17:6). We know how no century passes without the heroic testimony of the martyrs in one land or another, who bear witness to Jesus by shedding their own blood, the ultimate sacrifice for the love of the Savior. This has been the case throughout the history of the Church right to the present day.

The preaching of the apostles kindled in the hearts of the young communities the spark of brotherly love, the most winning element in the witness to Christ. The brotherly fellowship welded the hearts and spirits of the believers into a unity, as the 'company of those who believed were of one heart and soul'. The faithful held all things in common and cared for one another in such a way that 'there were no needy persons among them' (Acts 4: 32-35). It is through the 'koinonia' or the authentic communion of the faithful, revealed in their caring and sharing that the early Church witnessed to the Gospel of Jesus Christ. The acts and attitudes of brotherly love are more urgently relevant than ever before in our world so much torn apart as it is, by social and religious conflicts. The Christians are called upon to witness to the Lord in word and in deed. Transformed by the power and the values of the Gospel and by the Holy

Spirit into new creation, the Christians are called upon to lead exemplary lives that are filled with goodness, kindness, self-control and brotherly love and to proclaim the Gospel to the whole world, as 'the witnesses' of Lord Jesus Christ.

She made all the difference: There was a great scientist, who thanked only his primary school teacher in tremendous gratitude, on the day of receiving the greatest honor of his country. He explained during his acceptance speech the reason for thanking his good teacher Mme Maria. His father, an attorney by profession and was addicted alcohol had neither time nor kindness for him. His mother, heavily burdened with the task caring for her drinking husband who abused her with ill temper, could hardly find a way to provide support to her only child. At the end of that particular academic year, when things were really bad at home, the scientist, then a student in the primary school, met his teacher Mme Maria to discuss the final evaluation report. Ahead of him, all the children came, one by one, with their parents who keenly raised questions and asked for clarifications from Mme Maria about the academic performance of their children. Going last and alone without parents, the future scientist felt encouraged by the inspiring talk of Mme Maria who told him that he was the best and he could do better. Like a good mother, she offered him her love and guidance. Loved and encouraged by a good woman, he could forget the difficult situation at home, worked with determination and finally became a great scientist. Like Mme Maria, God tells us that He cares for us, though our situation in the world is difficult. The Son of God, who died for us and now walks with us, leads us in faith and hope and above all, offering us, all the time, the unconditional love and blessings of the heavenly Father.

Quote: We shall have to repent in this generation, not so much for the evil deeds of the wicked people, but for the appalling silence of the good people- *Martin Luther King*

Scripture reading for Day 16: Jn 5: 31-45

Prayer for the Day 16: Father, you clothed your only Son, our Lord Jesus Christ in human nature and sent Him to the world as your witness to testify to your everlasting love! Clothe us with the nobility of the soul and the kindness of the heart so that we may live in unity and charity as 'witnesses' to the Gospel of your son Jesus Christ! Amen.

17

CHRIST

We call our blessed savior 'Jesus Christ'. The first half of the name 'Jesus' was given by the angel (Mt 1:21) and the second half of the name 'Christ' was derived from Latin 'Christus' and the Greek 'Christos'. The LXX, the Greek Old Testament, regularly used the word 'Christos' to translate the Hebrew word 'masiah' from which the word Messiah came into use. 'Masiah' means 'the anointed one'. In the Old Testament, priests (Ex 29:29; Lv 4:3), kings (1 Kgs 10:1; 24:7) and prophets (Is 61:1) were supposed to be anointed for their respective offices. For centuries the Jews had referred to their expected Deliverer as 'the Anointed'. Perhaps this designation alludes to Is 61:1 and Dn 9:24-26 or even to Ps 2:2; 20:7; 45:8. Thus the term Christ or Messiah was evidently a title rather than a proper name. When the disciples recognized Jesus as the promised savior, they proclaimed Him as 'the Christ' to their fellow Jews, who could easily understand the significance of this title (Acts 5:42). The definite article was necessary in their designation in Greek. However, when the Greek-speaking Gentiles became converts to Christianity, they did not understand the full significance of the Jewish concept of 'Messiah' that did not mean much to them. They understood 'Christ' as one of the names of Jesus. Therefore in the New Testament, 'Christ' is used without the definite article as a simple name for the Lord as in Rom 5:6 or together with the name 'Jesus'. Thus, it occurs as 'Jesus Christ' (Acts 2:38) or as 'Christ Jesus' (Acts 24:24). Jesus, as the Christ or the Messiah combined in His person the offices of prophet (Jn 6:14), of king (Lk 23:2) and of priest (Heb 2: 17). He fulfilled all the predictions of the Old Testament about the expected Messiah in a fuller and higher sense.

The Development of Jewish Messianism

What is the origin of Jewish messianism? Can we associate it with the Mesopotamian cult and the dualism of Persian religion? Mesopotamian and Canaanite religions contain the myth of the annual dying and rising god whose death and resurrection was the heavenly event that assured the renewal of the cycle of fertility. Persian dualism exhibits a struggle between the god of light, Ahura Mazda, and the god of darkness, Ahriman or Angra Mainyu, which issues in the victory of light. Israelite messianism does not exhibit the cyclic conception of history that imitates the conception of nature, upon which the Mesopotamian-Canaanite myth rests. It does not also present any similarity with the dualism of Persian religion. The unique character of Hebrew messianism arises from the biblical conception of history as a process that under the singular direction of Yahweh, moves toward a final term that is designated as the kingdom of Yahweh. Israel, in particular the king of Israel, is the medium through which the kingdom of Yahweh was to be established. This conception obviously exhibits several stages of development that reflect the evolution of Israelite cultural and political institutions and the catastrophes of Israelite history. Above all, Israel's growing awareness of the character of Yahweh as the one and the only God of the universe and the Lord of history played a major role in the unfolding of Hebrew messisanism in the pages of the Old Testament.

Our conclusion is that it is Israel's own history and religious experience that gave birth to the messianic hope that begins with a promise: 'Her seed will crush your head' (Gn 3: 15). This assurance of God points to a struggle between humanity and evil, in which the human race will not be defeated. Here the passage takes broad view of the conflict between the human race and evil and it looks at the entire humanity and not merely at Israel. Already, in the very first pages of the Old Testament, we find the strong hope among the people of Israel that God will help humanity to triumph over evil. God who revealed Himself to the patriarchs assures them of His blessings. His promises refer explicitly to the possession of the land and the growth of Israel as His people. Implied in the promises of God is the assurance of the final victory and glory of Israel. No doubt, such an expectation of future prosperity and glory would certainly enflame the hopes of Israel for a secure future, in spite of the sufferings and oppressions that might come along the way, as Israel journeys towards its assured destiny, based on God's promise. The covenant between Yahweh and Israel at Mount Sinai constituted Israel as a people who are the chosen subjects of Yahweh, their ruler. The covenant gave them the hope that Yahweh their king would protect them as His subjects, as long as they would be loyal to Him. With the establishment of the monarchy, David and his dynasty became the dominant element in Hebrew messianism. A 'son of David' was expected to assure the perpetuity of the Davidic dynasty and the messianic hope came to rest on him. Throughout the Old Testament, we see many hints that God would send a great king to Israel who would someday rule the world. In Genesis, Jacob, as he gives blessings to all of his sons, thus speaks of Judah: 'The scepter will not depart from Judah nor the ruler's staff from between his feet, until he comes to whom it belongs and the obedience of the nations is his' (Gn 49:10). This is a foundational assurance regarding the eternal Davidic king who would rule not only over Israel but also over the whole earth. The prophecy about this future messianic king becomes much more explicit from King David's time. David revealed to God his desire that he wanted to build Him a 'house', meaning a temple. But God said to him that his son Solomon would build the temple. Then God promised David that He would build a 'house' for him, meaning that God would establish his family line after him in perpetuity. 'I will set Him over my house and my kingdom forever; His throne will be established forever' (1 Chr 17: 11-14). This prophecy is the seedbed of all of the messianic prophecies that talk about the 'son of David' and the expected messianic king.

The anointed in the Old Testament

In the Hebrew religious tradition, anointing was a key element of religious ceremony by which specific people were explicitly marked as sacred or set aside for a specific role: priests, kings, and prophets. The Jews came to expect a savior who would embody the elements of priest, king and prophet, whom they termed 'the Messias', which served as a title. The association with being anointed and being a savior occurs in several passages in Old Testament particularly in their prayers, what we call the Psalms. These passages often make reference to God and 'His anointed' many of which Christians interpret as prophetic and as foretelling the coming of Jesus, the Son of God. The pre-exilic psalms give a conspicuous place to the royal Messiah in the life and faith of Israel. The anointing which he received is a sign of divine preference (Ps 45: 8). It has made of him the adopted son of Yahweh (Ps 2:7; 2 Sm 7: 14). He is also certain of the protection of God and hence revolt against him is folly (Ps 2: 2). God will not fail to intervene to save him and 'exalt his horn' (1 Sm 2: 10). He is prayed for (Ps 84: 10). In relying on the promises made to David, therefore, it is hoped that God will never fail to perpetuate his dynasty. After the fall of Jerusalem, the people of Israel felt abandoned by their God, Yahweh, especially, when they saw that their king, the anointed of Yahweh, was taken prisoner by the pagans (Lam 4: 20): 'Why has God so rejected His Messiah, so that all the pagans behave outrageously to him?' (Ps 89: 39). It is in this context of sadness that the Jewish eschatology brought hope to the people of Israel. The expected Messiah finds the central place in the post-exilic Jewish eschatology: everywhere a royal messiah and only in certain places a sacerdotal Messiah. But the scriptural promises are not reduced to this Messianism in the strict sense of the word. They equally announce the setting up of the kingdom of God. They present also the artisan of salvation under the features of the Servant of Yahweh and of the Son of Man. The coordination of all this data on the expected Messiah is not easily or clearly presented and hence different groups of Judaism developed varied expectations regarding the Messiah. Only the coming of Jesus dissipated the ambiguities on this point.

Jesus, the anointed of Yahweh

In the New Testament, it is indicated that the savior, the long awaited messiah did come to the world in the person of Jesus. However, there is no record of His being officially anointed with oil as Messiah, priest or king in the Gospels. Instead Luke says that His heavenly Father inducted Him into His messianic office: 'The Holy Spirit descended upon Him in bodily form like a dove. And a voice came from heaven, 'You are my beloved Son; with you I am well pleased' (Lk 3.22). A woman also anoints Jesus and it happens just before His death: 'She has done what she could. She has anticipated anointing my body for burial' (Mk 14: 3-9). As Jesus demonstrates, over time, to His disciples that He is the promised savior, they began to call Him by the name of 'Messiah' or Christus in Greek. After the resurrection, this title 'Christ' became a proper name of Jesus and was used regularly to refer to Him. What does the name Jesus 'Christ' mean? It is always fascinating and enriching to bring the Hebraic cultural context into understanding the most important words that express our Christians faith. One of the most important the words is the title 'Christ'. What does it mean to call Jesus, the 'Christ' or what implications does it have for us to say that Jesus is the 'Christ'? To be the Christ is to be 'the anointed one of God'. But what does that mean? To be anointed literally means to have sacred anointing oil poured on one's head, because God has chosen the person for a special task. Priests and kings were anointed, and occasionally also the prophets. Kings were anointed during their coronation. Even though prophets and priests were anointed, the phrase 'anointed one' or 'the Lord's anointed' was most often used to refer to a king. For instance, David used it many times to refer to King Saul, even when Saul was trying to murder David: 'Far be it from me because of the Lord that I should do this thing to my lord, the Lord's anointed, to stretch out my hand against him, since he is the Lord's anointed' (1 Sm 24: 6). So, the main picture of the word 'Messiah' or 'Christ' as the 'anointed one' was of a king chosen by God. While Jesus also has a priestly and a prophetic role, the main inference that the word 'Christ' brings to our understanding is the role of a king or a ruler. The Gospels tell us many times that Jesus is this great King who has come. The wise men came to pay their respects and they brought presents to the king whose star they have seen in the east (Mt 2: 1-12). This was a fulfillment of the oracle of Balaam: 'I see him though not now. I behold him though not near. A star shall advance from Jacob and a staff shall rise from Israel' (Nm 24:17). Also, the Psalm 72 foretells the coming of a great king and describes how representatives from nations everywhere would come to give him tribute: 'He will endure as long as the sun, as long as the moon, through all generations. He will rule from sea to sea and from the River to the ends of the earth. The desert tribes will bow before him and his enemies will lick the dust. The kings of Tarshish and of distant shores will bring tribute to him; the kings of Sheba and Seba will present him gifts. All kings will bow down to him and all nations will serve him' (Ps 72: 5, 8-11). In Jesus, all prophesies concerning the Messiah find fulfillment.

The King of the Jews

Soon after He began His ministry, when Jesus came to Nazareth, He announced that the passage from Isaiah 61:1-2 had been fulfilled in Him: 'The Spirit of the Sovereign Lord is upon me, because the Lord has anointed me to preach good news to the poor. He has sent me to bind up the broken-hearted, to proclaim freedom for the captives and release from darkness for the prisoners, to proclaim the year of the Lord's favor' (Lk 4:17-20). In his oracle, the prophet Isaiah portrays the enthronement of the messianic King who would declare the good news of the jubilee year right after God anoints him. When a new king came into power especially in some Middle Eastern countries, the Jubilee year was announced. When Jesus applied the prophecy of the prophet Isaiah to Himself, there was a very strong reaction from His audience to His bold claims as the anointed of Yahweh. We see yet another picture of Jesus as King when He rode on the donkey into Jerusalem. This was very much a kingly image, often part of the annunciation of a new king, as it was done in the case of king Solomon: 'They went down and mounted Solomon on king David's mule, escorted him to Gihon. Then, Zadok the priest took the horn of oil from the tent and anointed Solomon. They blew the horn and all the people shouted, 'Long live King Solomon' (1 Kgs 1:38-39). Also, we see the fulfillment of another oracle about the triumphal entry of the messianic king: 'Rejoice greatly, O daughter of Zion! Shout, O daughter of Jerusalem! Behold, your king is coming to you; He is just and endowed with salvation, Humble, and mounted on a donkey, Even on a colt, the foal of a donkey' (Zec 9:9). During Jesus' trial, the main question that is asked of Him is 'Are you the Christ? Jesus seems to answer affirmatively: 'If I tell you, you will not believe me and if I asked you, you would not answer. But from now on, the Son of Man will be seated at the right hand of the mighty God' (Lk 22:67-69). Taking Him to Pilate, the Jewish religious leaders began to accuse Him, saying, 'We found this man misleading our nation and forbidding the people to pay taxes to Caesar and saying that He Himself is Christ, a King'. So Pilate asked Him, 'Are You the King of the Jews?' Jesus replied, 'Yes, it is as you say' (Lk 23:2-3).

The crucified Messiah is proclaimed as savior

In the light of the resurrection, the first Christians called Jesus the Messiah-Christ, a title that is freed from all ambiguities in the proclamation of the early Church. The Jews must be shown that the Christ, the expected Messiah, the object of their long-standing hope, has finally come to the world in the person of Jesus. Jesus is presented as the veritable son of David, destined from His conception through the power of the Holy Spirit to receive the throne of David His father. He was to lead the Israelite royalty to its completion by establishing the kingdom of God on earth. It is the resurrection that has enthroned Him in royal glory: 'Therefore let all Israel be assured of this: God has made both Lord and Christ this same Jesus whom you have crucified' (Acts 2: 36). United indissolubly to the personal name of Jesus, the word 'Christ', from then onwards, had an immense broadening with all the titles that the prophets assigned to the expected Messiah were given to Jesus with their proper explanation and illustration such as the servant of Yahweh, 'He whom God has anointed is His holy servant Jesus' (Acts 4: 27) and the irreproachable Lamb pictured by prophet Isaiah (Is 53: 7; 1 Cor 5: 7). It was written that Christ should suffer (Acts 3: 18). The Psalmist in Ps 2 described in advance the plot of the nations 'against Yahweh and against His Messiah' (Acts 4: 25). The gospel of Paul is also a proclamation of the Christ crucified (1 Cor 1: 23).

Personal reflection- 'Jesus Christ, the Messiah'

Did Jesus declare or acknowledge that He was the messiah? Yes. He accepted this title, though, with a lot of hesitation because of the political significance this title carried. Jesus gave His own interpretation of this title that was quite different from the popular expectation of the people of Israel. In the Gospel, we find that the confession of Peter regarding Jesus as the messiah (Mt 16: 16) is followed by the prediction of passion by Jesus: 'From that time on, Jesus began to explain to His disciples that He must go to Jerusalem and suffer many things at the hands of the elders, chief priests and teachers of the law and that He must be killed and on the third day be raised to life (Mt 16: 21). The Gospel identifies the messianic mission of Jesus with His suffering, death and resurrection. Jesus asks the disciples of Emmaus: 'Did not the Christ have to suffer these things and then enter his glory? (Lk 24:26). Later, Jesus told all the disciples: 'This is what is written: The Christ will suffer and rise from the dead on the third day' (Lk 24: 46). The theme of the suffering Messiah not drawn from any Old Testament messianic passage but only from the passages regarding the Servant of Yahweh and the Son of Man. The early church especially the apostles presented Jesus as the messiah. However, they focused on His passion, death, and resurrection. Peter tells the people after healing a crippled beggar, 'This is how God fulfilled what He had foretold through all the prophets, saying that His Christ would suffer' (Acts 3: 18). He explained the resurrection of Jesus as glorification and exaltation by God who has made Him Lord and Christ: 'Therefore let all Israel be assured of this: God has made this Jesus, whom you crucified, both Lord and Christ' (Acts 2: 36). The messiah accomplished His mission through His suffering and death on behalf of the sinners: 'When we were still powerless, Christ died for the ungodly' (Rom 5:6). Now, Jesus is enthroned in glory and exercises the threefold function of the Messiah, as king, priest and prophet for the salvation of the world. Through the saving work of Jesus, we have been united to Him. It was baptism that incorporated us into the death and resurrection of Jesus and conferred upon us new life (Rom 6: 3). Every baptized Christian, through dying with Jesus and rising with Him again, shares with Jesus the dignity of a king, priest and a prophet. Jesus exercised His kingship as a servant to all. John says that Jesus knew that the Father had put all things into His hands (Jn 13: 3). Though the hour of humiliation was near, He also knew that the hour of His glorification had also come. With the knowledge of His power and glory as a king, who would be exalted and enthroned in glory, Jesus, instead of feeling any sense of pride took the role of a servant and washed the feet of His disciples.

To wash the feet of the guests at the feast was the role of a slave. He showed us, we Christians, how to exercise our kingship that we received in our baptism. Instead standing for dignity, honor and power and glory, Jesus showed us that true and lasting greatness comes from the service of charity and of loving care for others. He said: 'The greatest among you should be the last and the one who rules should be like the one who serves' (Lk 22: 26). When we think of the messiah, instead of seeing a royal figure vested in purple garments as the people of Israel expected, let us always see the Son of God girt with the towel washing the feet of His disciples. In baptism, we receive also the office of the priesthood. The entire life of the Christian people, surrendered totally to the Lord, is a priestly act. We are to offer our entire life as a living victim holy and agreeable to God. This is the spiritual act of worship we offer (Rom 12: 1). Through baptism, we are also made prophets. Prophecy exists in the Christian community 'in order to build up, exhort and console' (1 Cor 14: 3). United to Jesus Christ, our Messiah, we exercise the threefold office as king, priest and prophet as we serve the Lord and the others in imitation of the example of Jesus, who became the Christ, the servant of God.

Martin and the Beggar: In the old town of Amiens in France, in the year 337, near the city wall, Martin saw a starving beggar. As a soldier he went on a horse along with a number of other soldiers who passed by the city wall. Many other people, rich men and wealthy ladies, old people, young boys and girls went by the beggar who was shivering in the cold. Nobody paid him any attention. The soldiers who passed by the beggar also completely ignored him. Martin was touched by the plight of the beggar. He carried no money and he could not offer the beggar any money. But Martin felt that he should do something. He took his sword, cut his cloak hanging from his shoulders and covered the beggar in that warm cloth against the cold. He spoke a few nice words to him and went on his way. That night martin had a vision. He saw Jesus in heaven surrounded by a company of angels. Jesus was wearing the cloth that Martin gave to the beggar. He showed it to the angels saying, 'See, here is the garment, Martin lovingly gave me'. In his fraternal service, Martin exercised the threefold function of a king, a priest and a prophet.

Quote: It is infinitely easier to suffer with others than to suffer alone. It is infinitely easier to suffer as public heroes than to suffer apart and in ignominy. It is infinitely easier to suffer physical death than to endure spiritual suffering - ***Dietrich Bonhoeffer***

Scripture reading for Day 17:Jn 13:1-17

Prayer for Day 17: Almighty God! You call each of us to follow your ways in union with your son you made us royal priesthood, and holy nation. You know the strength of our faith and the longing of our hearts. Guide us to do your holy will especially through our fraternal service to others! Amen.

18

SAVIOR

We lovingly and gratefully address Jesus as 'savior'. In our personal prayers we call upon Him as 'my savior'. Referring to His redemptive death and resurrection, we proclaim Him as the 'savior' of the world. It is one of the titles we find especially in the gospel according to John: 'Many Samaritans, upon the testimony from the Samaritan woman, believed in Jesus. They said to the woman, 'We no longer believe just because of what you said; now we have heard for ourselves, and we know that this man really is the Savior of the world' (Jn 4: 42). The Greek terms 'sozein' which means 'to save' and 'soteria' which means 'salvation' and 'soter' which means 'savior' were used in New Testament to designate the salvific ministry of Jesus. Those terms were also in use in the Greek and Hellenistic literature to refer to the activities of gods and the kings and some distinguished men, who had rendered public service. The devotees frequently applied the title 'savior' to pagan gods whom they sought in times of need, such as sickness, shipwreck or war in order to save them from peril. Asklepios received this title because he was the god of healing. Zeus was called savior because he was a helper in daily necessities. The gods of the mystery religions were addressed as 'saviors' because they were supposed to free their devotees from death and dispense life to them. Later the title was given to various Hellenistic kings, such as Alexander the Great and Ptolemy I, since the divinized rulers were symbol of peace and order. In the 1st century BC, Roman Emperors appropriated the title. In Rome, the royal title 'Soter' reflected the deification of the Roman emperors. Augustus became the 'world savior' because in his reign men saw the fulfillment of their desire for peace. The early Christians presented Jesus to the pagan world as the one and only true 'soter' or 'savior' who offers salvation to the entire humanity. This does not mean that the title 'savior' as applied to Jesus, has only a Gentile background. In an impressive theological and eschatological tradition, the pages of the Old Testament portray Yahweh as the savior. The early Christians, who were all Jews, drew a lot of inspiration from their Jewish heritage when they presented Jesus to the Gentiles as the savior of the world.

Yahweh, the Savior in the Old Testament

In the LXX, the Greek verb 'sozein' (to save) translates especially the Hebrew verb *YS* and it signifies primarily the possession of space and implied freedom and security that is gained by the removal of constriction. '*YS*' stands in opposition to '*SRR*' which signifies narrowness and constraints. Positively, the notion of 'salvation' involves an exercise of strength that gains victory;

negatively, it connotes liberation from danger, misfortune, sickness, famine and from hostile powers, especially from death. Hence to 'save' means to render help or protection in any straits. Yahweh is frequently called the savior of His people. 'That Yahweh saves' or ' Yahweh is salvation' is stated 266 times in the Old Testament, of which the verb is used 131 times: 'On that day, it will be said: 'Behold our God, to whom we looked to save us! This is the Lord for whom we looked; let us rejoice and be glad that He has saved us' (Is 25:9).). 'The Lord is my light and my salvation' (Ps 27:1).Yahweh is not only the God of Israel but also of the pagans and that is why He saves even the pagans: 'There is no just and saving God but me and there is no other' (Is 45.21-22). The salvation that God brings becomes personal, spiritual and eschatological as revelation progresses through the pages of the Old Testament. In the beginning, the sacred writers spoke of deliverance of Israel by God from merely temporal evils, such as war, famine and invasion: 'The God saves you from all your evils and calamities' (1 Sm 10:19). They especially focused on the deliverance of the chosen people from Egypt: 'The strength and courage is the Lord who is our savior. Pharaoh's chariots and army He hurled into the sea; the elite of his officers was submerged in the Red Sea' (Ex 15:1-4). There was also the reference to the deliverance from the Babylonian Exile: 'Israel, the Lord saves you! You are saved forever! You shall never be put to shame or disgrace in future ages' (Is 45:17). Yahweh, though occasionally, does save through human means and it is understood that He raised men to be saviors. This is the conception of the charismatic leaders who guided and ruled over the people of Israel. The judges of Israel were saviors: 'The Lord raised up judges to save them from their despoilers' (Jgs 2:16). 'When the Israelites cried out to the Lord, He raised up for them a savior, Othniel, who rescued them' (Jgs 3:9). The same conception was transferred to the kings in the beginning of the monarchy: 'Saul shall save my people from the clutches of the Philistines, for I have witnessed their misery and accepted their cry for help' (1 Sm 9:16). The kings were supposed to be the saviors of those who because of their weakness most need a savior, especially the poor: 'May the king defend the oppressed among the people and save the poor and crush the oppressor' (Ps 72:4). 'The king may show pity to the needy and the poor and save the lives of the poor' (Ps 72:13). However, many kings turned out to be unworthy rulers who did evil in the sight of the Lord. As a result, they were incapable of saving the people of Israel (1 Sm 8: 14).

Israel knew that besides her God there is no other savior: 'I am the Lord your God. You know no God besides me and there is no savior but me' (Hos 13: 4). God was in no way dependent upon human beings, for bringing His salvation to Israel. He might have made use of inadequate human beings and circumstances to offering His salvation. Nevertheless, it is God alone 'who works salvation' (Ex 14: 13). Indeed He is the 'salvation' (Ex 15:2). That is why, in every time of disaster, Israel confidently turned to God in order to be saved. The siege of Jerusalem by Sennacherib, the king of Assyria, is a classic example of such a situation. The king of Assyria dared Yahweh to save Israel: 'Has any of the gods of the nations ever rescued his land from the hand of the king of Assyria? Which of the gods rescued his land from my hand? Will the Lord then rescue Jerusalem from my hand? (2 Kgs 18: 30-35). But the Lord indeed saved His people: 'I will shield and save this city for my own sake and for the sake of my servant David' (2 Kgs 19:34). In fact, the angel of the Lord went forth and struck down one hundred and eighty-five thousand men in the Assyrian camp (2 Kgs 19:35) and thus completely destroyed the army of Sennacherib.

The Messianic hope in the Savior

For Israel, salvation is a gift from her God and it meant the conferring of God's blessings in order to be an instrument of Yahweh to the whole world: 'I will make you a light to the nations that my salvation may reach to the ends of the earth' (Is 49: 6). Yahweh Himself is salvation, as He saves not only the nation of Israel but also the individuals in need of His mercy: 'You answer us with awesome deeds of justice, O God our savior, the hope of all the ends of the earth' (Ps 65:6). So many people when they were in danger, cried out to God and He saved them: 'In their distress, they cried to the Lord who saved them in their peril' (Ps 107: 13). A number of prayers of thanksgiving testify to the mighty deeds of salvation that God performed in order to save people from danger, from trial and from imminent death. It is at the time of great national trial that Israel looked with most confidence to God for salvation. His title 'savior' became the major theme of prophetic eschatology: 'You know that I, the Lord, am your savior' (Is 60:16). The prophecies concerned with 'the last days' described the expected final salvation of Israel under various aspects. The most important assurance of the prophets to the people of Israel as they encountered the definite fall of the monarchy was that their salvation would come by the messiah, 'the savior'. The prophets foretold that Yahweh would send a messiah-king to His people for their 'salvation': 'Behold, the days are coming, says the Lord, when I will raise up a righteous shoot to David. As king, he shall reign and govern wisely; he shall do what is just and right in the land. In his days, Judah shall be saved. Israel shall dwell in security' (Jer 23: 5-6). Yahweh would save His people by gathering them together: 'The Lord has delivered His people, the remnant of Israel. Behold, I will gather them from the ends of the world' (Jer 31:7-8).

As 'salvation' for Israel, gradually approached the idea of liberation from all evil, collective and personal, and the acquisition of complete security, their expectation was pointed towards a perfect king, the messiah. The messianic king is a savior in a way in which the historic kings never were: 'See your king shall come to you. A just savior is He. He shall proclaim peace to the nations. His dominion will be from sea to sea (Zec 9: 9-10). The messianic salvation is eternal: 'My salvation will remain forever and my justice shall never be dismayed' (Ps 51: 6). Another important aspect of salvation as the prophets looked forward to the messianic times was the deliverance not only from evil but also from sin: 'I will order the grain to be abundant and I will not send famine against you. I will save you from all your impurities' (Ez 36: 29). The supreme threat to the salvation of Israel in both historical and prophetic literature is the sins of Israel, in particular, its disloyalty to Yahweh. The eternal salvation of the messianic Israel is inconceivable without the removal of the sins of Israel. Though not said explicitly, we find the implied hope in the Old Testament that the promised messiah or savior would take away the sins and assure people eternal salvation. In Jesus Christ, this messianic hope would be totally fulfilled.

Jesus, the savior of the world

Jesus Christ, the God-Man, the Messiah, is the savior sent by God into the world: 'And you shall call His name Jesus, for He shall save His people from their sins' (Mt 1: 21). Jesus reveals Himself as the Savior through significant acts that are presented to us in the Gospels. Jesus saved Peter as he walked on the water from drowning (Mt 14: 29-30) and He saved His disciples when they were caught in the storm (Mt 8: 25). He saved the sick by curing them. The word 'save' in the Synoptic Gospels meant a healing accomplished by Jesus (Mk 3: 4). The saving acts of Jesus, as healing, were attributed to the faith of the person cured (Mt 9: 22). The essential thing was to have faith in Jesus, because it was the faith that saved the sick (Lk 8: 48). Thus, frequently the verb 'to save' is used in the accounts of Christ's miracles: in healing the Samaritan leper (Lk 17.19), the woman suffering from hemorrhage (Mk 5.34) and the blind Bartimeus (Mk 10.52). It was also used when Jesus forgave the penitent woman. Jesus said to her: 'Your faith has saved you' (Lk 7.50). The verb 'save' is also used to refer to Christ's work of delivering people from sin and eternal death and conferring messianic salvation (Lk 19: 10). The healing is only a visible sign of the saving power of Jesus that confers a far greater salvation than just the restoration of the health of the body. The salvation, which Jesus confers, is above all, a salvation from sin. He gives repentance and forgiveness of sins (Acts 5: 31). Therefore, salvation includes the liberation of mankind from sin, a gracious deliverance of man by God in the person of His Son, Jesus: 'Christ Jesus came into the world to save sinners' (1 Tim 1:15). Indeed, salvation comes to the world through Jesus Christ: 'Salvation is found in no one else, for there is no other name under heaven given to men by which we must be saved' (Acts 4:12). Jesus is called as 'the Savior' from the earliest preaching (Acts 5.31) to the later apostolic catechesis (Ti 1:4; 2:13). The Church proclaims and testifies that Jesus is the savior of the world: 'We testify that the Father has sent His Son to be the savior of the world' (1Jn 4:14).

From the numerous texts in New Testament that designate or address Jesus as the 'savior' it is apparent that the New Testament develops and brings to perfection the notion of Yahweh as savior as portrayed in the Old Testament. God the Father Himself is the initiator of salvation and His son, Jesus Christ brings to completion the work of salvation through the Holy Spirit. Thus the title 'savior' suits equally well the Father (Ti 1:3; 2:10) and Jesus (2 Pt

1:11; 2:20). But both God the Father and Christ are called saviors principally because they deliver men from sin and confer eternal life. Jesus carries out the work of salvation on both the temporal level as well as the spiritual level. His miracles of healing are a deliverance from temporal evils. They belong also to the spiritual sphere or realm insofar as they are sign for the inauguration of spiritual salvation (Acts 4.9-12). Salvation is essentially an eschatological reality (Phil 3: 20), but already begins on earth (Ti 3:5; 2 Tim 1:9). A synthesis of this twofold aspect of salvation is found in Titus 3: 4-7: 'God saved us not because of righteous things we had done, but because of His mercy. He saved us through the washing of rebirth and renewal by the Holy Spirit, whom He poured out on us generously through Jesus Christ, our savior, so that having been justified, by His grace, we might become heirs having the hope of eternal life'.

Personal reflection – 'Jesus saves us'

The shepherds heard and saw the hosts of heaven praising God who extended His peace to all of mankind. They went to Bethlehem to see the wonder. Full of joy, they returned to their flocks in the pastures on the hills beyond Bethlehem. They glorified and praised God for all the things they have heard and seen, which were just as they had been told' (Lk 2:8-20). On the eighth day, the Child was given the Hebrew name that means 'Savior', the name the angel had given Him before He had been conceived (Lk 2:21). The title of Jesus as 'savior' refers to the divine action of restoring mankind to the state from which it had fallen by the sin of Adam. The experience of suffering and guilt is universally found in every man. Judeo-Christian revelation teaches us that the disobedience of the first man, Adam, deprived mankind of the relationship with God, its creator and brought it to the life of suffering, pain, sorrow, social injustice, violence and death. The appetites of man's own soul and body would entice him to sin. The existential situation of humanity in this world, in the midst of suffering, misery, sin and death is portrayed in the pages of the Bible as a 'fallen state' that needed restoration, through redemption. God's holy will was that all humanity should enjoy perfect happiness with Him forever. It was 'sin' that placed a hurdle in the path of mankind to be with God forever in eternal happiness and peace. But God is not the one to let sin and above all the devil, the source of sin and evil, dictate to Him the destiny of humanity and destroy His holy will for the human race. After promising salvation for fallen humanity (Gn 3:15), God prepared the human race to receive the 'savior' of the world at His appointed time for its restoration and for regaining the lost paradise.

God chose the people of Israel to be the privileged instruments that would prepare the way for the coming of the savior. He gave Israel the experiences of His salvation in her history. He liberated Israel from the hands of the oppressive king, the Pharaoh of Egypt and thus gave them a foretaste of final 'salvation' that He would accomplish for all humanity in His Son.

Exodus was a political salvation but it led the people of Israel to believe strongly that God alone is the savior and He alone saves humanity (1 Sm 14:39). By raising up human leaders and using them as His instruments to bring relief and victory to the people of Israel, God revealed to them that He is always active in their history. Numerous judges and kings became the powerful instruments of God to reveal God's salvation as liberation from oppression, victory in war with enemies, redemption from tyranny or relief from natural disasters like famine and hunger. Israel was given to understand that God alone is the master and author of history and human destiny is firmly in His control. To those who called upon Him, as individuals or as communities, God, the savior, came to their rescue. Israel saw her God as the Lord of salvation.

God sends His own Son as the savior of the world

At the appointed time, the Son of God became man and saved mankind by His expiatory death and resurrection. His salvation was the liberation of human race from the sins of the world, both the original sin and the actual sins of the entire humanity. During His earthly life, Jesus performed many miracles that brought healing to the sick. He even raised the dead back to life, as seen in the case of Lazarus (Jn 11: 38-44). In this way, Jesus showed to the world that the healer of humanity, the savior who restores both the soul and the body to health and the fullness of life has finally come to the world in His person (Lk 7: 18-23). Humanity was defiled and the precious blood of the savior washes it clean. Human race lost the friendship with God through the guilt of their sins. The savior of the world offered His own life on the cross as expiation for the sins of the world and thus erased the guilt of human race and nullified the conviction of humanity, by bearing their debt of punishment on Himself: 'Jesus is the atoning sacrifice for our sins, and not only for ours but also for the sins of the whole world' (1 Jn 2:2). That is why the Apostles, the privileged witnesses to the earthly life of Jesus, announced to the world, after the resurrection of Jesus that He alone saves (Acts 4: 9-12). Into the confused humanity thrown in the darkness of the error, the divine savior came as the victorious liberator, who by his death and resurrection conquered death and the devil as the light of the world (Jn 8: 12). The human race was enslaved by the dread of death and the Son of God freed mankind as the life and the resurrection (Jn 11:25). Jesus is the savior sent by the Father to restore humanity back to His friendship and to offer the privilege of becoming the children of God. From the state of being the enemies of God, men are reconciled to Him by the one mediator Jesus Christ, through His sacrifice on the cross (Rom 5:10). From captivity, men are redeemed, purchased by His Blood: 'You were bought at a price' (1Cor 6:20). From the exile and from dispersion men are brought back to the Fatherland (Jn 17:24). Out of spiritual chaos, the redeemer of the world recreates the image of God in every human being, restores him to God's own likeness and makes him pleasing to God as His beloved child (Col 3:10). In the person of Jesus, the good Shepherd, today, God leads the human race towards the promised land of heaven, the appointed destiny of mankind. The Good Samaritan Jesus heals the human race that became wounded and sick by the affliction of sin and the devil. From heaven Jesus continues to be our savior through the operation of His Holy Spirit, in the ministry of the Church. Today the Church, as the Body of Christ, proclaims this message of salvation to all the nations and invites all men to repentance and conversion. To be saved, men must respond with authentic conversion and bear good fruit that is possible only in union with Christ Jesus. Let us confidently seek the mercy of the Savior and remain always united to Him, for He alone is our Lord and Savior.

He ran and ran to get his crown: Once upon a time there was a little child who wanted to wear a crown and be a king. When he was a young man he asked his neighbors and the villagers from the surrounding areas whether they would make him a king. Some laughed at him, some mocked at him and some shook their head in disbelief about his desire. But nobody offered him a crown. The young man grew up to be an old man and in the long years he forgot completely about his crown. He saw people in hunger and he fed them as much as he could. He saw people without clothes and he clothed them as much as he could. He saw people in sorrow and he comforted them as much he could. He saw people in sickness and visited them and assisted them as much as he could. In his busy life of doing good to others, the thought of a crown never came to his mind. He died a very weary, tired old man. After his death he met the angel of God at the gate of Heaven and there the angel received him and crowned him with a shining priceless beautiful crown. The angel told him: 'when you serve others in genuine charity and authentic kindness, you win the lasting glory of the heavenly crown'.

Quote: The God of the Bible is indeed a universal God, but He is also a God who nevertheless chooses places in which to reveal Himself to men. He is a God without frontiers, omnipresent, never the prisoner of any particular place but not an impersonal God floating everywhere and nowhere. He breaks into history and geography because He speaks to men and enters into dialogue with them; and a dialogue always takes place at a particular time and place- ***Paul Tournier***

Scripture reading Day 18: 1 Jn 4: 1-21

Prayer for Day 18: Loving God, keep us in your light and in your love, now and for all eternity! You sent Jesus your only son as our savior. May we live in this world as your saved people through the new life that bears much fruit and be pleasing children to your loving heart! Help us to always abide in the love of your son so that we may be found worthy to enjoy everlasting peace in heaven! Amen.

19

JUDGE

*H*e will come again to judge the living and the dead'- the expectation of Christ's return as judge of the living and the dead has become part of the Christian Credo. Every man will appear before Him to render an account of his actions. Such a theme of a judging God is not unusual in the history of religion. In most of the religious traditions, there is found the belief in the 'judgment' of God after the death of human beings. But the manner in which the New Testament presents Christ as the 'judge' can be understood only in relation to its previous development in the Old Testament. The judgment of God was already an article of faith in the Old Testament.

The imperfect human judges in the Old Testament

Judgment 'mispat' is that which was pronounced by a judge 'sopet'. The same word also meant a governor who guided his people' (Dn 9: 12). One of the important duties of all the governors was to render just decisions in lawsuits, so that justice would prevail in society. The governors restored justice and condemned the offenders. For example, Moses sat in judgment over his people (Ex 18: 13). Samuel judged Israel as long as he lived. He made a yearly journey passing through Bethel, Gilgal and Mizpah and judging Israel at each of these sanctuaries. Then he used to return to Ramah for that was his home. There, too, he judged Israel (1 Sm 7:16-17). David as king rendered justice to his people (2 Sm 15: 1-6). There were many judges and officials who administered justice in Israel: 'You shall appoint judges and officials throughout your tribes to administer true justice for people in all the communities which the Lord, your God, is giving you' (Dt 16: 18). Some priests also administered justice: 'You may go to the levitical priests for justice. They shall study the case and then hand down to you their decision. You shall act, being careful to do exactly as they direct' (Dt 17: 8-13). In practice, despite the regulations laid down, injuries were far from being always redressed. The rights of each man were not always respected and justice was not always exactly observed. The people were looking forward to an ideal Judge and King. The Messiah was to fulfill their hopes for the perfect judge: 'He shall not judge by appearance. He shall not decide by hearsay. He shall judge the poor with justice and decide aright for the Land's afflicted. He shall strike the ruthless with the rod of his mouth and with the breadth of his lips he shall slay the wicked. Justice shall be the band around his waist' (Is 11: 3-5). The prayer of the people was, 'O God, give judgment to the king; your justice to the son of kings, that he may govern your people with justice, your oppressed with right judgment' (Ps 72: 1-2)

God as the perfect Judge

Even if the human agents of justice were faltering numerous times, Israel's faith in the judgment of God was never put in doubt. Yahweh governs the whole world and in particular, He rules over human beings. He knows perfectly the just and the sinners 'for He alone probes the mind and test the heart, to reward everyone according to his ways' (Jer 17:10). His word determines the law and establishes the rules of justice. Since He dominates history and the events of the world, He cannot fail to shape them in such a way that in the end the just will escape from their trials and the wicked will be punished. It is evident that 'the Lord will not sweep away the innocent with the guilty' (Gn 18: 23). That is why one spontaneously has recourse to Him as to the supreme dispenser of justice and the healer of injuries. As sovereign judge, God always renders perfect justice. In executing His judgment God distinguishes between the just and the sinful. In fact, His intent in punishing the sinful is to deliver the just (Ez 34:17-22). Moreover, God's judgment will not be directed solely toward Israel, because all peoples are subjects to Him. Jeremiah depicts the broad outlines of this judgment of the nations in 25: 1-17: 'I will repay them according to their own deeds and according to their own handiwork' (Jer 25: 14). Some of the psalms contain appeals to God from just men suffering persecution and tribulation: 'Grant me justice Lord! I have walked without blame and I have not faltered (Ps 26: 1). Sometimes the psalmists praise Him because He judges the whole earth in perfect justice: 'May the nations be glad and shout for joy; for you govern the peoples justly, you guide the nations upon the earth' (Ps 67: 5). At other times they urge Him to defend against the injustices of human judges: 'O God, defend the lowly and the fatherless; render justice to the afflicted and the needy. Rescue the lowly and the poor; deliver them from the hand of the wicked' (Ps 82: 3-4).

In the post-exilic period

The modes of expression of the post-exilic prophets tend toward apocalyptic, as we see in the prophecies of the last judgment. It encompasses the sinners of the whole world: 'The Lord God shall judge all mankind by fire and sword and many shall be slain by the Lord' (Is 66: 16). He will assemble the nations in the valley of Jehoshaphat which means 'God-Judge': 'Hasten and come, all you neighboring peoples, assemble there! Let the nations bestir themselves and come up to the valley of Jehoshaphat; For there will I sit in judgment upon all the neighboring nations (Jl 4:12). The book of Daniel describes the judgment that will bring this age to an end and open the eternal reign of the Son of Man: 'Then the kingship and dominion and majesty of all kingdoms under the heavens shall be given to the holy people of the Most High. His kingdom shall be everlasting and all dominions shall serve and obey him' (Dn 7: 26). In the book of Wisdom, we find the description wherein the just and unjust appear together to render an account. The sinners only need to fear, for God Himself will protect the just: 'The wicked shall be shaken with dreadful fear. They shall say among themselves, rueful and groaning through anguish of spirit: 'This just man is he whom once we held as a laughingstock and as a type for mockery, fools that we were! His life we accounted as madness and his death dishonored. See how the just man is accounted among the sons of God. How his lot is with the saints' (Wis 5: 3-5). The holy ones of the Most High will have a share in the kingdom of the Son of Man (Dn 7: 27). The prophetic appeal to the God-Judge frequently seems to be an effort to hasten the hour of the last judgment: 'Rise up, O Judge of the earth! Render to the proud what they deserve!' (Ps 94: 2).

We see on one side an assurance from God to the people of Israel that He stands by them. The whole history of Israel from the victory over Pharaoh and the Egyptians (Ex 6:6-9) to the conquests of David (2 Sm 5: 17-25) was interpreted as the judgment of Yahweh in favor of His people. When Israel trusts in the Lord and is loyal to Him in obedience, the Lord passes judgment in her favor. But when she forsakes the Lord, then Yahweh passes terrible judgment on her. The prophets denounce 'a sinful nation, a people laden with iniquity, offspring of evildoers, sons who deal corruptly and who have forsaken Yahweh (Is 1:4). The judgment of the Lord was seen first as national tragedy with the ruin of both kingdoms (Jer 16: 11-13) as well as accompanying calamities such as pestilence, hunger, sword, desolation and imprisonment (Jer 15: 2-9). However, even among the punished people of Israel God will bring up 'Remnant of Israel', the purified people, as the beginnings of a new people of God: 'I will bring about the restoration of my people, Israel. They shall rebuild and inhabit their ruined cities. I will plant them upon their own ground, never again, shall they be plucked from the land I have given them (Am 9:11-15). Even in the case of pagan nations, God will look upon with favor. Yahweh will heal Egypt and also Assyria (Is 19:22-25) and lead the nations to repentance (Jer 18:7). God will allow a holy remnant of the nations to have a share in the salvation of His own people (Is 24:6). Thus God's favorable judgment will come to pass for the holy remnant of Israel with whom will also be united the holy remnants from all the nations. At the time of Jesus, the expectation of the judgment of God understood in this eschatological sense was well established, although the concrete representation of it was by no means uniform and coherent. Nevertheless, the whole of Israel looked forward to the glorious establishment of the kingdom of God, through the divine messiah, who would pass terrible judgment on the evil ones, including the devil and reward the holy ones of God.

Jesus, the Judge

Jesus proclaimed the arrival of the kingdom of God. He also announced the coming judgment. This is shown in every phase of His activity, as He spoke to the disciples, to the Pharisees and to the people. According to the teaching of Jesus, man can only attain a share in the eschatological Kingdom of God and free himself from the eschatological judgment when he listens to the word of Jesus and puts it into practice (Mt 7: 24-27). Jesus frequently referred, in the course of His preaching, to the judgment on the last day. At that time all men must give an account of their lives (Mt 25:14-30). A severe condemnation awaits the hypocritical scribes (Mk 12:40), the cities around the Sea of Galilee which have not listened to Jesus preaching (Mt 11: 20-24) and the unbelieving generation which did not receive His representatives (Mt 10:14). The judgment of Sodom and Gomorrah will be nothing in comparison with theirs. They will suffer the judgment of Gehenna (Mt 23: 33). Jesus demanded appropriate response to His Gospel and in the absence of it, invoked God's judgment upon the hard-heartedness of the unrepentant people. Along with the absolute trust in the love of the heavenly Father, the Gospel called for a charitable and compassionate attitude towards one's neighbor. In the Mosaic Law, every murderer was subject to human judgment; according to the law of the gospel, one can be guilty of far less than murder and still be in danger of hell (Mt 5: 21). Everyone will be judged according to the way he has judged his neighbor (Mt 7: 1-5). The description of the solemn sessions in which the Son of Man is the dispenser of justice (Mt 25: 31-46) shows that men will either be welcomed into the kingdom or delivered over to eternal punishment, according to the fraternal love and kindness that men have shown for one another. Christ is presented in this section, as the judge of the nations. He acts like a shepherd king who separates the sheep from the goats. Christ is portrayed as the judge seated on the great white throne. The wicked people are wiped out, and Satan is cast into the fire that was prepared for him and his angels. The earth and the heavens then flee away from His presence. All the resurrected wicked unbelievers are brought to stand before the great white throne. The Lord Jesus Christ righteously judges them according to their work. They are then cast into the lake of fire that burns with brimstone. They share in the eternal judgment of the evil one and his hosts (Rv 20:9-15). On that day when Jesus separates the sheep from the goats, the wicked will find that it is a terrible fate to face the living and just God and His Son, Jesus Christ.

The Judge of the living and the dead

The New Testament continues the tradition of the Old Testament in presenting God as the just judge: 'This is how my heavenly Father will treat each of you unless you forgive your brother from your heart' (Mt 18:35). 'Why do you judge your brother? Or why do you look down on your brother? For we will all stand before God's judgment seat (Rom 14:10). At the same time Jesus is also presented as the judge. Jesus Himself states that He will one day appear as judge: 'Many will say to me on that day, 'Lord, Lord, did we not prophesy in your name and in your name drive out demons and perform many miracles? Then I will tell them plainly, 'I never knew you. Away from me, evildoers! (Mt 7:22). 'The Father judges no one, but has entrusted all judgment to the Son' (Jn 5:22). 'This will take place on the day when God will judge men's secrets through Jesus Christ, as my gospel declares' (Rom 2:16). Jesus' consciousness of His role as judge and His self-proclamation about this role reveal to us that He was not just any prophet of doom who spoke about the end of the world. He is rather the one 'who is mightier' than John the Baptist. His winnowing fork is in His hand, and He will clear His threshing floor, gathering His wheat into the barn and burning up the chaff with unquenchable fire' (Mt 3:11-12). God has given over all judgment to the Son, and the angels and the holy community represented by the Apostles will be with Him as He judges: 'I tell you the truth, at the renewal of all things, when the Son of Man sits on His glorious throne, you who have followed me will sit on twelve thrones, judging the twelve tribes of Israel (Mt 19:28). As presented in the New Testament, the identity of the one who announces the judgment and the one who judges is the same, Jesus, the judge. It was Jesus who proclaimed the Gospel: 'The time has come. The kingdom of God is near. Repent and believe in the good news' (Mk 1:15). When the demand for conversion was not taking place, Jesus judges the unrepentant people: 'Woe to you, Korazin! Woe to you, Bethsaida! If the miracles that were performed in you had been performed in Tyre and Sidon, they would have repented long ago in sackcloth and ashes. But I tell you, it will be more bearable for Tyre and Sidon on the day of judgment than for you' (Mt 11:20-24).

Jesus, the judge, will come to judge on the day of wrath when the just judgment of God will be revealed. It will be impossible to flee the judgment. Jesus will be 'the judge of the living and the dead' (2 Tim 4:1). 'I saw heaven standing open and there before me was a white horse whose rider is called Faithful and True. With justice, He judges and makes war' (Rv 19: 11). Jesus will judge even the hidden actions of men: 'The Lord will bring to light what is hidden in darkness and will expose the motives of men's hearts' (1 Cor 4: 5). Since the day when sin entered the world through the fall of the first man, all men have sinned and been judged worthy of condemnation (Rom 5: 16-18). No one is innocent before God (Rom 3: 10-20). No one can escape condemnation by his own merits. But when Jesus, the Son of God became flesh, God condemned in Him, the sin of the flesh to free us from its yoke: 'God sent His own Son in the likeness of sinful man to be a sin offering. And so He condemned sin in sinful man' (Rom 8:3). As the result, the justice of God is revealed not as justice that punishes, but that which brings justification and salvation (Rom 3: 21). All men face judgment of God and deserve condemnation. When they believe in Jesus Christ and receive His grace of salvation, they are gratuitously justified. The faithful are no longer condemned, 'for there is no condemnation for those who are in Christ Jesus' (Rom 8:1). Our confidence to face the 'Day of Judgment' comes from God's love for us already manifested in Christ, so that we have nothing more to fear: 'We have confidence on the day of judgment, because in this world we are like Him' (1 Jn 4: 17). The threat of judgment now weighs only upon evil men who do wicked things. Jesus has come to deliver from judgment those who believe in Him and follow His ways of righteousness. At the same time, the wicked men who refuse His grace will be judged unworthy to be the heirs of His heavenly kingdom.

Personal reflection – 'Jesus will come again to judge'

Jesus says: 'My judgment is just because I seek not my own will but the will of Him who sent me' (Jn 5: 30). Even in judging, Jesus is insisting that He is doing the holy will of His Father. He asserts that there is coming an hour in history when all the dead, all of them, good and evil, will be judged. Those who have 'done good' shall experience the resurrection of life. A consistent good life marks their path of the righteousness in this world. Those who have 'done evil' shall be condemned to eternal death. How often we hear people say that a God of love would not cast people into an eternal hell! It is a conclusion that is not based on the New Testament. In His nature, God is love as He is just. As He is love, He does everything in His power to bless us. This gives us hope. However, as He is a just God, He must always act righteously. This should give us assurance. God's love was active in sending His only begotten Son into this world in order that we might be saved from the power, guilt and judgment of sin. God's justice demanded that His Son should die in order to achieve this end. During three hours of darkness on Golgotha's tree, Christ endured the judgment of God against sin. In Him, the humanity received justification and thus escaped the condemnation arising out of the just judgment of God. There is a judgment to come and there is a judge to come. The exalted Christ sits upon a great white throne awaiting the time appointed by the Father to judge the living and the dead. He alone is worthy to determine the fate of every person, for He is perfect in all His ways. Jesus is an impartial judge. He shed His own blood on the cross at Calvary for all the members of the human race. He settled sin's score once and for all and brought our redemption. Jesus is also a powerful Judge, for He rose from the dead, defeating death and its dark forces.

The day of the Lord

Christ is the judge of all the earth. The Second Coming of Christ as a judge is one of the central doctrines of the Christian faith. The people of Israel called the 'Day of Judgment' as the day of the Lord, a day of the direct intervention of God, a day of cosmic agony and a day of the birth-pangs of the emergence of the new universe. It would also usher in the golden age that will be the age of plenty, the age of peace and prosperity and the age of friendship with God and men. It would also be the Day of Judgment when the wicked would be finally obliterated. The coming of Jesus as Judge was indeed the expected day of the Lord in the Old Testament and the Day of Judgment of the New Testament. The Christian life is an expectation of and waiting for the coming of Christ as Judge. Renewed in Christ Jesus through Baptism and strengthened by the Eucharist, the disciples of the Lord Jesus Christ engage in loyal service to the Lord and in fraternal service to the people in this world, in the hope that the just judge, Jesus Christ, will recompense them on the last day. But this day of Christ would come suddenly: 'The day of the Lord comes as a thief in the night' (1 The 5:2).

It would be the day Jesus the Judge will let loose His holy wrath on the wicked of the world. The righteous ones will find their rest. The evil ones will receive their condemnation. Judgment is an essential principle of the Christian faith along with forgiveness, reconciliation and grace. Through reconciliation with God and forgiveness of sins, the grace of our Lord Jesus Christ makes the sinful human beings the adopted children of God to inherit the eternal kingdom. Those who respond to the grace of Christ in this world will encounter a favorable judge who will justly reward them. The people who fail to respond to the gracious gift of Jesus Christ condemn themselves to the loss of eternal life. Christ is the judge who will separate those who responded to His grace and salvation in this world from those who rejected it.

The honest farmer: Once during a war in Germany, a section of soldiers were stationed in a rural area beside the farmlands. One of the captains who had many men and horses to feed was desperate to get some food. He walked towards a village and knocked at the door of the small cottage. An old man opened the door and received the captain with respect. The captain asked the old man where he could cut the grain and carry it off for the army. The old man led the captain and the soldiers who accompanied him to the nearby valley. He went across the first field that had very good barley and reached the second field, which was further away. The solders dismounted from their horses, cut down the grain, tied it in sheaves and carried it away. The captain asked the old farmer why he left the first field that had better barley and moved over to the second field. The old man replied, 'The first field does not belong to me, Sir! I can give only what is mine'. Appreciating the honesty of the old man the captain paid him a big reward. Honesty and truthfulness before God brings greater rewards.

Quote: Truly at the day of judgment we shall not be examined on what we have read, but what we have done; not how well we have spoken, but now religiously we have lived - *Thomas A Kempis*

Scripture reading for Day 19:Mt 25: 31-46

Prayer for Day 19: All-knowing God, we have confidence in your justice and we trust your mercy. We await your judgment in hope. Guide us to walk the ways of justice and truth, goodness and love, so that when your Son comes on the last day to judge all the living and the dead, we may be found worthy of receiving internal reward! Amen

20

BREAD OF LIFE

*J*esus said to the people after the multiplication of the bread, 'The bread of God is He who comes down from heaven and gives life to the world. I am the bread of life. He who comes to me will never go hungry and he who believes in me will never be thirsty' (Jn 6: 33-35). Jesus calls Himself the 'bread'. The word 'bread often refers to food in general (Gn 3: 19). Bread was the staple article of diet both in OT and NT times. Common bread was made of barley flour; wheat bread was a luxury. The bread was baked daily, usually done by wives or slaves. There were also professional bakers (Jer 37: 21). The bread was baked either leavened or unleavened and the latter method was used if quick baking was necessary especially in situations like when the family received guests (Gn 18:6). To understand the significance of the title of Jesus as 'the bread of life', we explain the significance of 'bread' in the Old Testament.

Bread in the Old Testament

Food as nourishment is God's gift to man. Having created man, God blessed him and said: 'See, I give you every seed-bearing plant all over the earth and every tree that that has seed-bearing fruit on it to be your food' (Gn 1: 29). After the fall of man, as the result of original sin, God ordained that sinful man would be assured of what is necessary as food only at the price of hard labor: 'By the sweat of your face shall you get bread to eat, until you return to the ground, from which you were taken' (Gn 3: 19). After the flood, God blessed Noah and his sons and made known to him what they might eat: 'Every creature that is alive shall be yours to eat. I give them all to you as I did the green plants. Only flesh with its lifeblood still in it, you shall not eat' (Gn 9: 3). In the Bible, the abundance or scarcity of bread had the value of a sign of divine blessing or curse. Abundance of bread was a blessing from God: 'Neither in my youth, nor now in old age have I ever seen the just abandoned or their children begging bread' (Ps 37: 25). The two incidents of the multiplication of bread by Jesus and the reference to the gathering of the leftovers points to the abundance of blessings that Jesus brings to the world. The first was feeding four thousand men besides women and children, with the leftovers gathered in seven baskets (Mt 15:29-39). The second incident was the feeding of the five thousand men, besides women and children and the leftovers were gathered in twelve baskets (Mk 6:30-44). While the abundance of bread symbolized God's blessing, the scarcity of bread was the sign of punishment from God for the sins: 'Beware, I will bring against you a nation from afar, O house of Israel, an ancient nation, a people whose language you know not. They will devour your harvest and your bread' (Jer 5: 17). 'When a nation sins against me, I stretch out my hand against it and break its staff of bread. I will let famine loose upon it and cut off from it both man and beast' (Ez 14: 13). In this way, bread, the staple food of the Jewish society, was considered a gift from God, and its scarcity, a punishment from Him.

Bread was good for man, as it was a source of strength: 'You raise grass for the cattle and plants for our beasts of burden. You bring bread from the earth and wine to gladden our hearts, food to build our strength' (Ps 104: 14-15). Bread was so essential that to lack bread is to lack everything: 'Jacob then made this vow. If God gives me enough bread to eat and clothing to wear, the Lord shall be my God' (Gn 28: 20). 'Though I have made your teeth clean of food in all your cities and have made bread scarce in all your dwellings, yet you returned not to me, says the Lord' (Am 4: 6). In the prayer, that Christ taught His disciples, 'bread' takes on the same significance and seems to sum up all the things which are necessary for daily life (Lk 11:3). In everyday life, a situation is described by the taste of the bread. A suffering person, whom God seems to have abandoned, 'eats a bread of tears': 'You have fed them the bread of tears, made them drink tears in abundance (Ps 80: 6). The sinner eats the bread of impiety or of falsehood: 'The evil ones eat the bread of wickedness and drink the wine of violence' (Prv 4:17). The sluggard eats the bread of idleness: 'The ideal wife eats not the bread of idleness' (Prv 31:27). To eat bread regularly with someone is to be his friend, an intimate friend (Ps 41:10). The duty of hospitality is sacred and it is bread that is shared with the guests (Gn 18:5). Jesus chose bread as a sign of the greatest of gifts that is the body of Christ: 'While they were eating, Jesus took bread, gave thanks and broke it and gave it to the disciples, saying, 'Take it; this is my body' (Mk 14:22).

Bread in the worship of Israel

The priestly legislation accords a great importance to the loaves 'of proposition', placed in the temple on a table: 'The priests display the shewbread on the pure table and the lamps of the golden lampstand burn evening after evening (2 Chr 13: 11). Perhaps it is a reflection of the old religious practice among many peoples that offered nourishment to the divinity. But, Yahweh refuses all such nourishment as He does not need feeding for strength. The Lord said, 'I will not partake of your food' (Jgs 13: 16). For Israel, these loaves become the symbol of communion between God and His faithful and the priests have the right to consume them: 'You shall take fine flour and bake it into twelve cakes, using two tenths of an ephah of flour for each cake. These you shall place in two piles, six in each pile, on the pure gold table before the Lord. On each pile, put some pure frankincense that shall serve as an oblation to the Lord, a token offering for the bread. Regularly on each sabbath day this bread shall be set out afresh before the Lord, offered on the part of the Israelites by an everlasting agreement. It must belong to Aaron and his sons, who must eat it in a sacred place, since, as something most sacred among the various oblations to the Lord, it is his by perpetual right' (Lv 24: 5-7).

While prescribing the Passover meal, the Lord said to Moses and Aaron, 'Keep, then, this custom of unleavened bread. Since it was on this very day, that I brought your ranks out of the land of Egypt, you must celebrate this day throughout your generations as a perpetual institution. From the evening of the fourteenth day of the first month until the evening of the twenty-first day of this month, you shall eat unleavened bread' (Ex 12:18-19). Thus, the unleavened bread became associated with the Passover meal. The unleavened loaves also accompanied the sacrifices (Ex 34:25). The leaven was excluded from the cultic offerings; perhaps it revealed a symbol of corruption: 'Every cereal offering that you present to the Lord shall be unleavened, for you shall not burn any leaven or honey as an oblation to the Lord (Lv 2: 11). God provided the people of Israel with bread from heaven, the manna: 'The Israelites ate this manna for forty years, until they came to the settled land. They ate the manna until they reached the borders of Canaan' (Ex 16: 35). The people of Israel always recalled that God gave them 'bread from heaven for their hunger (Neh 9: 15). 'God rained manna upon them for food; bread from heaven, He gave them' (Ps 78: 24). 'With bread from heaven, He filled them' (Ps 105:40). Already, the bread was presented as a symbol to the 'Word of God': 'He fed you with manna, a food unknown to you and your fathers, in order to show you that not by bread alone does man live, but by every word that comes forth from the mouth of the Lord' (Dt 8:3). As the bread nourishes the body, the 'soul' or 'spirit' is nourished by the Word of God. This way, the bread was portrayed as a symbol for the Word of God. It is in this sense that in announcing the hunger for the Word of God, the prophet Amos compares bread to the Word (Am 8:11). As they describe the Messianic banquet, prophets speak of the bread which stands for the living Word of God: 'Why spend money for what is not bread; your wages for what fails to satisfy? Heed me and you shall eat well. You shall delight in rich fare. Come to me heedfully! Listen that you may have life' (Is 55:2-3). Bread also stood for the divine wisdom that is gratuitously given by God: 'Wisdom sings her own praises. He who eats of me will hunger still and he who drinks of me will thirst for more' (Sir 24: 19-22).

Jesus, the bread from heaven

Jesus declares that He is the bread of God from heaven (Jn 6:32-33) and the bread of life (Jn 6: 35, 48). Jesus made this remarkable pronouncement after performing the miracle of the multiplication of bread. It was in response to the presence of a crowd of people who had sought Jesus because they had witnessed this miracle, Jesus revealed Himself as the life-giving bread. For want of sound reasons to believe that Jesus could give them eternal life, the crowd asked for some sign, perhaps similar to the giving of the manna in the Old Testament, which they attributed to Moses. Jesus spoke about His future sacrifice on the cross at Calvary as His sign. It is there that He would give His life as a 'ransom for many'. At specific points in His ministry, Jesus would teach about freely offering Himself for the salvation of the world: 'I am the good shepherd. The good shepherd lays down his life for His sheep' (Jn 10:11). 'We are going to Jerusalem, and the Son of Man will be betrayed to the chief priests and the teachers of the law. They will condemn him to death and will turn him over to the Gentiles to be mocked and flogged and crucified. On the third day, he will be raised to life' (Mt 20:18-19). Finally, at the Last Supper, Jesus dramatized the significance of His coming suffering and death: 'While they were eating, Jesus took bread, gave thanks and broke it, and gave it to His disciples, saying, 'Take and eat; this is my body'. Then He took the cup, gave thanks and offered it to them, saying, 'Drink from it, all of you. This is my blood of the covenant, which is poured out for many for the forgiveness of sins' (Mt 26: 26-28).

The New Testament writers tell us that the Lord's Supper was conducted in the course of a Passover meal. We understand the significance of this meal in Exodus 12. Passover was to be a memorial to God's act of mercy in sparing the firstborn sons of Israel while He judged the Egyptians and their gods and killed the firstborn sons of Egypt. The memorial itself involved the killing of a sacrificial lamb, applying its blood on the doorframes, eating the roasted meat along with bitter herbs and bread without yeast. Wine was also drunk during the Passover meal. Its essence was to remind the Israelites that God saved them by substitution, by the shedding of blood of the lamb. When Jesus spoke those solemn words, 'This is my body and this is my blood', He was referring to His coming sacrifice on the cross. Through His blood, the ratification of God's new covenant with the entire humanity was effected, whereby those who would believe in Jesus Christ would receive the forgiveness of sins. On the basis of His sacrificial death, God would credit Christ's righteousness for humanity. Since He, who is the Son of God, bore all our sins, the righteous one for the unrighteous people, we became reconciled to God and were restored to God's friendship. Jesus already through a parable points out that He is offering Himself to the whole of humanity without any restriction. It is for the people to accept Him or to reject Him, thereby accept or reject the salvation Jesus offers to the human race. In the parable, referring to those invitees that made excuses to absent themselves from partaking of the banquet, the master told his servant, 'Go out to the roads and country lanes and make people come in, so that my house will be full. I tell you, not one of those men who were invited will get a taste of my banquet' (Lk 14:24). In giving a very strong teaching context to the first account of the multiplication of the loaves, Mark seems to portray the bread as the symbol of the 'word' of Jesus. 'Jesus had compassion on the large crowd, because they were like sheep without a shepherd. So, He began teaching them many things (Mk 6: 34). At the same time, the bread is a symbol of His body handed over for the redemption of humanity. We see the reference in the Eucharistic gesture presented by Mark: 'Taking the five loaves and the two fish, and looking up to heaven, Jesus gave thanks and broke the loaves. Then He gave them to His disciples to set before the people. They all ate and were satisfied' (Mk 6: 41-42). According to John, Jesus reveals that He is the true bread (Jn 6: 32), after performing the miracle of multiplication of the loaves.

The discourse on 'bread of life' in the Gospel according to John

In the first section of the discourse on 'the bread of life', Jesus presents Himself as the divine 'Word' that came down from heaven (Jn 6: 35) and everyone who believes in His word, have everlasting life' (Jn 6: 47). This word incarnate is to be offered in sacrifice for the salvation of the entire humanity. Through communion with the 'Lamb of God' who takes away the sins of the world', through the sacrifice on the cross, man receives everlasting life: 'I tell you the truth: 'unless you eat the flesh of the Son of Man and drink His blood, you have no life in you. Whoever eats my flesh and drinks my blood has eternal life, and I will raise him at the last day. For my flesh is real food and my blood is real drink' (Jn 6:54-57). Jesus talks about the necessity of eating His flesh and drinking His blood in order to have eternal life. In so doing, Jesus explains that He is the spiritual food to humanity, just as the bread is material food, a staple diet for the human race. Jesus' insistence on the necessity of eating His flesh and drinking His blood depicts the need for us to be fully united to Christ in order to receive eternal life, in the same way as food and drink are assimilated in a person to produce physical life. 'Bread' signifies both Jesus' Word and His Body that are essential for us to receive spiritual nourishment and thus to continue our life as spiritual beings. Without Jesus, we lose our spiritual life. As we consume food for the continuity of our physical life, we need to consume the word and the sacred body of Jesus for the continuity of our spiritual life. We see that the discourse on the 'bread of life' in John is strongly sacramental in character. Already John prepares us for the institution of the Eucharist by Jesus at the Last Supper by the discourse (Jn 6: 35-58). During the Last Supper, 'while they were eating, Jesus took bread, gave thanks and broke it and gave to the disciples saying, 'Take it; this is my Body' (Mk 14:22). Then, He took the cup, gave thanks and offered it to them, saying, 'This is my blood of the covenant, which is poured out for many' and they all drank from the cup' (Mk 14: 23-24). Paul points out that 'whenever you eat this bread and drink this cup, you proclaim the Lord's death until he comes' (1 Cor 11: 26). Paul further states, 'Because there is one loaf, we who are many are one body, for we all partake of the same loaf' (1 Cor 10:17). Paul's testimony makes it clear that there was no other primitive cult in the Church other than partaking of the body and blood of Christ through the symbols of bread and wine. It was celebrated on the day after the Sabbath, because it was the day of resurrection of Jesus, the day of the Lord.

Personal reflection - 'I am the bread from heaven'

This is one of the most significant claims made by the Lord Jesus Christ during His earthly ministry. He is the heaven's bread that has power to save, secure and satisfy every person who comes to Him by faith. Jesus promises eternal life, salvation, security, satisfaction and absolute safety for the soul of man. Physical bread can sustain human life for long periods of time. However, after a time, the body will still die, even though it has been well fed. Jesus, on the other hand, is bread that gives everlasting life. When Jesus is received, He gives a salvation that lasts for all eternity. Bread represents the food that is a most basic need for survival. A meal is incomplete without bread and also for a lot of people, the meal is bread. No matter what all else we may consume spiritually, nothing will ever be more essential, basic and foundational than the Living Bread, that is the word and body of Jesus Christ. John presents Jesus as the One who completely satisfies the deepest spiritual needs of mankind. He is the gift of God to satisfy man's deepest hunger, just as, in a parabolic manner, the manna was bestowed upon a fainting and dying Israel. The bread remains the privileged symbol in the Eucharist, which is a memorial of the sacrifice of Jesus on the cross. The Eucharist celebrated under the symbol of bread and vine procures the believers physical contact and unity with the Risen Christ. In the Eucharist, the bread is changed into the body of Christ: 'You nourished your people with the food of the angels and furnished them bread from heaven, ready to hand, untoiled-for, endowed with all delights and conforming to every taste' (Wis 16:20). It is the 'bread' that becomes the marvelous food that the book of Wisdom talks about, through the sacrament of Eucharist. In every celebration of Eucharist, where bread stands as the symbol of the body of Christ, the Church unites all believers in everyplace and until the end of time in praises and offerings to the perfect sacrifice that Jesus offered on the cross. The manner in which the bread becomes the body of Christ is the mystery of Faith. In the Eucharist the Christian apprehends and unites himself/herself to the enduring reality of the atoning death and resurrection of Jesus.

Jesus affirms that He is the bread of life, the living bread, which gives life to the world. He makes the eating of this bread the condition of eternal life. Jesus identified the bread that He gives for the life of the world as His own flesh. He dwells in the person who eats His body and drinks His blood and raises him up to everlasting life. Jesus makes it clear that He is the bread of life, first of all, by His preaching and teaching. His words become nourishment for the believers like the nourishing bread. Jesus also makes it clear that the sacramental consumption of the 'bread turned His flesh' is also very essential for everlasting life. The sacrament of His body and blood brings union with Christ by which the Eucharist becomes the source of the eternal life. In a way, the symbol of 'bread' points to the humanity of Christ. Jesus, the Son of God, took on human life, faced our human situation, struggled with human problems, battled with human temptation, and dealt with human relationships. He became fully man while always remaining fully God. When we partake of the body of God-man Jesus, the divine life that is in Him is communicated to us. We are enabled to live by Him, with Him, and for Him. That is the beauty of the sacramental character of the Holy Eucharist. The symbol of 'bread' signifies to us and realizes within us, the life-giving presence of Jesus in our midst.

They shared the burden together: Once a woman lost her only brother, whom she loved so dearly, in an accident. She was questioning God, while praying in the Church, why He should bring such a terrible sorrow to her. As she was walking from the Church, she met a man who was weeping. When she asked the reason why he was crying he replied that he lost his eyesight that day. A good painter he was, he was too much hurt by the thought that he could no more paint. As she guided him to return home, there walked towards them a young man who looked grief-stricken and sad. Upon enquiry, he told that his sweetheart of many years ditched him and went with another man. As they talked together another young woman was sobbing nearby. She told them that her little child passed away a couple of days ago. All of them decided to return to the Church and ask Jesus why He permitted such sufferings to them. They saw that He was crying too. He told them that He has to bear the sorrow of all of them. They began to comfort Jesus. Then, Jesus told them that He can not prevent pain but can heal it. 'How?' they asked Him. 'By sharing it' He replied and disappeared. They comforted each other and found consolation and strength in the solidarity they experienced together, by sharing their sorrow and pain, and calling upon Jesus to heal their hurting wounds.

Quote: He was made what we are that He might make us what He is Himself - *Irenaeus*

Scripture reading for Day 20: Jn 6:25-59

Prayer for Day 20: Almighty God! You sent your only Son to be the bread of life. Make us, in your loving kindness, always eager to partake of the bread from Heaven. Nourished by the word of Christ and by His Eucharistic body may we be transformed into His image to become co-heirs with Him in your everlasting Kingdom! Amen.

21

LIGHT

*L*ight conveys to the human mind a sense of joy, optimism, goodness, purity, beauty, festiveness, dignity and life, while darkness signifies ignorance, error, sadness, gloom, desolation, death and evil in general. That is why in all the celebrations of feasts and festivities, people use lights so profusely, whether the festivities are religious or civil. Divinity and goodness are associated with light and evil spirits and wickedness are associated with darkness. Christianity has special reason to associate the light with divinity because Jesus Himself declared that He is the 'light' of the world. Jesus said to the people, 'I am the light of the world. Whoever follows me will never walk in darkness, but will have the light of life' (Jn 8: 12). 'I have come into the world as a light, so that no one who believes in me should stay in darkness' (Jn 12:46). Describing Jesus as the 'light', John states that 'the true light that gives light to every man was coming into the world' (Jn 1: 9). He further makes the verdict: 'Light has come into the world, but men loved darkness instead of light because their deeds were evil. Everyone who does evil hates the light, and will not come into the light for fear that his deeds will be exposed' (Jn 3:19). In order to understand the rich and profound thoughts of John about Jesus being the 'light' of the world, let us examine how the Old Testament described God and His works in relation to light.

God and light in the Old Testament

When God created the world, His first act as creator was the separation of light and darkness. In the beginning God created the heavens and the earth. The earth was a formless wasteland and darkness covered the abyss. Then, God said, 'Let there be light' and there was light. God saw how good the light was. God then separated the light from darkness. God called the light 'day' and the darkness He called 'night' (Gn 1:5). Again God set the lights in the dome of the sky. He said, 'Let there be lights in the dome of the sky, to separate day from night. Let them serve as luminaries in the dome of the sky to shed light upon the earth. And it so happened. God made the two great lights, the greater one to govern the day and the lesser one to govern the night. He made the stars. God set them in the dome of the sky to shed light upon the earth, to govern the day and the night and to separate the light from the darkness. God saw how good it was' (Gn 1: 14-18). If in the beginning of history, God created the light, in the end of history, iat the new creation, God Himself will be the light: 'He who was seated on the throne said,' I am making everything new' (Rv 21:5). The new Jerusalem does not need the sun or the moon to shine on it, for the glory of the God gives it light and the

Lamb is its lamp (Rv 21: 23) because 'God is light and in Him there is no darkness at all' (1 Jn 1: 5). The history of mankind as it unfolds between the beginning of creation and the end of the world witnesses a form of conflict between light and darkness. This conflict between light and darkness is quite similar to the conflict between life and death. Man's destiny is very much part of this conflict between light and darkness and between life and death. Jesus, as life and light, assures victory for mankind as a whole and also for individual persons who believe in Him. For 'In Him is life, and that life is the light of men' (Jn 1:4). However, the Old Testament does not engage in any dualism as seen in some other religions like Zoroastrianism that presented the conflict between the gods of light and the gods of darkness. Rather, it presents God as the absolute master who created everything. In fact, God fashioned both light and darkness. The same can be said of life and death. 'I am the Lord, there is no other. I form the light and create the darkness. I make the well-being and create woe. I, the Lord, do all these things' (Is 45:7). Therefore both light and darkness sing the glory of their master who created them: 'Light and darkness, bless the Lord; praise and exalt Him above all forever (Dn 3: 72). However, as with life and death, light and darkness have their own significance and symbolic meaning in relation to God and also with men.

God's manifestation is always portrayed as dazzling light. In fact light is God's clothing: 'You are clothed in majesty and glory, robed in light as with a cloak' (Ps 104:2). God is surrounded by fire: 'Mount Sinai was all wrapped in smoke, for the Lord came down upon it in fire (Ex 19:18). 'When our God comes, devouring fire precedes, storming fiercely round about' (Ps 50:3). 'As God comes, His splendor spreads like the light; rays shine forth beside Him' (Hb 3:4). God lets His face shine on men as blessing: 'May God be gracious and bless us. May God's face shine upon us' (Ps 67: 2). Light is the deliverance wrought by Yahweh: 'The people who walked in darkness have seen a great light. Upon those who dwelt in the land of gloom, a light has shone' (Is 9:1). Yahweh Himself is the light: 'The Lord is my light. Whom do I fear?' (Ps 27:1). Yahweh gives life, which is to see light, prosperity, and joy: 'O God, with you is the fountain of life and in your light we see light' (Ps 36:10). He illumines the paths of men by His Law: 'Your word is a lamp for my feet, a light for my path' (Ps 119: 105). Hence Yahweh is a guiding lamp: 'He kept His lamp shining above my head and by His light I walked through darkness' (Jb 29: 3). The servant of Yahweh is also called a light to the nations: 'I, the Lord, formed you and set you as a covenant of the people, a light to the nations' (Is 42: 6). He is also an agent of salvation: 'I will make you a light to the nations that my salvation may reach to the ends of the earth' (Is 49:6).

The darkness and the light

As for darkness, it can not exclude God's presence, since He probes and sees what happens there: 'Darkness is not dark for you and night shines like the day. Darkness and light are but one' (Ps 139: 12). 'God reveals deep and hidden things and knows what is in the darkness' (Dn 2: 22). In the darkness, God sees but is not seen. The most perfect darkness is that of Sheol, where men are far from the saving hand of God: 'You plunged me into the bottom of the pit, into the darkness of the abyss. Your wrath lies heavy upon me' (Ps 88: 7-8). Thus what we see in the Old Testament is the light and the darkness are contrasted as good and evil and as a consequence they represent the two different destinies of human beings. Such a contrasting terminology of light and darkness is very much seen in some philosophical and religious systems of thought. A good example for a Jewish religious system is the Essenian sect whose Qumran sectarian writings very much focused on the contrast between the light and darkness. We present a representative sample of the Qumran writings. At the eschatological battle God will destroy iniquity, bring darkness low and magnify light: 'For you have appointed the day of battle from ancient time, to come to the aid of truth and to destroy iniquity, to bring darkness low and to magnify light to stand forever and to destroy all the sons of darkness' (1QM 13.14-16). 'Those born of truth spring from a fountain of light, but those born of falsehood spring from a source of darkness. From the source of light are those born of truth, whereas from the source of darkness are those born of falsehood' (1QS 3.19). In Qumran writings, light/righteousness and darkness/falsehood are co-ordinate pairs of concepts. The children of righteousness are said to walk in the ways of light, and be ruled by the prince or angel of light, whereas the sons of falsehood walk in the ways of darkness and are ruled by the angel of darkness: 'All the children of righteousness are ruled by the Prince of light and walk in the ways of light, but all the children of falsehood are ruled by the angel of darkness and walk in the ways of darkness' (1QS 3.20-21). Thus, what is presented to the human beings in the world is a choice: man must choose to be 'a son of light' or 'a son of darkness'.

Jesus as the light of the world

Jesus refers to Himself as the 'light of the world' or simply as 'light'. Also, similar to Qumran writings Jesus makes a distinction between 'people of this world' and the 'people of light'. 'For the people of this world are shrewder in dealing with their own kind than are the people of light' (Lk 16:8). 'Put your trust in the light while you have it, so that you may become sons of light' (Jn 12:36). The distinction is similar as 'the sons of the kingdom' and 'the sons of the evil one'. Jesus remarks: 'The good seed stands for the sons of the kingdom and the weeds are the sons of the evil one' (Mt 13:38). The contrast between light and darkness is a leading theme of the Gospel according to John and of his first Epistle. The constant association of light and life is also seen in those two writings. In the fourth Gospel, John sets light as opposed to darkness, which aims to overcome the light. 'The light shines in the darkness, but the darkness has not overcome it (Jn 1:5). John also states that 'men love darkness more than light, because their works are evil. Everyone who does evil hates the light and will not come into the light for fear that his deeds will be exposed' (Jn 3: 19-20). With solemn reiteration, John proclaims, 'God is light, and in Him is no darkness at all (I Jn 1:5). He further states that 'the darkness is passing away and the true light is already shining' (1 Jn 2:8) for the believers. Christ reveals Himself as the light. His words and deeds manifest Him as the light of the world. The miracles that involved restoring the sight to the blind had a special meaning for they revealed Jesus as the source of light (Mk 8: 22-26). John stresses this perspective in recording the episode of the man born blind (Jn 9) wherein Jesus states: 'as long as I am in the world, I am the light of the world (Jn 9:5). Jesus is the light for the revelation to the Gentiles (Lk 2:32). Fraternal love is the sign of being in the light: 'Anyone who claims to be in the light and hates his brother is still in the darkness. Whoever loves his brother lives in the light, and there is nothing in him to make him stumble. But whoever hates his brother is in the darkness and walks around in the darkness; he does not know where he is going, because darkness has blinded him' (1Jn 2: 9-11). It is God who has brought the believers out of darkness into light: 'He has called you out of darkness into His wonderful light' (1Pt 2:9).

The Christian through his participation in the light and life of God through Jesus becomes himself a medium of light to those who are in darkness: 'You were once in darkness, but now you are light in the Lord. Live as children of light for the fruit of the light consists in all goodness, righteousness and truth. Find out what pleases the Lord (Eph 5: 8-10). Those who are sons of God are called sons of light: 'You are all sons of the light and sons of the day. We do not belong to the night or to the darkness' (1 Thes 5:5). God made His light shine in our hearts: 'God who said, 'Let light shine out of darkness' made His light shine in our hearts to give us the light of knowledge of the glory of God in the face of Christ' (2 Cor 4: 6). God dwells in inaccessible light (1 Tim 6:16). 'God is light itself, and in Him is no darkness at all' (1Jn 1:5). Therefore, everything which is light comes forth from Him, from the creation of physical light on the first day to the present illumination of our hearts by the light of Christ. Because the Christian has received the divine light through Christ the Christian himself becomes the light of the world: 'You are the light of the world. A city on a hill can not be hidden. Neither do people light a lamp and put it under a bowl. Instead, they put it on its stand, and it gives light to everyone in the house. In the same way, let your light shine before men, that they may see your good deeds and praise your Father in heaven' (Mt 5:14-16).

Personal reflection – 'I am the light of the world'

Jesus declared to the crowd at the temple: 'I am the light of the world. Whoever follows me will never walk in darkness, but will have the light of life' (Jn 8:12). Jesus made the discourse about light, at the temple, after the adulterous woman was set free from her life of sin. Jesus declared to the people that He is indeed the light of the world. Then, through listening to Jesus' teaching we can learn who Jesus is and we can walk in the light of life by following Him: 'Whoever follows me will never walk in darkness but will have the light of life'. The implication is just as Jesus satisfies the hungry and thirsty soul, so Jesus gives light to the soul lost in darkness. The woman caught in adultery was not expecting to become a trap for the Pharisees to catch Jesus. She had just followed her sinful desires one time, whatever the reason may have been. From that time on, she had been drawn into a world of darkness. She became the slave of her own sinful desires and the sinful desires of others. The Pharisees were only using her to trap Jesus. But Jesus did not condemn her for her life of sin. Jesus forgave her sins and commanded her to leave her life of sin and to live as a daughter of God. No one could set her free from her life in the darkness. But Jesus, the light of the world, reached down and pulled her out from her sinful life. Jesus set her free so that she might live from then on in His light. Jesus exposes the darkness of sin and drives it out because He is the light of the world. Jesus said: 'Whoever follows me will never walk in darkness, but will have the light of life'. Jesus wants us to believe in Him and follow Him. Faith in Jesus is the beginning of a journey. It is a long journey, or pilgrimage, and requires us to pass through many hardships and trials so that our faith may be refined and purified, thereby becoming purer than gold. Through the forgiveness of sins, Jesus makes it possible for anyone to start this journey with a fervent hope to receive the eternal life in Him. But we cannot make this journey alone. We need a guide to lead us in our journey to heaven, our eternal home. Jesus is the one we must follow in order to walk in the light of life.

The revelation of Jesus as the light of the world brings into focus the darkness-light contrast. Light defines the kingdom of God and His Son Christ, as that of goodness, love, peace and justice. Darkness specifies the domain of Satan as one of evil and ungodliness, although Satan sometimes disguises himself as an angel of light to deceive man (2 Cor 11: 14). Man exists between these two; he must choose to become 'a son of darkness' or 'a son of light'. By birth, as the result of original sin, all men belong to the kingdom of darkness, especially the Gentiles who, unlike the Jews, received no special revelation from God. As a result, 'they are darkened in their understanding and separated from the life of God because of the ignorance that is in them due to the hardening of their hearts' (Eph 4:18). Though we are Gentiles, it is God 'who called us from the kingdom of darkness and has transferred us into the kingdom of His son to share the destiny of the saints in the light' (Col 1: 12). This was the decisive grace experienced at baptism and we were brought into the light. Once we were darkness, but now we are light in the Lord. This determines our standard of conduct: 'to live as sons of light' (Eph 5:8; 1 Thes 5: 5)

The life of 'the sons of light'

A man should not allow his interior light to grow dark. Jesus told them, 'You are going to have the light just a little while longer. Walk while you have the light before darkness overtakes you. The man who walks in the dark does not know where he is going. Put your trust in the light when you have it so that you may become the sons of light' (Jn 12:35). 'The eye is the lamp of the body. If your eyes are good, your whole body will be full of light. But if your eyes are bad, your whole body will be full of darkness. If then, the light within you is darkness, how great is that darkness' (Mt 6:22). Paul echoes the same advice: 'The night is nearly over; the day is almost here. So, let us put aside the deeds of darkness and put on the armor of light' (Rom 13: 12). 'You are not darkness so that the day of the Lord should surprise you like a thief. Since we belong to the day, let us be self-controlled, putting on faith and love as breastplate and the hope of salvation as helmet' (1 Thes 5: 4-8). All the teachings of Jesus and Paul bring this perspective to us: the product of light is all that is good, just and true. The deeds of darkness include sins of all kinds. The men who live as the true sons of the light make the divine light that is present in them shine brilliantly before all men. Lighted by the true and eternal light that is Jesus Christ and thereby becoming the light of the world in his turn (Mt 5:14), a believer carries out the responsibilities that is given to him by Christ in this world in truth and love. That is how he becomes the light in this world that shines in darkness.

Towards the eternal light

Committed to the light, men can hope for the marvelous transformation God promised to the just in His kingdom, 'where the righteous will shine like the sun in the kingdom of their Father' (Mt 13: 43). In the heavenly Jerusalem where the righteous will finally arrive, God Himself will be the light of the just: 'No longer shall the sun be your light by the day or the brightness of the moon shine upon you at night. The Lord shall be your light forever' (Rev 22: 23) and 'your God shall be your glory' (Is 60: 19). Then, this light will illumine the elect, who are privileged to contemplate the face of God, in His heavenly glory. Such is the hope of the sons of light; such also is the prayer, which the Church addresses to God for her deceased members. The importance of this light theme in the Christian life is shown in the numerous hymns that set the prominence of the Christ, the eternal light over against the rise and the decline of the natural light of the day. The whole of the Christmas liturgy is centered upon the coming of the divine light into the world and the light shining in the darkness. The eternal word, the light of the world, is born as a human being in the obscurity of this world. His human birth is accompanied by the splendor of the heavenly bodies manifested to the shepherds (Lk 2: 9). Simeon proclaimed that the infant would be 'a light of revelation to the Gentiles and a glory to the people of Israel' (Lk 2: 32).

The Easter season portrays the slow conquest of the darkness of sin by 'the light of the world'. During Lent, Jesus is seen to struggle with the powers of darkness that seem to triumph on Good Friday. But, Christ rises on the third day, from the darkness of the tomb with greater radiance and splendor than ever. In many churches the glorious victory of light over darkness is brought out dramatically in the ceremonies of the Easter Vigil. The striking of the new fire in utter darkness, the lighting of the paschal candle and its gradual dispelling of the darkness of the church building as its flame is extended to the smaller candles of the participants, accompanied by acclamations of 'light of Christ'. The magnificent strains of the hymn resound in praise of the paschal candle, the symbol of Jesus Christ, who, as the new pillar of fire, leads redeemed new Israel out of the shadow of darkness and the slavery of death into everlasting light and life. It is obvious that the Christian use of light, especially the paschal candle in the liturgy for the dead has a very deeper significance. The body of the deceased Christian has been the temple of the Holy Trinity, a tabernacle of the Light that is God. It is waiting for that day of the glorious resurrection when in its glorified state it will share in 'the splendor of the saints'. The use of light recalls the sacredness of the body, the immortality of the soul, and the Beatific Vision to which both body and soul are destined and for which the Church prays: 'Let perpetual light shine upon him/her'.

We are preaching: Once a Franciscan Brother, Juniper by name, asked Francis of Assisi to teach him to preach eloquently and Francis agreed to teach him the next day. As they met next day morning, Francis took him to the market place smiling to the laborers, merchants and the children and exchanged kind and affectionate words of encouragement and fellowship. They helped an old man to walk back to his home, an old lady to carry her grand child and a hungry man to find some food. An exasperated Juniper asked Francis when he was going to teach him to preach. Francis replied: 'we are now preaching the best homily'. Deeds speak louder than mere words. In the silence of the tomb, Jesus proclaims loudly His message of love: God so loved the world that He gave His only Son.

Quote: It is not the constant thought of their sins, but the vision of the holiness of God that makes the saints aware of their sinfulness - *Metropolitan Anthony Bloom*

Scripture reading for the Day 21: Jn 9: 13-41

Prayer for Day 21: O, Eternal light! You, in your goodness and loving kindness, sent your only Son, Our Lord Jesus Christ, to be the light of the world. In Him, we are called out of darkness into your wonderful light, so that we may shine before the world as the lamps of your glory. Help us to open our hearts to the warmth of your light so that we may always be instruments of your compassion and love! Amen.

22

GATE

*T*he designation 'the gate' is used only by John. Jesus declares, 'I tell you the truth. I am the gate for the sheep' (Jn 10: 7). He repeats it with an explanation, 'I am the gate. Whoever enters through me will be saved. He will come in and go out and find pasture. I have come that they may have life and have it to the full' (Jn 10:9-10). A gate gives us access to something. We go through a gate to get to what is on the other side. Jesus is saying that it is through Him that we can go to heaven. A gate provides a way through a barrier. In Jesus, the barrier between the divinity and the humanity has been broken down and He became the gate through which humanity may now enter to reach heaven.

The 'gate' in Old Testament

During the Bronze Age, the city walls had only one or two gates. In the Iron Age, more gates were constructed around the fortified cities. Thus, during the time of the monarchy, Jerusalem had at least seven gates. The gates were often as deep as the thickness of the city walls. The gate, as the weakest point of the defenses, was the most strongly fortified position in the city. In the times of the Old Testament, the width of the principal gate was 13-14 feet. Other gates were usually quite narrow and were used for the passage of the pedestrians or the animals like donkey or camel. The narrow gate in contrast to the wide gate was the subsidiary gate. The main gate that was usually wide could accommodate the vehicular traffic and was the most frequented passage. When speaking about the narrow gate and the wide gate, we remember the words of Jesus: 'Enter through the narrow gate. For wide is the gate and broad is the road that leads to destruction, and many enter through it. But small is the gate and narrow the road that leads to life and only a few find it' (Mt 7: 13-14). The gates, when open, allowed people to come and go, thereby permitting free circulation. When shut, they prevented people from passing. Thus the idea of the 'gate' implies the sorting out of the people as between those who were permitted to come inside the city and those denied admission. The fortified gates, while allowing the inhabitants and the friends to come in and go out freely, protected the inhabitants from the attacks of the enemy. In this way, the gates ensured the security of the inhabitants and enabled the town to set itself up as a community. To possess the gates was to conquer the city. When the enemy entered through the gate, the fall and the defeat of the city was imminent. A usual place for the gathering of the people, it was also the place where departures were made in the time of war (1 Kgs 22:10). It was necessary for reasons of defense to keep the area inside the gate clear of buildings in order that at times of conflict, armed forces that defended the city could be amassed.

The common gathering of the people of the city was in those areas behind the gates: the meetings took place, business matters were settled and political maneuvers were worked out there. Also, judgments were pronounced regarding the disputes and crimes as the open space behind the gate served as the forum of justice, the place where the elders sat: 'The father and mother of the unruly son shall have him apprehended and brought out to the elders at the gate' (Dt 21:19). 'Let there be honesty and peace in the judgments at your gates' (Zec 8: 16). In the Iron Age gate at Tell en Nasbeh, long stone benches were found in the gate area that were probably intended for the elders and the judges. The gates were in some way identified with the city itself. To take possession of the gates meant to make oneself master of the city. After testing Abraham's fidelity through the demand of sacrifice of Isaac, his only son, God blessed Abraham saying, 'Your descendants shall take possession of the gates of their enemies' (Gn 22: 17). To receive the keys of the city was a sign of being invested with power: 'I will place the key of the house of David on his shoulder. When he opens, no one shall shut. When he shuts no one shall open' (Is 22: 22).

God and the gate of Jerusalem

God loved the holy city of Jerusalem: 'The Lord loves the city founded on the holy mountains. He loves the gates of Zion more than any dwelling in Jacob. Glorious things are said of you, O, city of God' (Ps 87: 1-3). Yahweh Himself had strengthened its gates: 'O, Jerusalem, glorify the Lord who has strengthened the bars of your gates and blessed the children within you' (Ps 147: 12). Jerusalem was the city that had the ancient gates through which the Lord, the king of glory, might enter: 'Lift up your heads, O gates; rise up, you ancient portals that the king of glory may enter. Who is the king of glory? The Lord, a mighty warrior, the Lord, mighty in battle' (Ps 24:7-8). The pilgrim passing through the gates of Jerusalem experienced peace and sang in joy: 'I rejoiced when they said to me, 'Let us go to the house of the Lord'. And now, our feet are standing within your gates, O, Jerusalem. Jerusalem, built as a city, walled round about. Here the tribes of the Lord come to give thanks to the name of the Lord. Here are the thrones of justice, the thrones of the house of David' (Ps 122: 1-5). Even if Jerusalem, the holy city of Israel, reputed to be impregnable, could offer its inhabitants security by shutting its gates, justice was not always done at the gates: 'On that day, the evil doers whose mere word condemns a man, who ensnare his defender at the gate and leave the just man with an empty claim will be cut off'' (Is 29: 21). 'The rulers of the house of Israel abhor what is just and pervert all that is right. They build up Zion with bloodshed and Jerusalem with wickedness. Her leaders render judgment for a bribe, her priests give decisions for a salary, her prophets divine for money' (Mic 5: 9-11).

The Prophets spoke of the city of God, the New Jerusalem that would be open to other nations and would be established in peace and justice: 'On that day, there will be the song in the land of Judah,' A strong city have we; our God sets up walls and ramparts to protect us. Open the gates to let in a nation that is just, one that keeps faith. A nation of firm purpose you keep in peace, for it trusts in you' (Is 26: 1-3). The glory of the Lord would shine on Jerusalem: 'Your gates shall stand open constantly; day and night they shall not be closed, but admit to you the wealth of the nations and their kings in the vanguard' (Is 60: 11). Yahweh, as the sign of this final blessing opens the gates of heaven in order to send down rain and manna and every kind of blessing on the earth. 'God commanded the skies above and the doors of heaven He opened. He rained manna upon them for food; bread from heaven He gave them' (Ps 78: 23-24). The author of the book of Revelation would clarify to us that the New Jerusalem would come down from heaven. There 'God will wipe every tear from the eyes of His people, and there will be no more death or mourning or crying or pain' (Rv 21: 1-4).

The first man Adam, who lived in friendship with God, saw the closing of the gate to the Paradise as the result of his fall. Since then, it is the act of worship that establishes relationship between the two worlds, divine and earthly. God slowly reopened the gate of heaven to humanity. That is how, Jacob recognized in Bethel 'the gate of heaven': 'Then, Jacob had a dream; a stairway rested on the ground, with its top reaching to the heavens and God's messengers were going up and down. And there was the Lord standing beside him. When Jacob awoke from his sleep, he exclaimed, 'Truly the Lord is in this spot, although I did not know it'. In solemn wonder he cried out, 'That is the gateway to heaven' (Gn 28: 12-17). In due course, the Jerusalem temple became the holy place, 'the gate way' to heaven. The Israelites presenting themselves at the gates of the temple knew that they approached Yahweh, the living God. They were also aware that only God expected the just and the virtuous and not the wicked to enter through the 'gates' of the Temple: 'Open the gates of victory. I will enter and thank the Lord. This is the Lord's own gate, where the just enter' (Ps 118: 19-20). It has been told to the people of Israel that faithfulness to the covenant and justice in their ways were required of the devotees of Yahweh who went through the gates of the Temple to worship God: 'With what shall I come before the Lord and bow before God most high? Shall I come before Him with holocausts, with calves a year old? You have been told, O, man, what is good and what the Lord requires of you: only to do the right and to love goodness and to walk humbly with your God' (Mi 6: 6-8).

The promise of the new 'gate'

The Temple of Jerusalem lost its significance as the 'dwelling place' of God, when the rulers and the scribes of the Temple were more concerned about 'shutting its gates' to the nations than 'removing evil' in their midst. Standing at the 'gate' of the Temple, Jeremiah cries out in the name of Yahweh: 'The people of Judah have done what is evil in my eyes. In the cities of Judah and in the streets of Jerusalem, I will silence the cry of joy and the cry of gladness, for the land will be turned to rubble' (Jer 8: 1-34). When the Temple was destroyed in 587 BC, as foretold by Jeremiah, the people of Israel realized that without the Temple, they could not approach God. They began to pray asking God to come down from heaven: 'Be not so very angry Lord! Look upon us, who are all your people. Zion is desert and Jerusalem a waste. Our holy and glorious temple in which our fathers praised you has been burned with fire. All that was dear to us is laid waste (Is 64: 9-11). 'Oh, that you would rend the heavens and come down with the mountains quaking before you' (Is 63:19). God responded by assuring them that He would come down from heaven and gather them as the shepherd gathers his flock: 'I will gather you, O Jacob, I will assemble all the remnant of Israel. I will group them like a flock in the fold' (Mi 2: 12). In Jesus this promise of God to His people has been fulfilled. Jesus is not only the new Temple but also the 'gate' and through Him the entire humanity can enter and approach God.

Jesus the 'gate'

Jesus begins His famous discourse in John 10, by saying that 'the man who does not enter the sheep pen by the gate but climbs in by some other way is a thief and a robber' (Jn 10:1). In the villages, there were communal sheep-folds where all the village flocks were sheltered, when they returned home at night. These folds were protected by a strong door or gate of which only the guardian had the key. Only thieves and robbers would not have access of the key and hence would climb in some other way. Jesus appears to have in mind, the numerous claimants to be the 'messiah' prior to Him who promised liberation of Israel from the Romans through war and violence. The zealots, for example, believed in war, murder and assassination. Through their recourse to violence and engagement in war, hundreds of people perished. Instead of violence, Jesus spoke the message of love. According to Him, only love and fraternal service would save humanity. It is only through loving and serving others and caring for them and sharing with them, as Jesus taught us by His own example, that humanity would have life, and have 'life' abundantly.

Speaking about thieves and robbers, Jesus also refers to the religious leaders of His time, who were obsessed with external rules and regulations like observing sabbath or washing hands before the meals, without the basic attitude of spiritual life, which is compassion and love, honesty and justice. Thus, when Jesus explains to His disciples that He is the door of the sheep, He does so by way of contrasting Himself with the thieves and robbers. In the life of a shepherd and his sheep there were always such sheep-stealers to deal with. These people had no love for their sheep; thus, they did not really care for them. They only came to harm the sheep. For this reason they did not enter the sheepfold through the gate. They climbed in some other way. Jesus takes this earthly reality and applies to the religious reality of His own time. Jesus refers to the fact that the religious leaders of His day were spiritual thieves and robbers of God's true people. They were not really interested in their spiritual welfare. They did not really care for them. The proof of that is that they themselves did not enter the sheepfold through the 'gate' and they did not teach the sheep to go through the 'gate', that is Jesus Himself. The religious leaders of Jesus' time did not believe in Jesus the 'gate', and they did not seek to enter the kingdom of God through Him. Also, they did not teach the people to enter the kingdom through Jesus Christ. Jesus insists that as 'the gate', He alone has authority to give admittance to reach God. Moreover, He has the power to bestow life (Jn 10:1). 'To be saved' is to have the gift of eternal life here and now, and 'to find pasture' is to obtain constant and unfailing spiritual food through union with Christ. A good shepherd conducts his flocks to the fields where good pasturage is to be found, watches over them while there and brings them back again and secures them in the fold.

The gate of new Jerusalem

The Apocalypse presents to us the fulfillment of the prophecies of the prophets who foretold the establishment of New Jerusalem. At the end of time, city of God and heaven become one and the same. The heavenly Jerusalem has twelve gates. The author of Revelation further states: 'It had a great high wall with twelve gates and with twelve angels at the gates. On the gates were written the names of the twelve tribes of Israel. There were three gates on the east, three on the north, three on the south and three on the west' (Rv 21: 12-13). The gates are always open and yet evil no longer enters there. Peace and justice abound in the city of God and there is the perfect exchange between God and Humanity. 'Nothing impure will ever enter it, nor will anyone who does what is shameful or deceitful, but only those whose names are written in the Lamb's book of life' (Rv 21:27). Jesus will write down, in His book of life, the names of those who go through Him as the 'gate' to enter the kingdom of God.

Personal reflection- 'Jesus, the gate to the eternal life'

The people of Israel, after the destruction of the Temple of Jerusalem, prayed that God would tear open the heavens and come to the world to establish the 'gate' to go to heaven. God answered their prayers by sending Jesus to the world. Jesus became the 'gate' through whom all can approach God, our heavenly Father. We have access to the Father only through Jesus Christ: 'Through Jesus, we have access to the Father by one Spirit' (Eph 2:18). 'We have confidence to enter the Most Holy Place by the blood of Jesus by a new and living way opened for us through the curtain, that is his body' (Heb 10: 19). Jesus is the true 'gate' of heaven for us. Jesus said: 'I tell you the truth. You shall see heaven open and the angels of God ascending and descending on the Son of Man' (Jn 1: 51). He is the gate leading to pastures where divine blessings are offered freely. Jesus points out that 'the one who enters through Him will come in and go out and find pasture' (Jn 10: 9). To be able to come and go unharmed was the Jewish way of describing a life that is absolutely secure and safe. Jesus as gate opens not to a place of isolation or exclusion. Rather, He leads us to a place of good pasture, a place of belonging and welcome and above all to a place of safety from the attacks of the evil one.

Jesus holds the keys of David: 'He, the holy and true one, holds the key of David. What he opens no one can shut and what he shuts no one can open' (Rv 3: 7). That is why Jesus has the right to make demands about the entry into the kingdom. He makes a demand to enter through the narrow gate. Those who do not take care to walk in the ways of Jesus will find the door shut (Mt 25: 10). Jesus states, 'Once the owner of the house gets up and closes the door, you will stand outside knocking and pleading, Sir, open the door for us'. But he will answer, 'I do not know you or where you come from'. Then, you will say, 'We ate and drank with you and you taught in our streets'. But he will reply, 'I don't know you or where you come from. Away from me, all you evildoers!' (Lk 13: 25-27). Jesus presented the entry into life and salvation as a great banquet (Lk 14: 15-24) or a wedding feast (Mt 25: 1-13). Jesus holds the keys of death and of hell. 'I am the Living One; I was dead and behold I am alive forever and ever! And I hold the keys of death and Hades' (Rv 1: 18). Jesus has conquered death and hell and now He has the power to save us from everlasting death and hell. What is essential is that we should enter through Him, the 'gate' to heaven, which implies that we walk in His ways in this earthly life.

The unique way of Jesus

If not for the 'gate' that is Jesus Himself, we cannot get in to the house of our Heavenly Father. There is no way to get over or around the wall to go to heaven: 'There is salvation in no one else; for there is no other name in all of heaven for people to call on to save them' (Acts 4:12). A gate controls who can come through and who may not. Entering through the gate that is Jesus represents a new way of living for a Christian who chose to follow Jesus. In this world, there are so many people who claim to possess the capacity to lead us to God. In Jesus' own time, the Pharisees were obsessed with practicing the external rules and regulations to enter the kingdom of God. The Sadducees who controlled the temple were insisting on the rituals, especially the sacrifices to receive God's favor. The Essenes, supposed to be the people of Qumran sect, lived a life of separation and seclusion as a distinct community and were preoccupied with the observation of their own rules and traditions. The zealots proposed the way of violence and war to please God. According to Jesus, all these ways are like climbing the wall, instead of entering through the 'gate', that is Jesus Himself. Jesus proposed His unique way- loving God totally and fully with one's heart and mind and loving and serving others in His name. Then let us keep Jesus, the crucified and risen savior before our eyes as we reflect on the true meaning of love. It is in Jesus that the unconditional love of God to the entire humanity is revealed and communicated. Let us joyfully respond to the love of our Heavenly Father, by walking in the ways of Jesus, the 'gate' to heaven.

The blind men and the elephant: Once there were six blind men, who were sitting together and talking and a tamed elephant passed by them. The first blind man reached out and touched the elephant's ear and said that the elephant was like a rug. The second blind man felt the elephant trunk and told that the elephant was like a giant snake. The third blind man touched the elephant's leg and insisted that it was like a tree. The fourth blind man rubbed around the elephant's side and stated that the elephant was like a wall. The fifth blind man put his hands on the elephant's tusk and said that elephant was like a spear. And the sixth blind man touched the elephant's tail and declared that the elephant was like a long thin rope. Each one insisted that he was right. After all, they all touched the elephant. The owner of the elephant heard the heated discussion and told them that each of them was right to some extent and each of them was wrong to a large extent. The elephant was beyond their limited description. In this world, many systems and traditions may promise the way to go to heaven and experience salvation. But Jesus offers us the perfect way because He is the 'gate' to heaven.

Quote: Christ believed it possible to bind men to their kind, but on one condition- that they were first bound fast to Himself - *John Seeley*

Scripture reading for Day 22: Jn 10: 1-10

Prayer for Day 22: Heavenly Father! You loved us so much you sent your only begotten Son into the world to bring us eternal life. Enkindle in hearts the desire to love you, deliver us whatever would estrange us from you. In you alone, we find peace partly here on earth and perfectly with you in heaven. May we always follow the ways of Jesus so that we may attain everlasting life through Him, who is the 'gate' to Heaven! Amen.

23

GOOD SHEPHERD

*T*he title of Jesus as the 'Good Shepherd' is presented in the Gospel according to John. Jesus declares: 'I am the good shepherd. The good shepherd lays down His life for the sheep' (Jn 10: 11). He clarifies further, ''I am the good shepherd. I know my sheep and my sheep know me' (Jn 10: 14). Jesus is designated as 'good shepherd' in the Synoptic tradition also, though implicitly. Thus, it is implied in the statement of Mark: 'When Jesus landed from the boat and saw the large crowd, He had compassion on them, because they were like sheep without a shepherd' (Mk 6: 34). Matthew repeats the same fact: 'Jesus went through all the towns and villages, teaching in their synagogues, preaching the good news of the kingdom and healing every disease and sickness. When he saw the crowds, He had compassion on them, because they were harassed and helpless, like sheep without a shepherd' (Mt 9:36). Jesus told His disciples, 'Do not be afraid, little flock, for your Father has been pleased to give you the kingdom' (Lk 12:32). Thus, we see that all the evangelists present Jesus as the good shepherd who cares for His sheep. We also find two more references in the Gospel according to Matthew. 'When they had sung a hymn, they went out to the Mount of Olives. Then, Jesus told them, 'This very night you will all fall away on account of me, for it is written (as found in Zechariah 13:7): I will strike the shepherd, and the sheep of the flock will be scattered' (Mt 26: 30-31). Jesus sent out the twelve with the instruction: 'Go rather to the lost sheep of the house of Israel' (Mt 10:6). Having told us that He is the gate, Jesus also brings us the comforting truth that He loves us and takes care of us like a good shepherd. The image of the good shepherd describes Jesus as the pastor who leads and rules his people in mercy and love and saves them at the cost of his life. Jesus is the good shepherd who not only loves His sheep but is also fully equipped to protect them and supply all their needs. Not only does He have the strength to protect them but also has the wisdom to understand what is good for His sheep. He knows that the Father entrusted them to Him to feed, watch over, guide and protect from the wolves that fill this world. In order to understand and appreciate the meaning of this beautiful title of Jesus, let us first examine how the shepherd is presented in the Old Testament.

Shepherd in the Old Testament

In the ancient Near East (Babylonia and Assyria), the title 'shepherd' was applied both to kings and gods. For example, the god Shamash was invoked as shepherd. Also king Hammurabi was also called the 'shepherd' of the people. There are two designations in the book of Genesis and two invocations in the psalms that directly referred to God as the shepherd. The first designation is seen in the benediction of Jacob, who blessed the two sons of Joseph with these words: 'May the God who has been my shepherd form my birth to this day, who delivered me from all harm, bless these boys' (Gn 48: 15). The second instance is when Jacob called his sons before his death and made his farewell instruction. 'By the power of the Mighty One of Jacob, because of the Shepherd, the Rock of Israel, the God of your father who helps you, may you have the blessings of the heavens above' (Gn 49: 24). The first invocation, in the psalms, is the famous hymn on 'the Lord, who is the Shepherd' (Ps 23:1). Another invocation is found in the prayer of the psalm 80: 'Shepherd of Israel, listen! Guide of the flock of Joseph! O, come to save us and restore us' (Ps 80:2). However, even if the usage of the explicit title is not found in numerous instances, throughout the Old Testament, the relationship between God and His people is described in terms that reveal the relationship between a good shepherd and his sheep. Israel is God's own flock: 'This is our God, whose people we are. God's well-tended flock' (Ps 95: 7). Yahweh leads and guides Israel: 'God led forth His people like sheep. He guided them through the desert like a flock' (Ps 78:52). Prophet Isaiah compares God's loving care of Israel to the care of the good shepherd: 'Like a shepherd he feeds his flock; in his arms he gathered the lambs, carrying them in his bosom and leading the ewes with care' (Is 40:11). Prophet Jeremiah weeps over the captivity of Israel, the Lord's own flock: 'My eyes will run with tears, for the Lord's flock will be led away to exile' (Jer 13: 17). Prophet Hosea regrets that Israel is quite a stubborn people: 'Israel is as stubborn as a heifer; will the Lord give them broad pastures as though they were lambs? (Hos 4:16). After the return from exile, Prophet Zechariah assures Israel that God cares for them: 'I will whistle for them to come together and when I redeem them they will be as numerous as before' (Zec 10: 8). The psalmist reminds Israel that they are God's own people: 'Know that the Lord is God, our maker, to whom we belong, whose people we are, God's well-tended flock' (Ps 100: 3). 'We, your people, the sheep of your pasture, will give thanks to you forever; through all ages we will declare your praise' (Ps 79:13). While, God's loving care was described to the shepherding of the flock, the title 'shepherd' is given to the rulers of the people including the king, the royal officers, the elders and all who had authority like the judges and the heroes of the judges.

The shepherds of Israel

God appointed shepherds to take care of His flock, the people of Israel. He guided them by the hand of Moses: 'You led your people like a flock under the care of Moses and Aaron' (Ps 77: 21). Later, God appointed Joshua as the shepherd of Israel: 'Moses said to the Lord, 'May the Lord send a man over the community that the Lord's community may not be like sheep without a shepherd' (Nm 27:15-20). God anointed David to graze His people as a shepherd, saying 'You shall shepherd my people Israel and shall be commander of Israel' (2 Sm 5: 2). The judges were called the shepherds of the people: 'I charged judges to tend to my people Israel' (2 Sm 7: 7). God appointed Cyrus, the Persian emperor as shepherd to His people so that he might help Israel rebuild Jerusalem and it's Temple: 'God says, 'I say of Cyrus: My shepherd, who fulfils my every wish' (Is 44: 28). Many of the rulers of Israel failed in their mission of shepherding the people of God. They did not seek Yahweh and were unfaithful to Him. Prophet Jeremiah points out their failure: 'The shepherds were stupid as cattle, the Lord they sought not; Therefore they had no success, and all their flocks were scattered' (Jer 10: 21). The prophet further states: 'Woe to the shepherds who mislead and scatter the flock of my pasture. I will appoint new shepherds for them' (Jer 23: 1-4).

The prophet Ezekiel condemns their selfishness, saying, 'Thus says the Lord God: Woe to the shepherds of Israel who have been pasturing themselves! You have fed off their milk, worn their wool and slaughtered the fatlings but the sheep you have not pastured. My sheep were scattered over the whole earth with no one to look after them or to search for them. I will claim my sheep from them and put a stop to their shepherding my sheep' (Ez 34: 1-11). According to the prophet, there will be only a single shepherd, the new David: 'I will appoint one shepherd over them to pasture them, my servant David. He shall pasture them and be their shepherd' (Ez 34: 23). He further states: 'My servant David shall prince over them and there shall be one shepherd for them all. They will live with my statutes and carefully observe my decrees' (Ez 37:24). Prophet Micah offers the hope of a single leader who will gather the people of Israel: 'I will gather you, Jacob, like a flock in the fold. With a leader to break the path, they shall burst open the gate and go out through it' (Mi 2:12). Even after the exile, the shepherds of the community of Israel did not live up to the expectation of God that kindled His anger against them: 'My wrath is kindled against the shepherds and I will punish the leaders' (Zec 10: 3). Prophet Zechariah speaks of a 'pierced' shepherd whose death was salutary. He states: 'They shall mourn for him as one mourns for an only son, and they shall grieve over him as one grieves over a firstborn' (Zec 12:10). This shepherd is identified with the servant Yahweh, of whom prophet Isaiah spoke thus, 'We were all gone astray like a sheep each following his own way. The Lord laid upon him the guilt of us all' (Is 53:6). 'Through suffering my servant will justify many and their guilt he shall bear' (Is 53:11). In Jesus Christ, the good shepherd, all the above prophecies were fulfilled.

Jesus is the good Shepherd

In the time of Jesus, the shepherds had low status in Palestine. They were ranked with the thieves and murderers as impure people. It is because it was hardly possible for them to faithfully observe all the regulations regarding ritual purity, due to their nomadic life-style. Jesus Himself as well as His disciples encountered much criticism from Pharisees for failing to observe the rules regarding sabbath and washing of hands (Mk 7: 1-15). Nevertheless, the people of Israel remembered well and awaited eagerly the fulfillment of the prophecy regarding the single shepherd who was to come. They expected the messiah to be that good shepherd. In His person, Jesus fulfills the expectant hope of the people of Israel who awaited their good shepherd. The birth of Jesus in Bethlehem fulfilled the prophecy of Micah: 'But you, Bethlehem-Ephratha, too small to be among the clans of Judah, from you shall come forth for me one who is to be the ruler in Israel. He shall stand firm and shepherd his flock by the strength of the Lord' (Mi 5: 1-3). The lowly shepherds, considered to be the lower classes, were the first among all the sections of the Jewish society to receive the good news of the birth of the savior of the world (Lk 2: 8-20). They became the first among the 'little ones' who, like the publicans and prostitutes, joyfully received the good news (Mt 11: 25-26). Faithful to the biblical tradition, Jesus depicts the forgiving and compassionate love of God under the figure of the shepherd who goes to look for the lost sheep (Lk 15: 4-7).

Moses prayed to God to give the community of Israel a leader who will guide the community in the ways of God (Nm 27: 17). Jesus is the good shepherd that God sent in response to the prayers of Moses. The flock will be persecuted by the wolves from without and from within by those disguised as sheep: 'Watch out for false prophets. They come to you in sheep's clothing, but inwardly they are ferocious wolves. By their fruits, you will recognize them' (Mt 7: 15). Jesus referred to them as thieves who 'come to steal and kill and destroy' (Jn 10: 10). John presents the beautiful image of Jesus as the good shepherd. Jesus feeds His sheep and leads them to the green pasture. The 'one shepherd' foretold by the prophets, Jesus states, 'It is I' (Jn 10: 11). He gives His life in full liberty for the welfare of the sheep (Jn 10: 11). Jesus is the prince of the shepherds: 'When the Chief Shepherd appears, you will receive the crown of glory that will never fade away (1 Pt 5: 4). He healed His sheep by His own death: 'He Himself bore our sins in His body on the tree, so that we might die to sins and live for righteousness. You were like sheep going astray, but now you have returned to the Shepherd and Overseer of your souls'. (1 Pt 2: 25). Finally at the end of time, the Lord of the sheep shall separate the good from the wicked in the flock, by knowing them by their fruits (Mt 25: 31). Then, He will lead His flock to the source of eternal life: 'The Lamb at the center of the throne will be their shepherd. He will lead them to springs of living water. And God will wipe away every tear from their eyes' (Rv 7: 17). Peter, after the resurrection of Jesus, received from Him the mission of feeding the flock' (Jn 21: 15-17). Other shepherds in the Church are elders and the bishops' (Eph 4: 11). Following the example of the Lord, who laid down His life for His flock, they must feed the people of God lovingly and compassionately, without seeking their self-interest.

Personal reflection- 'The Lord is my Shepherd'

The oldest representation of Christ found in the Catacombs represents Jesus as a shepherd, carrying a sheep on His shoulders. Jesus chose this symbol to describe Himself as the good shepherd and the kind of authority He exercises over His flock. The gentlest of the masters, He cares about us, watches over us and preserves us. A good shepherd knows and judges the needs of His sheep diligently. He seeks the lost sheep and brings them home again. A good shepherd has the necessary skills for pasturing his sheep and for bringing them into a green and fruitful ground. He lets not his sheep to feed upon rotten soil, but in wholesome pastures. He knows the straying nature of his sheep. That is why he watches over them with utmost care. At any time they go astray, he brings them back again. There are the contented and the happy ones who are in no danger of getting lost or into mischief. There are others that are restless and discontented, jumping into everybody's field, climbing into bushes and even into leaning trees whence they often fall and break their limbs. These sheep bring the good shepherd incessant trouble as do the lost sheep. But the good shepherd cares for all the sheep, even the wandering and troublesome ones. The Lord Jesus, our good shepherd, deals mercifully towards us, the poor wandering sinners. He forgives us our sins and restores us to His flock even if we have failed. A good shepherd is provided to defend his flock against the thieves and robbers as well as against the wild animals. The shepherd goes before, not merely to point out the way, but to see if it is practicable and safe. He is armed in order to defend his charge and in this he is very courageous. And when the thief and the robber come to steal the sheep, the faithful shepherd has often to put his life in his hand to defend his flock. Jesus defends us against the evil one and against the evildoers. If any of his sheep be weak and feeble or his lambs young, the good shepherd will bear them in his arms for their safety and recovery. The Lord is not wanting to us herein. He carries us with utmost care in our journey of life. A good shepherd rejoices when the strayed sheep is brought home. The Lord does rejoice at the conversion of the sinner (Lk 15:7)

Jesus knows His own

The good shepherd, when he puts forth his own sheep, goes before them and they follow him (Jn 10.4). They are so tame and so trained that they follow their keeper with the utmost docility. He leads them forth from the fold or from their houses in the villages, just where he pleases. As there are many flocks, each shepherd takes a different path and it is his business to find pasture for them. The shepherd calls sharply from time to time to remind them of his presence. They know his voice, and follow on. But, if a stranger calls, they stop short, lift up their heads in alarm, and if it is repeated, they turn and flee because they know not the voice of a stranger. Each of the sheep has a name, to which it answers joyfully. Jesus knows each one us, the sheep of His flock. The knowledge of Jesus is the knowledge of divinity that is all-wise, almighty and full of mercy. He knows our strengths and weaknesses and what to expect from us. He knows us far better than we know ourselves. However, His knowledge is a loving knowledge that is laden with grace. What is important is that we must trust Him and make use of the graces that He offers so abundantly and so lovingly. Let us remember the words of the apostle Paul: 'I can do all things in Him who strengthened me' (Phil 4:13).

Mine know me

As the shepherd's call sound at the door of the common fold, his own sheep recognize his voice and flock to him. They follow him, feeling safe under his protection. They understand the slightest sign of his hand, the slightest modulation of his voice and follow him. We have become the flock of Jesus; first of all, it pleased Him to call us. Jesus declares that His Father has given Him His sheep. In baptism, we were made His own. Since then whenever we surrender ourselves entirely to Him, we can experience how good He is. Even after being with Jesus for several years, the disciples knew Him not quite well and did not comprehend what He taught. They needed the light of the Holy Spirit to lead them to the truth. In the same way, let us always be alert to the prompting of the Holy Spirit, as Jesus speaks to us in His gentle voice in so many ways in order to guide us.

Intruders, hirelings and true shepherd

The true shepherd who seeks the well-being of his sheep is simple and straightforward in all his dealings. He need not use violence or ruse to gain access to the flock. He simply enters by the door of the sheepfold. The thief climbs up by another way in order to steal the sheep. He uses deceit and violence to gain access to the sheep so that he may slay them for gain. As far as hirelings are concerned, he works for his wages and the welfare of the sheep is not his concern. When dangers come, the sole thought of the hireling is his own safety and he betakes himself to flight. The Gospel according to John enumerates eight characteristics of the true shepherd. He enters by the door. The porter opens the door to him. The sheep recognizes his voice and come to him. He calls his own sheep by name. He leads them out. He goes before them. The sheep follow him. He gives his life for the sheep. In Jesus we find all the eight characteristics to the utmost perfection and that is why He is our good shepherd. Let us always remember that we are not one in the crowd and we are not a mere number to Him. He knows each one us individually by our name and by our innermost thoughts and desires, our character and qualities and addresses each one of us according to our need. He speaks to us personally. Assuredly we are all human beings and we have to battle against our intemperate and inveterate self-love. From Jesus, the good shepherd, we can learn how to be really loving and caring people for others without any self-interest. Let us examine whether we have the dedication like Jesus in our commitments to our families, churches and communities.

One fold and one shepherd

When Jesus spoke of one fold and one shepherd, He had only a little flock around Him. He would send a handful of men to the whole earth. He would be with them through the guidance of the Holy Spirit. Today His flock embraces the entire world and is counted nearly two billion, one third of the population of our planet. The Father has given Jesus the whole of humanity and He died on the cross for the redemption of the entire human race. It is thrust upon us to bring the good news of Jesus Christ to those who have not yet so far heard or understood. Through our own witnessing lives, we can assist Jesus to bring those other sheep to His fold. To Him and to us, it is saddening to see so many divisions that have arisen in the flock of Christ. Nothing will be more pleasing to the one true shepherd than the zeal and the efforts of those who labor to bring all Christians together in Christ, in order to make them understand one another and to love one another. In this way, His fold will become more holy, more united and more universal. As we pray for the Christian unity, let us also seek to broaden our outlook and raise us above the petty conceits and narrow prejudices that hinder true unity.

The man and his piece of cloth: A man in the east, where they do not require as much clothing as in colder climates, gave up all worldly concerns and retired to the woods, where he built a hut and lived in it. His only clothing was a piece of cloth, which he wore round his waist. But, as ill-luck would have it, rats were plentiful in the wood, so he had to keep a cat. The cat required milk to keep it, so a cow had to be kept. The cow required tending, so a cow-boy was employed. The boy required a house to live in, so a house was built for him. To look after the house a maid had to be engaged. To provide company for the maid a few more houses had to be built and people invited to live in them. In this manner a little township sprang up. The man said, 'the further we seek to go from the world and its cares, the more they multiply!. What is important for us is to be rooted in Christ. The rest will occur to us through the guidance and care of Him, who is our good shepherd.

Quote: Lead us, heavenly Father, lead us over the world's tempestuous sea; Guard us, guide us, keep us, feed us, For we have no help but you, yet possessing every blessing, if you God our Father be- *James Edmeston*

Scripture reading for Day 23:Psalm 23

Prayer for Day 23: O God, you know the greatness of the dangers that envelop us, and the inability of our weak nature to withstand them. As our shepherd, keep us safe in soul and body, and grant us strength to bear the sufferings and sorrows. Lead us always in the green pastures in this life and bring us home, in the life to come! Amen.

24

RESURRECTION

*J*esus made one of the enduring statements, 'I am the Resurrection and the Life' (Jn 11:25). He identifies Himself as the source of eternal 'life' through the 'resurrection'. The resurrection of the dead can be viewed in two ways. The first is the restoration of a deceased person to the conditions of the present life. Jesus brought back to life three dead persons: the daughter of Jairus (Mt: 18-26), the son of widow of Nain (Lk 7: 11-17), and Lazarus (Jn 11: 1-44). The second is the transformation through conferring upon the deceased, a new and permanent form of life. It is the second that is 'resurrection' in the strict sense. Christ Himself has returned to life, in the role of 'the first born from among the dead' (1 Cor 15: 20). The resurrection of Jesus is the principle assurance for the resurrection of the Christians to the eternal life of glory. Jesus, who is the resurrection and the life, will raise on the last day all those who believe in Him (Jn 11: 25-26).

In the Religious traditions and in the Old Testament

The Greeks believed that the soul of the person is incorruptible by nature. According to them, after death, the soul severed its ties with body and entered into divine immortality. This is the belief also in many of the religions. In the ancient Orient, in imitation of the natural cycle of the season of winter and spring, a primordial myth of the god who died and rose again arose in the popular religions. Osiris in Egypt, Tammouz in Mesopotamia, Baal in Canaan were the best examples for such a god. The sacred rites, performed in honor of those gods during the beginning of agricultural season, were thought to contribute to the fertility of the earth. The Old Testament broke completely from this mythology and the related sacred rites and rituals from the very beginning. The one and the only God is the sole master of life and death. It is God who sends rain to water the earth and spring-time to revive the nature to freshness. God blessed Noah and said: 'As long as the earth lasts, seedtime and harvest, cold and heat, summer and winter and day and night shall not cease' (Gn 8: 22). Agricultural seasons and harvest of the produce are the blessings of Yahweh that He mercifully imparts according to His holy will so that creatures may have food in abundance, for which the Psalmist praises God: 'All of the creatures look to you to give them food in due time. When you open your hand, they are filled. When you hide your face they are lost' (Ps 104: 27-29).

The Hebrew conception of man made it impossible for a belief in an 'afterlife'. That is why the books of the Law and the Prophets of the Old Testament are silent on the 'afterlife' in any form. Israelites did not conceive of the living man as an incarnate spirit like the Greeks but as an animated body. It is the strength and the vigor of the body and its functions, especially its capacity for pleasure that made up the fullness of life. Death is total annihilation of bodily functions and Israel knew of no vital activity that survived death. As the prophet Isaiah states, 'Dead they are, they have no life, shades that cannot rise. For you have punished and destroyed them and wiped out all memory of them' (Is 26:14). We can safely draw a conclusion that the early books of the Old Testament do not speak of eternal life after death. Indeed, death was considered terminal. When a person died, the 'spirit' departed and the deceased continued to exist as a 'self' in Sheol, but was incapable of any vital activity or passivity. Death was accepted as the natural end of man and Sheol was the abode of the dead. The ideal death was to die at the ripe old age with undiminished powers (Gn 25:8), unlike a victim of premature death or of a lingering wasting disease. The first book of the Old Testament explained how humanity was excluded from paradise as the result of the sin of the first man (Gn 3: 23). There was no hope of immortality for human race as the consequence of the fall of Adam that closed the door to paradise once for all. Within such a belief system about death, resurrection could be only the 'restoration' of life in this world.

The conviction that Yahweh has power over life and death has been embodied especially in the narratives of the lives of prophets Elijah and Elisha that contain accounts of the reawakening of dead children. God had sent Elijah to the home of a widow in the small town of Zarephath to receive food and shelter. But then her only son took sick and finally died. The widow was deeply distressed. Elijah took the dead boy and prayed. The Lord heard Elijah's cry and the boy's life returned to him and he lived (1 Kgs 17:22). A wealthy woman and her husband had befriended the prophet Elisha by giving him food and a room to stay in, especially during is journeys. Deeply touched by their kindness, Elisha asked what he might do for them. She had everything she needed, except that she had no son who would carry on her husband's name. She was terribly grieved about her sterility. Furthermore, her husband was too old. But Elisha prophesied the blessing of a child to be born to her and so it was. But one day, tragedy befell the family. The boy took very sick and he died. Elisha prayed for him and life returned to the boy (2 Kgs 4:35). Resurrection in these narratives was only the 'restoration' of the life that was lost and the restored persons continued to live in this world till their end of life.

The belief in Resurrection in the Old Testament

After exile, we see a progressive development of the belief in the resurrection of the dead, not restoration, among the people of Israel. It began with the usage of the image of resurrection to express their collective hope. In several passages, Israel is compared to a dead man after suffering divine punishments particularly the exile, and is promised revival. The earliest of the passages on resurrection is from the book of prophet Ezekiel 37: 1-14. It refers to the restoration of Israel under the image of the resurrection of the dead. After the trial of exile, God would raise up His people, as one would restore life to dry, dead bones: 'These bones are the whole house of Israel. I will open your graves and have you rise from them and bring you back to the land of Israel' (Ez 37: 11-13). Prophet Isaiah spoke about the restoration of the dead: 'He will destroy death forever. He will wipe away tears from all faces' (Is 25:8). 'Your dead shall live. Their corpses shall live. Awake and sing, you who lie in the dust' (Is 26:19). Prophet Hosea insisted that God would triumph over death for the benefit of His people: 'Come let us return to the Lord! He has struck us, but He will bind our wounds. He will revive us after two days. On the third day, He will raise us up to live in His presence' (Hos 6:1). Hosea also foretold the conquest of God over death and Sheol, the abode of the dead: 'Shall I redeem them from death? Where are your plagues, O death! Where is your sting, O, nether world?'(Hos 13:14).

From the collective revival of the people of Israel, the reflection on resurrection moves towards the resurrection of the individuals during the Maccabean period. During the persecution of Antiochus, the heroism of the martyrs raised questions about their restoration. Daniel responded with the assurances of their victory and the punishment for the evildoers: 'Many of those who sleep in the dust of the earth shall awake, some shall live forever and others shall be for an everlasting horror and disgrace' (Dn 2: 2). The new life is not a restoration but a transfiguration. A special feature of the resurrection is 'the wise shall shine brightly like the splendor of the firmament and those who lead the many to justice shall be like the stars forever and ever' (Dn 2: 3). We can count seven references to the 'resurrection' in the second book of Maccabees. The mother and her sons, the Maccabean martyrs, are convinced that God will give them back 'breath and life' (2 Mc 7: 23). A clear statement about the belief in resurrection was made by the third of the Maccabee martyrs. He put forth his tongue and stretched out his hands, as told by the torturers, saying: 'These I have received from heaven. For the laws of God, I now despise them. I hope to receive them again from Him' (2 Mc 7:11). From Josephus, the Jewish historian of the first century AD and from the New Testament we learn that the Pharisees believed in the resurrection, but the Sadducees and the Samaritans did not (Mt 22:23; Acts 23:8). The Jewish Apocalyptic literature also affirmed the belief in the resurrection of the dead.

Jesus the first-born from the dead - in the Gospels and Acts

Jesus expressly taught about the resurrection of the dead. He spoke about final judgment: 'The time is coming when all those who are in their graves will hear His voice and come out. Those who have done good will rise to life and those who have done evil will rise to be condemned' (Jn 5: 28-29). He also taught that He would give food that assures eternal life (Jn 6:54) and that He would raise up those who believe in Him on the last day: 'This is the will of

Him who sent me that I shall lose none of all that He has given me, but raise them up at the last day. For my Father's will is that everyone who looks to the Son and believes in Him shall have eternal life' (Jn 6: 39-40). He defended the belief in resurrection against the Sadducees, whom He charged with ignorance of the power of God and of the Scriptures. He said: 'Those who are considered worthy of taking part in the resurrection can no longer die, for they are like the angels. They are God's children, since they are children of the resurrection. In the account of the bush, even Moses showed that the dead rise, for he calls the Lord, 'the God of Abraham, and the God of Issac and the God of Jacob. He is not the God of the dead, but of the living, for to Him all are alive (Lk 20: 35-38). Christ also declared: 'I am the resurrection and the life. He who believes in me, even if he dies, shall live forever' (Jn 11: 25). He also made predictions that the 'Son of Man' must die and rise on the third day (Mk 8:31). In fact, 'the Son of Man would be three days and three nights in the bosom of the earth' as the 'sign of Jonah' (Mt 12: 40). After resurrection, Jesus reserved His appearances to His chosen witnesses (Acts 2:32). The Apostles saw and touched Him (Jn 20: 19-29) and they ate with Him (Lk 24: 36-43). He was in their midst, not as a phantom, but with His own body (Mt 28:9), that was in a glorified state (Jn 20:19-20). Jesus rose from the dead in conformity with the Scriptures and fulfilled the promise of the glorious exaltation of the Messiah at the right hand of God (Acts 2:34-36), the glorification of the servant of Yahweh (Acts 4:30) and of the enthronement of the Son of Man (Acts 7: 56).

In the Epistles

Paul places the general resurrection on the same level of certainty with that of Christ's Resurrection: 'If the dead are not raised, then Christ has not been raised either. And if Christ has not been raised, your faith is futile. But Christ has indeed been raised from the dead, the first fruits of those who have fallen asleep. For since death came through a man, the resurrection of the dead comes also through a man' (1 Cor 15: 16-21). He preached the resurrection of the dead as one of the fundamental doctrines of Christian faith at Athens (Acts 17: 31), at Jerusalem (23:6), before Felix (24: 15) and before Agrippa (26: 8). He insists on the same doctrine in his Epistles: 'If the Spirit of Him who raised Jesus from the dead is living in you, He who raised Jesus from the dead will also give life to your mortal bodies through His Spirit, who lives in you' (Rom 8: 11). 'By His power, God raised the Lord from the dead, and He will raise us also' (I Cor 6: 14). 'Jesus will transform our lowly bodies so that they will be like His glorious body' (Phil 3: 21). The Christian awaits the final transformation of his body from present misery to a glorified state (Phil 3:10), when at the call of the Son of man the dead will rise, some to eternal life and others to damnation (Jn 5: 28-29). The elect enter into a new life in the heavenly Jerusalem that is the primeval Paradise (Rv 21-22), that was closed to humanity after the fall of old Adam, and now reopened with the resurrection of the new Adam, that is Jesus Christ, the Son of God.

Personal reflection - 'I am the Resurrection'

For some Christians, Jesus' own resurrection was the greatest of all the signs that He had performed during His earthly life. It affirmed beyond any doubt that He is the Son of God and that all what He taught is true. But in the New Testament, the resurrection of Jesus is not presented as an argument for having faith in Jesus. Rather it is presented not as the proof to have faith but as the first revelation in the journey of Faith. When we have faith, then, we encounter the risen Jesus. To recognize the resurrection of Jesus as a historical fact in itself means nothing unless it is part of the faith journey of the believer with the risen Jesus. What is important is to perceive the event of resurrection of Jesus as the climatic event in the salvation history and to receive the redemption that is achieved by the death and resurrection of Jesus. Jesus tells Thomas: 'Because you have seen me, you have believed. Blessed are those who have not seen and yet have believed' (Jn 20:29). Instead of presenting the resurrection as the proof of His divinity, the early Church proclaimed the saving effect of the resurrection of Jesus on the entire humanity.

The redemption of humanity was accomplished together by the death and resurrection of Jesus. The redemption of mankind is the work of the Father, through the Son, in the Holy Spirit. Through His resurrection, the Son of God communicates the divine life that comes from the Father by defeating sin and death. It is for this reason that the resurrection of Jesus was the primary object of the apostolic proclamation from the very beginning. As Luke points out, 'with great power, the apostles testified to the resurrection of the Lord Jesus' (Acts 4:33). They proclaimed that 'the God of our fathers raised Jesus from the dead and exalted Him to His own right hand as Prince and Savior that He might give repentance and forgiveness of sins. We are witnesses of these things and so is the Holy Spirit, whom God has given to those who obey Him' (Acts 5: 30-32). The apostles announced the person of risen Jesus as the good news of salvation. Paul would go to the extent of insisting that by His resurrection Jesus was declared as the Son of God, for our salvation. He says, 'I am set apart for the gospel of God regarding His Son, who as to His human nature was a descendant of David and who through the Spirit of Holiness was declared with power to be the Son of God by His resurrection from the dead' (Rom 1: 1-4). For Paul, it is the resurrection that completed the redemptive work of Jesus and manifested Him in His role as Savior of the world, the role assigned to the Son of God. It is in the resurrection of Jesus that the full and profound significance of His earthly life as the divine instrument of salvation of the entire humanity is revealed. Christ became the first of the risen from the dead by conquering death and sin. The resurrection of the faithful completes this victory of Christ over sin and death. The resurrection of Jesus becomes the guarantee that those who believe in Him also will rise to eternal life, by overcoming the clutches of sin and death that hold humanity in bondage and slavery as the result of the fall of first man, Adam.

The resurrection of the whole person

Paul describes in some length the scenario of the general resurrection: the sound of the angel's voice, the trumpet call to assemble the elect, clouds of parousia and the procession of the elect: 'The Lord Himself will come down from heaven, with a loud command, with the voice of the archangel and with the trumpet call of God and the dead in Christ will rise first. After that, we who are still alive and are left will be caught up together with them in the clouds to meet the Lord in the air. And so we will be with the Lord forever' (1 Thes 4: 16-17). The important conclusion that we draw from the above description and other similar narratives in the New Testament is that the resurrection in the Christian belief looks for the restoration and transformation of the whole person. This expectation is quite different from the beliefs of resurrection as found in the Greek tradition and in many religions all over the world. These religious traditions look forward to the freedom of the soul from the constraint of the body to enjoy immortality. It is the soul or 'self' of the person that is liberated from the clutches of the body that will enter into eternal bliss. The Christian view of resurrection, on the contrary, looks toward to the transformation of the entire person, in his body and soul, to become spiritual, immortal and incorruptible being. Paul clearly explains, 'The body that is sown is perishable, it is raised imperishable. It is sown in dishonor, it is raised in glory; it is sown in weakness, it is raised in power. It is sown a natural body, it is raised a spiritual body. The spiritual did not come first, but the natural and after that the spiritual. The first man was of the dust of the earth, the second man from heaven. As was the earthly man, so are those who are of the earth; and is the man from heaven, so also are those who are of heaven. And just as we have borne the likeness of earthly man, so shall we bear the likeness of man from heaven' (1 Cor 15: 42-49).   That is why the Creed professes faith in the doctrine of the 'resurrection of the body'. The resurrection is not a return to the conditions of the earthly life, but to a new life in the Spirit. This new life is possessed by Jesus as the Son of God, who rose from the dead and is communicated from Him to those who believe in Him.

Baptism unites us with the risen Christ

The Christians are united to the risen Christ through the sacrament of Baptism. Paul explains this reality in these words: 'All of us who were baptized into Christ Jesus were baptized into His death. We were therefore buried with Him through baptism into death in order that just as Christ was raised from the dead through the glory of the Father, we too may live a new life' (Rom 6: 2-4). Baptism symbolizes not only the beginning of a new life in Christ but also death to the old life of sin. By baptism, the Christian is washed, sanctified and made righteous in the name of Lord Jesus Christ (1 Cor 6:11): 'Having been buried with Him in baptism, we are raised with Him through faith in the power of God who raised Jesus from the dead' (Col 2:12).   Paul exhorts the Christians to lead the new life that begins in baptism here and now: 'Clothe yourselves with compassion, kindness, humility, gentleness and patience. Bear with each other and forgive whatever grievances you may have against one another. And over all these virtues, put on love, which binds them all together in perfect unity' (Col 3: 12-14). The new life that begins in baptism and is manifested in our virtuous life on earth, reaches its fullness by the final transformation through our resurrection from the dead.

A fruitful tree: A farmer had a brother in the nearby town. He was a gardener and possessed a magnificent orchard full of finest fruit trees. The fame of the tasty fruits from his trees was well known all over the region. One day the farmer went to the town to visit the garden of his brother who handed over an apple tree, one of the best from his garden and asked his workmen to take it to the farm of his brother. The farmer thought about where to plant the apple tree. He said to himself, 'if I plant it near the hill, the wind might shake the fruits before they are ripe. If I plant it near the road, people shall steal the fruits. So let me plant it behind my house', and so he did. The tree without much sunshine did not blossom much. The farmer sent word to his brother who came and saw what had happened. He rebuked him and said, 'without sunshine and warmth, how could you expect the tree to bear fruits!'. Without being united to Christ, the Son of God, who nourishes our spiritual life, we cannot have resurrection and the eternal life.

Quote: Christian theology has never suggested that the 'fact' of Christ's resurrection could be known, apart from faith -*Alan Richardson*

Scripture reading for Day 24:Jn 11:17-44

Prayer for Day 24: Lord Jesus, true God and true man, you are the Resurrection and the Life. Graciously teach us to be perfectly human, as you are, with a large, tender, and stout heart! Grant us an unshakable faith in you and guide our steps to follow you faithfully, until the day, when we shall forever abide with you! Amen.

25

LIFE

*J*esus proclaimed: 'I am the resurrection and the life' (Jn 11:25). He also assured the people that they would obtain eternal life through faith in Him: 'Just as Moses lifted up the snake in the desert, so the Son of Man must be lifted up that everyone who believes in Him may have eternal life' (Jn 3:15). 'Whoever believes in the Son has eternal life, but whoever rejects the Son will not see life, for God's wrath remains on him' (Jn 3: 36). Jesus presented Himself as the source of life: 'I tell you the truth, whoever hears my word and believes Him who sent me has eternal life and will not be condemned. He has crossed over from death to life' (Jn 5:24). 'My Father's will is that everyone who looks to the Son and believes in Him shall have eternal life and I will raise Him up on the last day' (Jn 6: 40). 'I have come that they may have life and have it to the full' (Jn 10: 10). Jesus prayed: 'This is eternal life: that they may know you, the only true God, and Jesus Christ whom you have sent' (Jn 17: 3). The above verses are from the gospel according to John that refer to Jesus as the life or the source of life. The synoptic gospels also present Jesus as the source of eternal life, a theme that is more fully developed in other New Testament writings such as the Fourth Gospel. Let us begin our exposition on the theme of life with an examination of life as understood and presented in the Old Testament.

Life in the Old Testament - Yahweh, the living God

In the creation narrative, life appears at the last stages of creation as its crowning point. God said, 'Let the water teem with abundance of living creatures and on the earth let birds fly beneath the dome of the sky' and so it happened. God created the sea monsters and all kinds of swimming creatures with which the water teems, and all kinds of winged birds. God saw how good it was and God blessed them saying: 'Be fertile, multiply and fill the water of the seas and let the birds multiply on the earth'. Then God said: 'Let the earth bring forth all kinds of living creatures: cattle, creeping things and wild animals of all kinds'. And so it happened' (Gn 1: 20-25). Then God said, 'Let us make man in our image, after our likeness' (Gn 1:26). Thus, finally, God created the most perfect living thing in His own image and likeness- man. God blessed our first parents saying, 'Be fertile and multiply; fill the earth and subdue it' (Gn 1: 28). The Old Testament saw life as a blessing from God who is always addressed as the 'living God'. The designation of Yahweh as the 'living God' implied that as opposed to the lifeless images of other gods, Yahweh possessed unlimited power, freedom and movement. Joshua said to the Israelites, 'This is how you will know that there is a living

God in your midst, who at your approach will dispossess the Canaanites, Hittites, Hivites, Perizzites, Girgashites, Amorites and Jebusites' (Jos 3: 10).

As living God, Yahweh alone imparts life as His blessing. It is Yahweh alone who confers and sustains life. Man became a living being, when Yahweh breathed into his nostrils: 'The Lord God blew into the nostrils of man the breadth of life and so man became a living being' (Gn 2: 7). For the Hebrew mind that saw Yahweh as the 'living God', life was always observable by its motion and action. A living thing as opposed to the dead thing was that which had the power to act. Losing life meant the cessation of vital activity. As far as human beings are concerned, life was the basic good from God, without which no other good is possible. To have life means to enjoy the good things in this world. Sennacherib, the king of Assyria, declared to the people of Israel: 'Choose life and not death. Make peace with me and surrender. Then each of you will eat of his own vine and of his own fig-tree and drink the water of his own cistern, until I come to take you to a land like your own, a land of grain and wine, of bread and orchards, of olives, oil and fruit syrup' (2 Kgs 18: 31-32). Seen in this way, to have life means to be in health, to have the good functioning of the body and to have the capacity to enjoy good things such as food and drinks and also to have those good things in abundance.

Choice of life and death

For the people of Israel, in so far as all the good things of life came from the land, especially in the land that God gave, the Promised Land is the land of the living or the land of life. God said, 'Now, Israel, hear the statutes and decrees which I am teaching you to observe, that you may have life, and may enter in and take possession of the land which the Lord, the God of your fathers, is giving you' (Dt 4:1). Justice and justice alone should be your aim that you may have life and may possess the land which the Lord, your God is giving you' (Dt 16:20). Seen in this way, life was more than the exercise of the vital functions of the body in good health, but also the enjoyment of good things in this world. Through observing the precepts of the Lord, Israel could enjoy the abundance of good things as blessing from Him. Yahweh, the Lord of life, is also the Lord of death. He alone has the power to give life as well as to impose death. Israel is called upon to choose between life and death, depending on the choice between good and evil. When Israel chooses good over evil, then, life comes as a blessing from God. When Israel chooses evil over good, then, death comes as a curse from God. What we see here is the portrayal of life not simply as physical and biological reality, but as an ethical option, chosen as a free choice on the part of the people of Israel. When Israel observes the will of Yahweh, then, it is assured of life. The choice before Israel was clear - life or death. Israel could choose life only by loving Yahweh and observing His commandments. God said, 'Here, then, I have today set before you life and prosperity, death and doom. If you obey the commandments of the Lord, your God, which I enjoin you today, loving Him and walking in His ways, and keeping His commandments, statutes and decrees, you will live and grow numerous and the Lord, your God, will bless you in the land you are entering to occupy. I have set before you life and death, the blessing and the curse. Choose life, then, that you and your descendants may live, by loving the Lord, your God, heeding His voice and holding fast to Him. For that will mean life for you, a long life for you to live on the land which the Lord swore He would give to your fathers Abraham, Isaac and Jacob' (Dt 30: 15-20).

Life as portrayed by the prophets

The prophets insist on the same theme of choosing good leads to life and choosing evil leads to death. According to the prophet Amos, to live, one must seek Yahweh: 'Thus says the Lord to the house of Israel: seek me that you may live' (Am 5:4). Also, one must seek good and not evil to live: 'Seek good and not evil that you may live. Then truly the Lord, the God of hosts be with you as you claim. Hate evil and love good and let justice prevail' (Am 5:14-15). Isaiah would insist that in order to live Israel should hearken to the word of the Lord: 'Heed me and you shall eat well, you shall delight in rich fare. Come to me heedfully, listen, that you may have life' (Is 55:2-3). Prophet Ezekiel proposes that by turning away from wickedness, the people of Israel could escape death and be blessed with life: 'If a man is virtuous, if he lives by my statutes and is careful to observe my ordinances, he shall surely live. If he practices all the abominations, he shall surely die. His death shall be his own fault' (Ez 18: 5-13). 'Turn and be converted from all your crimes that they may be no cause of guilt for you. Cast away from you all the crimes you have committed and make for yourselves a new heart and a new spirit. Why should you die, O, house of Israel? For I have no pleasure in the death of anyone who dies. Return and live' (Ez 18: 30-32). 'Turn, turn from your evil ways. Why should you die, O, house of Israel? (Ez 33: 11). In the books of the prophets, life is portrayed as a good that is received from God as a blessing by walking in His ways and observing His ordinances, especially following by the ways of justice and fraternal love.

Life in Wisdom and Apocalyptic literature

In Wisdom literature life is presented as well-being, as success, health and good fortune. The man who pursues wisdom and righteousness will find life. 'Wisdom said, 'O children, listen to me; instruction and wisdom do not reject. Happy the man who obeys me and happy those who keep my ways! For he who finds me finds life and wins favor from the Lord' (Prv 8: 32-36). 'In the path of justice there is life, but the abominable way leads to death' (Prv 12: 28). 'He who pursues justice and kindness will find life and honor' (Prv 21:21). The wicked are doomed to death: 'God rejects the obstinate in heart. He preserves not the life of the wicked' (Jb 36: 5).

It is the song on the Servant of Yahweh that introduces, for the first time, the concept of life beyond death. A person can die for something other than his sins and in dying, can find life: 'A grave was assigned him among the wicked and burial place among the evildoers, though he had done no wrong nor spoken any falsehood. He shall see the light in the fullness of days' (Is 53: 9-11). During the persecutions of Antiochus Epiphanes, the people of Israel saw that death could come from one's fidelity to God. Such a death accepted heroically with courage and loyalty to God was not a separation or punishment from Him but a path to receive worthy reward from God that would bring eternal life through resurrection. The mother of the martyrs, who were seven brothers, encourages them saying, 'God, the creator, in His mercy, will give you back both breadth and life, because you now disregard yourselves for the sake of His law' (2 Mc 7: 23). The just are assured of eternal reward and the wicked everlasting horror: 'From the dust of the earth, the wise will awake to shine brightly like the stars forever and the wicked will receive everlasting horror and disgrace' (Dn 12:2-3).

The book of Wisdom carries the hope of eternal life further. The souls of the just are in the hand of God and no torment shall touch them. But the wicked shall receive a punishment since they neglected justice and forsook the Lord' (Wis 3: 1-10). 'The just will live forever and in the Lord is their recompense. They shall receive the splendid crown, the beauteous diadem from the hand of the Lord' (Ws 5: 15-16). The concept of life in the Old Testament remains, right from the beginning, open to development. We see a picture of man, who was at first created immortal but lost this immortality through the fall of Adam. Sin is therefore the reason why death entered the world. God promises life to the just and death to the sinner. Life and death are correlative with good and evil. Life is dependent on the moral conduct of each one and his observance of the law of God. Life is progressively portrayed not only as a joyous earthly life, but also as the life everlasting.

Life in the New Testament - the synoptic Gospels

In the fullness of time, Jesus, the Son of God, came to the world and promised 'life' in abundance to those who believe in Him. The concept of life as found in the New Testament focuses on 'eternal life'. The synoptic gospels present 'life' as not of the earthly existence and its enjoyments but as something that finds completion after death, as the 'fullness of life'. Eternal life can be obtained by keeping the commandments of God. A man asked Jesus, 'Teacher, what must I do to get eternal life? Jesus replied, 'If you want to enter life, obey the commandments' (Mt 19: 16-17). On another occasion, an expert of the Law asked Jesus, 'What must I do to inherit eternal life? Jesus asked in reply, 'What is written in the Law? How do you read it? He answered, 'Love the Lord your God with all your heart and with all your soul and with all your strength and with all your mind' and 'Love your neighbor as yourself'. Jesus said: 'You have answered correctly. Do this and you will live' (Lk 10: 25-28). It is love for God and neighbor that constitutes the ethics of the kingdom of God and guarantees eternal life. Those who make sacrifices for the sake of the kingdom of God in loving and serving God and neighbors will be rewarded with eternal life. Jesus said to the disciples, 'No one who has left home or wife or brothers or parents or children for the sake of the kingdom of God will fail to receive many times as much in this age, and in the age to come, eternal life' (Lk 18:29-30). The path to eternal life is narrow and only a few walk through it: 'Small is the gate and narrow the road that leads to life and only a few find it' (Mt 7: 14). For Jesus, life is more precious and important than mere food and clothes. He asks the disciples, 'Is not life more important than food and the body more important than clothes? (Mt 6:25). To save life is more pleasing to God than the observation of the Sabbath (Mk 3:4). Jesus heals the sick and restores health and life to people, as God's unique messenger of life.

Life as portrayed in the writings of John

In the gospel according to John, Jesus refers to Himself as having life in Himself (5: 26) or as being the life (11:25; 14:6). He also refers to Himself as giving life to others (5:21; 6:33). By this, Jesus means that He is the source of eternal life and that salvation is mediated through Him. This is why He can give (eternal) life to others. Jesus also says that the Spirit gives life and that His words are Spirit and they are life (6:63). The Spirit gives life in the sense that the Spirit is the means by which one understands the identity of Jesus as the source of life and thereby enters into salvation: 'I say to you, unless one is born of water and the Spirit, he cannot enter the Kingdom of God. That which is born of the flesh is flesh and that which is born of the Spirit is spirit' (3:5-6). When He says that His words is Spirit, Jesus means that His teaching is from the Spirit, being Spirit-inspired; this is why His words 'are life': his teaching mediates the possibility of entering into eternal life. Christ, the eternal word, possessed life from all eternity: 'In Him was life and that life was the light of men' (1: 4). He is 'the light of life' (8:12). He gives living water which in the recipient becomes 'spring of water bursting forth to eternal life' (4:14). Jesus is also 'the bread of life' (6:35) and 'the one who feeds on this bread will live forever' (6:58). Jesus, the good shepherd has come to the world so that His sheep 'may have life and have it to the full' (10:10). He laid down His life for His sheep only to take it up again (10:17), because death had no power over Him (10:18). Whoever lives and believes in Jesus shall not die (11: 25). His Father granted authority over all people so that He might give eternal life to all those whom the Father has given Him (17: 2) and the eternal life is to know His Father, the only true God and Him, the Christ whom the Father has sent' (17:3). Jesus is 'the Word of life' (1 Jn 1:1) In Jesus Christ 'life' which was with the Father appeared to the world (1 Jn 1:2).

Life in the Pauline Epistles

According to Paul, God gives eternal life 'to those who persevere in doing good' (Rom 2:7), for 'the gift of God is eternal life in Christ Jesus, our Lord' (Rom 6:23). Those who believe in Christ 'receive eternal life' (1 Tim 1:16). Then, the believers have 'by being rich in good deeds will lay up treasure for themselves as a firm foundation for the coming age, so that that may take hold of the life that is truly life' (1 Tim 6: 19). In this way, 'having been justified by His grace, they might become heirs having the hope of eternal life' (Ti 3:7). For Paul, eternal life is not a future life that is to come after death or at the end of time. Rather, eternal life is a present reality that begins in baptism. It is a new life that is created by the sacrament of baptism: 'We were baptized into His death. We were, therefore, buried with Him through baptism into death in order that just as Christ was raised from the dead through the glory of the Father, we too may live a new life' (Rom 6: 4). The Spirit, who dwells in the Christian as the result of baptism, 'and who raised Christ from the dead will also give life to the mortal bodies' (Rom 8:11) of the Christians.

Personal reflection - 'I am the Life'

Jesus explains that the purpose of His coming to the world is that 'we should have life and have it abundantly' (Jn 10:10). Through His death on the cross, He destroyed death and restored life to the entire humanity. Now, He communicates 'life' to all those who believe in Him. Through baptism, Jesus establishes relationship between the believer and the Father, in the Spirit. As a result, the Christian no longer lives to himself. Rather, he 'lives for Him who died for him and was raised again' (2 Cor 5:15). 'He lives by faith in the Son of God' (Gal 2:20). Christ is his life (Col 3: 4). The new life is thus instituted by the participation, through baptism, in the redeeming death and the saving resurrection of our Lord Jesus Chirst. This life is a sharing in the glory of the risen Jesus, here and now, in this world that moves to the fulfillment in the resurrection of the baptized at the end of time. The Christian continues to live in this world, in his mortal body, but he has received the power from Jesus Christ who continues to strengthen him in the Spirit, so that the Christian is able to conquer sin in his life and as a result, he conquers death itself. He can pass through death unharmed to live forever. Through the passage of death the corruptible puts on immortality. For this reason, every person goes through bodily death. Instead of preventing life, death establishes life permanently and expands it in God: 'When the perishable has been clothed with the imperishable and the mortal with the immortality, then the saying that is written will come true': 'Death has been swallowed up in victory' (Is 25:8). O death, where is your victory? O death, where is your sting? (1 Cor 15: 53-55).

Eternal life is indeed life with Christ. After death, as the fruit of resurrection, the believers attain the fullness of life with the risen Christ. At that time, the believer can see God as He is (1Jn 3: 2), face to face: 'Now we see but a poor reflection as in a mirror. Then, we shall see face to face. Now, we know in part. Then, we shall know fully (1 Cor 13:12). This vision of God in His heavenly kingdom is given to the believer as the result of individual resurrection. The entire redeemed humanity will attain the full perfection of life at the end of time. Then,

God's abode with men, the heavenly Jerusalem will appear: 'I saw a new heaven and a new earth for the first heaven and first earth had passed away and there was no longer any sea. I saw the Holy City, the new Jerusalem coming down out of heaven from God. And I heard a loud voice saying, 'Now the dwelling of God is with men and He will live with them' (Rv 21: 1-3). There the river of the water of life flows and the tree of life flourishes: 'Then the angel showed me the river of the water of life, as clear as crystal, flowing from the throne of God and of the Lamb down the middle of the great street of the city. On each side of the river stood the tree of life' (Rv 22: 1-2). At that time, there will be no more death' (Rv 21:4), for 'death will be thrown into the lake of fire' (Rv 20:14). In the heavenly Jerusalem, the saints of God will participate in the very life of the Father, through Jesus Christ, in the Holy Spirit, where God will be all in all (1 Cor 15: 28).

King Solomon and the Ants: Once king Solomon rode out of his palace in Jerusalem towards countryside. Many commanders of his large army and the Queen of Sheba accompanied him on the journey. Wisest of men, Solomon knew the languages of all the creatures. Across an ant-hill, he heard the ants talking to each other saying, 'here comes the king to crush us in the dust'. The king told the queen of Sheba what the ants said. She replied that the little ants should not have murmured against the great king. The king answered, 'The wise and strong should seek the welfare of the weak'. Then, he turned around the ant-hill and left the ants unharmed. Then the queen of Sheba praised the king saying, 'Now I know the secret of your wisdom. Happy must be the country whose ruler heeds more the murmur of the poor than the flatteries of the great'. The greatness of Jesus is that He died for us, ordinary human beings, dust from dust, so that we might have life in abundance in eternity.

Quote: One short sleep past, we wake up eternally and death shall be no more. O, death, thou shall certainly die- *John Donne*

Scripture reading for Day 25:   I Cor 15: 1-28

Prayer for Day 25: O, God of life! You overcame sin and death through your only-begotten Son and opened to us the gates of everlasting life. May the solemn reception of baptism purify your people from their old nature and transform them into new creatures so that they may be found worthy to share the glory of your angels and saints! Amen.

26

SERVANT

*I*t is the apostolic preaching that applied to Jesus the title 'servant'. Peter proclaimed to his Jewish listeners: 'The God of Abraham, Issac and Jacob, the God of our fathers, has glorified His servant Jesus' (Acts 3: 13). 'When God raised up His servant Jesus, He sent Him first to you to bless you by turning each of you from your wicked ways' (Acts 3: 26). The Christian community prayed, 'Indeed Herod and Pontius Pilate met together with the Gentiles and the people of Israel in this city to conspire against your holy servant, Jesus, whom you anointed' (Acts 4:27). Matthew presents Jesus as the Servant of Yahweh who came to proclaim justice to the nations and quotes from the prophet Isaiah 42:1-4. He writes, 'This was to fulfill what was spoken through the prophet Isaiah: Here is my servant whom I have chosen, the one I love, in whom I delight; I will put my delight on him and he will proclaim justice to the nations' (Mt 12: 17-18). Jesus Himself tells His disciples, 'I am among you as one who serves' (Lk 22: 27). He washed the feet of the apostles like a servant (Jn 13: 1-17). The title of Jesus as 'servant' reveals to us the sacrificial life and death of Jesus for our salvation. The only Son of God, Jesus became the Servant of God par excellence. To present the significance of this title for Jesus, let us first examine the meaning of this title in the Old Testament.

Servants of God in Old Testament

The word 'servant' in the pagan world referred to a person in slavery. The slaves were treated like animals. In the Old Testament, on the contrary, the name servant denotes honor. The title 'servant of the king' is an honorific title of an official who held high position in the court of the monarch. When such an official presented himself before the king and addressed as 'your servant' he expressed his humility in the royal presence. In the presence of Yahweh, the living God, the same humility is shown for example by Moses: 'O Lord God, you have shown your servant your greatness and might' (Dt 3:24). Yahweh names those whom He calls to collaborate in His plan as His 'servants'. Abraham (Gn 26: 24), Issac (Gn 24:14) and Jacob (Ex 32:13) are called the servants of God. Moses is presented as the servant of God par excellence in the Old Testament: 'Israel beheld the great power that the Lord had shown against the Egyptians, they feared the Lord and believed in Him and in His servant Moses' (Ex 14:31). The Lord said, 'My servant Moses bears my trust. Face to face I speak to him' (Nm 12:7-8). 'In the land of Moab, Moses, the servant of the Lord died' (Dt 34:5). Joshua, who led Israel into the Promised Land was also called 'the Servant of the Lord' (Jos 24: 29).

King David is glorified as the 'Servant of the Lord' (1 Kgs 8:66; 11:36; 2 Kgs 19:34). 'I have chosen David, my servant. With olive oil, I have anointed him' (Ps 89:21). Prophet Elijah is also honored as servant of God: 'The Lord has accomplished all that he foretold through His servant Elijah' (2 Kg 10:10). Prophet Ahijah (1 Kgs 14: 18) and Zerubbabel (Zec 3:8) are also called the servants of God. In the second book of the Kings, 'my servants the prophets' (2 Kgs 9: 7; 17: 13, 23) is a common phrase to refer to the prophets who spoke in the name of God. The priests who conduct worship in the temple were also addressed as the servants of God: 'Come, bless the Lord, all you servants of the Lord, who stand in the house of the Lord' (Ps 133:1). Thus, we see that the title 'servant' of God is given to those who fulfill some definite mission in the social and religious life of the chosen people, as leaders and kings, as prophets and priests. It is in the same sense of mission from Yahweh that a pagan king is also called a servant of Yahweh. When the people of Israel were unfaithful to God, they were chastised by the exile through the agency of a Babylon king, Nebuchadnezzar, who carried out God's holy will and hence is called servant of God. The Lord says, 'Now I have given all the lands into the hand of Nebuchadnezzar, king of Babylon, my servant' (Jer 27: 6). This brief explanation leads us towards the mysterious figure that appears in prophet Isaiah 40-55 and is named as the Servant of Yahweh.

The Servant of Yahweh

In the oracles of the Book of Consolation (Is 40-55) that deal with the servant of Yahweh, the prophet presents the people of Israel as the servant of God: 'You are my witnesses, says the Lord, my servants whom I have chosen' (Is 43: 10). 'Hear then, O Jacob, my servant, Israel, whom I have chosen' (Is 44:1). O Israel, you are my servant. I formed you to be a servant to me' (Is 44:21). But Israel was not a worthy servant. The Lord says, 'I know that you are utterly treacherous, a rebel you were called from birth' (Is 48: 8). 'It was for your sins that you were sold, for your crimes that your mother was dismissed' (Is 50: 1). But God, who wills not the destruction of the sinners, chooses for Himself a remnant from His chosen people of Israel that will be always faithful to Him under the reign of His Servant, the new David (Ez 34: 23). It is this remnant that is personified as an individual and is addressed by the prophet as the Servant of Yahweh. The second half of the book of Consolation (Is 49-55) is dominated by this mysterious figure whom God calls His Servant. 'The Lord called me from birth. From my mother's womb He gave me my name. You are my servant, he said to me, Israel, through whom I show my glory' (Is 49: 1-3). The mission of the Servant is very different from the charismatic leaders, kings, prophets or priests that came before him. He makes himself a sin offering, heals others through his innocent suffering and brings judgment and righteousness through his death and not through conquests. He suffers and dies, possibly by condemnation and execution. His death is mysterious because he is innocent. His suffering and death are portrayed as vicarious atonement for the sins of others. God vindicates him through granting him the fullness of life. The prophecies about the mysterious servant of Yahweh would be fulfilled in Jesus Christ, who is not only the servant of God, but also the only Son of God. The conception of atoning and redeeming death that is described in the oracles regarding the Servant of Yahweh finds perfect resonance with the portrayal of the suffering and death of Jesus. The suffering of the servant is not an accident, but something he undergoes in obedience to God's will. There is mystery in his suffering, because in his death God's plan succeeds: 'The will of the Lord shall be accomplished through him' (Is 53: 10). God would restore the servant to peace and health: 'Therefore I will give him his portion among the great and he will divide the spoils with the mighty' (Is 53:12). No doubt, more than any other prophetic passage in the Old Testament, it is the oracles regarding the Servant of Yahweh that lead us towards a better understanding of the gospels especially their presentation of the passion and death of Jesus as the supreme sacrificial offering made for the forgiveness of the sins of all mankind and for its restoration to divine friendship

The servants of God in the New Testament

Jesus is presented in the pages of the New Testament as the true servant of God who fulfills the holy will of God without reserve. Jesus is the perfect model to serve God totally. From His childhood, He was always concerned about doing only His Father's holy will. He replied to His parents who were searching for Him in the temple, 'Why were you searching for me? Didn't you know I had to be in my Father's house?' (Lk 2: 49). The unfolding of His entire life reveals to us how in all the things He said or did, Jesus was always seeking to fulfill His Father's holy will. It is the obedience to His Father that took Him to the cross. Explaining the reason why He should undergo the passion, He says to the disciples: 'The Prince of this world has no hold over me. But the world must learn that I love the Father and that I do exactly what my Father had commanded me' (Jn 14: 30). In serving God so totally Jesus makes amends for the disobedience of the entire human race, starting with the disobedience of our first parents. He also presents Himself as the perfect model how to serve God. Serving God is, first of all, to love Him with all our heart and might. Jesus warns us that we can not serve two masters - God and mammon: 'No one can serve two masters. Either he will hate the one and love the other or he will be devoted to the one and despise the other. You can not serve both God and money' (Mt 6:24). Just like Jesus Himself did, serving God leads to the fraternal service to the members of our human race as one's own brothers and sisters. His compassionate service to the entire humanity led Jesus to the cross: 'The Son of Man did not come to be served, but to serve, and to give His life as a ransom for many' (Mk 10: 45). Jesus, after washing the feet of His disciples as a servant, says to His disciples, 'No servant is greater than the master. Now that I, your Lord and Teacher, have washed your feet, you also should wash one another's feet. I have set you an example that you should do as I have done for you' (Jn 13: 14-16).

Jesus sends out His disciples to be the servants of the Gospel in the world. Paul states this fact when he declares: 'I have become the servant of the Gospel that you have heard and that has been proclaimed to every creature under heaven' (Col 1:23). They have to preach the Gospel 'in all humility and if necessary with tears and in the midst of tribulations' (Acts 20:19). As the result of believing in the Gospel, the Christians have passed from slavery to sin to be the servants of God: 'You have been set free from the slavery to sin and have become the slaves to God. The benefit you reap leads to holiness, and the result is eternal life' (Rom 6:22). Though as the creatures of God, we are only the slaves of the Son of God, Jesus grants us the honor of becoming His friends. 'I no longer call you servants, because a servant does not know his master's business. Instead, I have called you friends, for everything that I have learned from my Father, I have made known to you' (Jn 15:15). What is more, by redeeming us with His blood, Jesus granted us the divine adoption and we have become God's own children: 'Formerly when you did not know God, you were slaves to those who by nature are not gods. Now, you are no longer a slave but a son; and since you are a son, God has made you also an heir' (Gal 4:7). Paul exhorts the believers how to be the servants of God: 'Hate what is evil and cling to what is good. Be devoted to one another in brotherly love. Honor one another above yourselves. Never be lacking in zeal, but keep your spiritual fervor serving the Lord. Be joyful in hope, patient in affliction and faithful in prayer. Share with God's people who are in need. Practice hospitality. Do not be overcome by evil but overcome evil with good' (Rom 12: 9-21).

Jesus, the true Servant of God

As did the apostolic preachers later, Jesus Himself portrayed His passion and death as the fulfillment of the prophecy of prophet Isaiah about the servant of God. Jesus made the mission of the Servant His own. Like the servant of Yahweh, He is meek and humble of heart (Mt 11: 29). He offers His life for the redemption of the multitude of sinners (Mt 20: 28). It is for their sake that He was treated like a criminal, died on the cross, knowing that He would rise again, as it was written of the Son of Man (Mt 10: 33-34). Contrary to the expectations of the people of Israel, as the expected Messiah, He did not come to establish a temporal kingdom but to lead the people to the eternal kingdom of God by Himself passing through death as the Servant of God. After Jesus was baptized in the river Jordan by John the Baptist, a voice came from heaven saying, 'You are my Son whom I love; with whom I am well pleased' (Mk 1:11). It is remarkable that this seems to be an almost exact quotation of Is 42:1 that speaks about the Servant of Yahweh, which states: 'Here is my servant whom I uphold, my chosen one with whom I am pleased'. Mathew quotes Isaiah 42:1-4 on the servant of Yahweh and comments that the prophecy is fulfilled in Jesus who does the will of His Father to the perfection. In his hymn, Paul refers to the self-emptying of Jesus who became a servant for our salvatioon: 'Although He existed in the form of God, He did not regard equality with

God a thing to be grasped, but emptied Himself, taking the form of a servant and being made in the likeness of men. Being found in appearance as a man, He humbled Himself by becoming obedient to the point of death, even death on a cross' (Phil 2:6-8). The portrayal of Jesus as the servant of Yahweh brings out the novelty of His character as the risen Christ who first suffered and died for the sins of others. At the same time it presents Him as perfectly fulfilling in His person all the elements of Israel's gifts and missions as the chosen people of God.

Personal reflection: 'The suffering servant of God'

Jesus said: 'I am among you as one who serves' (Lk 22: 27). Luke presents to us the context of this wonderful saying of Jesus: 'A dispute arose among them as to which of them was considered to be greatest. Jesus said to them, 'The kings of the Gentiles lord it over them; and those who exercise authority over them call themselves Benefactors. But you are not to be like that. Instead, the greatest among you should be like the youngest, and the one who rules like the one who serves' (Lk 22: 24-26). What kind of dispute did the disciples have during the Passover feast? They were probably arguing about who should sit in the place of honor at the table. Jesus did the unthinkable! He turned the world's value of greatness upside-down and he presented authority as loving-sacrifice and selfless-service. Authority without sacrificial love is meaningless in the Christian family of Jesus. The way of greatness in God's kingdom is the way of servant hood and humility, charity and kindness. Jesus showed us a perfect example about how to be a servant for others of which Peter illustrates: 'When they hurled their insults at Him, He did not retaliate. When He suffered He made no threats. Instead, He entrusted Himself to Him who judges justly. He Himself bore our sins in His body on the tree so that we might die to sins and live for righteousness' (1 Pet 2: 23-24). In Him is no sin. He appeared so that He might take away our sins (1Jn 3:5). He is the atoning sacrifice for our sins and not only for ours but also for the sins of the whole world (1Jn 2:2).

Faithful till the end

The title 'servant' furnishes a biblical basis for the atoning passion and death of Jesus. It also gives meaning to the suffering and death that all the human beings experience in this world. He, the Son of God, stooped down to serve us, His worthless creatures with a love that is beyond our imagination. He renounced as it were 'the form of God', emptied and made Himself totally the servant of sinful mankind. He teaches us a valuable lesson in fraternal service by kneeling before the apostles and washing their feet. Allowing Himself to be mocked, spat upon, scourged, crowned with thorns, nailed to the cross - in all these things, He was serving us. In all these humiliations, He carried out the holy will of His heavenly Father. He never hesitated, never faltered, never showed a sign of mental anxiety or uncertainty. Always serene and deliberate, He pursued a steady course towards His sacrificial death on the cross. He remained fully the master of Himself and of the situation, always appearing tranquil, unperturbed and dignified. He is the servant of Yahweh who died for taking away the sins of the world: 'The high-priest Caiphas said to the members of the Sanhedrin, the Jewish Council, 'You know nothing at all. You do not realize that it is better for you that one man die for the people than that the whole nation perish. He did not say this on his own, but as high priest that year, he prophesied that Jesus would die for the Jewish nation and not only for the nation, but also for the scattered children of God to bring them together and make them one' (Jn 11: 49-52). All the days of His life, Jesus never lost sight of Calvary and of the cross. He asked the sons of Zebedee, 'Can you drink the cup I am going to drink?' (Mt 20: 22). On another occasion He presented His passion and death as a baptism: 'I have a baptism to undergo and how distressed I am until it is completed' (Lk 12: 50). A couple of days before His terrible suffering, Jesus spoke about the hour: 'The hour has come for the Son of Man to be glorified. Unless a kernel of wheat falls to the ground and dies, it remains only a single seed. But if it dies, it produces many seeds' (Jn 12: 23-24). Then, Jesus interrupted His discourse and remarked: 'Now my heart is troubled, and what shall I say? Father! save me from this hour? No, it was for this very reason I came to this hour. Father glorify your name' (Jn 12: 27). Even at that time of so much stress and anxiety, Jesus remained firm to carry out God's plan for the salvation of the world.

A model for us

During the dreadful night at Gethsemane, sorrowful and troubled, Jesus pleaded to the Father: 'If it is possible, may this cup be taken from me. Yet, not as I will, but as you will' (Mt 26: 39). However, regaining His composure, He surrendered Himself totally to His Father: 'If it is not possible for this cup to be taken away unless I drink it, may your will be done' (Mt 26: 42). After the agony, He went to meet His passion and death with utmost obedience to the will of His Father. Having been obedient unto death, even death on the cross, Jesus, with the satisfaction of His mission fully accomplished, said: 'It is finished' (Jn 19:30). Thereafter, He trustfully turned to His Father and submitted His life: 'Into your hands, Father, I commit my spirit' (Lk 23:46). Thus ended the life of God's holy Servant, Jesus Christ on the croos, as the prophet Isaiah foretold, in the oracles regarding the servant of Yahweh. Jesus was not only guiltless but also infinitely good. Hence, God restored His servant to glory. The event of resurrection bears the hall-mark of the all-powerful intervention of God's omnipotence. In the risen Christ, the glorification and exaltation of the servant of Yahweh became complete and final. As servants of God, we are called upon to discern and follow the holy will of God in our daily life. At times, our journey in this world may take us through suffering, trials and even death. In any situation, especially at the time of suffering and sorrow, let us remember the suffering servant of Yahweh, our Lord Jesus Christ, and follow

His good example to be faithful and obedient to God at all times. Let us always bear in mind that though we are creatures and only the servants of God, God has given us the honor of being His adopted children in Jesus Christ. As God's servants who have also become His children, let us always seek to please Him through loving obedience and faithful service. Then, as we approach the doors of the heavenly kingdom, God, our master, would say to us: 'Well done, good and faithful servant! You have been faithful with a few things. I will put you in charge of many things. Come and share your master's happiness' (Mt 25: 23).

He gave his life for many: In the year 362 B.C., Rome was devastated by a terrible earthquake. A huge chasm suddenly opened up so deep that no one could see the bottom. The citizens brought stones and earth to fill in, but the yawning gulf remained the same. The Senate then consulted the soothsayers who informed them that the crater could not be filled until what was most valuable in Rome was cast into it. The people threw their valuable possessions like gold and silver but the hole remained always deep. At that time, a noble youth, Marcus Curtius by name, rode forward in his horse. He told them that sacrifice was the most valuable virtue of Rome and went on to show his own sacrifice for the city of Rome by leaping into the deep pit with his horse. Immediately the ground closed behind him and became a level ground as it was before the earthquake. As servant of God, Jesus sacrificed His life for us. In gratitude, we have to sacrifice our lives in His service for His glory.

Quote: To love sufferings and afflictions for the love of God is the highest point of most holy charity. For in this, there is nothing lovable save the love of God only - *Francis de Sales*

Scripture reading for Day 26:Is 53: 1-12

Prayer for Day 26: Father! Your only Son offered His life as atoning sacrifice for the remission of our sins. In this He fulfilled your holy will. Guide us through the Holy Spirit that we may faithfully follow your holy will in all the things we do and thus become your worthy servants in this world and be rewarded in the life to come! Amen.

27

WAY

The most remarkable statement of Jesus explaining the centrality of His role in the salvation of mankind is, 'I am the way and the truth and the life. No one comes to the Father except through me' (Jn 14:6). Jesus declares that He is the Way. As used in the Bible, the word for 'way' is 'derek' in Hebrew and 'hodos' in Greek and it refers to a path formed little by little through the repeated footsteps of those who used it. The ancient Semites were nomadic people. The 'way', referring to the route or path, was very important to their nomadic life-style, in order to reach their destination safely and surely. As the Son of God who became man for our redemption, Jesus is the mediator par excellence between God and mankind. In this role, He becomes the 'way' to God and to His heavenly kingdom. Let us explain the profound meaning of Jesus being our 'way' beginning with a presentation from the Old Testament.

The Way in the Old Testament

In the pages of the Old Testament, walking in God's way refers, first of all, to the religious adventure that is made through the trust and confidence in God. The first such adventure is seen in the faithful journey of Abraham. At the call of God, He set out to walk in the 'way' that God showed Him (Gn 12:1-5), leading to the covenant that God made with him (Gn 15:18), having a son at a very old age as a blessing from God (Gn 21:2), the trial of sacrificing his son that affirmed his unwavering fidelity to God (Gn 22:1-14) and the confirmation of divine blessings for his descendants (Gn 22: 15-18). Indeed, it was a remarkable 'way' that Abraham walked following God and His plan for him. The Exodus is another great religious adventure, when the people of Israel under Moses walked the 'way' of the Lord. God freed the people of Israel from the Egyptian slavery of Pharaoh after performing remarkable signs and wonders and guided them back to the Promised Land. He went before them marking out the route that they would walk with a column of a cloud and a column of fire: 'The Lord preceded them in the daytime by means of a column of cloud to show them the way and at night by means of column of fire to give them light. Thus they could travel both day and night. Neither the column of cloud by day nor the column of fire by night ever left its place in front of the people' (Gn 13: 21-22). The people of Israel escaped from being recaptured by the troops of Pharaoh when God walked them through the sea and let the Pharaoh's army perish in the waters of the Red sea. Israel always remembered this 'way' to liberation and freedom through the sea, led by the mighty hand of God. They would sing to the Lord praising Him: 'Through the sea was your path. Your way, through the mighty waters, though your footsteps were unseen. You led your people like a flock under the care of Moses and Aaron' (Ps 77: 20-21). In the desert, God supplied food and drink. Under His providential care, the people of Israel lacked nothing.

Moses reminded the people of Israel of God's compassionate care saying: 'The Lord God fought for you before your very eyes in Egypt as well as in the desert where you saw how the Lord your God carried you as a man carries his child all along your journey until you arrived at this place' (Dt 1: 30-31). 'The Lord your God has blessed you in all your undertakings. He has been concerned about your journey through this vast desert. It is now forty years that he has been with you and you have never been in want (Dt 2: 7). He fed you with manna. The clothing did not fall from you in tatters nor did your feet swell these forty years (Dt 8: 3-4). The Lord your God is bringing you into a good country, a land with streams of water, with springs and fountains welling up in the hills and valleys, a land of wheat and barley, of vines and fig trees and pomegranates, of olive trees and honey, a land where you can eat bread without stint and where you will lack nothing, a land whose stones contain iron and in whose hills you can mine copper' (Dt 8: 7-9). The memory of the 'way' of the exodus was recalled each year during the celebration of the Passover, the feast of the Tabernacles and the Pentecost, the three major festivals that were celebrated in the sanctuary of the Jerusalem Temple. Passover became the great national feast of Israel which celebrates its establishment as the chosen people of Yahweh. The feast of the Tabernacles is the festival of seven days with a carrying of palms and branches and the dwelling in booths made of leafy branches as commemoration of the desert sojourn of Israel. The Pentecost was celebrated fifty days later, after the celebration of Passover. A festival of the harvest, it became the celebration of the anniversary of the giving of the Law by God to the people of Israel through Moses. The prophets recalled the exodus experience to call upon the people of Israel to walk faithfully in the ways of Yahweh. For instance, the prophet Hosea reminded them saying, 'When Israel was a child, I loved him. Out of Egypt, I called my son' (Hos 11:1).

The Law as the way

While Israel was encamped in front of Mount Sinai, Moses went up the mountain to God and received the Law (Ex 24:12) as the bond of the covenant that God made with the people of Israel. Taking the book of the covenant, Moses read it aloud to the people, who answered, 'All that the Lord has said, we will heed and do'. Then Moses took the blood of the bulls, one half he splashed on the altar. The other half, he sprinkled on the people, saying: 'This is the blood of the covenant which the Lord has made with you in accordance with all the words of His' (Ex 24: 3-8). It was repeatedly made known to the people of Israel that the obligation to follow the Law flowed from the covenant. All Law was ultimately the will of Yahweh and became a part of covenant tradition. Following the Law is a religious duty that imposes a sacred obligation. The conception of Law as the revealed will of God is not paralleled in any other ancient Near Eastern collections. Indeed, following the Law as the sacred covenant obligation is unique to Israel. After arriving in the Promised Land, Israel had the obligation to continue 'journeying in the ways of the Lord' (Ps 128: 1), by following the Law.

Israel's knowledge of the ways of God, made known through the revelation of the Law, was a singular privilege granted to the chosen people. They must, therefore, faithfully 'walk' in the Law of the Lord: 'Happy those who walk by the teaching of the Lord and observe God's decrees. They do no wrong for they walk in God's ways' (Ps 119: 1-3). God had revealed to His people all the ways of understanding, identifying and following His 'ways', through the Law that endures forever: 'Such is our God. No other is to be compared to Him. He has traced out all the way of understanding and has given her to Jacob, his servant, to Israel, his beloved son' (Bar 3: 36-37). 'Blessed are we, O, Israel, for what pleases God is known to us' (Bar 4:4). Israel must obey the Law, because it is the way of God and thus the true way for Israel to always walk. In order to continue in the covenant and to progress toward light, peace, prosperity and life, Israel should not forsake the Law of Yahweh. The prophet Baruch exhorts the people of Israel to 'learn where the prudence, where strength and where understanding is; that you may know also where the length of days and life, where the light of the eyes and peace is- only in following the Law (Bar 3: 14). God Himself promises good life for walking in His ways: 'If you live in accordance with my precepts and be careful to observe my commandments, I will give rain in due season, so that the land will bear its crops and the trees their fruit. You will have food to eat in abundance so that you may dwell securely in your land. I will establish peace in the land that you may lie down to rest without anxiety' (Lev 26: 3-6).

Rejecting the way of the Lord

To disobey the Law is to turn toward destruction. The prophet Baruch asks the people of Israel in exile: 'How is it, Israel, that you are in the land of your foes, grown old in the foreign land, defiled with the dead, accounted with those destined for the nether world? You have forsaken the fountain of wisdom. Had you walked in the way of God, you would have dwelt in enduring peace' (Bar 3: 10-13). God Himself warns the people of Israel about forsaking the Law and suffering many evils as its consequence. The Lord said to Moses, 'They will forsake me and break the covenant which I have made with them. At that time, my anger will flare up against them. I will forsake them and hide my face from them so that they will become a prey to be devoured and many evils and troubles will befall them. At that time, they will indeed say, 'Is it not because our God is not among us that these evils have befallen us? (Dt 31: 16-17). The Lord warns also about returning to the desert, a way that would reverse the exodus: 'If you do not heed me and do not keep all the commandments, if you reject my precepts and spurn my decrees, refusing to obey my commandments and breaking my covenant, then I, in turn, will give you deserts. I will punish you with terrible woes. I will turn against you, till you are beaten down before your enemies and lorded over by your foes' (Lv 26: 14-17). However, God will not abandon His people for long. Once He purifies them and they make amends for their guilt, He will bring them back: 'I will not reject or spurn my people, lest, by wiping out, I make void my covenant with them, for I, the Lord, am their God' (Lv 26: 41-45). Walking back into the desert that is exile in foreign land and purified by the sufferings and hardships, Israel is comforted again: 'Comfort, give comfort to my people, speak tenderly to Jerusalem and proclaim to her that her servitude is at an end. Her guilt is expiated. In the desert, prepare the way of the Lord. Make straight in the wasteland a highway for our God' (Is 40: 1-3). 'They shall not hunger or thirst, nor shall the scorching wind or the sun strike them. For He who pities them leads them and guides them beside springs of water. Can a mother forget her infant, be without tenderness for the child of her womb? Even should she forget, I will never forget you. See, upon the palms of my hands, I have written your name. I will lift up my hand to the nations and raise my signal to the peoples. They shall bring your sons in their arms and your daughters shall be carried on their shoulders. All mankind shall know that I, the Lord, am your savior, your redeemer, the mighty one of Jacob' (Is 49: 10-26).

The ways of God and the ways of the wicked

As with the people of Israel in general, individuals have the responsibility to walk in the 'ways' of God. However, it is a free choice that man has to make between two ways, implying two kinds of moral conduct: the good way and the evil way. Man's way may be good, upright, righteous and perfect or evil, obstinate, lying and crooked. Faced with the two ways, man is free to choose and is responsible for his choice (Dt 30: 15-20). The just walk in the good way and the wicked walk in the evil way: 'God watches over the way of the just, but the way of the wicked leads to ruin' (Ps 1: 6). 'The path of the just is like shining light that grows in brilliance till perfect day. The way of the wicked is like darkness. They know not on what they stumble' (Pr 4: 18). The ways of God are not merely the ways of good conduct, but also they are the ways that lead to salvation. The righteous man keeps the ways of Yahweh, in observing the precepts of God. The way of the wicked is their wicked manners of life. God judges the wicked according to their evil ways and 'lay upon them the consequences of their abominations' (Ez 7: 8). The path of the wicked is crooked (Pr 21: 8), leading to foolishness (Pr 12:15) and sinful ways (Ps 1:1) and finally to disaster (Ps 1: 6) and to death (Pr12: 28): 'God, who alone probes the mind and tests the heart to reward everyone according to their ways and according to the merit of their deeds' (Jer 17:10) will repay the wicked for walking in the evil ways. However, God desires that the wicked should turn from his evil way and walk in the ways that He has made known in order to have the life that comes from Him: 'Do I indeed derive any pleasure from the death of the wicked?' says the Lord God. Do I not rather rejoice when he turns from evil way that he may live' (Ez 18: 23). That is why the

Psalmist brings hope to the sinners. Good and upright, forgiving and compassionate is the Lord who shows the sinners the way' (Ps 25: 8).

The way in the New Testament

Jesus teaches the way of God in accordance with the truth (Mk 12: 14) and that 'way', though narrow, certainly leads to life. On the contrary, the way that is broad leads to destruction, though many walk through it (Mt 7: 13-14). Comforting His disciples during the last supper, Jesus tells them: 'You know the way to the place where I am going' (Jn 14:4). Thomas objects and says to Jesus, 'Lord, we don't know where you are going, so how can we know the way?' (Jn 14: 5). Jesus makes use of this objection to make a profound pronouncement: 'I am the way, the truth, and the life' (Jn 14:6). The way of God is no longer the Law that God gave to the people of Israel through Moses, but the very Person of Jesus Christ: 'The Law was given through Moses, but grace and truth came through Jesus Christ' (Jn 1:17). In Him was life and that life was light of men (Jn 1: 4). Full of life and truth, the one and only Son of God also becomes the way for the entire humanity to reach the truth and the life. Commissioned by the risen Christ, the apostles 'preach the way to be saved' (Acts 16: 17) and they instruct the converts 'in the way of the Lord' (Acts 18: 25, 26). The most excellent way, according to Paul, is love (1 Cor 12: 31). While the apostles and those who follow their tradition are good teachers, the false teachers can misguide the believers to follow their own shameful ways and bring the way of truth into disrepute' (2 Pet 2: 1-2). 'It would have been better for them not to have known the way of righteousness than to have known it and then to turn their backs on the sacred command that was passed on to them' (2 Pet 2:21). The book of the Acts of the Apostles designates Christianity simply as 'the Way' (Acts 9:2). Paul admits to Felix, the governor: 'I admit that I worship the God of our fathers as a follower of the Way, which they call a sect' (Acts 24: 14). The early Christians saw their practice of Christian faith more than a set of propositions which could be taught or a code of moral principles that are to be followed. Rather, Christianity, according to them, was the revealed will of God operating in history through the person of Jesus Christ, who is the 'way' to salvation. As the author of the letter to the Hebrews tells us, 'we enter the Most Holy Place by the blood of Jesus, by a new and living way opened for us through the curtain, that is His body ' (Heb 10:19). Christianity is more than just a religious system. It is a way of life that is guided by the vision and the mission of Jesus Christ.

Personal reflection: 'Jesus, the way'

God freed the people of Israel from the slavery in Egypt and led them towards the Promised Land. Moses, chosen by God to be the leader and the guide of His people, presented the Law as the 'way' to the chosen people of God. In the messianic age of salvation

Jesus, the new Moses, is the guide, the escort and the leader of the people of the new Covenant. He freed us from the slavery of sin and death and is leading us to the Promised Land, the kingdom of heaven. He calls the entire humanity to follow Him (Mt 4:19) towards the eternal glory reserved for all God's children. However, the only way to the eternal glory is the way of the cross and so, it is necessary to stop first at Calvary. Jesus sets out resolutely for Jerusalem (Lk 9: 51) on a trip that ends with His supreme sacrifice on the cross. The 'way' of Jesus passes through the narrow path of the cross to reach the glory of the resurrection. Jesus asked the disciples of Emmaus, 'Did not the Christ have to suffer these things and then enter His glory? (Lk 24: 26). Following Jesus who is the 'way' is, first of all, becoming His disciple and leading an authentic Christian life in this world. We have to remember that Christian life does not consist merely in a series of outward observances or in simply avoiding certain things in life. Christian spirituality springs from the deepest attachment to the person of Jesus Christ. A true believer lives in Christ through the Spirit who molds his external actions as well as his interior dispositions. All his judgments, feelings, words and actions are guided by the Spirit who dwells in him. Above all, a Christian seeks to discover God's holy will, in the midst of changing conditions of this earthly life. It is Jesus, the 'way, truth and the life' that illumines his path, strengthen his spirit and guides him along, enabling him to lead holy life that is pleasing to God. Such a marvelous transformation in the life of the Christian can happen only when the believer surrenders his entire life to the person of Jesus. The development of intimacy with Jesus, through daily prayer, will lead to utmost proximity with Him, leading to a fruitful life that is pleasing to God.

God is with us, when Jesus is our way

We have to remember that man's heart is fickle. Perseverance for man is so terribly hard. It is difficult to keep one's faith and trust from wavering, when one stands face to face with stern reality. Bitter disappointment or frustration may bring discouragement in following Jesus. To be fervent is easy in the beginning and for a short while. What is important is to hold on till the end to our unshakable faith and unwavering trust in God. A strong faith in God is possible only when we are able to surrender our entire life in His loving hands. We may not have all the insights about the divine plan for us. But we do know that God rules the world and nothing happens without His permission. From heaven, His vision pierces all heights and fathoms all depths and nothing is hidden from His sight. He is almighty and infinitely wise and His divine power reaches from end to end, in time and space. His Providence, with a mighty yet gentle hand guides human destiny. There is no reason why human beings have to live in constant anxiety and fear. Ever alert to listen to the promptings of the Holy Spirit and ever determined to do our daily duties in this world, we walk trustingly in the ways of our heavenly Father without any fear for the future. Whatever may happen in the world or to each of us individually, if God is with us and we are with Him, we shall have the protection of His power and need to entertain no fear. The Psalm 91 is very meaningful to us as we choose to walk in the 'way' of God. 'Surely He will save you from the fowler's snare and from the deadly pestilence. He will cover you with His feathers and under His wings you will find refuge. No harm will befall you and no disaster will come near your tent. For, He will command His angels concerning you to guard you in all your ways' (Ps 91:3, 11). Indeed when Jesus is our 'way', it is God who walks with us.

Walking in the ways of God: Many years ago, there was a great famine in the Netherlands. The poor families suffered from lack of food. A rich man desired to feed the children in his village. He sent bread in a big basket for all the children that went to the school in the village. The children were pushing each other as they snatched the loaf of bread from the basket, though the rich man placed a loaf of bread for each child. The quarrel was about getting a bigger loaf. There was a little girl who stood patiently till all the rest got their share and then took the last little loaf in the basket. While the other children were busy eating their bread and had no time to thank the rich man, the little girl thanked him for the bread. The next day also the same thing happened. But when the little girl came home and her mother cut the loaf, she found six coins of silver. Prompted by the mother, the little girl ran back to give the money to the rich man. The rich man told her that it was the reward she received for being patient and also grateful. Like the rich man, God rewards us when we choose to walk in His way, though it is narrow.

Quote: Courage brother! Do not stumble! Though your path be dark as night, there is a star to guide the humble. Trust in God and do the right! - *Norman Macleod*

Scripture reading for Day 27: Lev 26: 1-35

Prayer for Day 27: O Lord, our God! Your anger lasts but a moment but your kindness and goodwill for a lifetime. You forgive the sinner and call the wicked to repentance and conversion. As we begin each day anew, be with us and guide us to walk in your ways. May your shoulders carry our burdens and enable us to look confidently at the uncertainties of our future always trusting your goodness and love for us! Amen.

28

TRUTH

*I*n Scripture, the word true is often used to describe what is eternal, heavenly and divine. When we examine the title of Jesus as the 'truth', we can not but remember the famous conversation between Jesus and the Roman Governor Pilate. Jesus said to Pilate: 'For this reason I was born, and for this I came into the world, to testify to the truth. Everyone on the side of the truth listens to me'. Pilate asked Jesus, 'What is truth?' (Jn 18: 37-38). The term 'truth' is used in various contexts in the Gospel of John who declares that 'grace and truth' came through Jesus Christ' (Jn 1:17). Speaking about the testimony of John the Baptist about His identity as the redeemer, Jesus says that John testified to the truth (Jn 5:33). Above all, we have the unforgettable statement of Jesus, 'I am the way, the truth and the life' (Jn 14: 6). Explaining the future role of the Holy Spirit, Jesus says, 'When the Spirit of truth comes, He will guide you into all truth' (Jn 16:13). The Greek word for truth is 'alêtheia' that signified the unveiled reality. Truth for the Greeks is reality as intellectually perceived and thus truth is something known rather than believed and trusted. In the Greek sense, something is true when it reveals itself clearly and evidently to the intellect. Hebrew vocabulary has no distinct word for 'true' and 'truth'. In Hebrew, the true is that to which one can give belief, whether it is a person or a thing. The foundation of the belief rests on the steadfast and unchanging character of the reality. It does not change upon testing or examination or stress. That is why it is reliable and will not betray the confidence. Seen in this sense, truth is something that demands personal commitment as the result of its trustworthiness and faithfulness rather than intellectual assent as the consequence of its perceptibility. For the Hebrews, truth is dependable and trustworthy as opposed to the lie that is undependable and spurious and hence can not be trusted. Seen in this way, for the Hebrews, truth is, above all, related to God's trustworthiness and fidelity.

Truth in the Old Testament

The Hebrew word for 'truth' is 'emet' and is formed from the word 'Aman' which means to be solid and stable and so reliable and it designated the one in whom or that in which one can trust. As an attribute of God, emeth is connected with covenant and its promise and refers to the trustworthiness and reliability of God. Yahweh is the trustworthy God. Moses tells the people of Israel: 'Understand that the Lord, your God, is God indeed, the faithful God who keeps His merciful covenant down to the thousand generation toward those who love Him and keep His commandments' (Dt 7: 9). 'A faithful God without deceit, just and upright He is' (Dt 32:4). Old Testament sees Yahweh's trustworthiness in the context of the covenant and the promises that He made to the people of Israel. Also, Yahweh's truthfulness (emet) is inseparable from His loving kindness (hesed). Yahweh is 'rich in loving-kindness (hesed) and fidelity (emeth) and He keeps loving kindness (hesed) for a thousand generations' (Ex 34: 6-7). The entire eighty-ninth psalm is devoted to the praise of God's loyalty with reference to the promise He made to David about establishing his dynasty forever: 'Lord, God of hosts, who is like you? Mighty Lord, your loyalty is always present' (Ps 89: 9). The psalmist praises Yahweh especially for 'His fidelity and love' (Ps 138: 2). Yahweh's faithfulness is joined to justice. After the return from exile, Ezra prays to God saying, 'Now, O, our God, great, mighty, and awesome God, you who in your mercy preserve the covenant! In all that has come upon us you have been just, for you kept faith while we have done evil' (Neh 9: 32-33). That is why Yahweh's fidelity is a source of protection and support for the just man seeking divine help since 'God's faithfulness is a protecting shield' (Ps 91: 4). The psalmist prays, 'Lord, do not withhold your compassion from me; may your enduring kindness ever preserve me' (Ps 40:12). Since God is always faithful to His promises, His words are true. Remembering the promise of Yahweh regarding the perpetuity of his dynasty, David expresses his confidence in the words of Yahweh saying, 'Lord God, you are God and your words are truth; you have made this generous promise to your servant' (2 Sm 7: 28). In keeping with the fidelity of God, His words, as revealed in the Law, are true: 'The statutes of the Lord are true, all of them just' (Ps 19:10).

To walk in the truth

Men walk the way of truth when they serve God in faithfulness. Hezekiah, the king, 'who did what was good, upright and faithful before the Lord, His God' (2 Chr 31:20), makes his prayer to God for healing in the time of his grave illness: 'O Lord, remember how faithfully and wholeheartedly I conducted myself in your presence, doing what was pleasing to you' (2 Kgs 20: 3). Also, an Israelite is true and virtuous, when he follows the Law of the Lord faithfully: 'If he lives by my statutes and is careful to observe my ordinances, that man is virtuous- he shall surely live' says the Lord God' (Ez 18: 8). In some instances, the Law was called as the truth: 'Guide me in your truth and teach me for you are God my savior' (Ps 25: 5). In the Wisdom literature, wisdom becomes synonymous with the truth: 'Get the truth and sell it not- wisdom, instruction and understanding' (Prv 23: 23). Those who trust in God shall understand the truth (Wis 3:9). God's plan for the world is written in the 'Book of Truth' (Dn 10: 21). The Jewish religion as the revealed religion of the one true God is also called as 'truth' (Dn 8:12).

Truth in the New Testament

Jesus is known as a teacher who instructs the people in the way of God in accordance with the truth: 'The Pharisees and the Herodians spoke to Jesus saying, 'Teacher, you are a man of integrity and that you teach the way of God in accordance with the truth' (Mt 22:16; Lk 20:21). It is in the gospel according to John that we have a profound presentation on the meaning of truth. For John, it is Jesus who is the truth: 'I am the Way, the Truth and the Life' (Jn 14:6). Jesus is the way that leads to the Father, precisely because as the Truth, He communicates the divine revelation of the Father to the world leading to the divine Life in those who believe in Him. Jesus is the Truth, precisely because He is the eternal Word, 'the Word who is nearest to the Father's heart' (Jn 1:18) as the one and the only Son. For the people of Israel, the Law was the truth in so far as it made known to them the holy will of Yahweh. However, in God's plan, 'the Law was put in charge to lead us to Christ' (Gal 3:24), the fullness of truth and life. 'The Law was given through Moses. Grace and truth came through Jesus Christ' (Jn 1:17). In Jesus, the Law finds completion and fulfillment (Mt 5: 17). Jesus tells the truth that He heard from the Father (Jn 8: 40). The devil is the father of lies, as there is no truth in him (Jn 8: 44). Jesus declares the truth (Jn 8: 45), because He is full of grace and of truth (Jn 1: 14). According to John, it is God's word that is truth (Jn 17: 17). God's eternal Word became flesh and dwelt among us (Jn 1:14) in the person of Jesus Christ. Then, only in the person of Jesus Christ, that truth is revealed to us. Everyone who is on the side of truth listens to Jesus (Jn 18:37) and so he shall not perish but have eternal life (Jn 3: 16), because Jesus is the true light (Jn 1:9) and the true food (Jn 6:55) for eternal life: 'Whoever lives by the truth comes into the light' (Jn 3:21).

The Holy Spirit is called the Spirit of truth. Jesus says, 'I will ask the Father and He will give you another Counselor to be with you forever- the Spirit of truth' (Jn 14: 16-17). 'When the Counselor comes, whom I will send to you from the Father, the Spirit of truth who goes out from the Father, He will testify about me' (Jn 15: 26). 'When He, the Spirit of truth, comes, He will guide you into all truth' (Jn 16:13). Led by the Spirit of truth, 'the believers, as true worshipers, can worship God in spirit and truth, for they are the kind of worshipers, the Father seeks. God is spirit and His worshipers must worship in spirit and truth' (Jn 4: 23-24). Guided by the Spirit, the believers walk in the truth. John states, 'It has given me great joy to find some of your children walking in the truth, just as the Father commanded us' (2 Jn 4). 'It gave me great joy to have some brothers come and tell about your faithfulness to the truth and how you continue to walk in the truth (3 Jn 3). John states further that only by loving one another in the Spirit, we walk in the truth: 'Let us not love with words or tongue but with actions and in truth. This then is how we know that we belong to the truth' (1 Jn 3: 18-19). Only when we are truthful to God, by being steadfast, loyal and faithful to Him, we shall be able to love and serve one another as the children of God.

The Gospel as the truth

The Jews prided themselves on possessing the explicit formulation of the truth in their Law where they found the entire will of God recorded for them. For the Jewish expression the truth of the Law, Paul substitutes 'the truth of the gospel' or 'the word of truth': 'Faith, love and hope that you have already heard about in the word of truth, the gospel that has come to you. All over the world, this gospel is bearing fruit and growing, just as it has been doing among you since the day you heard it and understood God's grace in all its truth' (Col 1: 5-6). 'You heard the word of truth, the gospel of your salvation' (Eph 1:13). The gospel is 'the revelation of mystery, hidden for long ages past, but now revealed and made known through the prophetic writings by the command of the eternal God so that all nations might believe and obey Him' (Rom 16: 25-26). At the end of age, 'the unbelievers perish because they refused to love the truth and be saved' (2 Thes 2:10) by rejecting the Gospel. Faith is acceptance of the truth of the gospel and arriving at the knowledge of the truth: 'From the beginning God chose you to be saved through the sanctifying work of the Spirit and through the belief in the truth' (2 Thes 2:13). 'Arriving at the knowledge of truth' becomes a stereotyped expression for adhering to the gospel and embracing Christian faith. Believers are precisely those who know the truth (1 Tim 4: 3). The apostles are servants of God commissioned to preach the knowledge of the truth, that is the gospel: 'A servant of God and an apostle of Jesus Christ for the faith of God's elect and the knowledge of the truth that leads to godliness' (Ti 1:1). The believers must not stray from the truth of the gospel once they accept it (Jas 5:19), because through the gospel 'they are firmly established in the truth' (2 Pt 1:12). Those who teach false doctrines and not the gospel of Christ have wandered away from the truth' (2 Tim 2:18), 'oppose the truth' (2 Tim 3:8), 'turn away from the truth' (2 Tim 4: 4) and 'reject the truth' (Ti 1:14). Knowing the truth leads to the practice of fraternal love: 'Now that you have purified yourselves by obeying the truth so that you have sincere love for your brothers, love one another deeply from the heart. For, you have been born again, not of the perishable seed but of imperishable, through the living and enduring word of God' (1 Pt 1: 22-23).

Personal Reflection - 'Jesus, the truth'

For the Christians, the 'truth' is the eternal Word of the Father, present in Jesus Christ and illuminated by the Spirit, now proclaimed as the gospel. We must welcome the gospel as good news in faith, so that it may transform our lives as new creation and lead us to eternal life. As the incarnation of the eternal Word, Jesus is both the mediator and the fullness of truth. As Paul states, 'Jesus Christ is the truth and the truth is in Him' (Eph 4: 21). Jesus told those who believed in Him, 'If you hold to my teaching, you are really my disciples. Then you will know the truth and the truth will set you free' (Jn 8:31-32). As the object of human knowledge, truth refers not merely to correct understanding of facts but to God's revelation. Faith gives assent to the truth that can lead to the liberty of the children of God. Freed from the bondage of sin and death, man becomes the heir to the eternal kingdom in Jesus Christ through the Holy Spirit. Truth is different from fact in the biblical sense. Human knowledge seeks the certutitude of the facts for the earthly affairs of mankind. Science and mathematics assure humanity this certitude of facts through experimentation and verification. Man has so many questions about the ultimate concerns of life such as the destiny of man and the salvation of humanity. However, a finite being as he is, man cannot answer questions with certitude about his destiny, eternity and above all, about God. The divine is in a way 'hidden' from man who can get only a glimpse of the eternal and everlasting God through the divine manifestation in the nature. The nature reveals God as creator and lord of nature. As per the conviction of Israel, while other religious traditions received only the glimpses of divine glory through divine manifestation in nature, Israel alone was privileged to experience the one true God as the master of history who intervened on behalf of the people of Israel to save them and guide them.

Israel experiences divine revelation

A fundamental characteristic of the experience of Israel about Yahweh is that He is a living God. The vigor and vitality of Yahweh is perceived in His words and actions that together constitute His self-manifestation or revelation. Even if man is a free agent who may accept or reject God's offer of salvation, yet Yahweh directs the history of the world and the destiny of humanity as the Lord and Savior. The first experience of the power of Yahweh for Israel is the direct intervention of Yahweh in favor of Israel against the Egyptians. From the liberating experience of Exodus, the people of Israel see Yahweh as the God of creation, who brought order from chaos and established the universe in it's place. All the peoples of the earth can also experience, like the people of Israel, the self-manifestation of God in nature and in history. But, God reveals Himself to the people of Israel in a very special way, through election and covenant. Of course, this revelation of God was to be communicated to all the nations and to all the peoples through the people of Israel that was chosen by God to be the light to all the nations. The prophet Isaiah speaks of the universal mission of Israel saying, 'In days to come, the mountain of the Lord's house shall be established as the highest mountain and raised above the hills. All nations shall stream toward it. Many peoples shall come and say, Come, let us climb the Lord's mountain, to the house of the God of Jacob, that He may instruct us in His ways and we may walk in His paths' (Is 2: 2-3).

What is very special about the divine revelation to Israel is that, unlike to other peoples who saw only His actions in nature and history, God spoke His 'word' as truth to Israel and His truth was communicated to Israel in a triple stream at the head of which stands Moses. The first of the stream is Law that revealed the covenant will of Yahweh as the truth. In Law, truth was codified in writing and the priests interpreted the codified Law to reveal the holy will of Yahweh to the people of Israel. The second stream is prophecy. The prophet is sent by God to interpret the present events and tell the plan of Yahweh for the future thus revealing the holy will of God to the people of Israel. The third stream is wisdom. The wisdom literature does not deal with the cosmic and historical events and speak of the will of God for the entire people of Israel as the Law and the prophets have done. Rather, the wisdom literature gives guidance to the individual behavior and manifests the holy will of Yahweh to the individual Israelite. What we find in this triple stream of revelation is the 'truth' that Yahweh communicates to the people of Israel as a community of God and to the individual Israelite as the servant and the child of God in order to guide them to walk in His ways. The revelation of God through the Law, the Prophets and the Wisdom literature is not a knowledge to be known by human intelligence, but the 'truth' that has to be received in faith and to be followed in total submission as the holy will of Yahweh.

The fullness of divine revelation in Jesus who is the truth

In Jesus, the 'Word' of God itself comes down as the fullness of divine revelation. The author of the letter to the Hebrews says: 'In the past, God spoke to our forefathers through the prophets at many times and in various ways, but in these last days, He has spoken to us by His Son, whom He appointed heir of all things and through whom He made the universe' (Heb 1:1-2). Jesus Himself implies this meaning when He says: 'Blessed are your eyes because they see and your ears because they hear. For I tell you the truth, many prophets and righteous men longed to see what you see but did not see it and to hear what you hear but did not hear it' (Mt 13: 16-17). Jesus asserts that He is the full revelation of the heavenly Father as His one and only Son: 'All things have been committed to me by my Father. No one knows who the Son is except the Father and no one knows who the Father is except the Son and to those to whom the Son chooses to reveal Him' (Mt 11: 27; Lk 10:22). In Jesus, the revelation of the Old Testament reaches its fullness (Mt 5: 17-18). Thus, Jesus Himself becomes the 'truth' of divine revelation for the salvation of mankind (Jn 14:6). He is not only the truth, but also the revealer and the communicator of the truth to the world. The Holy Spirit, whom Jesus would send, would teach the believers all the truth that Jesus has: 'The Spirit of truth will guide you into all truth. He will not speak on His own. He will speak only what He hears and He will tell you what is to come. He will bring glory to me by taking from what is mine and making it known to you. All that belongs to the Father is mine. That is why I said, the Spirit will take from what is mine and make it known to you' (Jn 16: 13-15). Now, Jesus Christ, the incarnate 'Word of God', is proclaimed as the Gospel to the entire humanity. The Gospel becomes the 'truth' because, 'it is not something man made up, but received by revelation from Jesus Christ' (Gal 1:12). In biblical sense, 'truth' is truth of salvation that is passed to us in the sacred books, beginning with the Law, the Prophets and the Wisdom literature in the Old

Testament and finding fulfillment in the person of Jesus and now proclaimed by the Church as the gospel or the good news of Jesus Christ. Let us receive the truth in faith and let it transform our lives through love.

You are a person I can trust: Once a hunter lost his way in the forest and asked the shepherd boy who was tending his sheep nearby for the route to return to his town. The shepherd boy replied that it was a difficult route and he needed assistance not to be lost in the forest. The hunter promised to pay him huge money if he would leave the sheep for sometime and come with him to show the way. The shepherd boy replied that he could not leave his sheep alone because of the wolves who might attack the sheep and that his employer trusted him to take care of the sheep. When the friends of the hunter came in search of him, the shepherd boy understood that he was indeed talking to the prince of his country. After a couple of days, the prince offered the shepherd boy a good job in his palace, in appreciation of his dependability, loyalty and dedication to his work. The shepherd boy, after he found someone to take care of the sheep went to the palace and served the prince with the same trustworthiness and dependability with which he tended his sheep. We receive Jesus as the truth because he is trustworthy and dependable, always faithful and loyal to those who trust in Him.

Quote: To your own self, be true and it must follow as the night the day. You can not be, then, false to any man - ***William Shakespeare***

Scripture reading for Day 28: Jn 8: 31- 47

Prayer for the Day 28: Heavenly Father, we thank you for the gift of your Son who is the truth and the Holy Spirit who is the Spirit of truth. Grant us a humble and docile heart to receive and be instructed by the Spirit of truth that is dwelling within us. By surrendering our lives in faith to the truth of the Gospel of your Son, may we be found worthy to see you face to face! Amen.

29

VINE

When Jesus said, 'I am the vine and you are the branches' (Jn 15: 5), His Jewish disciples would have clearly understood that He was calling Himself and the disciples as the New Israel. Over and over again, in the Old Testament, Israel was presented as the vine or the vineyard of God. Hence, the Jews saw the vine as the symbol of their nation. The Jerusalem temple was adorned with a large golden vine resplendent with valuable gemstones as fruit. When the rays of the sun reflected on the golden vine, it illuminated the temple. Archaeologists have discovered ancient Jewish coins minted with the design of the vine and the branches. Jews proudly called themselves as God's vineyard. Using the well-known symbol that stood for the nation of Israel, Jesus declares, 'I am the true vine' (Jn 15:1). True means what is divine, heavenly and eternal. God established Israel as His messenger to the world for a certain period of time and took care of her like a gardener. Jesus implies that the time has come for Him to replace the temporary and earthly vine that is Israel, with Himself as the eternal vine in whom the new community of God will be united, nourished and supported as the branches.

Vine in the Old Testament

Noah was the first to plant a vineyard (Gn 9:20). Palestine was full of vineyards and the product of the vine was a blessing from God: 'O Lord, you bring wine to gladden our hearts' (Ps 104: 15). The lack of wine is a curse from God. When the people of Israel fail to observe the commandments of God, 'they may plant a vineyard, but will not enjoy its fruits' (Dt 28:30). 'They will not drink or store up the wine, for the grubs will eat the vines clean' (Dt 28: 39). Vine was one of those crops that is so completely dependent on the careful and skillful attention of the workers and on the rhythm of the season. The ground must be cleared of stones and terraced. The vineyard was secured against the damaging animals by an enclosing wall or hedge. Sometimes, a watchtower was built for additional protection. After all the hard work that it required, the vine was worth only in the fruits, as the branches were good only for the fire. There are so many references in the Old Testament, portraying Israel as the vine or God's vineyard. Prophet Isaiah portrays Israel as God's vineyard. God gave utmost care to the vineyard, but at the harvest time, He found nothing but sour grapes. God had done all that was required to make Israel bear fruit, yet it bore none. So He took away its wall and left it unprotected. As a result, tt was trampled down by foreign nations and laid waste. God says, 'What more was there to do for my vineyard that I had not done? Why, when I looked for the crop of grapes, did it bring forth wild grapes? Now I will let you know what I mean to do with my vineyard. Take away its hedge, give it to grazing, break through its wall, let it be trampled! Yes, I will make it a ruin. It shall not be pruned or hoed, but overgrown with thorns and briers. I will command the clouds not to send rain upon it' (Is 5: 4-6). The prophet concludes, 'The vineyard of the Lord of hosts is the house of Israel' (Is 5: 7).

Through the prophet Jeremiah God demands Israel: 'I had planted you a choice vine of fully tested stock. How could you turn out obnoxious to me, a spurious vine?' (Jer 2:21). Through prophet Ezekiel God states, 'Like the wood of the vine, which is destined as fuel for fire, do I make the inhabitants of Jerusalem' (Ez 15: 6). 'Israel was like a vine, planted by the water. Fruitful and branchy was she because of the abundant water. She was torn up in fury and flung to the ground. The east wind withered her up, her fruit was torn off. Then her strong branch withered up, fire devoured it' (Ez 19: 10-14). The psalmist prays to God to restore His favor to Israel: 'You brought a vine out of Egypt. You drove away the nations and planted it. You cleared the ground. It took root and filled the land. Why have you broken down the walls so that all who pass by pluck its fruit? Turn again, Lord of hosts, look down from heaven and see. Attend to this vine, the shoot your right hand has planted. Lord of hosts, restore us; let your face shine upon us that we may be saved' (Ps 80: 9-20). God promises to restore His favor: 'On that day, I, the Lord is the keeper of the pleasant vineyard. I water it every moment. Lest anyone harm it, night and day I guard it. In days to come Jacob shall take root, Israel shall sprout and blossom covering all the earth with fruit' (Is 27: 2-6). In Jesus Christ, the true vine and the believers as the branches, God, the gardener, fulfills His promise to establish a pleasant vineyard.

The vine in the New Testament

Jesus summarizes salvation history through the parable of the tenants (Mk 12: 1-8). Rather than receiving the message of the prophets and turn back to walk in the ways of God, the people of Israel ill-treated their prophets and rejected their message. Finally, God sent His only son, calling the chosen people to conversion. They not only rejected Him but handed Him over to the Romans to be crucified. The Son's death on the cross opens a new chapter in the salvation history: 'The kingdom of God will be taken away from the people of Israel and be given to people who will produce its fruit' (Mt 21: 43). Through the parable of two sons (Mt 21: 28-31), Jesus points out that the only criterion to be a worthy son of God is fruitful work. Through the parable of the workers in the vineyard (Mt 20: 1-16), Jesus insists that God gathers the workers for the vineyard as it pleases Him. The call to work in the Lord's vineyard is a gratuitous gift and no man can claim his reward as his right.

Jesus Christ, the true vine

In the hands of Jesus, during the last supper, wine, the fruit of the vine, became the symbol for His blood to be shed to seal the new covenant (Mt 26: 27-29). During that Passover meal, Jesus presents Himself, together with the disciples, as the true Israel that would give abundant fruit as desired by the Father (Jn 15:1). He also describes the special intimacy that exists between Himself and His disciples: 'I am the vine and you are the branches' (Jn 15:5). Jesus describes His relationship to His Father, referred to as the cultivator. God, the Father, removes any branches emanating from Jesus, which do not bear any fruit. God also prunes those branches which bear fruit so that the fruitage is made more abundant. The branches represent Jesus' disciples. These branches bear great fruitage only when they remain united to the true vine that is Jesus. When these branches remain cut off from the true vine, they become incapable of bearing any fruit. Indeed they become dry and inevitably die as the result of being cut off from their source of nourishment. The life of a Christian is the same. If Christians drift away from Jesus, who is the source of everlasting life, then they will also lose their spiritual life and will be dead spiritually. The disciples have to abide in Jesus in order to bear much fruit in this world. Otherwise they will be cut off from Him and remain fit only for burning (Jn 15:5-8). Jesus firmly insists: 'Apart from me, you can do nothing' (Jn 15:5). He makes it clear that a very close relationship between the community of believers and Himself is very essential in order that they may truly lead an authentic Christian life that is fully pleasing to God, our Father. Christ unambiguously presents Himself as the very life of His community: 'If a man remains in me and I in him, he will bear much fruit' (Jn 15:5). He also warns that 'if anyone does not remain in me, he is like a branch that is thrown away and withers; such branches are picked up, thrown into the fire and burned' (Jn 15:6).

The vine and the branches

How can Christians remain in union with Jesus, the true vine? Jesus gives the answer. 'As the Father has loved me, so have I loved you. Now, remain in my love. If you obey my commandments, you will remain in my love, just as I have obeyed my Father's commands and remain in His love' (Jn 15: 9-10). Clearly, a Christian is required to observe the commandments of Jesus Christ in order to remain in union with Jesus and to remain in His love. There is a direct correlation between the way in which Christians are rooted in Christ and the fruitage they bear. When we are firmly attached to Jesus, our lives will be nourished by the Holy Spirit and we will thereby produce much fruitage. The secret of fruit-bearing in a natural vine is having an adequate supply of sap. If the connection between the branch and the stem of the vine is not solid, the sap cannot freely flow to the branch. Jesus is using this analogy to illustrate the oft-repeated concept of abiding in Christ and having Christ abide in His followers. The branches that do not bear fruit are removed and burned in the fire. On the contrary, by bearing fruit, the disciples are assured of being with Jesus in the heavenly kingdom forever. Reminding this assurance of Jesus, Paul writes to the Ephesians: 'I pray that out of His glorious riches, the Father may strengthen you with power through His Spirit in your inner being, so that Christ may dwell in your hearts through faith. And I pray that, being rooted and established in love, you may have the power together with all the saints, to grasp how wide and long and high and deep is the love of Christ and to know that this love surpasses all knowledge- that you may be filled to the measure of all the fullness of God' (Eph 3:16-19).

The fruit of the Spirit - love

Paul states further that 'the fruit of the Spirit is love, joy, peace, patience, kindness, goodness, faithfulness, gentleness and self-control' (Gal 5: 22- 23). The word 'fruit' is a singular word but this fruit of the Spirit is displayed in nine different forms that are progressively attained. All virtues begin with love. That is why, Paul would say, 'Follow the way of love' (1 Cor 14:1). From the beginning to the end of New Testament, the love of the neighbor seems to be inseparable from the love of God. Jesus proposed them together as the way to inherit eternal life. He said, 'Love the Lord your God with all your heart and with all your soul and with all your strength and with all your mind and 'love your neighbor as yourself' (Lk 10:27). He demonstrated that fraternal love has to be revealed in humble service by washing the feet of the disciples. They had already seen, during His public ministry, how He was always moved with compassion for all in need. The apostles would witness the sacrificial love that Jesus had shown for humanity by sacrificing His life on the cross. They would see a new dimension of sacrificial love, a love that would lead one to die for those He loved. The human family did not deserve such a sacrifice from God's one and only Son. Paul expresses this fact so well: 'God demonstrates His own love for us in this: While we were still sinners, Christ died for us' (Rom 5:8). Jesus says to the disciples, 'My command is this. Love each other as I have loved you. Greater love has no one than this that he lay down his life for his friends. You are my friends if you do what I command' (Jn 15: 12-14). Now, love of Christ continues to be expressed in the world through the fraternal goodness and charity that the followers of Christ manifest within the Christian community. Jesus states: 'A new command I give you: Love one another. As I loved you, so you must love one another. By this all men will know that you are my disciples, if you love one another' (Jn 13: 34-35).

Joy, peace and patience

It is love that leads to joy. Obeying the command of Jesus by loving one another leads to the joy of the believer: 'If you obey my commands and remain in my love, my joy may be in you and that your joy may be complete' (Jn 15: 10-11). Joy, in turn, leads the believer to peace which is the state of the man who lives in harmony with nature, with himself and above all with God. This harmony comes by the complete surrender of one's life in God's hands in love and trust. Jesus assures peace to his disciples with the confidence of victory over sin and evil. He says 'Peace I leave with you; my peace I give you. I do not give to you as the world gives. Do not let your hearts be troubled and do not be afraid' (Jn 14:27). Peace, in turn, leads to patience. Any patience we show can never be equal to what the Lord has shown. Patience is required of the believer who is devoted to do the will of the Lord in daily life. Paul urges the Ephesians: 'I urge you to live a life worthy of the calling you have received. Be completely humble and gentle. Be patient, bearing with one another in love' (Eph 4: 2). It is patience that enables us 'to get rid of all bitterness, rage and anger, brawling and slander, along with every form of malice' (Eph 4:31) and in this way, with a good heart, to forgive others. By being patient, kind, compassionate and forgiving others, we can show true goodness and kindness to others: 'Be kind and compassionate to one another, forgiving each other, just as in Christ God forgave you' (Eph 4: 32).

Goodness and kindness

The next fruit is goodness. It is God who is perfectly good and hence goodness is present in a man only when he is with God who imparts goodness to his heart, leading in turn to generosity and sharing. Paul advises Timothy, 'Command them to do good, to be rich in good deeds and to be generous and willing to share' (1 Tim 6: 18). Paul also tells Titus, 'I want you to stress these things so that those who have trusted in God may be careful to devote themselves to doing what is good' (Ti 3: 8). The next fruit is faithfulness. Fidelity or faithfulness is an attribute of God that is manifested fully in Jesus Christ. Paul tells Thessalonians: 'The one who calls you is faithful' (1 Thes 5: 24). He further states, 'God who has called you into fellowship with His Son, Jesus Christ our Lord, is faithful' (1 Cor 1: 9). A believer is faithful, who holds fast in the faith, through the test of time. The next fruit is gentleness. Paul insists that 'the servant of the Lord must not quarrel, but be gentle unto all men, able to teach, not resentful' (2 Tim 2:24). Paul himself showed this caring gentleness to the Thessalonians: 'We were gentle among you, like a mother caring for her little children' (1 Thes 2:7). The last fruit is named as self-control, which is maintaining control over our passions and desires. We have to behave like the free children of God who has set us free from sin through Jesus Christ. Paul tells Galatians, 'Stand firm, then, and do not let yourselves be burdened again by a yoke of slavery' (Gal 5:1). Only if we remain in Christ and let His graces nourish us, we can bear the fruit of the Spirit that is revealed in the practice of the above explained nine virtues.

Personal reflection- 'Jesus is the vine and we are the branches'

In first-century Palestine, vinedressers removed shoots in several ways. Sometimes the tip was pinched off so the shoot would grow more slowly. Larger branches were pruned to prevent them from becoming too long and weak. In our spiritual lives too, pruning is, at times, necessary. God prunes us with a vinedresser's knife as He permits us face suffering and hardships. Sometimes it hurts badly and we wonder if He knows what He is doing. It may seem to us that we are the only branches getting pruned, while other branches, it may appear to us, need it more than us. But the Vinedresser knows what He is doing. Spiritual pruning can take many forms. It may be sickness, hardships or loss of material possessions. It may be persecution or slander. For some it is the loss of a loved one or grief in a relationship or it may be a combination of several difficult and sorrowful situations. Pruning is never comfortable, but it leads us to bear more fruit in the end. In the case of believers, becoming a more profound and dedicated Christian will be the outcome. Whatever the method of pruning God uses, we can be assured that He cares about us and wants us to bear much fruit. He continues His care throughout our lives to keep us spiritually healthy and productive. Knowing the Father's love and concern for us should change the way we look at trials. He does not allow us to experience problems and struggles for no purpose. The problems He permits are designed to develop fortitude and strength so that we can bear more fruit. He prunes us because He loves us.

There are times when cares of the world distract us from our relationship with God. We desperately need to let go of the preoccupations and unworthy attractions. God will at times intervene to prune away our distractions. This pruning is called as 'the testing of faith'. James says, 'Consider it pure joy, my brothers, whenever you face trials of many kinds, because you know that the testing of your faith develops perseverance. Perseverance must finish its work so that you may be mature and complete, not lack anything' (Jas 1: 3-4). God's pruning action makes room in our lives for God: 'We know that in all things God works for the good of those who love Him, who have been called according to His purpose' (Rom 8: 28). If we remember that God is trying to make us more fruitful, we can look past the the painful pruning process to the final goal of bearing abundant fruit. The author of the letter to the Hebrews encourages us to have a proper perspective on God's perfecting process: 'Endure hardship as discipline. God is treating you as sons. For what son is not disciplined by his father? God disciplines us for our good that we may share in His holiness. No discipline seems pleasant at the time but painful. Later on, however, it produces a harvest of righteousness and peace for those who have been trained by it' (Heb 12: 7-11). The Father uses affliction only to make us more responsive to His grace thereby to bear much fruit in our lives as the children of God. Jesus states, 'If you remain in me and my words remain in you, ask whatever you wish, and it will be given you' (Jn 15:7). What an assurance of goodness, compassion, trustworthiness and abundant generosity from Jesus, if only we totally remain with Him! It seems like more than anyone could ever hope for. The vine provides all nourishment. Jesus is the source of all spiritual strength and nourishment. When He is united to us, we may ask the heavenly Father for our needs in all confidence and trust.

Jesus was a master teacher. He used ordinary things and ordinary experiences of life to express extraordinary and eternal truths. Jesus' disciples could easily understand Jesus' use of the symbol of the vine and the branches, pruning and fruit-bearing. The heavenly mystery is taught by the earthly vine in the teaching of Jesus wqho presented Himself as the true vine. Jesus is not saying that Israel was a false vine. What He means is that He is the true vine of which the nation of Israel was a symbol. It is He who will produce at last the fruit that God was looking throughout the history of salvation, the true vine, in whom both the Jews and the Gentiles would be united together as branches. The Jews, as the chosen people of God, preserve their definite place in the plan of salvation. In Jesus, both Jews and the Gentiles are brought together as the branches in the true vine, Jesus Christ. Jesus declares, 'My Father is the gardener'. The Greek word is 'georgos' which means 'earth worker'. It is from this Greek word that we get the name 'George'. Our heavenly Father is the gardener who takes care of the vine and the branches in His vineyard. In the loving hands of our heavenly Father, we are happy and safe.

The happy man: Once there was a king who wanted to find a happy man. In spite of his power and riches, he was always sad. An astrologer told him that if he wears the shirt of a happy man, he will find happiness. That is why the king was so eager to find a man of contentment. So, the king sent forth his messengers. They rode far and wide throughout the kingdom and nowhere could they find a happy man. No one seemed content and everyone had some complaint. If a man was rich, he never had enough. If he was not rich, it was someone's fault. If he was healthy, he had a bad wife. If he had a good wife, he was sick. One night, as the messengers were passing by a small cottage, they heard someone pray in contentment: 'O Lord, thank you for the day! I have finished my daily labor. I have helped my neighbors. Now, I can sleep peacefully'. The messengers were glad that at last they found a happy man, but they could not get his shirt, for he had none. For our happiness, it is just one thing that matters. If we are united to Christ, we have everything. Without Him, we have nothing.

Quote: The saints of God in heaven might have had their trials too on earth - failing health, declining years, the ingratitude of men - but they have endured as bearing for Him who is invisible- ***Benjamin Jowett***

Scripture reading for Day 29:Jn 15: 1-17

Prayer for Day 29: O God of strength! We can be hard pressed and falling, but you are at our side to help us and guide us. May we be always united to your Son Jesus Christ in love and faith as the branches are in the vine! May He be the source of our peace and joy, strength and courage as we journey towards your kingdom! Amen.

KING

30.

<h1 align="center">KING</h1>

The inscription on the cross of Jesus read: 'Jesus of Nazareth, king of the Jews' (Jn 19:19). During His trial, before the crucifixion, Pilate asks Jesus, 'Are you the king of the Jews? (Jn 18:33). Jesus does not reject the title, but He clarifies that His 'kingdom is not of this world' (Jn 18: 36). 'Are you king, then!' asked Pilate. Jesus answered, 'You are right in saying that I am a king' (Jn 18:39). In the gospel according to Mark, Jesus answers, 'Yes, it is as you say' (Mk 15: 2). All the gospels, though they present Jesus as the messianic king, insist that the kingship of Jesus is not political but spiritual and eschatological. The different order of His kingship and the paradox associated with it is best seen in what takes place during His passion and crucifixion: after the scourging, the soldiers mockingly saluted Him as the king of the Jews (Mk 15: 18). The chief priests, the teachers of the law and the elders were deriding Him mocking His royalty: 'He is the King of Israel! Let Him come down now from the cross, and we will believe in Him' (Mt 27: 42; Lk 23: 37). Pilate himself presented Jesus to the Jews who had Jesus arrested and set up for trial: 'Behold your King!' (Jn 19: 14). Pilate attempted to reason with the mad mob by asking them, 'Shall I crucify your King?' (Jn 19: 15). In connection with the crucifixion, Pilate wrote a title and placed it on the cross and the writing was, 'Jesus of Nazareth, the King of the Jews' (Jn 19: 19). When the Jews wanted the title changed, Pilate refused to make any change (Jn 19: 21-22). Seeing the divinity in Jesus, the good thief prayed, 'Jesus, remember me when you come into your kingdom' (Lk 23: 42). The nature of Jesus' royalty and His kingship shines out on the cross if we can see things from the viewpoint of faith. In order to understand the full significance of the title of Jesus as king, let us first examine kingship in the Old Testament.

Kingship in the Old Testament -Yahweh as the King of Israel

In the ancient Orient, the royalty was considered as divine, an idea common to many civilizations in the history of the world. In Egypt, the reigning Pharaoh was seen as an incarnation of god Horus and all his acts were, therefore, viewed as divine by nature. In Babylon, the king was honored as the representative of god Marduk who designated him to the rule of the 'four regions' that means the entire earth. As divine representative, the king was both civil and military head as well as the high priest. Later, under the influence of the Orient, the Greek and Roman emperors were also honored as gods on earth and were offered cultic worship. The king not only had to assure justice, victory, and peace in

216

his kingdom but also mediate all divine blessings, including the fertility of the earth and the fecundity of both man and beast. Naturally, the king functioned as the center of the cult for the gods.

To the people of Israel, Yahweh alone reigns for ever in heaven and on earth as the one true God. He reigns over all the nations. Hence the conception of the kings as divine incarnation or mediators as viewed in other civilizations was a practice of idolatry to Israel. Prophet Jeremiah declares, 'The Lord is true God. He is the living God, the eternal King. He made the earth by His power, established the world by His wisdom and stretched out the heavens by His skill' (Jer 10: 10). Among all the nations, He has chosen the people of Israel as His own domain. Moses tells the people of Israel, 'You are a people sacred to the Lord, your God. He has chosen you from all the nations on the face of the earth to be a people peculiarly His own. It was not because you are the largest of all nations that the Lord set His heart on you and chose you, for you are really the smallest of the nations' (Dt 7: 6-7). Through covenant, Israel became Yahweh's kingdom. Yahweh, as the king of Israel, resides in the midst of His subjects, His own chosen people in Jerusalem: 'Great is the Lord and highly praised in the city of our God. The holy mountain, fairest of the heights, the joy of all the earth, Mount Zion is the city of the great king' (Ps 48: 2-3). Prophet Jeremiah, condemning the worship of the idols of foreign gods, asks the people of Israel, 'Is the Lord no longer in Zion, is her King no longer in her midst?' (Jer 8: 19). From the temple of Jerusalem, Yahweh, the king, blesses His people (Ps 134: 3), guides them, protects them and gathers them as the shepherd does with his flock (Ez 34: 11-12). He directs His people in His ways through the Law. Thus, the reign of Yahweh over Israel is not a political rule but a spiritual and moral government that distinguishes nation of Israel as a unique kingdom and sets apart the people of Israel as the chosen people.

The rule of the kings of Israel

Since Yahweh is the real king, the kings of Israel were treated as human as any Israelite. Like other Israelites belonging to the Jewish nation, he was also subject to the exigencies of the covenant and the Law. The prophets never failed to remind the kings that they should also walk in the ways of the Lord. For instance, we see the prophet Nathan rebuking king David for his sin: 'You are the man that sinned against the Lord. Why have you spurned the Lord and done evil in His sight?' (2 Sm 12: 7-9). Speaking in the name of God, the prophet Ahijah tells Jeroboam, 'I will tear away the kingdom from Solomon's grasp and will give you ten of the tribes. He has not followed my ways or done what is pleasing to me, according to my statutes and decrees' (1 Kgs 11: 31-39). It is Yahweh who reigned over as the king of Israel, in virtue of the covenant. When the Israelites said to Gideon to rule as king, he replied, 'The Lord must rule over you' (Jgs 8: 23). Again, when the elders of Israel asked Samuel to appoint a king over the people of Israel, he prayed to Yahweh, who responded, 'Grant the people's every request. It is not you they reject, they are rejecting me as their king' (1 Sm 8:1-9). Kingship emerged in Israel after much tension and reluctance. We find the entire episode in 1 Samuel 8: 10-22. When Samuel resisted the demand of the people for a king, 'they refused to listen to Samuel's warning. They said, 'There must be a king over us. We too must be like other nations, with a king to rule us and to lead us in warfare and fight our battles'. Thereupon, the Lord said to Samuel, 'Grant their request and appoint a king to rule them' (1 Sm 8:19-22). It was God who appointed Saul and later David as the kings of Israel: 'When Samuel caught the sight of Saul, the Lord assured him, 'This is the man of whom I told you; he is to govern my people' (1 Sm 9: 17). In the same way, showing David to Samuel, the Lord said, 'There- anoint him, for, this is he' (1 Sm 16:12). The king is the anointed of God and hence must be respected (1 Sm 24:11). God promises that He will protect the king if he is faithful. With God's blessings, the king can assure the prosperity of his people, win victories over enemies and govern the kingdom in justice (Ps 45: 4-8). Further, as the leader of the people of God, he occasionally exercises some of the functions of worship. 'David offered holocausts and peace offerings before the Lord. When he finished making these offerings, he blessed the people in the name of the Lord of hosts' (2 Sm 6: 17-18).

The prophetic critique of the kings

In so far as the kings lived up to the ideals assigned to them as the anointed of Yahweh, they received the support of the prophets. Such was the case with David, Asa (1 Kgs 15: 11-15), Jehoshaphat (1 Kgs 22: 43), Hezekiah (2 Kgs 18: 3-7) and Josiah (2 Kgs 23: 25). Bad kings were numerous and the prophets denounced the abuses of kingship. The failures of the kings led to national calamities, finally leading to exile. Several prophets evaluated kingship as disaster for Israel. Hosea foretold its end: 'The People of Israel shall remain many days without king or prince' (Hos 3: 4). Prophet Jeremiah announces the humbling of Davidic dynasty: 'No descendant of Coniah, king of Judah, shall achieve a seat on the throne of David as ruler again over Judah' (Jer 22:30). The experiment with the kingship ended in 587 BC, with the fall and the destruction of Jerusalem. The prophets, disappointed with the infidelity of the human kings, foretold that Yahweh would send the ideal king to govern the people of Israel in perfect justice. Already in the eighth century, the prophet Isaiah turned his eyes toward the future king whose birth he hailed: 'His dominion is vast and forever peaceful; from David's throne and over his kingdom, which he confirms and sustains by judgment and justice both now and forever' (Is 9: 1-6). Guided by the Spirit of Yahweh, he would make justice reign to such an extent that the land would become an earthly paradise for he would give the people of God joy, victory, peace and justice (Is 11: 1-9). Micah even identifies the place from where the future perfect ruler will come: 'But you, Bethlehem-Ephratha, too small to be among the clans of Judah, from you shall come forth for me one who is to be ruler of Israel. He shall be peace' (Mi 5:1-5).

The prophet Jeremiah, at the very hour of the Davidic dynasty's fall which he so correctly foretold, announces the future perfect reign of the son of David: 'Behold, the days are coming, says the Lord, when I will raise up a righteous shoot to David. As king he shall reign and govern wisely and he shall do what is just and right in the land' (Jer 23: 5). Prophet Ezekiel speaks of the future king as shepherd: 'Thus says the Lord, 'I will appoint one shepherd over them to pasture them, my servant David. He shall pasture them and shall be their shepherd' (Ez 34: 23). After the exile, pagan empires, the Persians, the Greeks and the Romans, governed Israel one after another. Neither the rule of Hasmonaean dynasty of the Maccabees nor the reign of the puppet kings like Herod would stop the great expectation of the people of Israel who looked forward to the arrival of the messianic king, as their eyes turned toward the 'last times' announced by the prophets. Expectation of the kingdom of God, to be established by the messianic king constituted the central point of eschatological hope. The ancient royal psalms like 2, 45 and 72 were sung by the people as their fervent prayer in anticipation of his future reign. The image appearing on the horizon was that of a just, victorious and peaceful king about whom the prophet Zechariah says: 'Rejoice, O daughter of Jerusalem, your king shall come to you; a just savior is he, meek and riding on an ass, on a colt, the foal of an ass' (Zec 9: 9).

Jesus, the anticipated messianic king

It was at the time of great expectation for the messianic king that Jesus began His public ministry. He did not oppose the political rule of the tetrarch Herod, who suspected a competitor in Him (Lk 13: 3). He did not question the Roman government to whom tribute was due (Mk 12: 13-17). When Nathanael declared, 'Rabbi, you are the Son of God; you are the King of Israel' Jesus did not contradict him, but only assured him saying, 'You shall see greater things. You shall see heaven open and the angels of God ascending and descending on the Son of Man' (Jn 1: 49-51), thereby pointing to a heavenly kingdom rather than an earthly rule. When the multitude wanted to take Him and make Him king by force, after the multiplication of the loaves, 'Jesus withdrew to a mountain by Himself' (Jn 6:15). Conforming to the prediction of the prophet Zechariah, He rode meekly on a donkey and the colt (Mt 21:5), as He permitted the crowd to acclaim Him as the Son of David and the king of Israel (Lk 19: 38). During the interrogation before Pilate, Jesus does not reject the title of king, but made sure to clarify that His 'kingdom is not of this world' (Jn 18: 36). Thus, Jesus, while affirming that He is indeed king, nevertheless, always prompt to clarify that His kingship does not belong to this world and hence not political. Like the rule of Yahweh, over the people of Israel, His reign is moral and spiritual. His government is not over a definite territory but a universal reign over the hearts and lives of people. After his resurrection from the dead, Jesus received all authority as a ruler (Mt 28: 18), that was foretold by angel Gabriel during the annunciation to Mary: The Lord God will give Him the throne of His father David and He will reign over the house of Jacob for ever and his kingdom will never end' (Lk 1: 32-33). Jesus is 'the ruler of the kings of the earth' (Rv 1:5) and 'the Lord of lords and the King of kings' (Rv 17: 14). Jesus, the King, who ascended to heaven and is seated at the right hand of the Father, will come again: 'When He shall come in His glory, and all the holy angels with Him, then He will sit on His throne in heavenly glory. All the nations will be gathered before Him and He will separate the people one from another, as a shepherd separates the sheep from the goats. He will put the sheep on His right and the goats on the left. Then the King will say to those on His right, 'Come, you, who are the blessed of my Father. Take your inheritance, the kingdom prepared for you since the creation of the world' (Mt 25: 31-46).

Personal reflection - 'The King of Kings'

It is important to remember that in the gospels, the focus is not so much on Jesus as the king, but on the kingdom of God, that He preached and inaugurated and will bring to completion on the last day. The term 'Kingdom of God' or the more rabbinic formulation preferred by Matthew, 'Kingdom of Heavens', is found rarely in the Old Testament. In the New Testament, the expression occurs overwhelmingly in the Synoptic Gospels, almost always in sayings of Jesus - some 90 times, as against only twice in John, about six times each in Acts and Paul and once in the book of Revelation. Thus, the frequency with which Jesus uses the expression is quite unique. Jesus regards the founding of the kingdom of God as His mission to which He had been sent by the Father. He replies to the people of Capernaum, 'I must preach the good news of the kingdom of God to the other cities also; for I was sent for this purpose' (Lk 4:43). He preached primarily not about Himself, but about the kingdom of His Father. He saw the Kingdom of God as God's loving and saving presence in the midst of mankind, the realization of God's salvific plan to unite all men by the bond of His saving love. God's kingdom is a process, and a growth that takes place through the power and initiative of God. The kingdom of God, as Jesus proclaimed, consists of those who follow the way of love and justice, in as much as they treat one another with compassion and kindness. The Kingdom of God is the central theme of preaching of Jesus, the referent of most of his parables and the subject of a large number of sayings. It is also the content of the symbolic actions which form so large a part of his ministry: his table-fellowship with tax-collectors and sinners and his healings and exorcisms. In a certain way, the kingdom of God has become present in the person of Jesus Christ, in his words, teachings, and actions. To the listeners of Jesus' preaching, his

Aramaic formula, 'malkutha', would have indicated not so much a place ruled over by God, that is what the English word 'Kingdom' suggests, but as the activity through which God reveals Himself as King. In this sense, 'Kingdom of God' is synonymous with 'God reigns'. Although nominal in form, the expression is verbal in meaning. The Kingdom of God is God's kingly activity that He exercises in supreme love always guided by justice.

The Kingdom of God as portrayed by Jesus

The proclamation of the Kingdom of God and the call to repentance belong to the core message of Jesus (Mk 1:15). If we are to understand the vision of Jesus for a new society, we must ask ourselves what exactly Jesus meant when He spoke of the 'kingdom of God' and what exactly He meant by 'repentance' as human response to God's rule. Jesus nowhere tells us clearly just what the Kingdom really is. He described it in the elusive language of the parables. This is because the Kingdom of God is in fact a symbol and not an idea or a concept. As a symbol, it can represent or evoke a whole range of series of conceptions or ideas. In fact, Jesus' proclamation of the coming of the kingdom provoked all of Israel's dreams and longings for the future. The deepest and the most fundamental human aspirations were packaged in that phrase. It was so rich that it could stimulate infinite associations and meanings. With the kingdom's advent, God would right all that is wrong with the present world. Jesus' use of the symbol touched the human desire for a better future and the fulfillment of God's every promise in the salvation history.

For Jesus, it is not God's power, but God's love which is the key of salvation and that is what Jesus offers when He proclaims the arrival of God's kingdom. Drawing from His own experience of God as 'abba', the dear Father, He proclaims God's unconditional love for human beings. The Kingdom of God, proclaimed by Jesus, then, is ultimately the revelation of God's unconditional love for humanity in the one and only Son of God. When we encounter this love in Jesus Christ, through the Holy Spirit and respond to it appropriately in trusting surrender, we experience salvation and God's rule in our hearts. Jesus offered a new relationship with God through Himself as the way, the truth and the life. Jesus revealed God's attribute as love in relation to the world and to humanity. When the revelation of God's love (kingdom) meets its appropriate response in men's trusting acceptance of this love (repentance), there begins a mighty movement of personal and social redemption that sweeps through human history. It fosters fellowship, because it empowers free individuals to exercise their concern for each other in genuine community. And it leads on to justice because it impels every true community to adopt just social structures, which alone can make freedom and fellowship possible. Justice becomes the foundation of true freedom and of an authentic fellowship among human beings. Peace as true liberty and fellowship as the sign of authentic community, is possible only within the foundation of justice.

Towards establishing God's community in every generation

A new society is implicit in the dynamics of the kingdom. Jesus definitely had a vision, explicit or implicit, of a new society, though He offered no blue print for it. It is a summons, an inspiration that spells out the values of the new society, which are freedom, fellowship, justice and above all, love. Love of God leads to love of neighbor and love becomes the summation of ethics of the Kingdom. It is for the humanity to elaborate the concrete social structures through which the values of the kingdom are realized in each generation. The new community that arises as a consequence of the kingdom is always an unfinished task, summoning us to a permanent creativity of love of God and the love of neighbor, in solidarity with all our brothers and sisters who constitute humanity in the world. To the extent that we are open to the saving revolution of God's unconditional love, to the extent that we are prepared to live by the values of Jesus and commit ourselves to the building of God's community in the world, to that extent the Kingdom of God comes among us. Human beings as we are, we understand that we can never build a 'perfect society' in history. However, the vision of Jesus is a never-ending call to engage in ceaseless activity that will produce in every age new blueprints for society ever more consonant with the vision of the Gospel. Lying on the horizons of human history, and yet part of it, the Kingdom of God is offered to us as God's gratuitous gift, yet, at the same time, confronting humanity as a continuous challenge for its realization in each and every generation, until the King returns in His glory at the end of time (Mt 25:31).

Abraham and the old man: Once an old man, nearly hundred years old, rested in front of Abraham's tent on his way home. Abraham, a hospitable and charitable man, received him and gave him good food. Abraham noticed that the old man ate food without saying a prayer to God. Surprised, Abraham asked the old man why he did not say a prayer to God before eating for which the old man replied that he worshipped only the fire and he knew no other God. Angry at his idolatry, Abraham thrust the old man out of his tent. God who could see from heaven what happened spoke to Abraham and told him: 'I have endured the old man for hundred years though he did not honor me and still gave him food, health and long life always desiring his salvation. Would not you endure him for just a day? Perhaps, he may learn about me, the one true God from you'. Abraham rushed out searched and found the old man, brought him back to his tent, served him with utmost care and spoke to him about the one true God. God rules us with patient kindness, utmost goodness and above all with a forgiving love.

Quote: The best portion of a good man's life is his little, nameless, unremembered acts of kindness and love- *William Wordsworth*

Scripture reading for Day 30: 2 Sm 7: 1-17

Prayer for Day 30: God of majesty and King of glory! Yours is a kingdom for all ages and your dominion endures through all generations! Your goodness extends to the entire creation and your merciful love surrounds the whole of humanity. May we welcome your reign of justice and love in our hearts and work unceasingly towards establish your kingdom of love, peace, fellowship and justice in our communities and in the world. May your kingdom come on earth as it is in heaven! Amen.

31

CORNERSTONE

*J*esus after telling the parable of the two sons (Mt 21: 28-32) and the parable of the tenants (Mt 21: 33-41) says to His Jewish audience, 'Have you never read in the Scriptures?: The stone the builders rejected has become the cornerstone. The Lord has done this and it is marvelous in our eyes? Therefore I tell you that the kingdom of God will be taken away from you and given to a people who will produce its fruit. He who falls on this stone will be broken to pieces but he on whom it falls will be crushed. When the chief priests and the Pharisees heard Jesus' parables, they knew He was talking about them' (Mt 21: 42-45). Jesus quotes the Psalm 118: 22-23 and refers to Himself as the stone that was rejected by the Jewish establishment but God has made Him the cornerstone. In any construction, the cornerstone is that stone at the base which binds two walls and is chosen for its size. The cornerstone can be at the foundation of the building or can be the principal stone of the summit. In any case, it holds the structure together and hence is the most important stone. In the same way, God's entire plan of salvation is held together by Jesus Christ, the Son of God, whose life, death and resurrection accomplished the victory over sin and evil, over death and devil. The glorified Christ serves as the most important piece, the cornerstone, of the entire structure of the new temple of God that is the community of God's redeemed people. Jesus, like the heavy stone, will crush the source of all evil, that is Devil, and all those who choose to belong to him, on the last day, when He returns in His heavenly glory.

Cornerstone in Old Testament

In human point of view and in the symbolism of many cultures, solid and weighty stone is a sign of strength and durability. For this reason, we still find the worship of sacred stones still prevalent in the religious practices of numerous peoples in many parts of the world. In Palestine, since the stones are abundantly present, they are always found at hand. The heavy stones present the image of strength to the mind of the Hebrews. That is why, the Bible presents, quite often, the image of rock to refer especially to the steadfast fidelity of God. Moses sings the praise of Yahweh thus, 'I will sing the Lord's glory and proclaim the greatness of our God. The rock - how faultless are His deeds, how right all His ways! A faithful God, without deceit, how just and upright He is' (Dt 32: 3-4). The worship of sacred stones, quite developed in primitive religions, was considered as a practice of idolatry and was hence forbidden in Israel. However, without any act of worship or veneration bordering on magical purposes, the sacred stones were used as symbols to convey the special presence of Yahweh. For instance, Jacob raised up a sacred stone at Bethel: 'Jacob took the stone that he had put under his head, set it up as a memorial stone and poured oil on top of it. He said, 'This stone that I have set up as a memorial stone shall be God's abode' (Gn 28: 16-22). Although the distinction between the sacred stone and the memorial stone is not always very clear in the Old Testament, the concepts of unchangeableness and durability were especially attached to both the stones. Thus we find Jacob and Laban, his father-in-law, erecting a memorial stone and also making a mound with sacred stones. Laban said to Jacob: 'Here is this mound and here is the memorial stone that I have set up between you and me. This mound shall be witness and this memorial stone shall be witness that with hostile intent neither may I pass beyond this mound into your territory nor may you pass beyond it into mine' (Gn 31: 45-52).

The Israelites were required to make the altar with untrimmed stones. By means of these altars made of stones, God received offerings and sacrifices and in return, blessed His people. God tells the people of Israel, 'If you make an altar of stone for me, do not build it of cut stone, for by putting a tool to it, you desecrate it' (Ex 20: 25). Moses wrote down all the words of the Lord after the people agreed in one voice to follow the ordinances of the Lord. 'Rising early the next day, he erected at the foot of the mountain an altar and twelve pillars for the twelve tribes of Israel' (Ex 24: 4). Evidently, the altar symbolically represented God and the twelve pillars stood for the twelve tribes of Israel as Moses, on behalf of the people of Israel, ratified the covenant with God by sprinkling the blood of the bulls on the altar and on the people. The stones, erected intentionally to serve as the memorials, reminded the people of Israel the mighty deeds that Yahweh performed in order to help and guide His people. For instance, Joshua says to the twelve men whom he selected among the Israelites, one from each tribe: 'Bring one stone each from the bed of Jordan. In the future, these twelve stones are to be sign among you. When your children ask you what these stones mean to you, you shall answer them, 'The waters of Jordan ceased to flow before the ark of the covenant of the Lord, when it crossed the Jordan'. Thus, these stones are to serve as a perpetual memorial to the Israelites' (Jos 4: 4-7).

The 'stone' in the prophets

The prophet Jeremiah refers to the cornerstone when making prophecy against Babylon for bringing devastation to Jerusalem and foretelling its ruin at the hands of the Persians: 'Thus says the Lord. 'I will stretch forth my hand against you, roll you down over the cliffs and make you a burnt mountain. They shall not take from you a cornerstone or a foundation stone. Ruins forever shall you be' (Jer 51: 26). It was the stony heart of the people of Israel that was the reason for their forgetting their faithful God and for failing to observe His ordinances, leading to their divine chastisement at the hands of the Babylonians. Through prophet Ezekiel God promises to remove the stony heart and to replace it with a natural heart: 'Though I have removed them far among the nations and scattered them over foreign countries, they shall return to the land of Israel and remove from it all its detestable abominations. I will give them a new heart and put a new spirit within them. I will remove the stony heart from their bodies and replace it with a natural heart so that they will live according to my statutes and observe and carry out my ordinances. Thus, they shall be my people and I will be their God' (Ez 11: 16-20). Prophet Isaiah, while foretelling the disasters that would befall on the Israelite kingdoms, assures that God would, however, fulfill His promise to David, by firmly establishing Davidic rule through the messiah, who is called cornerstone: 'Thus says the Lord God: See, I am laying a stone in Zion, a stone that has been tested, A precious cornerstone as a sure foundation; he who puts his faith in it shall not be shaken' (Is 28:16). The same promise is affirmed by the psalmist, who would have thought of the image of the cornerstone of the Jerusalem temple, while assuring the durability of the Davidic dynasty: 'The stone the builders rejected has become the cornerstone. By the Lord has this been done; it is wonderful in our eyes' (Ps 118: 22). Prophet Amos promises the reconstruction of Jerusalem by God Himself: 'Thus says the Lord, your God, 'On that day, I will raise up the fallen hut of David. I will wall up its breaches, raise up its ruins and rebuild it as in the days of old' (Am 9: 11). Prophet Jeremiah assures that never again the city will suffer destruction: 'The days are coming, says the Lord, when the city shall be rebuilt as the Lord's. Never again, shall the city be rooted up or thrown down' (Jer 31: 38-40). All the promises of the prophets are to be fulfilled in Jesus Christ, the cornerstone of the new edifice of God.

Christ the rejected and glorified cornerstone

As He foretold in the parable of the Tenants that portrayed the evil actions of the murderous workers of the vineyard (Mt 21: 33-41), Jesus was rejected by His own people, through crucifixion on the cross. However, through the resurrection, God establisheed Him as the cornerstone of the new edifice that would replace the old one, the people of Israel, who rejected Jesus (Mt 21: 42-45; Mk 12: 10-12). The risen Christ, exalted by the Father and now seated at His right hand, is the source of new life and salvation. Everyman, in order to receive salvation as God's gift, has to choose the light or the darkness, goodness or evil, God or devil. For those who reject God and His infinite goodness, Jesus becomes a stumbling stone that would crush them on the judgment day: 'Everyone who falls on that stone will be broken to pieces, but he on whom it falls will be crushed' (Lk 20: 18). When speaking to the same Jewish establishment that arrested John and himself, after the ascension of Jesus and the reception of the Holy Spirit, Peter would declare with boldness: 'Know this, you and all the people of Israel: It is by the name of Jesus Christ of Nazareth, whom you crucified but whom God raised from the dead, this man (crippled beggar at the temple - Acts 3: 3-8) stands before you healed. Jesus is 'the stone you builders rejected which has become the cornerstone. Salvation is found in no one else, for there is no other name under heaven given to men by which we must be saved' (Acts 4: 10-12).

Christ, the cornerstone of the new people of God

Christ has been appointed by His heavenly Father as the cornerstone of the new edifice or the new people of God, fulfilling the promise that God made through the prophets. It is, in a certain sense, a continuation of Israel and of her institutions such as the election, the covenant, the law and the prophets that constituted them as God's chosen people. There is also a discontinuity, however, between the old people of God and the new people of God. It consists in the centrality of the person of Jesus Christ in the new edifice, the same Jesus whom the old people of God rejected. Now, God constitutes His new people not on institutions as covenant and law, but on the person of His only Son, Jesus Christ, as Lord and savior. That is why, Paul insists, 'no one can lay any foundation other than the one already laid, which is Jesus Christ' (1 Cor 3: 11). He states further, 'You are no longer foreigners or aliens, but fellow citizens and members of God's household, built on the foundation of the apostles and prophets with Christ Jesus Himself as the chief cornerstone. In Him the whole building is joined together and rises to become a holy temple in the Lord. And in Him you too are being built together to become a dwelling in which God lives by His Spirit' (Eph 2: 20-22). Peter explains that as the cornerstone of the new economy of salvation, in the plan of God, Jesus can be a precious stone that brings rejoicing or a heavy stone over which men stumble and hurt themselves, depending on their acceptance or rejection of Jesus: 'As you come to Him, the living stone, rejected by men but chosen by God and precious to Him, you also, like living stones, are being built into a spiritual house to be a holy priesthood, offering spiritual sacrifices acceptable to God through Jesus Christ. For in Scripture it says: See, I lay a stone in Zion, a chosen and precious cornerstone, and the one who trusts in him will never be put to shame. Now to you who believe, this stone is precious. But to those who do not believe, the stone the builders rejected has become the cornerstone and a stone that causes men to stumble and a rock that makes them fall, they stumble because they disobey the message, which is also what they were destined for' (1 Pt 2: 4-8).

Jesus and the spiritual Temple

Both Paul and Peter refer to the new edifice of God as holy temple or as spiritual house. This apostolic image about the new people of God comes from Jesus Himself. Clearing the temple of the traders and condemning the business operation as making the 'house of prayer' into a 'den of thieves' (Mk 11: 15-17), Jesus declared: 'Destroy this temple and I will raise it again in three days'. John concludes that the temple He had spoken of was His body (Jn 2: 13-

22). Jesus spoke of the community of the people of God that is constituted in Him as the new temple in which the true worshipers, consisting of both the Jews and the Gentiles, would not sacrifice animals for appeasing God, but 'worship Him in spirit and truth' (Jn 4: 21-24). Guided by the spirit of truth, the true believers not only sing the praises of God but also offer the sacrifices of good deeds of kindness and sharing which alone pleases God: 'Let us continually offer to God a sacrifice of praise- the fruit of the lips that confess his name. And do not forget to do good and to share with others, for with such sacrifices, God is pleased' (Heb 13: 15- 16). Reminding them to lead a life that reflects the dignity of their Christian calling, Paul writes to the Corinthians, 'Don't you know that you yourselves are God's temple and that God's spirit lives in you? If anyone destroys God's temple, God will destroy him; for God's temple is sacred and you are that temple' (1 Cor 3: 16-17).

What is important to remember is that Jesus is not only the cornerstone of the new edifice, the new people of God, but He is also the builder of this edifice, which is 'His Church'. He named Peter as the 'rock' or the foundation: 'I tell you that you are Peter (that means rock) and on this rock, I will build my Church' (Mt 16: 17-19). Jesus also placed the apostles and the prophets as the foundation (Eph 2: 20). The apostles worked in the name of Jesus and built up the local churches by establishing Christian communities as Paul has done (1 Cor 3: 10). However, it is the Father, through Jesus Christ, in the Holy Spirit who makes the churches grow all over the world from its inception (1 Cor 3: 6). In order to build up His Church, Jesus 'made some to be apostles, some to be prophets, some to be evangelists and some to be pastors and teachers' (Eph 4: 11). There are different gifts in the Church, given by the Holy Spirit, for the common good of the entire Church. However, it is love and fraternal service that brings together all these different gifts so that all the members of the Church, through common and mutual work, may build up the edifice of the Church as the new people of God, always receiving from Jesus unfailing help and strength (I Cor 14:12). Any edifice needs a certain order and structure and it is also true with the Church, the spiritual house of God. All the gifts are to be made use of 'in a fitting and orderly way' (1 Cor 14: 40), for the good of the entire Church. Made efficacious by the various gifts of its members that they receive from the Holy Spirit, the Church seeks new members by proclaiming the Gospel till the end of time, as commissioned by the Lord Jesus Christ. On the last day, the new Jerusalem will appear as the eternal edifice, with God and Jesus Christ as its temple. On the twelve gates will be found written the names of the twelve tribes of Israel. The names of the twelve apostles will be found on the twelve foundations of the wall of the city (Rv 21: 12-14). The implication of the writing of the names of the twelve tribes and the twelve apostles is clear: the glorious edifice of God, to be revealed to us on the last day, as the everlasting community of the saints in heaven, that is to share eternal joy with the angels of God in the kingdom of heaven, was first established in the old Israel with the twelve tribes and later extended to the peoples of all nations who became the new Israel through the twelve apostles. The builder of the edifice is the Father and the cornerstone is Jesus Christ and the structure is held together in the Holy Spirit, for the eternal glory of the Triune God.

Personal reflection – 'Jesus, the cornerstone'

The early Church first consisted of the Jewish converts. Later on, numerous Gentiles became Christians especially through the missionary efforts of Paul and his companions. When Christian community became a mixed community of the Jews and the Gentiles, many questions arose about the religious practices of the Gentile converts. For instance, the question of their circumcision was a major point of discussion in the primitive Church. Reflecting and praying together, the early Church saw Jesus Christ as the cornerstone that brought two walls together as one singular edifice of spiritual temple. One wall represented the Jews, the chosen people of God and the other wall represented the Gentiles who came from all the nations and all the peoples: 'Jesus made the two one and has destroyed the barrier, the dividing wall of hostility' (Eph 2:14). God initiated the history of salvation for the world, with the people of Israel as the center. He manifested Himself to them as the one true God, the creator of all things, in the midst of the polytheistic practices of the Gentiles. Saving them from Egyptian slavery and thus revealing Himself as a liberating God, He made covenant with them thereby making them His chosen people. In the fullness of time, God sent His only Son born as a Jew. He preached the gospel to the chosen people, but the religious leaders rejected His message. In the divine plan, this rejection constituted the refusal of salvation for which God instituted Jesus Christ as the only mediator. The stone rejected by the builders became the cornerstone. The risen Christ, exalted and enthroned as the savior of the world through His death and resurrection, offers salvation not only to the Jews but also to all the nations and to all the peoples (Mt 28:19-20). In the new age, apart from Jesus Christ, the eternal Word made flesh, there is no salvation. Jesus was rejected by Israel, the original builders of the earthly temple (Ps 118: 22). As the rejected cornerstone, He became a stumbling stone: 'He shall be a snare, an obstacle and a stumbling stone to the house of Israel, a trap and a snare to those who dwell in Jerusalem. And many among them shall stumble and fall, broken, snared, and captured (Is 8:14-15). The religious establishment of Israel stumbled over the 'stumbling' stone, Jesus Christ (Rom 9: 32). As a result, the entire establishment, together with the temple that represented them, was annihilated by the Romans in 68-70 AD.

Through His victory on the cross, Jesus is the cornerstone of God's new spiritual temple that has replaced the Jerusalem temple. He is the Lord and Savior to all those who believe in Him, both the Jews and the Gentiles. Having been led by His grace to faith in Him, now we place our hope and confidence in Him and build our lives around him, with Him and upon Him. Jesus has to be the cornerstone of our lives. It is He who can bear the weight of our lives, as we encounter difficulties and trials, sufferings and sorrows. Jesus says, 'Everyone who hears these words of mine and puts them into practice is like a wise man who built his house on the rock. The rain came down, the streams rose and the winds blew and beat against that house; yet it did not fall, because it had its foundation on the rock. But everyone who hears these words of mine and does not put them into practice is like a foolish man who built his house on sand. The rain came down, the streams rose, and the winds blew and beat against that house and it fell with a great crash' (Mt 7:24-27). Let us follow the teachings of Jesus and thereby establish our lives on solid 'rock', the mighty cornerstone, so that we may be able to withstand the 'storms' in our lives in safety and security, until that day when we shall see Him face to face, as our Lord and Savior, in His heavenly Kingdom.

Three heavy stones: Once there lived a saintly monk in the solitude of a monastery in the mountain. He spent much time in prayer. He also served happily those who passed by the monastery with water and food and cared for the sick in times of pestilence in the nearby villages. His name inspired veneration and people sought his prayers and blessings. There was a rich robber, the head of several hundred lawless men and the owner of numerous slaves who stored up all his ill-gotten wealth in his treasury. He was amazed at the fame of the old simple monk among all the people who also despised the robber as an evil person. He desired so much to be respected and venerated by the people. He went to the monk and told his desire. The monk asked him to carry three heavy stones on his shoulders and walk with him to see the beautiful countryside from the cliff of the mountain. The man found it very difficult to walk with the burden. With the permission of the monk, as he dropped off the three stones, one by one, he could walk comfortably towards the cliff. The monk told him that unless he drops of his attachment to power, riches and pleasure and became a free man, he cannot become a holy man who will be venerated by all the people. Jesus told us to abandon the earthly things and to build our lives on Him alone, our rock and our cornerstone.

Quote: The living Church, though never neat, keeps God's world from complete disaster - *George F. Macleod*

Scripture reading for Day 31:Eph 2: 1-22

Prayer for Day 31: Blessed are you, heavenly Father, for carrying with us our burdens each day! You are the rock in whom our lives are established in safety and security. You rejoice in our joys and share our sorrows as we place them on your steadfast shoulders. Help us to be kind-hearted and helpful to others in all that we do and say! Amen.

32

HEAD OF THE BODY

*P*aul calls Jesus 'the Head of the Body, the Church' (Col 1:18). He also says, 'Christ is the Head of the Church, His Body, of which He is the Savior' (Eph 5: 23). In the literal sense of the word, 'head' stands for the head of a living creature, especially for the head of a human being. It is evident that the head is the most essential part of the human body. A living body without head is unthinkable, because without the head, the body cannot function at all. When the head is absent, the body will be without life or activity. The union of the head and the body is of an organic nature, wherein the head cannot exist without body that carries it and the body cannot function without the head. A person exists, moves and lives only when the head and the body are integrated together, thereby constitute the distinct individual being. Of all the analogies or images used in the Bible to describe the People of God or the Church, the analogy of the Head and Body is unique in the sense that it has no Old Testament reference. Hebrew language has no particular word for body except to designate a corpse. Hebrew thought did not conceive body as a unified totality but only as a collection of different organs. The Greek word for body, 'soma' of the New Testament can hardly be translated into any appropriate Hebrew or Aramaic term. Even if it belongs to the specifically Pauline theology, the analogy of the head and the body carries profound meaning for the reality of the Church. Just as a human body, without the head, cannot function, cannot have direction, above all, cannot receive nourishment, so it is with the Church, without the Head, that is Christ Jesus. The very existence of the Church is indelibly linked to Jesus Christ, her Lord and Savior. Since our focus is on Jesus, the 'head', let us first discuss the role of the head in the Old Testament.

The Head in the Old Testament

In Hebrew thought, unlike the Greek concept, 'head' was not considered as the seat of thought, consciousness or decision. The Hebrew word, 'ro's' meant, in the strict sense, the head of the man or animal. However, it was also used in the metaphorical sense, to signify everything that comes first in order, rank or quality among the persons and the things. Thus the term 'head' signified, among the things, the beginning of a road or a year, the top of a tree or a mountain or a monument and among the persons the chief or the ruler. As a result, the word 'head', as used to in the Old Testament, indicated things as diverse as the top of mountain (Gn 8:5), the first month of a year (Ex 12:2), the front place in the crowd (Dt 10:11), the beginning of the night watch (Jgs 7:19) and the top of a pillar (1 Kgs 7:16). To lift up the head of a person means that this person is honored: Joseph interpreted the dream of the chief cupbearer of Pharaoh saying, 'Within three days, Pharaoh will lift up your head and restore you to your post' (Gn 40:13). Promising blessings to the people of Israel, if they obey the ordinances of Yahweh, Moses says, 'The Lord will make you the head, not the tail and you will always mount higher and not decline, as long as you obey the commandments of the Lord, your God' (Dt 28: 13). 'If you do not hearken to the voice of the Lord, your God and are not careful to observe all His commandments, the aliens residing among you will rise higher and higher above you, while you sink lower and lower. He will lend to you, not you to him. He will become the head, you the tail' (Dt 28: 43-44). The ruling classes of Israelite society are referred to as the 'head' of the people, in contrast to the 'tail' -the mass of the people which follows them and is subordinate to them (Is 9:14).

Jesus as the Head and Church as the Body in the New Testament

Naming Jesus as the Head and the Church as the Body is one of the most creative and profound contribution of Apostle Paul to Christian theology. Various explanations of its origin have been proposed by numerous biblical scholars, especially tracing its source to Stoic and Gnostic philosophies. The likely source of inspiration seems to be Paul's own dramatic encounter with Jesus Christ on the road to Damascus, when Jesus asked Paul a straight question that changed his life forever: 'Why do you persecute me?' (Acts 9: 4). Paul remembered that question so well that he would repeat it, at least twice, first as he spoke to the people of Israel at the Jerusalem temple (Acts 22: 7) and again to King Agrippa and Festus, the Roman Governor (Acts 26: 14). Saul, before becoming Paul, was actually persecuting the Christians: 'Saul was breathing out murderous threats against the Lord's disciples. He went to the high priest and asked him for letters to the synagogues in Damascus, so that if he found any there who belonged to the Way, whether men or women, he might take them as prisoners to Jerusalem' (Acts 9: 1-2). The complete identification of Jesus with the Christian community, in His question to Paul, impacted the thinking of Paul to such an extent that he proposed several theological expressions to explain the profound unity between Jesus Christ and His Church. One such theological analogy is Christ as the Head and the Church as the Body.

The image of the city or state as a body was quite well known in political philosophy of Paul's time and hence he was familiar with it. In fact, the body was the most common 'topos' in ancient literature for unity. The famous fable of Menenius Agrippa, about the other parts of the body failing to co-operate and feed the belly and as a result, all of them losing their strength, was the best example for such a 'topos'. The unity of the state depended on the mutual co-operation of all the members of the geographical location. In the case of the Church, it is the allegiance to Jesus Christ, made in faith, and expressed through the rebirth in Baptism and partaking of the Eucharist that constituted the unity of the believers. Surely, Paul would have seen the connection between the Body of Christ, that is Eucharist and Body of Christ that is the Church. That is why, in the first letter to the Corinthians, he speaks first about the Body of Christ that is Eucharist: 'Is not the bread that we break a participation in the body of Christ?' (1Cor 10:16). 'Therefore whoever eats the bread and drinks the cup of the Lord in an unworthy manner will be guilty of sinning against the body and blood of the Lord' (1 Cor 11: 27). Later, in the same letter, in the following chapter, Paul speaks about the body of Christ that is the Church: 'Now, you are the body of Christ and each one of you is a part of it' (1 Cor 12: 27). Paul's conclusion is that the Christian community that worships together and partakes of the Eucharist together constitutes the body of Christ, of which Christ is the Head. When Paul says that the members of the Christian community are the parts of one Body (Rom 12:5) it is not a metaphorical expression but a theological reality that actually takes place. The Lord Jesus actually establishes the members as the parts of His Body, the Church, first by Baptism: 'We were all baptized by one Spirit into one body- whether Jews or Greeks, slave or free' (1 Cor 12: 13) and later by the Eucharistic communion: 'Because there is one loaf, we, who are many, are one body, for we all partake of the one loaf' (1 Cor 10: 17). As the head of the body, Jesus is the source of the life of the Church as He directs, governs, nourishes and strengthens the members of the Body, the Church.

Christ as the Head of the Universe and the Church

First of all, Paul points out that Jesus is the Head of the universe. He states, 'God placed all things under the feet of Jesus and appointed Him to be head over everything for the Church, which is His body' (Eph 1:22). Jesus is the Head of everything because 'He is the image of the invisible God, the firstborn of all creation. For by Him all things were created; things in heaven and on earth, visible and invisible, whether thrones or powers or rulers or authorities; all things were created by Him and for Him. He is before all things and in Him all things hold together' (Col 1:16-17). Glorified in resurrection, Jesus is 'seated at the right of the Father in the heavenly realms, far above all rule and authority, power and dominion, and every title that can be given, not only in the present age but also in the age to come' (Eph 1: 20-21). As the result of His exaltation, 'Christ is the Head over every power and authority' (Col 2:10). At the same time, as Paul states, 'Jesus is the head of the body, the Church' (Col 1:18). The head belongs to the human body and it guides and directs the parts and conditions the growth within the essential unity existing between the head and all the parts of the body. The entire human body is joined and held together of its various muscles and ligaments by the head. As the head, Christ is the unifying and central principle of the Church: 'From Jesus Christ, the Head, the whole body, joined and held together by every supporting ligament, grows and builds itself up in love, as each part does its work' (Eph 4:16). As the Head, Christ is also the source from which the Church gains sustenance and the means by which it continues to grow. He nourishes and cherishes it (Eph 5:29). Christ is also the ultimate goal to which the church is moving, until all its members reach unity in the faith and in the knowledge of the Son of God and become mature, attaining to the whole measure of the fullness of Christ' (Eph 4:13). Till then, the members of the body, who are 'God's chosen people, holy and dearly beloved, must clothe themselves with compassion, kindness, humility, gentleness and patience, forgiving one another and above all, putting on love that binds them all together in perfect unity' (Col 3: 12-14) as they journey together towards the heavenly kingdom to meet Christ, the Head.

The Church and the Universe

We have seen that Christ is the Head of the Universe, yet at the same time, He is also the Head of the Body, that is the Church. Because, Jesus is the Head of both of them, He directs their destinies that are bound together in Him. What is the important insight of Paul, in his theological discourse, is that it is through the Church that the universe is led to the fullness in Jesus Christ. The Church, created by God, built up by Christ and inhabited by the Spirit exists in the world to be at the service of Jesus Christ, who restores the entire creation to the fullness, for the glory of the heavenly Father. Seen this way, the Church does not exist only to meet the needs of her members or to ensure institutional survival but to fulfill the redemptive purpose of Christ of reconciling the world in Christ (2 Cor 5: 19).United to Jesus Christ the Church is oriented towards the world by the very nature of her mission. Christ, as the Head, directs the Church to be His instrument in order to reconcile all things whether things in on earth or things in heaven (Col 1: 20) and thereby making all things new in the fullness of His divine glory (Rv 21:5). Christ fills her with His fullness and she in turn fills Him, as she completes His body through her progressive growth in this world (Eph 4:13). Seen this way, it is evident to us that the Church has a definite mission in this world that she received from Jesus Christ.

No doubt, the Church is distinct from Christ, yet she is united to Him inseparably. Paul presents the analogy of the Body and the Head to illuminate the role of the Church to function as an effective instrument of salvation in this world, in union with Jesus, her Head. There are different functions for the members of the Church. Paul explains, 'Just as each of us has one body with many members and these members do not all have same function, so in Christ, we who are many form one body and each member belongs to all others. We have different gifts, according to the grace given us. If a man's gift is prophesying, let him use it in proportion to his faith. If it is serving, let him serve; if it is teaching, let him teach; if it is encouraging, let him encourage; if it is contributing to the needs of others, let him give generously; if it is leadership, let him govern diligently; if it is showing mercy, let him do it cheerfully' (Rom 12: 4-8), for 'in the Church, God has appointed first of all apostles, second prophets, third teachers, then workers of miracles, also those having the gift of healing, those able to help others, those with gifts of administration, and those speaking in different kinds of tongues' (1 Cor 12: 28), so that the body of Christ may be built up' (Eph 4:12). 'There are different gifts, but the same Spirit. There are different kinds of service, but the same Lord. There are different kinds of working, but the same God works all of them, in all men' (1 Cor 12: 4-6).

Unity and Fellowship

Explaining through the analogy of the functioning of the parts of the Body, Paul insists that 'all the different gifts are from the same Spirit who gives them to each one, just as He determines' (1 Cor 12: 11). He further states, 'God has arranged the parts in the body, every one of them, just as wanted them to be. If they were all one part, where would the body be? As it is, there are many parts, but one body. The eye can not say to the hand, 'I don't need you!' And the head cannot say to the feet, 'I don't need you!'. On the contrary, those parts of the body that seem to be weaker are indispensable and the parts that we think less honorable, we treat with special honor. And the parts that are unpresentable are treated with special modesty, while our presentable parts need no special treatment. But, God has combined the members of the body and has given greater honor to the parts that lacked it, so that there should be no division in the body, but that its parts should have equal concern for each other. If one part suffers, every part suffers with it; if one part is honored, every part rejoices with it' (1 Cor 12: 18-26).

In spite such a wonderful teaching and an inspiring exhortation of Paul to the members of the Church to work together in equality and dignity for the common good of the mission of the Church, the preservation of the unity as well as the equal dignity of all the members within the Church had been always a problem. Even today, as we see so many denominations of the Christian people, we cannot but feel sorry for the conditions of disunity in the one Body of Christ. But let us not be disheartened as this disunity is not something new. From its inception, the Church, consisting of human members, has to face the challenge of disharmony. Acts 6: 1-3 presents the situation of conflict between the Grecian Jews and the Hebraic Jews among the early Christians in Jerusalem. We also know that disharmonious conditions as well as internal strife existed in the church in Corinth to whom Paul was writing the famous analogy of the Body of Christ. Made up of the human beings whose conduct has been not always spotless, the Church has to struggle for unity and peace within, even as she strives to bring the divine fullness of Jesus Christ to the entire universe as her proper mission. In spite of the presence of sinful human beings as the members of the Church, since the Head is Jesus Christ, the sinless Son of God, the Church is able to go forward, unhindered by the challenges of sin and evil in the world. Guided by the Holy Spirit, she preaches the Gospel to all the nations and to all the peoples, thereby bringing continued growth to the Body of Christ until the end of time, when Christ will make her spotless and pure, holy and perfect, clothing her with the fullness of His divine glory.

Personal reflection - 'The Church is the Body of Christ'

Paul added a unique title to Jesus in relation to the Church: He is the head of the Church, which is His Body. In Christ, the Church exists as a divine institution. She was conceived in the mind of God (Eph 3:10-11), foretold by the prophets (Is 2: 2-4), built by Jesus (Mt 16:16-18), purchased with His blood (Acts 20:28) and constructed under the immediate direction of the Holy Spirit working through the apostles of Christ (Acts 2: 42-47). Because Christ is the Head of the Body, Christ and the new people of God are inseparably joined together. Christ works through His Body and the Body does the work of Christ (1 Cor 12:12-27). This makes it impossible to reject the Body without also rejecting the Head, 'from whom the whole body, supported and held together by its ligaments and sinews grows as God causes it to grow' (Col 2:19). Christ cannot be received apart from His Body. It is the Father who calls the Church into being, constitutes its identity in Christ and empowers it through the Spirit. The Church exists in the gathering together of believers in Jesus, who express their faith in their celebrations, in their lifestyle and in their service: 'For as many of you as were baptized into Christ have put on Christ, there is neither Jew nor Greek, there is neither slave nor free, there is neither male nor female; for you are all one in Christ Jesus' (Gal 3:27-28).

The idea of call is basic to Paul's understanding of Church, for God calls the Church into being because of His graciousness and His love. The one God of Israel who always remains faithful to His promises to Abraham, but now extends His call to all who believe, attaching no conditions to His free gift of eternal life in Christ Jesus (Rom 3:24). In baptism, Christians 'put on Christ' (Gal 3:27), being also 'baptized into one body...and all...made to drink of one Spirit' (1 Cor 12:13). Baptism washes, sanctifies and justifies us (1 Cor 6:11) and through the Lord Jesus Christ, we receive 'our reconciliation' (Rom 5:11). However, something more profound occurs. In Baptism we 'put on the new person', for we 'have been baptized into Christ Jesus, buried, therefore, with him by baptism into death, so that as Christ was raised from the dead by the glory of the Father, we too might walk in newness of life' (Rom 6:3-4). Being baptized into Christ marks the beginning of our Christian existence, and as such, initiates our new life in Christ.

Eucharist, the Body of Christ

The Spirit of Christ makes us holy, forms us into one body and gives us gifts for use in the service of the church. The community of the baptized are gathered together to share a meal and to remember the Lord, in a common table: 'Do this in remembrance of me...For as often as you eat this bread and drink the cup, you proclaim the Lord's death until he comes' (1 Cor 11:24.26). This ritual imitates the ritual meal Jesus shared with His disciples 'on the night when he was betrayed' (1 Cor 11:23), celebrating the meaning of Christ's death for the community and anticipating the eternal banquet. The body of Christ is the Church and this makes the Eucharist, also the body of Christ, an effective sign of Christian unity. The community shares its common faith through many expressions of prayer. Paul urges the community to 'let your requests be made known to God' in 'prayer and supplication, with thanksgiving' (Phil 4:6). The Church, the Body, prays to Christ, the Head, who is also the Lord of history and thus directs her towards the perfection and glory that will be hers on the last day. Dictators come and go; kingdoms rise and fall; civilizations wax and wane but the Church will continue to proclaim the good news of Christ to the end of age, in spite of the vicissitudes of human history. Problems and strife may arise among the members, challenges may abound, difficulties may hurt, divisions may divide, yet the Church will continue to fulfill the redemptive purposes of God for the world, in Christ Jesus and through the Holy Spirit, always being assured of the presence and power of her Head, that is Jesus, who promised to be with her, 'to the very end of the age' (Mt 28: 20).

Sharing till it hurts: This incident happened in the life of Mother Theresa of Calcutta. One evening, a gentleman came to the convent of Mother Theresa in Calcutta and told her that there was a Hindu family in his neighborhood that has not eaten for a couple of days since they had no food. Anxious to feed the family as soon as possible, Mother Theresa took some rice and went immediately to meet the starving family and offered them the rice that she brought with her. The mother of the starving family took half of the rice that Mother Theresa brought and went out to meet another family. When she returned after a few minutes, Mother Theresa asked her what she did with the rice that she took with her. She replied that the neighboring Muslim family also was starving for several days and she shared some rice with them. That day two starving families shared their meal and rejoiced in their fellowship that transcended religious divide. Sharing till it hurts is the true Christian love, because Jesus loved us till it hurt Him on the cross to the point of death.

Quote: We need to think of the Church as the body through which our risen and ascended Lord is seeking to redeem the world from all the evil with which the world is infected - *Leonard Hodgson*

Scripture reading for Day 32:1 Cor 12: 4-31

Prayer for Day 32: Lord God! Be pleased to watch over your Church and guide her through your Holy Spirit. Enable each one of us, the members of your Church, to contribute to the growth and discipline, to the loyalty and to the fraternal service that may preserve the family spirit and the fellowship within your Church! Amen.

33

HIGH PRIEST

*J*esus is the high priest who sacrificed Himself on the cross for the redemption of the world. The Epistle to the Hebrews uses this title no less than ten times. We present some instances: 'For destroying him who holds the power of death - that is the devil, Jesus had to be made like His brothers in every way, in order that He might become a merciful and faithful high priest in service to God and that He might make atonement for the sins of the people' (Heb 2: 14-17). 'Therefore brothers, fix your thoughts on Jesus, the high priest whom we confess' (Heb 3: 1). 'Since we have a great high priest who has gone through the heavens, Jesus, the Son of God, let us hold firmly to the faith we profess' (Heb 4:14). 'Jesus was designated by God to be high priest in the order of Melchizedek' (Heb 5: 10). 'Jesus, the high priest meets our need- one who is holy, blameless, pure, set apart from sinners and exalted above the heavens' (Heb 7: 26). 'We have a high priest who sat down at the right hand of the throne of the Majesty in heaven' (Heb 8:1). In the letter to the Hebrews, we find the most systematic theological exposition of the priesthood of Christ. Before we examine its contents, let us present the salient features of the priesthood in the Old Testament, for a better understanding of the priesthood of Jesus.

Priesthood in the Old Testament

Priesthood exists in all periods and regions in some form or another, as part of the religious practice throughout the history of humanity. In the Near East, as seen in the ancient Mesopotamia and Egypt, priesthood seemed to have been hereditary and wielded great influence over the society as the priests functioned as the officials of religion as well as the teachers and at times as the judges. The temples had large land holdings and numerous personnel of labor such as the slaves, received huge revenue through the temple properties and the regular offerings thereby making the clergy rich and powerful. Not much is known about the priesthood of the immediate neighbors of Israel, the Canaanites, except that those priests were designated by the same word as the Hebrew 'kohen', which meant priest.

In Israel, the book of Genesis presents the patriarchs as building altars in Canaan (Gn 12: 7) and offering sacrifices: 'Abraham took the ram and offered it up as a holocaust in place of his son' (Gn 22: 13). Laban, together with Jacob, his son-in-law, offered a sacrifice on the mountain and invited his kinsmen to share in the meal (Gn 31: 54). The patriarchs seemed to have exercised the familial priesthood practiced among some of the ancient peoples. The tribe of Levi was still an unconsecrated tribe like any other tribe, without any sacred function of priesthood (Gn 34: 25-31). Jacob gave the Levites no blessing: 'Simeon and Levi, brothers indeed, weapons of violence are their knives. In their fury they slew men in their willfulness they maimed oxen. Cursed be their fury so fierce and their rage so cruel! I will scatter them in Jacob, disperse them throughout Israel' (Gn 49: 5-7). The priests that appear in the book of Genesis are strangers: Melchizedek, the priest-king of Jerusalem (Gn 14: 18-20) and the priests of Pharaoh (Gn 41: 45; 47: 22).

The origin of Levite Priesthood

It is with Moses, a Levite himself, that the association of this tribe with the priestly functions got started. The book of Exodus presents the origin of the Levite priesthood: 'When Moses realized that Aaron had let the people run wild with the worship of the golden calf and dancing, he stood at the gate of the camp and cried, 'Whoever is for the Lord, let him come to me'. All the Levites then rallied to him and he told them: 'Thus says the Lord, the God of Israel: 'Put your sword on your hip, every one of you! Now go up and down the camp, from gate to gate, and slay your own kinsmen, your friends and neighbors'. The Levites carried out the command of Moses, and that day there fell about three thousand of the people. Then, Moses said, 'Today you have been dedicated to the Lord, for you were against your own sons and kinsmen, to bring a blessing upon yourselves this day' (Ex 32: 25-29). Thus, the tribe of Levites was chosen by Moses and consecrated for divine service as priests. Moses blessed the Levites saying the prayer, 'O God, the Levites keep your words and they uphold your covenant. They promulgate your decisions to Jacob and your law to Israel. They bring the smoke of sacrifice to your nostrils and burnt offerings to your altar. Bless, O Lord, Levi's possessions and accept the ministry of his hands' (Dt 33: 9-11). Before the construction of the temple of Jerusalem by the king Solomon, the Israelites worshipped at numerous sanctuaries scattered through the land of Israel. The Levites became the priests par excellence, serving the people of Israel in those sanctuaries by their hereditary priesthood. About their privileges, Moses had commanded this: 'The whole priestly tribe of Levi shall have no share in the heritage with Israel; they shall live on the oblations of the Lord and the portions due to him. The priests shall have a right to the following things from the people: from those who are offering a sacrifice, whether the victim is from the herd or from the flock, the priest shall receive the shoulder, the jowls and the stomach. You shall also give him the first fruits of your grain and wine and oil as well as the first fruits of the shearing of your flock; for the Lord, your God, has chosen him and his sons out of all your tribes to be always in attendance to minister in the name of the Lord' (Dt 18: 1-5).

Priesthood during and after monarchy

During the time of monarchy, the kings performed priestly functions, like offering sacrifices and blessing people on special occasions, as did the kings among the neighboring peoples. They also appointed priestly families to serve in the sanctuaries. David accepted the priesthood of Abiathar but added the priestly line of Zadok (2 Sm 8:17). Solomon displaced the house of Abiathar in favor of Zadok (1 Kgs 2:26). In the first book of Chronicles, we find the genealogy of Levi that connect Aaron and Zadok with Levi (1 Chr 5: 27- 6: 66). The Levite priests served not only in the Jerusalem temple but also in the sanctuaries all over the land of Israel. The reform of Josiah in 621 BC, suppressed the local sanctuaries, centralized the rituals especially the sacrifices in the temple of Jerusalem and reserved the exercise of priesthood to the descendants of Zadok alone. In this context of sweeping reforms, there arose the distinction between the Priests and the Levites (Ez 44: 10-19). The simultaneous disappearance of monarchy and the Jerusalem temple in 587 BC, freed the priesthood from the political power and established it as the only religious guide of the nation, leading to the appearance of the 'high priest' in post-exilic Judaism. The high priest was the most important person in the Palestinian Jewish community in the post-exilic period. He was not only the head of the cult; he was the president of the Sanhedrin, the the highest Jewish Council and the chief representative of the people to the ruling officers of the foreign powers who ruled Palestine during these centuries. The house of Zadok held the office by hereditary succession down to Onias II (175 BC), who was replaced by Jason (175-172), the last Zadokite appointed by the Seleucid kings. As the result of the Maccabean rebellion, Jonathan was invested as high priest in 153 BC. His brother Simon, who succeeded him in 143 BC, was the first of the dynasty of the Hasmoneans who governed as high priests till the year 37 BC. They generally met with opposition from the Pharisees as well as from the traditional clergy who opposed them on account of their non-Zadokite origin. Finally, with the beginning of Herod's reign in 37 BC, the high priests were appointed by the political authority which chose them from the great sacerdotal families in Jerusalem.

The exercise of priestly functions

The fundamental character of Israel, as designated by God, was to be a kingdom of priests and a holy nation: 'You shall be to me a kingdom of priests, a holy nation' (Ex 19:6). Israel was to be 'a holy nation'-reconciled through the 'sprinkling of blood; brought near to, and kept in fellowship with God by that means. The priesthood, as the representative officers for sprinkling the blood for the forgiveness of sins of the people and as their authorized mediators, were required all the more to show forth the 'holiness' of Israel. The bodily qualifications required in the priesthood, the kind of defilements which would temporarily or wholly interrupt their functions, their mode of ordination, and even every portion, material and color of their distinctive dress were all intended to express in a symbolical manner this characteristic of holiness. In Israel, the priests always exercised, first of all, the office of worship. As the man of the sanctuary, a priest gathered the faithful into the house of Yahweh and presided over the liturgies at the time of the feasts of the people. He presented to God the offering of His faithful and he transmitted to the faithful the divine blessing. Once a year, on the Day of Atonement, the high priest officiated for the pardon of all his people's faults (Lv 16). In addition, the priest also performed the rites of consecration and purification such as the purification of lepers (Lv 14) and of the mothers after the childbirth (Lv 12: 6-8). The priests were also the ministers of the Word of God as they explained to the people the narratives from the sacred scripture on which the Jewish faith was based. Of course, in Israel, the Word of God came to His people through another voice: that of the prophets prompted by the Spirit. However, the priests were the custodians of the sacred scripture and they insured the written redaction of the Law. In the last centuries of Judaism, before the destruction of Jerusalem, the synagogues multiplied all over Roman empire and the priesthood concentrated on their ritual duties in the Jerusalem Temple, leaving the interpretation of the sacred scripture to the scribes or the teachers of the Law, often called the Rabbis.

The Levites were to act as priests' assistants, as singers and musicians, as gate keepers and guards, and as officers and judges. It had been their duty to look after the sacred vestments and vessels, the store-houses and their contents and the preparation of the shewbread, of the meat-offerings and of the spices. They were also generally to assist the priests in their work, to see to the cleaning of the sanctuary and to take charge of the treasuries. The service of the week was subdivided among the various families which constituted a course. Just like the priests, the Levites had been arranged into twenty-four courses. Each course of priests and of Levites came on duty for a week, from one Sabbath to another. On Sabbaths the whole course was on duty. On feast-days any priest might come up and join in the ministrations of the sanctuary. At the Feast of Tabernacles all the twenty-four courses were bound to be present and officiate. When actually engaged in service within the Temple, the priests were not allowed to drink wine, either by day or by night. The law even made provision to secure that the priests should come up to Jerusalem properly trimmed, washed and attired so as to ensure the decorum of the service. The priests had to undergo a course of instruction and were examined before being allowed to officiate.

The promise of the perfect high priest

The prophets never questioned the institution of the priesthood itself. However, while they proclaimed its perpetual durability, they also predicted the reform of worship and the renewal of the priesthood in the last days. A prophetic oracle is found both in Isaiah (2:1-5) and in Micah (4:1-3) predicting that 'in the last days' the mountain of the Lord and the House of God would be raised above the hills and that the nations would flow to it. The book of Ezekiel concludes with a magnificent vision of the future Temple and it lays down the duties and functions of the priests. Jeremiah, who had been bold enough to foretell the destruction of the Temple, had nonetheless declared on God's authority that the Levitical priests would never lack successors to offer sacrifices. For his part, the prophet Malachi, while sharply berating the negligence of the priests (Mal 2:1-9), does not remain at this negative level, but proclaims that the Lord 'will enter into his sanctuary' and he will purify the sons of Levi and will refine them like gold and silver, and they will become for the Lord persons who will present the offering as it ought to be. Then the offering of Judah and Jerusalem will be pleasing to the Lord as in the days of old' (Mal 3:3-4). In the first book of Samuel, a mysterious man of God came to Eli and spoke about the promise of God that would often be referred to regarding the renewal of priesthood: 'I will raise up for myself a faithful priest, who will behave according to my heart and according to my desire; I will assure to him lasting house and he will walk always before my Anointed one (1 Sm 2:35). The book of Sirach recalled with insistence that the priesthood of Aaron had been guaranteed by an eternal pact (Sir 45:7-15). The messianic expectation was centered on a unique personage, who would receive both the priestly anointing and the royal coronation at the same time and this eschatological expectation was very much alive at the beginning of the Christian era. We must recognize that it was an entirely normal feature of the Jewish religious aspirations of the period. The people of Israel were waiting for the total and definitive fulfillment of God's plan. It was only reasonable then to include also the priestly aspect, since the priesthood occupied the foremost place in biblical revelation and in the life of the people of God. In this historical context, the Christian community had undertaken to affirm that God had answered the expectations of His people and that the fulfillment has now become a tangible reality: by His life, His death and His glorious resurrection, Jesus became the perfect high priest in whom the messianic expectation finds fulfillment.

Jesus, the unique priest

In the gospels the word 'priest' is never applied either to Jesus or to His disciples, but always designates the Jewish priests. It was clear to everyone that Jesus was not a Jewish priest. It was known that He did not belong to a priestly family and that in consequence He had no right to perform any priestly function. Jesus belonged by birth to the tribe of Judah. Thus, according to the law, He was not a priest. No one thought of attributing priestly office to Him and He himself never laid any claim to it. Jesus' activities during His public ministry had nothing priestly about it in the then traditional sense of the word, but placed him rather in the line of the prophets. He had undertaken to proclaim the word of God, as the prophets had formerly done and to announce that the establishment of the kingdom of God was at hand. He expressed this message sometimes through symbolical actions (Mt 21:18-22), in this respect imitating Jeremiah, Ezekiel and other prophets. His miracles were reminiscent of the time of Elijah and Elisha: the multiplication of the loaves, the raising of the widow's son and the healing of the leper. In fact, many people recognized Him as a prophet, perhaps as the greatest prophet who was eagerly awaited by the people of Israel, in fulfillment of the promise God made to Moses (Dt 18: 19).

Jesus and the Temple

Though Jesus was not recognized as a priest within the Jewish religious system, yet, He challenged the priestly ideology of His times. He was especially rejecting the traditional manner of understanding holiness and was taking sides against the system of ritual separations. Instead of a holiness obtained by separating oneself from others, he proposed a holiness that people can obtain by welcoming them. The word thysia, which designates the ritual sacrifices and occurs very often in the Old Testament, occurs only twice on the lips of Jesus in the gospels and on both occasions he is recalling that God does not like this kind of ritual sacrifice. The first case is in Mark, where thysia occurs in a phrase spoken by a scribe and approved by Jesus and the perspective is the same: the love of God and one's neighbor 'is worth more than all holocausts and all sacrifices' (Mk 12:33). Without employing the word thysia, another saying of Jesus has the same sense: it prescribes that reconciliation with a brother should precede the offering of a gift at the altar of the Temple (Mt 5: 23-24). On the other hand, the gospels record a forceful intervention by Jesus within the Temple itself. In reproaching the sellers of animals destined for sacrifice, Jesus was effectively criticizing the whole sacrificial worship that was administered by the priests. John carefully notes that Jesus 'drove out of the temple the sheep and the cattle' (Jn 2:15), that is to say, the animals that were to be offered in sacrifice. Mark observes that the high priests were very angry with Jesus (Mk 11: 18) and it is not difficult to understand their position. Jesus was questioning their cultic ritual of offering animal sacrifices for the remission of the sins of the people. A connection can be seen between this initiative on the part of Jesus and the prophecy of Malachi: 'Suddenly the Lord whom you are seeking will enter his sanctuary. He is like a refiner's fire and He will purify the sons of Levi' (Mal 3:1-3). The negative part of the prophecy is thus accomplished, but there is nothing to show how its positive part will be fulfilled, that which announces the institution of a worship pleasing to God: 'Then the sacrifice of Judah and Jerusalem will please the Lord' (Mal 3: 4). With the sacrifice of Jesus on the cross at Calvary, the positive aspect of this prophecy would be fulfilled.

The sacrificial death of Jesus

From the point of view of Old Testament cult, the death of Jesus in no way appeared as a priestly offering; it was in fact the very opposite of a sacrifice. Ritual sacrifice did not consist in the putting to death of a living person, still less in his sufferings. In the rites of offering performed by the priest in the holy place, the Jewish laws carefully distinguished between slaughter and ritual sacrifice (Dt 12:13-16). Now Jesus death had taken place outside the holy city. It had not been accompanied by liturgical rites. The rites that accompanied a sacrifice made it a solemn and glorious act that would bring about a union with God and obtain divine blessings. Because it was offered during the course of religious ceremonies, the victim would be symbolically lifted up to God. A legal penalty like the crucifixion of Jesus, on the contrary, was a juridical and not a ritual act. Also, in themselves, Jesus' actions of rendering thanks to God for the bread and the wine, breaking the bread and passing the cup, do not constitute a ritual sacrifice, but belong to the normal course of a meal. Neither is the new value that Jesus confers on these traditional actions necessarily makes them sacrificial. To hand over one's body and to shed one's blood to save others is not a ritual sacrifice, but an act of heroic dedication. 'He died for us' (1 Thes 5:10). To die for someone is not a sacrifice in the ritual sense, but an act of supreme devotion. The leaders of the early Christian communities did not take the title of kohen or hiereus, the Hebrew and Greek words to designate a priest. They were given names which expressed the notion of mission or of service or of a position of responsibility and authority, such as apostolos, (apostle) which means, 'one who has been sent', diakonos (deacon) that means 'one who serves', episkopos from which the word 'bishop' comes and which means 'overseer', presbyteros which gives us the word 'priest' but actually means an 'elder' and hegoumenos which means 'leader'.

The specific intention of Jesus

It is the specific intention of Jesus that makes His death a sacrificial offering. Among the words spoken by Jesus, there is an expression that possesses an undeniably sacrificial connotation, for it unites the word 'blood' with the word 'covenant'. These words have an obvious connection with the words pronounced by Moses at the sacrifice accomplished on Mount Sinai as a way of sealing the covenant between the people of Israel and Yahweh. Moses, sprinkling the blood of the bulls on the people Israel, said: 'This is blood of the covenant which the Lord has concluded with you' (Ex 24:5-8). Seen in this background, the connection between the sacrifice of Jesus and the new covenant is particularly evident in the wording of Matthew and Mark, where the expression 'the blood of the covenant, is literally reproduced (Mt 26:28; Mk 14:24). It is also visible in the wording of Luke and Paul, who say: 'This cup is the new covenant in my blood' (Lk 22:20; 1 Cor 11: 25). It may also be noted that the date of this event also facilitates the connection with the story of the Exodus: the passion of Jesus took place at the time of the Feast of Passover. In his letter to the Galatians, Paul says of the Son of God: 'He loved me and gave himself up for me' (Gal 2:20). The Epistle to the Ephesians takes up the same expression, but extends it and gives it a sacrificial sense: 'Christ loved us and gave himself up for us, an offering and sacrifice to God in an odor of sweetness' (Eph 5:2). The Epistle to the Hebrews affirms insistently that we, Christians, have a priest, that too, 'an eminent high priest' and it identifies Him plainly: He is 'Jesus, the Son of God' (Heb 4:14). The clarity and the force of the affirmation leave not the slightest room for doubt. A comparison is made between His priesthood and the old priesthood affirming that it is in the very person of Christ Jesus that the old priesthood had found its fulfillment.

Personal reflection - 'Jesus, the High Priest'

Christ is the High Priest who unites the people to His priesthood, thereby granting them the priestly privilege of presenting sacrificial offerings to God: Christ has made us priests to serve His God and Father' (Rv 1:6). Peter declares, 'You are a royal priesthood' (1 Pt 2: 90). What will the sacrifices of the believers be? Obviously, it will not consist in ritual sacrifices of the kind prescribed in the Old Testament. Christian worship must model itself on the sacrifice of Christ and will therefore differ radically from the ritual sacrifice of the Old Testament. Like Jesus' own offering, the sacrifice of the believers consists in a transformation of human existence itself by means of divine love, the 'true fire from heaven'. The sacrifice of Christ presents two inseparable aspects, each being realized by means of the other. One concerns the relationship with God: this is the aspect of obedience, of personal faithfulness to the divine will. The other concerns the relationship with mankind: this is the aspect of fraternal solidarity, carried even to the total gift of oneself. Instead of 'aspects', we can call them the 'dimensions' and so we can speak of the vertical dimension and the horizontal dimension which come together to form the cross of Christ, the symbol of the supreme sacrifice of Jesus. The union of these two dimensions characterizes in a similar way the Christian sacrifice, the Christian transformation of human existence. The same expression 'to do the will of God' which first defined the sacrifice of Christ, now defines the Christian vocation. The desire to do what is pleasing to God moves Christians, as it did Christ, to devote themselves to others: 'Do not neglect to do good and to share what you have, for such sacrifices are pleasing to God' (Heb 13:16). In this verse, the author employs the technical term for 'sacrifice' and he applies it to the life of fraternal charity. Henceforth, worship can no longer be situated separately as 'sacred' alongside of a life considered 'profane'. Rather, the entire human life itself must be taken up and transformed into a generous offering of obedience to God and of fraternal service to others, especially the least of the brothers and the sisters. Such transformation of existence is possible only through the priestly mediation of Christ, who communicates to believers the purifying and renewing power of the Spirit. Receiving everything through Christ, the faithful are invited to 'offer through Him at all times a sacrifice of praise of God' (Heb 13:15), through their daily lives, fully devoted to God in love and fully dedicated to others in fraternal service.

I waited for you: Once there was a monk who was making his usual prayer in the chapel. He had the vision of Jesus standing before him. He was delighted and was grateful. At that time, he heard the call of the poor at the door of the monastery who came to get food. It was the duty of that monk to serve every noon some hot soup and food to the starving who came to the monastery for food. He hesitated for a while, since he would not like to miss the vision of Jesus, but then realized that serving the poor was a better service to Jesus than just seeing Him in the vision. He went out to serve the poor their meals. After several hours, he returned to the chapel and saw Jesus still waiting for him. Jesus told him, 'My son! If you had not gone to serve the poor, I would have left you immediately. Since you showed your deep love for me in serving the poor, I waited for you, and now you can have my vision as long as you want'. Jesus spent the entire day with the monk. True worship consists in authentic service to others, always for the love of God.

Quote: Preach not because you have to say something, but because you have something to say- *Richard Whately*

Scripture reading for Day 33: Heb 7: 1-28

Prayer for Day 33: God of mercy and compassion! We offer our entire life as a pleasing sacrifice to you through Jesus our high priest, so that this offering may free us and the world from the bonds of sin and death and win for us your eternal reward! Amen.

34

MEDIATOR

*J*esus is called as 'the mediator of the new covenant' (Heb 9:15; 12:24). Paul states: 'There is one God and one mediator between God and men, Christ Jesus, who gave Himself as a ransom for all men' (1 Tim 2:5). Mediator is the person who stands midway between two others for their communication or who intervenes between two separated parties in order to unite them. The mediator goes from one party to the other, intercedes with the party who is threatening on behalf of the party being threatened and brings peace to the latter, when he obtains it. The English terms mediate, mediator, and mediation are derived from the Latin word 'medius', which means 'in the middle'. The Latin word seems to have originated as a translation of the Greek word 'mesites' that was used in approximately the same basic sense and referred to a person who served as an intermediary between two separated parties who sought reconciliation. This word originated during the early centuries of the Christian era and was employed mostly in ecclesiastical literature, in dependence on the New Testament texts that speak of Christ as mediator. Christ is the unique mediator between God and mankind because in His very person, divinity and humanity are perfectly united.

The concept of mediation is fundamental to any religion as communication between the divine and the human is conceived possible only through some recognized intermediaries, who are acceptable to God and are recognized that way by human beings who seek his mediation. Most of the religions have sought to make up the distance that separates God and man through the intermediaries that can be priests, kings, heavenly heroes, magicians and even the incarnations of gods. In the ancient Near East, the people sought mediators to communicate with gods and obtain their blessings. In Mesopotamia, both gods and men served as mediators. An individual person was considered to live under the patronage of a particular god who, as his personal mediator, presented his petitions to the great gods. The principal human mediator was the king, who served as the representative of the god on earth, as his viceroy. The king represented the people in the cults, in prayer and worship before gods and communicated the will of gods and their blessings to the people. In Egypt, the Pharaoh served as the unique mediator. Himself a god, he incorporated his people in his person and brought the two worlds of god and man in communication.

Mediation in the Old Testament - the intermediaries of Yahweh

While other religions placed secondary divinities or spirits of men as mediators, Israel considered Yahweh as the unique and only God, who is alone in His absolute transcendence.

That is why in the Old Testament, there is no Hebrew word to express 'mediator' or 'mediation' to refer to the arbitrators or intermediaries. Paul explains this Jewish belief very well saying, 'Now there can only be intermediary between two parties, but God is one' (Gal 3:20). However, Yahweh does not exist in solitude in heaven but actively intervenes in history. He speaks to His people in order to guide them and to communicate His holy will. Thus we find the paradox in the Jewish religion whereby there can be no official mediators because Yahweh is one, yet He communicates with His people through intermediaries since He actively intervenes in the life of His chosen people as well as in the world history that He directs as the Creator and the Master of the world. Abraham is chosen by Yahweh to be His intermediary through whom all nations of the earth shall be blessed and Israel, as the chosen people, will receive the blessings of the earth and of posterity. Also, as the friend of God, Abraham played the role of intercessor with God when he intervened in favor of Sodom (Gn 18: 22-32) and the pagan king Abimelech (Gn 20: 17-18). Yahweh chooses Moses and uses him as His instrument to liberate the people of Israel from the Egyptian slavery, to conclude the covenant with them at Mount Sinai, to give them His Law and to establish His worship. Moses acts as head or lawmaker in the name of Yahweh before the people of Israel and represents Israel before Him, often interceding in favor of the people of Israel (Ex 32:11-14). His role as the intermediary in the Old Testament was so important that Moses is the only person in the Bible, apart from Jesus, to be given the name mediator though in a different sense than Jesus: 'The Law was put into effect through angels by a mediator, Moses' (Gal 3:19) who is the intermediary of God par excellence in the Old Testament. After his death his unique office of mediation branched out into three distinct streams.

The three streams of mediation in Israel

The first stream of mediation with God and people of Israel is the institution of Levitical Priesthood. Serving as cultic officials and leading the people in worship and offering their sacrifices, the priests obtained divine forgiveness for the people for their sins and brought down His blessings for the prosperity and peace of the devotees and submitted to God the praise and supplication of the community and of the individuals. As the guardians of the sacred Law, they interpreted the ordinances in the Law to the people thereby revealing Yahweh's holy will to them. They reminded the people of the steadfastness and the generous deeds of Yahweh in their history and invited their unwavering fidelity and loyalty to Him in return. They blessed the people with these words: 'The Lord bless you and keep you. The Lord let His face shine upon you and be gracious to you. The Lord look upon you kindly and give you peace' (Nm 6: 24-26). The second stream of mediation was the institution of kingship. In the history of Israel the kings actually succeeded the judges. The king was the anointed of Yahweh, who treated him as a son (2 Sm 7: 14). Before God, the king represented all his people and although he did not have the title of priest, he exercised the cultic function. He carried the ephod, offered sacrifices, pronounced the prayer in the name of Israel and blessed people. The third stream of mediation was the role of the prophet. While priesthood and kingship were hereditary, the prophet received a personal vocation. Yahweh intervened directly in his life to give him his mission. The prophet made known the holy will of God to the people always insisting that Yahweh spoke through him. At the same time, the prophet prayed to God for his people.

Along with these three streams, there emerged two portrayals of mediation in the Old Testament at a later date. The first is the portrayal of the Servant of Yahweh as presented in Is 40-55. He is a mysterious figure who personified the faithful remnant of Israel in his function as mediator between God and man. His mission was described as not only to preach the message of salvation but also to 'bear the sins of many' and to bring redemption by his own suffering (Is 52:14; 53:12). He would offer his own life as a sacrifice of expiation. Another figure of mediation is the Son of Man as portrayed in the book of Daniel 7: 13-18. He represented the glorified people of God, oppressed by the pagan powers before being exalted by the judgment of God. He was expected to reign over the nations and to assure the reign of Yahweh over the world. At this later date of the post-exilic period, along with these two portrayals, there was also focus on the angels who were presented as the messengers of God. The book of Tobit that describes the service of angel Raphael is the best example for such a presentation about the angels of God in heaven. At the threshold of the New Testament, the angel Gabriel came as the messenger of God to Zechariah and to Mary (Lk 1: 8-38).

The Mediator in the New Testament

That Christ is the definitive and indispensable mediator between God and man is the central doctrine of the New Testament. However, the term mediator itself is a rare occurrence and is found only in a few passages: Gal 3: 19; Heb 9:15; 12:24 and the famous text 1Tim 2:5. Nevertheless, the role of Christ as mediator is proclaimed throughout the New Testament in more concrete and particular terms. Jesus strongly affirmed that no one can approach the Father except through Him. Jesus said: 'No one comes to the Father except through me. If you really knew me, you would know my Father as well. From now on, you do know Him and seen Him' (Jn 14: 6-7). Peter declares, 'Salvation is found in no one else, for there is no other name under heaven given to men by which we must be saved' (Acts 4:12). Underlying all such assertions is the fundamental conviction that man's ultimate destiny is the attainment of union with God, failing which human life is a loss, a disaster. That this union can be reached only through Christ is the chief tenet of the Christian message. The reason for this dependence on Christ is twofold. On the one hand, union with God is, of its very nature, a grace that man by himself has no power to attain or right to expect. On the other hand, by sin man is so turned away from God that he can be restored only by a grace of pardon and conversion coming from God Himself. In the divine plan of salvation, it is through Christ, and through none other apart from Him, that God has chosen to extend to man the grace of His friendship, reconciliation and salvation. Even in the eternal life of the Trinity, the son has a mediatorial role in the sense that the Holy Spirit proceeds from the Father 'through the Son'. Furthermore, in the creation of the world, the Word was the mediator 'through whom' all things were made (Jn 1: 3). By the very fact of the incarnation, there has already been a certain mediation accomplished between divinity and humanity, in that they both are brought together in the one person of Jesus Christ, who is fully God and fully man, thereby, constituting Jesus as the perfect mediator between God and mankind.

Jesus Christ, the unique Mediator

Between God and mankind, Jesus Christ is the mediator of the new covenant, which is better than the old (Heb 7:22). It is henceforth through Him that men draw near to God (Heb 7: 25). Under different forms, this truth is repeatedly affirmed in the New Testament. As we examine the role of Jesus as mediator as explained in the New Testament, the first affirmation is that in being the eternal Son of the everlasting Father, who was with the Father from the beginning (Jn 1: 1-2), Jesus is mediating the Holy Spirit, to complete the divine life of the Holy Trinity. This mediation arises from His very Being as the Son, through whom proceeds the Holy Spirit, of course, from the Father, who is the eternal source of the one and unique Godhead of the Holy Trinity. In relation to the world, the mediation of Jesus is seen in creation. John insists, 'Through Him all things were made; without Him nothing was made that was made' (Jn 1:3). Paul clarifies this preposition: 'By Him all things were created, things in heaven and on earth, visible and invisible, whether thrones, or powers or rulers or authorities. All things were created by Him and for Him. He is before all things and in Him all things hold together' (Col 1: 16-17). In the fullness of time, Jesus comes into the world to bring about a new creation because the old creation was destroyed by the sin of humanity and needed reconciliation and restoration. He, who was 'the Son', shared the flesh and blood of humanity and became man. In Him, the eternal Word of God made flesh and dwelt among us' (Jn 1:14). In His incarnation, Jesus belonged to the two parties, divine and human, whom He came to reconcile in Himself and this He did by the blood of His cross. By himself man was incapable of reconciling himself with the Creator whom he has offended by sin. God reconciled us to Himself through Jesus Christ (2 Cor 5:18), in whom man is made a new creation (2 Cor 5:17). Reconciliation with God brings renewal of fallen human nature, restoration of the friendship with God, as the result of justification by the blood of Jesus (Rom 5:9). The material world, which remains always in solidarity with mankind, suffered degradation as the result of sin of humanity. In the reconciliation of humanity that came with the sanctification by the blood of Jesus, the world also shares in the restoration and becomes a new creation: Paul affirms this saying, 'Through Jesus, God reconciled to Himself all things, whether things on earth or things in heaven, by making peace through His blood, shed on the cross' (Col 1:20).

Personal Reflection – 'Jesus, the only mediator'

In Jesus, the one and only mediator, all the ancient mediations have come to an end. In Him, who is the 'descendant of Abraham', Israel and the nations inherit the blessings promised to Abraham, the father of God's chosen people. Jesus is the new Moses, the guide of the new exodus, who set humanity free from the slavery of sin and death and is leading the new people of God to their promised land of heavenly kingdom. In fact He is greater than Moses, the mediator par excellence of the Old Testament: 'Jesus has been found worthy of greater honor than Moses, just as the builder of a house has greater honor than the house itself. For, every house is built by someone but God is the builder of everything. Moses was faithful as a servant in all God's house, testifying to what would be said in the future. But Christ is faithful as a son over God's house' (Heb 3: 3-6). In Jesus, the three streams of mediation of the Old Testament come together again. First of all, 'Jesus is the perfect high priest who has a permanent priesthood. He is holy, blameless, pure, set apart from sinners, is exalted above the heavens. Unlike the other high priests, He does not need to offer sacrifices day after day, first for His own sins, and then for the sins of the people. He sacrificed for their sins once for all when He offered Himself' (Heb 7: 23-28). He is also the King of kings and the Lord of the lords (Rv 17:14), to whom the Lord God will give the throne of His father David, and He will reign over the house of Jacob forever and His kingdom will have never end (Lk 1: 32-33). Being Himself the Word of God, Jesus is also the prophet par excellence, the announcer of the kingdom of God (Mt 21:11). As the perfect high priest, the King of kings and the prophet par excellence, all the three streams of mediation of the Old Testament come together in Him and find perfection and fulfillment. Jesus is also the Servant of God foretold by Isaiah (Mt 12: 17-21), the Son of Man, who will judge on the last day (Mt 26: 64) and the angel of the covenant who purifies the temple by His coming (Jn 2: 14-17). In the temple which is 'not made by the hand of man' (Heb 9: 11), Jesus remains mediator 'always living to intercede' in favor of His brethren (Heb 7: 5). In fact, just as 'God is one and unique, so also is His mediator one and unique' (1 Tim 2:5), Jesus Christ, the mediator of the everlasting covenant.

Human instruments of mediation

The fact that Christ is the only mediator does not, however, put and end to the role of men as intermediaries in the history of salvation. God chooses and makes use of men and women for His service through the mediation of Jesus Christ who associates all the members of His Body, the Church, in His mediation. Through Jesus, the Head (Col 1: 18), the Church participates in His unique mediatory role, in the new economy of salvation. Already during His earthly life, Jesus called men to work with Him and commissioned them to proclaim the gospel. He gave them power to perform the signs which manifested the presence of God's kingdom in the world (Mt 10: 5-42). These envoys went with the power and authority of

Jesus, the only mediator, driving out the demons and curing the diseases (Lk 9: 1-6). No one knows who the Father is except the Son and those to whom the Son chooses to reveal Him (Lk 10:22) and the Son reveals the Father to the world through His disciples whom He sends because the harvest is plentiful though the laborers are few (Lk 10: 1-2). After the resurrection, with all authority in heaven and on earth, the unique mediator sends the disciples 'to go and make disciples of all nations' promising His presence till the end of age (Mt 28: 18-20). On the Pentecost, Jesus communicated to His Church the Spirit who proceeds from the Father, through Him. The Spirit, continuing the presence of Jesus among the new people of God, gives different gifts to each member in the Church, as He determines (1 Cor 12: 7-11). Thereby the Spirit enables the members of the body of Christ to participate in the mediatory role of Christ, the Head of the body, until that time, when all the members of the body will join the Head in the fullness of His divine glory. Till then, the victorious members of the body of Christ who have joined the company of the angels in heaven and are now associated with the royalty of the Mediator, seated with Him in heaven (Rv 2: 26; 3: 21). They present to God their prayers for the struggling saints on earth, especially asking God to hasten the hour of His justice.

I am going to die like an angel: Mother Theresa once spoke of the man she picked up from the drain. Sick and hungry, half eaten by worms and lying in the street unattended and uncared for, Mother Theresa picked him up from the street and brought him to her 'Home for the Aged'. There the Sisters washed him clean, fed him and cared for him. However, very sick, he was dying slowly. His last words were: 'Mother, I have lived like an animal in the street, but I am going to die as an angel, loved and cared for. Now, I am going home to God'. In every act of fraternal service, done for the love of God, the Christians, manifest the mediatory role of Jesus, the unique mediator, who has commissioned them to be the mediators of His grace to the world.

Quote: Jesus has now many lovers of the heavenly kingdom, but few bearers of His Cross - *Thomas Kempis*

Scripture reading for Day 34:Heb 9: 11-28

Prayer for Day 34: O God! Your only Son is our mediator and our guide to reach you and share your heavenly glory! Grant that we, who place our confidence in your protection may never fail to please you in everything we do and thus may we be the channels of your grace to the world! Amen.

35

PEACE

*P*aul writes to the Ephesians, 'For Christ Himself is our Peace' (Eph 2:14). The risen Christ greets the apostles saying, 'Peace be with you' (Jn 20:19). When sending the disciples on mission, Jesus tells them to greet the people saying, 'Peace be to this house' when they enter a house (Lk 10:5). Jesus leaves peace as His farewell gift to the apostles: 'Peace I leave with you; my peace I give you' (Jn 14: 27). When Jesus was born, the angels sang: 'Glory to God in the highest and on earth peace to men on whom His favor rests' (Lk 2:14). From the above verses, it is very evident to us that peace is closely related to the proclamation of the gospel and thereby it is an important theme in the New Testament. It is also presented as an important blessing of Yahweh in the Old Testament. Every man desires peace from the very depths of the heart and he searches to find it in many ways, especially through recourse to various religious practices, though most often he is left unsatisfied and frustrated. God offers true and lasting peace to His people, through the good news of Jesus Christ, His only Son. Let us explain how Jesus Himself becomes our authentic peace that lasts for ever.

Peace in the Old Testament

By peace, human beings understand a state of tranquility or quietness as a freedom from civil disturbance or a state of security or order within a community provided for by law or custom. Peace signifies also freedom from disquieting or oppressive thoughts or emotions, and harmony in personal relations. Also, peace points to a state or period of mutual concord between governments and a pact or agreement to end hostilities between those who have been at war or in a state of enmity. The Bible employs all these meanings and more when it speaks of peace. The Hebrew word in the Old Testament for peace 'shalom' means 'completeness, soundness and welfare' and is most often linked to God's presence and comes as His blessing. It is so rich in content that no single English word can adequately translate it. It covers good health, prosperity, security, friendship and salvation. It is the desired experience of individuals, families and the people of Israel as a nation. Because God's own presence is in the midst of His people to grant His favor to them, they have 'shalom'. In a secular sense, 'shalom' designates well-being, prosperity, or bodily health. It also expresses the state of mind or internal condition of being at ease, satisfied or fulfilled. It refers to a condition in which nothing is lacking.

Paulraj Lourdusamy

Know God, Know Peace; No God, No Peace

The opening chapters of Genesis describe how the human race came into existence, how and why man rebelled against God's rightful rule and the devastating consequences of the original sin on mankind and the entire creation. In the beginning, Adam and Eve lived in perfect peace with themselves, their surroundings and with God, their Maker. All of that tranquility came to an abrupt end, however, on the day they chose to disobey God. Their deliberate rebellion against God's rightful rule plunged both themselves and every human being after them into sin and death. As the result of their first sin, human beings are born into this world alienated from and at odds with themselves, the world and above all, with God, the Creator and Master. Coupled with this alienation is a deep and abiding yearning for true and lasting peace. Despite the fact that He had every right to do so, God chose not to turn His back on the human race. Rather, He desired to restore humanity back to His friendship and offer the gift of His salvation.

As first step in this direction, God chose Abraham to be the founding father of the nation of Israel, whereby He initiated His saving mission. Three times Scripture refers to Abraham as God's 'friend' (2 Chr 20:7; Is 41:8; Jas 2:23), a relationship involving loving care and resulting in peace. Although God had to take the first step, it was nonetheless up to Abraham to respond appropriately, with trusting and obedient faith. James explains the exemplary faith of Abraham: 'Don't you remember that our ancestor Abraham was declared right with God because of what he did when he offered his son Isaac on the altar? You see, he was trusting God so much that he was willing to do whatever God told him to do. His faith was made complete by what he did, by his actions. And so it happened just as the Scriptures say: 'Abraham believed God, so God declared him to be righteous'. He was even called 'the friend of God' (Jas 2:21-23). Abraham's example teaches that becoming God's friend is a two-step process consisting of God's taking the initiative and man responding with true, active faith. Peace is the gift from God to His friends. Abraham died in an old age happy and in peace (Gn 15:15). It was Israel's firm belief that all peace comes from Yahweh who is the foundation of peace. Gideon's altar had the title, 'Yahweh-shalom' (Jgs 6:24), which means 'Yahweh is peace'. When a person or community is in communion or friendship with Yahweh, there is peace given as a blessing from Yahweh. The priestly blessing invokes the peace of Yahweh upon Israel (Nm 6:26). The elements of peace are mentioned in Lv 26: 3-13: rain, abundant harvests, no enemy to terrorize, no wild beasts to terrify and above all, prosperity, all resulting from God's presence in the midst of His people. If the relationship with Yahweh is corrupted, there can be no peace (Jer 30:5). The false prophets of Jeremiah's time prophesied to the people of Israel the gift of peace when there would be no peace at all (Jer 6: 14; 8:11). Peace is not merely prosperity and well-being, but it is, above all, righteousness that comes from the obedience to the commandments of Yahweh. Such a righteousness would ensure that peace is flowing like a river for Israel (Is 48:18). In fact, peace is one of the fruits of righteousness (Is 32:17-18). The psalmist poetically describes the relationship between the two as righteousness and peace kissing each other (Ps 85:10). There is no peace for the wicked people (Is 48: 22) as God, who gives peace as His blessing to the righteous ones, creates woes for the evil ones (Is 45: 7).

Peace and the Prophets

Shalom becomes a pivotal term in the prophetic writings. The 'false' prophets, forgetting that the conditions of righteousness only would safeguard the national well-being within the covenant relationship, promised political peace forever: 'They led the people astray saying 'peace', when there was no peace' (Ez 13:10). Through the prophet Jeremiah, God says, 'Lies these prophets utter in my name. I did not send them. I gave them no command nor did I speak to them. By the sword and famine shall these prophets meet their end. The people to whom they prophesy shall be cast out into the streets of Jerusalem by famine and the sword' (Jer 14:14-16). Against the sense of false security, the pre-exilic prophets proclaimed the coming judgment precisely as a loss of this shalom due to Israel's persistent disobedience and unrighteousness. The prophet Jeremiah declares as God's word: 'It is because your fathers have forsaken me and followed strange gods which they served and worshiped; but me, they have forsaken and my law they have not observed. And you have done worse than your fathers. Here you are, every one of you, walking in the hardness of his evil heart instead of listening to me. I will cast you out of this land into a land that neither you nor your fathers have known' (Jer 16: 11-13). The prophet Micah states: 'The leaders render judgment for a bribe, the priests give decision for a salary and the prophets divine for money. Therefore, because of you, Zion shall be plowed like a field and Jerusalem reduced to rubble and the mount of the temple to a forest ridge' (Mi 3: 11-12). Israel's persistent moral and spiritual unfaithfulness, however, could not permanently thwart God's plans for peace. The prophets proclaimed with absolute certainty the coming of a day when peace would fill the earth through the reign of God's anointed, the Messiah: 'The messianic child would be a 'Prince of Peace' (Is 9:6). He was expected to end warfare in the world and to proclaim peace throughout the land (Zech 9:9-12). He would reunite families (Mal 4:6). He would bring lasting peace, above all, to Jerusalem -the holy 'city of peace' (Is 66: 12-13).

Isaiah provides a fascinating glimpse of the Messiah and His reign. The messiah will embody peace and bring it to the people. His reign will be the climax of Israel's history and the solution to their present difficulties. Various divine attributes are ascribed to this figure in the list of titles in Isaiah 9:5, the last of which is 'Prince of Peace'. But although he resembles God, he is also depicted in human terms. He will grow in power, sit upon the throne of David and establish an eternal kingdom (Is 9: 6). This imagery of the future Davidic king is developed more graphically in Isaiah 11, where the character of his rule is described. The chapter concludes with what many would see as a description of God's eternal reign (Is 11: 8-9). It has a corporate dimension; a faithful remnant of Israel is tied to the 'shoot' from the stump of Jesse (Is 11:10-16). Christians have traditionally taken this language to refer to the coming of Jesus Christ. In the age to come, peace will be universal as not only the nations but the entire creation will experience the peace of God through the reign of Jesus Christ over the entire earth. The Messianic reign will be an age of peace (Is 2:2-4) with the advent and the rule of the Prince of peace (Jer 33:15-18).

Peace in the New Testament

In the New Testament, the Greek word for peace 'eirene' incorporates the breadth of meaning conveyed by the Hebrew 'shalom' and specifically refers to either 'a set of favorable circumstances involving peace and tranquility' or 'a state of freedom from anxiety and inner turmoil'. It is the opposite of 'war; anguish, distress, confusion; disturbance, tumult, uproar; fight and strife'. The distinctive idea about 'eirene' in the New Testament is its mediation through Jesus Christ. He is described as the peace which ultimately unites humanity (Eph 2:14-17), reconciling humanity with God (Rom 5:1) through His death (Col 1:20). In Christ, true peace has come to the world (Lk 1:79; 2:14 29). By Him it is bestowed on the people (Mk 5:34; Lk 7: 50; Jn 20:19) and His disciples are its messengers (Lk 10:5; Acts 10: 36). So long as sin is not yet conquered in every man until the last day, perfect peace will not come to the world. However, Jesus has left His peace with the disciples (Jn 14:27). Jesus brought peace to Jerusalem (Lk 19:38), but His offer was refused, for which Jesus wept, saying: 'If you had only known on this day what would bring you peace - but now it is hidden from your eyes. The days will come upon you when your enemies will build an embankment against you and encircle you and hem you on every side. They will dash you to the ground, you and your children within your walls. They will not leave one stone on another, because you did not recognize the time of God's coming to you' (Lk 19:42-44). To those who believed in Him, Jesus said, 'Go in peace' and His blessing of peace brought forgiveness of sins (Lk 7: 50) and healing (Lk 8: 48). Just like prophet Jeremiah, Jesus warns about having false security and living in illusory peace that does not exist (Lk 17:26-36). The risen Lord greets the disciples assuring them His peace (Lk 24:36).

Jesus is our peace

In Christ, God became a man and dwelt among the human beings in order to bring God's His reconciliation to the sinful world and and fallen humanity thereby to grant mankind real and lasting peace. The peace that Jesus Christ spoke of was a combination of hope, trust, quiet tranquility and serenity in the mind and within the soul that is brought by a sincere reconciliation with God, the source of lasting peace. Such peace is possible because Jesus reconciled us with His Father through His atoning sacrifice on the cross. As we accept God's gift of peace through personal faith in Jesus Christ, we are expected to be peacemakers in the world. Jesus called His followers to live at peace with each other (Mk 9: 50) and He empowered them to bestow peace on those who are worthy (Mt 10:13). 'Blessed are the peacemakers', said Jesus, 'for they will be called God's children' (Mt 5:9). Peacemaking will sometimes be unsuccessful (Mt 10:34-37). Moreover, peacemaking is costly. It involved a cross for Jesus, and it involves a cross for us, His followers (Mt 10:37-39). According to Jesus, no cost is too great for the privilege of receiving, experiencing and sharing God's peace. At Jesus' birth, the shepherds hear the angels proclaiming that with the arrival of the savior, peace is available 'on earth' to people 'on whom God's favor rests' (Lk 2:14). In Luke's gospel 'peace on earth' comes in a special way, not only to the disciples but also to the outcasts, foreigners and to all those who will receive God's grace and respond with faith.

Peace cannot remain where it is not welcomed. If a home welcomes God's messenger, that messenger's 'peace' remains there; if not, the peace returns to the messenger (Mt 10:13). When the disciples and the peace of Jesus are rejected, they are to leave that house or that town, shaking off the dust of their feet against it. So Jesus defined two groups of human beings: those who could receive Him and His peace and those who would not receive Him: 'Do not think that I have come to bring peace on earth; I have not come to bring peace, but a sword. For I have come to set a man against his father, and a daughter against her mother, and a daughter-in-law against her mother-in-law; and a man's foes will be those of his own household' (Mt 10:33-36). Thus His gospel of peace may create division even in the same family (Lk 12: 51-53), because the gospel demands a definite response of faith leading to those who accept the gospel and those who reject it, thereby creating division even in the same family. However, the Christians are called to be the channels of peace. Peacemakers who sow in peace raise a harvest of righteousness (Jas 3: 18). Peace also is the fruit of the Holy Spirit (Gal 5:22). Sometimes God disciplines us through hardships that 'produces a harvest of righteousness and peace for those who have been trained by it' (Heb 12:11).

Personal reflection- 'Peace, I give you'

In Greek thought 'peace' is a relational word which speaks of a state of objective well-being, leading to harmonious relations between people or nations. Living at peace with others involves much more than the mere avoidance of open conflict or engaging in adversity. It is rather establishing authentic fellowship among the human beings leading to solidarity between peoples and nations in the world. A genuine fellowship among the human beings will come about only when the people feel that they are the children of the one and only God, who is the Father of us all. Without such a strong bond arising from the common fatherhood of

God, building sincere brotherhood among the human beings will be a very difficult task. For us, Christians, peace is being in harmony with God, with our fellow human beings and also with the entire creation. Our love for the Father and His only Son Jesus Christ must lead us to care for others, thereby building up bridges among the human beings and becoming the channels of peace in the world and among the peoples. For us, Christians, true and lasting peace can come only through a personal and committed relationship with Jesus and through Him with God, our heavenly Father.

The question arises: 'In what way does the Lord Jesus become our peace?' The answer to this question leads us at once to the great divine plan of atonement. Jesus presented to God a full, honorable, and accepted atonement for the sins of the world. The only thing that could separate between God and man was sin. Jesus is the Lamb of God who took away the sins of the world through His perfect sacrifice on the cross. By offering Himself as a sacrifice for the sin of the world, Jesus bore our sins on Himself, thereby suffering, bleeding, dying and so making peace by the blood of His cross. And now, by the great sacrifice of Christ once for all, we are made one with God, one with Him in mind, one in affection, one in will and one in fellowship. Also, through the power of Christ who removed the walls of separation between the human beings, we are empowered and enabled to love and serve others. Paul explains this fact to the Ephesians: 'But now you belong to Christ Jesus. Though you once were far away from God, now you have been brought near to him through the blood of Christ. For Christ himself has made peace between us Jews and you Gentiles by making us all one people. He has broken down the wall of hostility that used to separate us. By his death he ended the whole system of Jewish law that excluded the Gentiles. His purpose was to make peace between Jews and Gentiles by creating in himself one new person from the two groups. Together as one body, Christ reconciled both groups to God by means of his death, and our hostility toward each other ended' (Eph 2: 14-16). In the same way, today, Jesus can offer His peace to the hurting hearts, broken families, divided communities and warring nations if He is received and His Gospel is accepted as good news. In and of ourselves, we have neither the desire nor the ability to live at peace with God, that is, to enter into a relationship centered on knowing, loving and serving Him as well as serving other human beings for His sake. As seen in world's many and various religions, philosophies and belief systems, trying to get to God on our own terms and/or trying to force Him to accept us is an exercise in futility. And yet the true and lasting peace for which we all long is available only in and through a right relationship with God, which adds up to a real dilemma: Although we cannot get to God on our own merit, we cannot experience real peace apart from Him. The good news is that God, with whom our first parents have broken their friendship through their fall, seeks to make us His friends. He is so filled with love that He stoops down to our level, reaches out to us, and freely offers us the opportunity to enter into a real, lasting and personal relationship with Him, a relationship centered on peace. For this purpose, He has sent his only Son to the world, Jesus Christ, who is our peace.

Francis of Assisi and the brother Wolf: Once Francis of Assisi visited the people of the village of Gubbio. He found out that the people were scared of a wild wolf that was harming people and cattle alike. Francis went to the nearby forest where the wolf was hiding and gently persuaded him to come to the village. In front of the people gathered there, he asked the wolf to promise that he would never harm any cattle or people. The wolf made its promise by lifting its right paw and placing it in the hands of Francis. Then he asked the villagers to promise that they would feed the wolf everyday so that it would not starve and they readily agreed. For the next two years till it died of old age, the wolf went everyday to a house in the village where it was happily fed. It never harmed any person or animal till its death. The villagers shed tears of sadness when it died, because they loved the wolf, not only because it turned good, but it always reminded them of the visit of St. Francis of Assisi to their little village. Justice and charity only bring true peace.

Quote: <u>Prayer of Francis of Assisi</u>

Lord, make me a channel of your peace.
Where there is hatred, let me sow love.
Where there is injury, let me sow pardon.
Where there is doubt, let me show faith.
Where there is despair, let me give hope.
Where there is darkness, let me give light.
Where there is sadness, let me give joy.
O Divine Master, grant that I may
not try to be comforted, but to comfort;
Not try to be understood, but to understand;
Not try to be loved, but to love.
Because it is in giving that we receive,
In forgiving that we are forgiven,
And in dying that we are born to eternal life.

Scripture reading for Day 35: Lv 26: 3-13

Prayer for Day 35: O God! You are the author of peace! Preserve us in your peace and guide us in your love! Hear our prayers for peace in the world and fellowship among the human beings. Keep us, your children, always at your side so that we may taste your fatherly goodness in this life and enjoy your lasting peace in the eternal life! Amen.

36.

POWER OF GOD

*I*n the first letter to the Corinthians, Paul makes a remarkable statement naming Jesus the 'power'of God (1Cor1: 24). He further states, 'For the message of the cross is foolishness to those who are perishing, but to us who are being saved, it is the power of God. For the weakness of God is stronger than man's strength. God chose the weak things of the world to shame the strong' (1 Cor 1: 18, 25, 27). Every religion views God/ gods as having 'power' over not only the natural forces and but also over human beings. However, they differ in attributing the degree of that power to individual gods. In the ancient Near East as well as in the Greek and Roman religious mythologies, some gods were considered more powerful than others and some exercised authority over a specific natural force such as rain or wind, thereby they were addressed as rain god or wind god. In the midst of polytheistic religious beliefs and practices, the Jewish faith stated with unwavering firmness the belief in one and only true God, who created the heaven and the earth. The Christian faith formulates the first article of biblical revelation that it draws from the Jewish religious heritage as 'I believe in God, the Father almighty, creator of heaven and earth'. The formula expresses the Christian belief in the omnipotence of the one true God. In relation to the world, God, the creator, employs His power in relation to human beings, first of all, to save His people, thereby offering human race the gift of eternal salvation thereby making them the heirs of His heavenly kingdom.

The power of Yahweh as the creator

Yahweh, the God of Israel is all-powerful in heaven and on earth, because heaven and earth are His creation (Gn 2: 4). He created them by His word and the breath of His mouth: 'By the Lord's word, the heavens were made; by the breadth of His mouth, all their host. He spoke and it came to be, commanded and it stood in place' (Ps 33: 6, 9). He gives to the universe its stability (Ps 119: 90) as He controls the natural forces that can rise up to disturb the order that He has put in place such as the violent sea (Ps 65: 5). He does with His handiwork as He wills: The Lord says, 'It was I who made the earth, and man and beast on the face of the earth, by my great power, with my outstretched arm and I can give them to whomever I think fit' (Jer 27: 5) and 'nothing is impossible for Him' (Jer 32: 17). It is He who determined the order (Prv 8: 27) and as such He can change it at His will. By His power, He can make the large mountains leap or melt away (Ps 114: 4; 144: 5). The almighty power of the one true God is revealed to the entire humanity in His wonderful creation. Indeed, 'the heavens declare the glory of God and the sky proclaims its builder's craft' (Ps 19: 2).

The power of Yahweh as the God of Israel

God also manifests His power through His intervention in the history of the world, giving it direction and purpose, especially as He executes His plan of salvation for mankind. He created our first parents in His own image and likeness (Gn 1:27), to be the masters of His creation and to share His friendship. Through their disobedience to God, our first parents lost the friendship with God and disfigured His own image and likeness in them. God, ever faithful and true, did not abandon humanity, but in His infinite wisdom, executed His plan of salvation of humanity and the renewal of His entire creation through the people of Israel until that time, when He would send His only Son. First, God chose Abraham and revealed in his life of friendship that 'nothing is impossible' for Him, including the gift of a son in old age and sterility. God asked Abraham: 'Is anything too marvelous for me to do? (Gn 18: 14). In every situation, God showed that He could protect His chosen ones and realize for their benefit, whatever He has willed. God made Abraham 'a great nation' (Gn 12: 2) and He granted Promised Land to Jacob and his descendants (Gn 28: 13). God blessed Jacob and gave him the name of Israel, which means 'you contended divine being' (Gn 32: 27-30). The people of Israel, the descendants of Abraham, Issac and Jacob experienced the almighty power of Yahweh who revealed Himself in the burning bush to Moses as the God of their fathers, 'the God of Abraham, of Issac and of Jacob' (Ex 3: 15). By His strong hand and His outstretched arm, Yahweh liberated His people from the slavery of the mighty Pharaoh. Moses asks his people, 'Did any god venture to go and take a nation for himself from the midst of another nation, by testings, by signs and wonders, by war, with his strong hand and outstretched arm, and by great terrors, all of which the Lord, your God, did for you in Egypt before your very eyes? (Dt 4: 34). By this unprecedented deliverance, Yahweh revealed Himself as the one and all-powerful God, in heaven and on earth. Moses says, 'You must know and fix in your heart that the Lord is God in the heavens above and on earth below and that there is no other' (Dt 4: 39).

Yahweh secured victory for His people as the warrior. His name Sabaoth or the Lord of the hosts means Yahweh of armies. The psalmist sings, 'Who is the king of glory? The Lord, a mighty warrior, the Lord, mighty in battle' (Ps 24: 8). David tells Goliath, 'You come against me with sword and spear and scimitar, but I come against you in the name of the Lord of hosts, the God of the armies of Israel that you have insulted' (1 Sm 17: 45). At times Yahweh intervened to strengthen His people and their leaders as it happened with Gideon and with the king David who won victories for Israel. Judas Maccabeus declares, 'It is easy for many to be overcome by a few; in the sight of Heaven, there is no difference between deliverance by many or by a few; for victory in war does not depend upon the size of the army, but on strength that comes from Heaven' (1Mc 3: 18). On other occasions, God, in answer to the prayer of the people, intervened in such a striking way that the people had nothing to do themselves, as He destroyed the mighty army of Sennacherib, the king of Assyria (2 Kgs 19: 35). Yet, in every situation, it is Yahweh who is the strength of His people, as the psalmist declares, 'God is our refuge and our strength, an ever-present help in distress' (Ps 46: 2). Israel cannot fail to be saved, for her strength comes from God who loves Israel and He has the power to do what He wills in history.

The power of God who saves His servants

God, the almighty, has His own preferential compassion for the powerless in the world. How He comes to their aid to put an end to social servitude of the oppressed people is revealed as early as in the exodus experience of the people of Israel, who suffered slavery and oppression at the hands of the Egyptians. God, with His mighty hand, set them free. However, the liberated people of Israel always did not fully trust God and were faithful to Him. They made a golden calf and worshiped it in the desert (Ex 32: 1-5). They showed no faith in His power despite His mighty hand performing so many miracles during the march to the Promised Land. As punishment, the entire unfaithful generation was to die in the desert after having wandered about for forty years (Nm 14:22). But God, at the intercession of Moses, did not destroy completely this rebellious people, for Moses prayed: 'O Lord, why should the Egyptians say, 'With evil intent He brought them out, that He might exterminate them from the face of the earth? Let your blazing wrath die down; relent in punishing your people' (Ex 32: 12). God relented in the punishment He had threatened to inflict on His people (Ex 32:14). What we see throughout the salvation history is that God remains with the weak and the powerless against the mighty and powerful, in order to liberate the subjugated and oppressed people from their degradation and slavery so that His power over the entire creation would be revealed and recognized. Within the community of Israel, Yahweh condemned and punished those who abused their power and inflicted hardships over the poor refusing to deal with them justly. God says, 'Woe to those who enact unjust statutes and who write oppressive decrees. Depriving the needy of judgment and robbing my people's poor of their rights, making widows their plunder and orphans their prey. What will you do on the day of punishment, when ruin comes afar? To whom will you flee for help?' (Is 10:1-3).

As He intervenes in history, often He chooses the weak instruments to make them strong in Him. The little shepherd boy David could face and destroy the giant-like Goliath because 'the Lord delivered him into David's hands' (1 Sm 17: 47). Jeremiah, a person unable to speak, would become a fiery prophet by the power of God (Jer 1: 6-8). The best case for Yahweh standing in solidarity with the downtrodden in His power is the people of Israel themselves, who were left without any hope in a foreign land after the exile. Through prophet Ezekiel God assured to revive them and bring them back to homeland which He did. Above all, God sees the entire humanity, powerless and weak, in the face of sin that has destroyed the divine image of mankind. He takes pity and wishes to save the entire humanity from sin and death. He foretells through prophet Isaiah how He plans to accomplish His plan for the salvation of mankind - through His mysterious Servant (Is 53), who would die, weighed down by suffering and abuse. But by means of His suffering and death, he will make countless justified (Is 53: 11). Again, when the faithful Jews were facing persecution at the mighty and the powerful of the world during the rule of the Greeks, God assured their victory by the promise of resurrection of the dead that can happen only as the result of His power that brings eternal life (2 Mc 7:9). At His appointed time, He will end the power of the oppressors leading to their damnation, but give the faithful ones a share in the grant eternal dominion of the Son of Man (Dn 7:12).

The divine power of Jesus

God's power to end the reign of sin and death, of devil and evil is revealed to us, the believers, in the person of Jesus Christ, who manifests God's absolute power as 'love' 'grace' and 'blessing' for the eternal life of mankind. Jesus, the almighty Word, was made flesh in the womb of the young girl from Nazareth, as the power of the most High overshadowed her (Lk 1: 35). As the Son of Man, Jesus was anointed with the Spirit and Power. He went around doing good and healing all who were under the power of the devil, because God's power was with Him (Acts 10: 38). Jesus manifested His divine power by miracles, wonders and signs which God did through Him (Acts 2: 22) that proved not only that God was with Him and that He was sent by the Father, but in addition that He is truly Emmanuel, 'God with us' (Mt 1: 23).

Through the miracles of healing, Jesus manifested His power to save mankind not only from their sins but also from all the consequences of sins such as human infirmity, suffering and death. Jesus gave abundant proofs of His power and Godhead. The winds hushed as He uplifted His finger and ordered to be calm, the waves obeyed His voice and became docile, the tempest cowered at His feet, as before a conqueror it knew and obeyed. These stormy elements, the wind, the tempest and the water gave full proof of His abundant power. The lame man leaping, the deaf man hearing, the dumb man singing, the dead rising, these, again, were proofs that the 'power of God' was with Him. As the voice of Jesus startled the shades of Hades and rent the bonds of death, with 'Lazarus, come forth!' and when the carcass rotten in the tomb woke up to life, His divine power and Godhead showed forth before the world. Jesus cured diseases and raised the dead. He forgave sins and through the power of the Holy Spirit He expelled demons. He affirmed His power to lay down His life and take it up again, that is, to immolate Himself freely on the cross and to rise again in resurrection. Finally, He announced His coming on the last day to exercise His power as the sovereign judge (Jn 5: 21-29). He said, 'You will see the Son of Man sitting at the right hand of the power and coming on the clouds of heaven' (Mt 26: 64). After offering His life on the cross for the salvation of the world, Jesus was buried in the tomb. Not long, however, did he sleep, for he gave another proof of His divine power and Godhead, when He rose from the dead after three days, not being held by the bonds of death.

Jesus and the Mission

To draw all things to Himself, Jesus, before His ascension, sent out His disciples to give testimony to the world until the end of time that He has all power in heaven and on earth, to save the human race and to renew the entire creation. They have to proclaim the good news of salvation in Jesus Christ to all the nations and to all the peoples until the end of time. Those who believe the good news in faith and obedience will be made through the power of God His adopted children and inherit His everlasting kingdom. He promises 'to be with them always, to the very end of the age' (Mt 28: 18-20) as the mission of the Church continues to make new children of God in every generation. Jesus is especially present through the Holy Spirit whom He sent from the Father. Jesus tells the disciples, 'I am going to send you what my Father has promised; but stay in the city until you have been clothed with power from on high' (Lk 24: 49). The Spirit that filled the apostles on the Pentecost (Acts 2: 4), is the Counselor that the risen Christ gave them as farewell gift and the Spirit guided the disciples of Jesus as they proclaimed to the world the power of Jesus as the Lord and Savior (Acts 2: 32-36). Wherever the powerful preaching of the apostles converted the hearts of men they exercised the power to forgive their sins and to communicate the Spirit to them in order to make them the children of God (Acts 8: 17).

Paul declares to the Corinthians that the message of the cross is the power of God: 'For the message of the cross is foolishness to those who are perishing, but to us who are being saved, it is the power of God' (1 Cor 1: 18). That is why Paul is not concerned about preaching with wise and persuasive words but with a demonstration of the Spirit's power, so that the faith may not rest on men's wisdom but on God's power (1 Cor 2: 5). It is because 'God chose the foolish things of the world to shame the wise and the weak things of the world to shame the strong' (1 Cor 1: 27). It is the cross of Christ that gives the 'power to grasp how wide and long, and high and deep is the love of Christ' and to know this love surpasses all knowledge (Eph 3: 18-19). The Cross leads us to God through the understanding of His infinite love revealed in the sacrifice of His only Son for the salvation of the world. In this way, the message of cross becomes the power of God. The Disciples of Christ receive God's power to serve others especially to bring the good news of Christ: 'Jesus was crucified in weakness, yet He lives in God's power. Likewise, we are weak in Him, yet by God's power we will live with Him to serve you' (2 Cor 13: 4). Through them the gospel reaches the hearts of men with power and with the Holy Spirit (1 Thes 1:5). Those who accept the gospel and believe in Jesus Christ 'are shielded by God's power until the coming of salvation that is ready to be revealed in the last time' (1 Pt 1:5). The devil has power to make war with the saints as he was given authority over every tribe, people, language and nation and many will be guided by him (Rv 13:7-8), until that day when Christ 'will destroy all dominion, authority and power' and the last enemy to be destroyed is death' (1 Cor 15: 24-26). Then, the Lord God almighty will reign in power and glory along with the Lamb of God, in the company of the angels and the saints forever.

Personal reflection – 'Jesus, the power of God'

Jesus is the power of God, because in Him we see the greatest act of power that has ever or will ever be demonstrated and witnessed. He alone has the power to reconcile the world unto Himself, not counting their trespasses against them (2 Cor. 5:19). Jesus alone has the power to be both the just judge and the justifier of the one who has faith in Him (Rom 3:26). He alone has the power to forgive sins (Mark 2:7). He alone has the power to reckon an ungodly man righteous apart from works (Rom 4:5). He alone has the power to raise the dead to new life and then seat them in the heavenly places (Eph 2:5-6). We have all these spiritual blessings and more through the unfathomable power of the cross of Jesus Christ. In order to see real power, we, the believers, should look at the cross of Jesus Christ. There 'His power shines like the working of His mighty strength, which God exerted in Him when He raised Him from the dead and seated Him at His right hand in the heavenly realms far above all rule and authority, power and dominion, and every title that can be given, not only in the present age, but also in the one to come' (Eph 1:19-21). On the cross is present for us all the power we need to smell, taste, touch, hear, see and understand the infinite love of God that He manifested in His Son, the crucified Lord, for the salvation of the mankind. The cross preaches the gospel to us more than any words,   that gospel, which is the power of God for salvation to everyone who believes (Rom 1:16). The power of God, demonstrated most fully in the cross of Jesus Christ, should be seen as a paradox by men. After all, men are always impressed with the manifestation of power that is compelling physically, politically, financially, militarily or spiritually, in strength and might. The message of the world is that strength is good and weakness is bad. Power is proof that one is a winner while weakness is proof one is a loser. The cross is the symbol of cruel punishment that was not inflicted on Roman citizens, but only on the non-Roman citizens and the slaves. It represents the utter powerlessness and helplessness of a crucified person before the cruel expression of the human might and power of those who inflicted such a merciless and terrible punishment on him. As such it is the sign of utter weakness. But the weakness of God revealed on the cross is stronger than the man's strength (1Cor 1:25).   Indeed, God chose the lowly things of the world and the despised things among the human beings (1Cor 1:28) to reveal His power as we see in the symbol of the cross. Through the symbol of utter weakness, God reveals the mighty expression of His redeeming power for the salvation of the entire humanity and the renewal of the whole creation. Let us bow before Christ on the cross and crown Him with the songs of praises. He is worthy of it and unto Him is everlasting power and might. Let us bless His name, exalt Him, shout the songs of praise in a loud voice, above all, love Him and serve Him with all our might and strength, for in Jesus Christ, the crucified savior, is revealed the unconditional and compassionate love of God as His power. Let the whole world sing in one voice: O Christ, we adore you, for by your cross, you have redeemed the world.

In the cross shines the beautiful charity: Once when Catherine of Sienna was going to the Church for prayer, she met a man, pale and thin, begging for charity. He was a worker from nearby village. Sick for sometime, he did not work for many days. He would like to return to his village but had no food for several days and hence no strength to walk the long distance. Catherine had no money with her. Just a little food would not help the man much as he also needed money to buy medicine and also food for a couple of days till he could reach home. As she did usually, Catherine held her hands over the silver cross that she was wearing from her childhood and prayed for the man. With sudden inspiration, she took the silver cross that had a few precious stones and handed it over to the man and told him to sell it and get money. The man would have received much more money than what he required for his way home. That night, she had a vision in which Jesus appeared to her and beside Him was her little silver cross. He told her, 'In this cross shines your beautiful charity'. In the cross of Christ, shines for us the beautiful charity of God, as His power.

Quote: The Cross is where history and life, legend and reality, time and eternity intersect. There, Jesus is nailed for ever to show us how God could become a man and a man could become God - *Malcolm Muggeridge*

Scripture reading for Day 35: Rom 8: 18-39

Prayer for Day 36: Lord Jesus Christ! bound and forsaken for our salvation, betrayed by one who sat at your table, abandoned by all your own, delivered to the powers of this world, led to the slaughter as the Lamb of God, and crucified on the Cross! Grant us the grace to remember your sacred passion on the cross and to find the power from the cross to bear our sufferings courageously and to serve you joyously all the days of our life, till we shall share in your eternal glory in heaven! Amen.

37

WISDOM OF GOD

*I*n his theological discourse, another title assigned by Paul to Jesus is the 'wisdom of God'. He explains, 'Jews demand miraculous signs and Greeks look for wisdom, but we preach Christ crucified: a stumbling block to Jews and foolishness to Gentiles, but to those whom God has called, Jews and Greeks alike, Christ is the wisdom of God' (1 Cor 1: 22-24). The quest for wisdom is a trait of mankind and that is why in every culture, we find collections of wisdom literature. In the ancient Orient, both Egypt and Mesopotamia had a great reputation for their sages who bequeathed abundant literature of wisdom that consists of maxims on how to live free of anxiety that arises from hostility, opposition and failure and to foster one's success and advancement. A class of professional scribes, who worked in palaces and temples, seemed to be at the origin of this literature that offers wise counsel for a successful life. The sages, however, were also concerned about moral character as they counseled about honesty, kindliness, truthfulness and moderation. In some instances, the writings of the sages contain their reflections on the problem of good and evil, as they questioned the success of wickedness and the failure of righteousness and explained the proper attitude that man should take as he faced unhappiness. In Greece, in the sixth-century BC, such a reflection on the meaning of life took a speculative turn leading to the Greek philosophy.

Wisdom in the Old Testament

Israel seemed to have no contact with the wisdom literature of the Orient, until the settlement in Canaan. However, Joseph was hailed as a wise man in Egypt: Pharaoh said to Joseph: 'Since God has made all this known to you, no one can be as wise and discerning as you are' (Gn 41: 39). Moses grew up in the court of Pharaoh, as the adopted son of Pharaoh's daughter (Ex 2: 10-11) and as such, should have had some knowledge of the wisdom literature of Egypt. King Solomon had a great reputation as the wisest of the kings: 'God gave Solomon wisdom and exceptional understanding and knowledge, as vast as the sand on the seashore. Solomon surpassed all the Cedemites and all the Egyptians in wisdom. He was wiser than all other men and his fame spread throughout the neighboring nations' (1Kgs 5:9-11). The queen of Sheba, as she witnessed Solomon's great wisdom, said to him: 'Your wisdom and prosperity surpass the report I heard. Happy are your men, happy these servants of yours, who stand before you always and listen to your wisdom' (1Kgs 10: 6-9). 'King Solomon surpassed in wisdom and riches all the kings of the earth'

(1Kgs 10: 23). Of course, the Old Testament makes it clear that both Joseph (Gn 41:47) and Solomon (1Kgs 3: 6-14) received their wisdom from God. Israelite wisdom, like the wisdom of other peoples, was the product of the scribal schools and the scribal class that appeared in Israel during the time of monarchy. Israel always made it clear that true wisdom comes from Yahweh alone as evidenced in Joseph and Solomon. Though men might always attempt to gain knowledge by their own intellectual powers and efforts, as did the first parents (Gn 3: 1-7), for the people of Israel, true wisdom could come from God alone. God gave them, His chisen people, the divine Law as the foundation of authentic wisdom. Moses said to the people of Israel, 'Observe the statutes and the decrees as the Lord, your God, has commanded you, in the land you are entering to occupy. Observe them carefully, for thus you will give evidence of your wisdom and intelligence to the nations, who will hear of all these statutes and say, 'This great nation is truly a wise and intelligent people' (Dt 4: 5-8).

The folly of trusting human wisdom

The prophets called upon the people of Israel to find the wise and perfect path to holiness in the Law of the Lord and to remain faithful to Him by obeying Hos ordinances. They spoke against the temptation to judge everything according to human views and perceptions and seek guidance and light in godless human wisdom. God tells Jeremiah to tell His people, 'My people do not know the ordinance of the Lord. How can they say, 'We are wise, we have the law of the Lord? Why that has been changed into falsehood by the lying pen of the scribes? Since they have rejected the word of the Lord, of what avail is their wisdom? (Jer 8:7-9). God tells Isaiah, 'Therefore I will deal with this people in surprising and wondrous fashion. The wisdom of its wise men shall perish and the understanding of its prudent men be hid (Is 29:14) and the wise will be confounded, dismayed and ensnared (Is 8: 9). Isaiah further states: 'Woe to those who are wise in their own sight and prudent in their own esteem' (Is 5: 21). In the destruction of Jerusalem in 587 BC, the warnings of the prophets came true. The false wisdom of the royal counselors who assured the people of Israel security and protection of God, even though He firmly rejected their sinful ways and abandoned them to their destruction by the pagan powers. Jeremiah pointed out their folly of false wisdom and condemned them: 'Small and great alike, all are greedy for gain; prophet and priest all practice fraud. 'Peace, peace, they say, though there is no peace. They are odious; they have done abominable things, yet they are not at all ashamed. Hence they shall be among those who fall; in their time of punishment they shall go down' says the Lord (Jer 6: 14-15). The painful experience of exile reminded the people of Israel about their obligation to remain faithful to the Law of the Lord, even as they sought the clarity of the earthly things as knowledge.

The wisdom literature of Israel

After returning from exile, the scribes and writers integrated all their reflections on noble character and good and pleasant behavior within the framework of the Law and the fidelity to God. The sages of the Old Testament saw the powerful hand of God at work in history even as they admired nature and sought to identify those virtues and attitudes that lead to true happiness (Sir 42-43). They wrote about prudence, moderation in desires, hard work, humility, level-headedness, discretion and loyalty. Unlike the prophets, who spoke about the life and destiny of the people of Israel as a nation, the sages were concerned about the life of the individual at its best and worst. In the wisdom literature, we find discourses on the success, good behavior and happiness of the individuals as well as reflections on their personal problems such as solitude, wretchedness, anguish in the face of suffering and death. As the just men, who remained faithful to Yahweh, perished unjustly, as seen during the time of Greek persecution, especially during the fateful reign of Antiochus IV, the sages brought encouragement and hope to the people of Israel by the promise of the reward of eternal life (Wis 5:15). In the religious history of Israel, the belief in resurrection originated in this way, as the sages sought answers for the unjust sufferings and death of the loyal and unwavering people of Yahweh who remained faithful to Him till death.

Some salient features of Wisdom literature of Israel

The sages portrayed Yahweh as the only and truly wise God from whom originates all wisdom. He can communicate it to whomever He wishes to reveal because He is the sage par excellence. The wisdom of Yahweh is revealed, first of all, in the creation: 'The Lord by wisdom founded the earth, established the heavens by understanding' (Prv 3:19). As the sages contemplated the wonder of God's creation, they began to see His wisdom as a divine reality that exists from eternity and for eternity with God Himself. Wisdom speaks about her pre-existence: 'When God established the heavens, I was there, when He marked out the vault over the face of the deep; When He made the firm skies above, when He fixed fast the foundations of the earth; When He set for the sea its limit, so that the waters should not transgress His command; Then was I beside Him as His craftsman and I was His delight day by day' (Prv 8: 27-30). Wisdom is identified with the Law: 'All wisdom is the fear of the Lord; Perfect wisdom is the fulfilling of the Law' (Sir 19: 17). Present from creation, wisdom is associated with all that God does in the world: 'Indeed, she reaches from end to end mightily and governs all things well' (Wis 8: 1). It is purely a gift of God (Wis 8: 21) that brings all goods. Wisdom says, 'Happy the man who obeys me, and happy those who keep my ways. He who finds me finds life and wins favor from the Lord' (Prv 8: 33-36). Solomon, the wisest of the human beings, states: 'All good things together came to me in the company of the wisdom and countless riches at her hands' (Wis 7: 11). Another wise sage proclaims, 'Happy the man who finds wisdom, the man who gains understanding! For her profit is better than profit in silver and better than gold is her revenue. She is more precious than corals and none of the choice possessions can compare with her. Long life is in her right hand and in her left are riches and honor. Her ways are pleasant ways and all her paths are peace. She is a tree of life to those who grasp her and he is happy who holds her fast' (Prv 3:13-18).

Jesus as the Wisdom of God

The prophet Isaiah foretold that the messianic king would be endowed with 'a spirit of wisdom and of understanding' (Is 11: 2). This prophecy finds fulfillment in Jesus, the true wisdom of God. Jesus grew in wisdom and stature and in favor with God and men in Nazareth (Lk 2:52). At the beginning of His public ministry, when Jesus came to Nazareth and spoke in the synagogue, the people were amazed at His teaching and they asked: 'Where did this man get this wisdom and these miraculous powers? (Mt 13: 54), wondering how He received the wisdom that was unequaled and was accredited by miraculous works. Jesus understood this problem and answered that in His person, they saw someone greater than Solomon (Mt 12:42). To His disciples, Jesus promised to 'give the words and wisdom that none of the adversaries will be able to resist or contradict' (Lk 21:15). Jesus praised His Father because He had hidden the good news of salvation from the wise and the learned and revealed them to little children (Mt 11: 25). Jesus presented Himself as the true wisdom and He invited the people to come to Him and learn from Him promising them rest and peace (Mt 11: 28-29).

Pauline teaching of Jesus Christ as the wisdom of God

The title of Jesus as the 'wisdom of God' is an expression, specific to Paul. To explain this title, we have to examine Paul's presentation of Jesus as the wisdom of God in his epistles. First of all, Paul contrasts the wisdom of God with the wisdom of the world. He asks, 'Where is the wise man? Where is the scribe? Where is the debater of this age? Has not God made foolish the wisdom of the world?' (1Cor 1:20). Paul, then, speaks of a wisdom, not of this age, nor of the rulers of this age (1 Cor 2: 6), but the wisdom of God, which according to him, has a different content and a different character than that of the wisdom of the world or of this age. It has a salvific content, rather than a philosophic one, a revelatory and spiritual character rather than a rationalistic or empirical one. The wisdom of God originates in the all-knowing infinite divine mind. The wisdom of the world originates in the reasoning of the finite human intellect, in which Paul included also the metaphysical, epistemological and ethical speculations of the Greek philosophers.

The mystery of God

Paul indicates that formerly the wisdom of God, as His divine plan for the salvation of the world, was concealed, inaccessible to human understanding and deliberation. He identifies this concealed wisdom as 'mystery'. He states: 'But we speak God's secret wisdom, the wisdom that has been hidden and that God destined for our glory before time began. None of the rulers of this age understood it, for if they had, they would not have crucified the Lord of glory' (1 Cor 2: 7-8). The wisdom of God has its roots in eternity, having its source in God. God veiled it from human apprehension until the appointed dispensation of Jesus Christ and of His Spirit. In the pre-incarnate/pre-pneumatic dispensation of redemptive history, the wisdom of God remained a 'mystery' with respect to human understanding. This mystery pertains to the unknown, rather than to the unknowable. The mystery corresponds to the 'secret' of God, that remained locked up in His mind, destined to be disclosed at His appointed time, through His Son and the Holy Spirit to the apostles and prophets of Christ (Eph. 3:5) as the Gospel or the good news of salvation. The content of the mystery concerns the definitive actions of God in response to the condition of sin and damnation of His creatures and consists in the redeeming will of the Father, the atoning work of the Son, and the applying ministry of the Holy Spirit.

In the appointed time, the content of the divine mystery was proclaimed as the Gospel or the good news of salvation by Jesus Christ. The mystery has its roots in, and derives its significance from God's 'eternal purpose' (Eph 3:11). Paul insists that the mystery originates in the divine will and acquires particular impetus and actuality only through the divine purpose. God has purposed to redeem mankind from sin, death and above all from His wrath in order that the redeemed people might share in His divine glory. Thus, the mystery concerns the realization of redemption or salvation by the death and resurrection of Jesus, accomplished in history in three successive stages - the first is the coming of Jesus to the world for its redemption, the next is the time of the Church (Eph 3:9) as it prolongs the mission of Christ on earth guided by the Holy Spirit and the final stage is the consummation of the ages with the second coming of Christ. Paul makes it clear that the Gentiles are also to be heirs together with the people of Israel, to this divine gift of salvation, by becoming members of one body, the Church. Together, they become shares in the promise in Christ Jesus (Eph 3:6). Paul himself was chosen as an apostle to preach to the Gentiles the unreachable riches of Christ and to make plain to everyone the administration of this mystery (Eph 3:8-9).

The Cross of Christ and the true Wisdom

The wisdom of God is particularly expressed in or identified with the realities of righteousness, sanctification and redemption that came to humanity through Jesus Christ who brings the realization of these realities in the human beings through His saving action. From eternity past, God planned to save mankind through the person and work of the God-man, Jesus Christ. According to this divine plan, salvation was to be realized in and through the only Son of God who became God's divine answer to the problem of sin of the fallen humanity. True wisdom is to be found in this God's plan for the redemption of the world, which, for all its own wisdom, had fallen away from God. The wisdom of God that was concealed in the mind of God as the mystery, when revealed becomes the logos -the word or the message. Until God revealed His plan through Jesus Christ to the world, as the message of His Gospel, this wisdom was unknown to the world. Without the revelation of Jesus Christ, man could have never acquired the mystery by his own efforts. It is Jesus, the only Son of God, who proclaimed the Gospel or good news as the true wisdom and thereby revealed to us the divine plan of salvation. After His ascension, the Church continues to announce the same Gospel to the world as the good news of reconciliation, sanctificationa dn salvation. In so far as Jesus is the sum and the substance of the salvation of mankind, He becomes the Gospel or the good news and in this, He becomes the true wisdom of God.

In the plan of God, salvation came to the world in Jesus Christ only through the cross. The salvific plan of God to offer human beings a participation in the divine glory was accomplished by the sacrifice of Jesus on the cross. That is why, for Paul, the wisdom of God is the 'word or the message (logos) of the cross' (1 Cor 1: 18). Since the Greeks despised cross as the sign of condemnation, they viewed the wisdom of God, revealed in the cross of Christ as mere foolishness. It conflicted with their standards of philosophic and religious propriety. The heart of the Christian message, which Paul described as the 'word of the cross' ran counter not only to Roman political thinking, but also to the Jewish religious perspectives and to the whole ethos of religion of the ancient times, in particular to the perspectives of God held by the educated people such as the Greek philosophers. The 'word or the message of the cross' was apparently intellectually insipid and academically unrespectable, 'a stumbling block to Jews and foolishness to the Gentiles' (1Cor 1:23). But true wisdom is revealed in the cross that bore the savior of the world, the living God who died on the cross on behalf of the fallen creatures. The philosophic intellectuals of the world judge such a presentation as foolishness. The Roman cross was an exceedingly ignominious symbol. Crucifixion was a bitterly cruel and shameful punishment that, as a rule, was reserved for hardened criminals, rebellious slaves and rebels against the Roman state. The mystery of the crucified God appears irrational to the secular mind. It appears contrary to all sound and sane reasoning. However, for the believers, Christ, the crucified, becomes the personal figure of true wisdom about God's means of restoring humanity to Himself, because, 'the foolishness of God is wiser than man's wisdom, and the weakness of God is stronger than man's strength (1 Cor 1: 25). The good news or Gospel of Christ crucified, even if apparently seems foolish to the unbelieving world, is the revelation of God's saving action to the believers who see in Him the fulfillment of God's eternal purpose (Col 1:20) accomplished on the cross. That is why, for the believers, 'those whom God has called, both Jews and Greeks, Christ is the power and the wisdom of God' (1 Cor 1:24).

Personal reflection- 'Jesus, the wisdom of God'

Jesus Christ is the wisdom of God, in as much as He is God's answer to every believer's personal, social, relational, and metaphysical problems/questions. Having become the definite answer of God to the spiritual quest of the entire humanity, Jesus Christ alone is sufficient for us and for our salvation. In Him the Christian is complete. The high value attributed to wisdom marked not only ancient Hebrew and Semitic thought, but also ancient Greek and Oriental philosophy. The ancient civilizations and the great world religions have their own illustrious wisdom literature. For example, the Egyptians possessed the 'Wisdom of Ptah-hotep' (2500 BC), the Jews, the Torah (1400 BC), the Confucians, the Analects (sixth century BC), and the Hindus, the Vedas (2000-1000 BC). Also, today as humanity progresses in knowledge especially with the advancement of science and technology, mankind is able to accumulate knowledge in ways unimaginable just several decades ago. In this situation, Paul proposes to us a definite vision to be a wise people through our faith and hope in Jesus. Indeed, Christians have their own vision of wisdom and Paul presents this wisdom as Jesus Christ. To be more exact, Paul presents Christ 'crucified' as the wisdom of God. He writes to the Corinthians: 'When I came to you, I did not come with eloquence or superior wisdom as I proclaimed to you the testimony about God. For, I resolved to know nothing while I was with you, except Jesus Christ and Him 'crucified'. My message and my preaching were not with wise and persuasive words, but with a demonstration of the Spirit's power so that your faith might not rest on men's wisdom, but on God's power' (1 Cor 2: 2-5). In Corinth, Paul proclaimed only the message of the Christ crucified. Knowing Paul's journey to Corinth from Athens, we examine what He preached in Athens. Paul stood up in the meeting of Areopagus, the well known place of gathering of very wise men and made a great philosophical discourse using all his good learning and sound scholarship. But in that learned crowd that listened to him, some of them sneered and others indifferently said, 'We want to hear you on this subject' (Acts 17: 22-32). For all his fantastic skillful performance full of great eloquence among the crowd of the philosophers and other wise men, Paul could not harvest any faith from his learned audience. He learnt his lesson. As he reached Corinth from Athens (Acts 18:1), he made sure that he preached not a philosophical discourse of his own eloquence, but the good news of salvation that is Jesus Christ 'crucified'. Christian wisdom is not simply a rule of life or a collection of wise guidance or a system of philosophical speculation but the revelation of the mystery of salvation from God, made known to the world by Jesus Himself, proclaimed today through the Church as the good news of Jesus Christ, who is the true wisdom of God.

As we follow the good news of Jesus Christ as His faithful people in this world, let us never fail to appreciate whatever that is true, whatever that is honorable, whatever that is upright and pure, whatever is lovable and admirable and whatever is good and praiseworthy in the wisdom of the world, including the noble and sublime religious traditions that reveal the spiritual riches of the human race. However, as believers in Christ, we must seek definite response to every one of our life concerns, including peace to our restless souls and serenity to our anxious hearts always in Jesus Christ, the true wisdom of God. It is in His cross that we can find meaningful answers to our every question even about the ultimate principles and concerns of human life, especially about God, mankind and universe. Revealing God as love and life, designating the participation of humanity in this divine love and life as the destiny of mankind, and pointing to the total restoration of the universe as the purpose of creation, Jesus brings to us the true wisdom and His cross manifests what God accomplished for us and for our salvation through His only Son. When faced with problems, pained by sorrows, fallen by failures, confronted by conflicts, confused by controversies, enraged by enmities, and weakened by infirmities, even as the curious and the questioning humanity in us awakens and seeks definite answers to the great puzzles, mysteries and challenges of our human existence let us confidently raise our minds and hearts towards the crucified Savior for finding true wisdom and thereby lasting answers for all our yearnings, always in profound faith and absolute trust in Him, the wisdom and power of God.

Take me back to my dungeon: Long ago, a tyrant, by the name of Dionysius, ruled the city of Syracuse in Sicily. Often ruthless in his actions, he was also vain of his own talents. He wrote poetry that he wanted all his courtiers to admire and praise him, which they did out of fear. There was a learned man and philosopher in Syracuse, by the name of Philoxenus. Dionysius desired to be praised by this famous philosopher and hence invited him to the palace and recited his poetry. Known as a person who always told the truth, Philoxenus told the tyrant frankly that his verses did not deserve to be called poetry. Full of anger, the tyrant threw the old man in the dungeon, the worst prison cell. When the people learnt about the fate of the philosopher, they protested in large numbers. Taken aback, the tyrant wanted to save his face. He called the philosopher from the dungeon and hosted him a dinner and recited poetry that was of better quality, yet below standard. The philosopher, never hesitant to tell the truth, told the guards: take me back to the dungeon. Admiring the sincerity and the courage of the learned man, the tyrant set him free. Wisdom consists in being honest and truthful and Jesus who is the truth itself is also the true wisdom of God.

Quote: 'The first step of wisdom is to know what is false'- *Latin Proverb*

Scripture reading for Day 37: Sir 1: 1-18

Prayer for Day 37: Lord God, we pray to you to send your Holy Spirit in to our hearts, so that He may teach us the mysteries of your heavenly kingdom and reveal to us the majesty of your divine plan for our salvation. Illuminated by His wonderful light, may we always seek to acquire the true wisdom that is Jesus Christ and through Him obtain the gift of eternal salvation! Amen.

38

DIVINE FULLNESS

*P*aul is the most creative thinker in the history of Christianity. As the result of the missionary efforts of the Church to bring the Gospel to all the nations, as commanded by the risen Christ (Mt 28: 18-20), the Christian faith encountered the world civilization beyond the frontiers of Palestine, where it originated. In her mission, the Church has never learned a better language in which to address the world than the language of Paul, the apostle. Already we have reflected on some important titles that Paul assigned to Jesus Christ to explain the unique role of Jesus Christ in the history of salvation- the Head of the body, the unique Mediator, the Peace, the Power of God and the Wisdom of God. Under this title 'divine fullness' we shall reflect also on two other titles, all of them presented together by Paul, since they are inseparably linked to each other in his theological discourse. They are the 'firstborn over all creation' and the 'image of the invisible God'. Paul uses the term 'fullness' to mean the totality of the divinity that dwelt in Christ: 'God was pleased to have all His fullness to dwell in Him' (Col 1:19). Paul explains that God, in His divine plan, wanted to grant a share to humanity in this divine fullness of His only Son, Jesus Christ, through the ministry of the Church. In his discourse on the deification of humanity in the Son of God, Paul names Jesus as 'the image of the invisible God' and the 'first-born over all creation' (Col 1:15). Together, these titles present Jesus to us in a very profound light that can enlighten our Christian faith. The word 'fullness', which signifies perfection in abundance, is particularly apt to describe the divine glory of Jesus who received all power and authority in heaven and on earth and who communicates this divine glory to humanity and to the entire universe through the ministry of His Church.

The meaning of the word 'fullness'

The word 'fullness' (the Greek noun is pleroma) signifies completion or something which completes. Ordinarily it refers to what fills something, as we see in several instances in the Bible. Though used in many senses in other books of the Bible, such as abundance, totality or completion, in the theology of Paul, 'pleroma' has developed into a distinct discourse, whereby Paul speaks about how Christ is in complete possession of divinity and the faithful are granted a share in His divine fullness, through the ministry of the Church, His Body, that is progressing in history towards the perfect participation in the divine fullness of Christ at the end of time. The key verses that present the Pauline theology of 'divine fullness' are: 'God was pleased to have all His fullness dwell in Christ' (Col 1:19). 'In Christ, all the fullness of the Deity lives in the bodily form' (Col 2: 9). 'The Church, His Body, is the fullness of Christ who fills everything in every way' (Eph 1:23). 'The Body of Christ will be built up until we attain to the whole measure of the fullness of Christ' (Eph 4:13). 'You may be filled to the measure of all the fullness of God' (Eph 3:19). 'Christ fills the whole universe' (Eph 4:10). 'When the times will have reached their fulfillment, God will bring all things in heaven and on earth together under one head' (Eph 1:10). Paul explains that according to the saving plan of God, Christ, the Son of God, progressively fills the universe with His divine fullness through the Church.

The discourse of Paul on the 'divine fullness' of Christ

Paul explains that the divine plan of salvation originated as the holy will of God, the Father, who sent His only Son to be in solidarity with the fallen sinful human race and to be subjected to the power of death on the cross. Jesus, who was conceived by the power of the Holy Spirit, became fully human, sharing our human condition in every way except sin. In His victory through resurrection, the pernicious work of sin was repaired whereby humanity was restored, redeemed and reunited with God through the sacrifice of Jesus on the cross. Now, the saved and sanctified mankind progressively comes to the possession of divine life from the divine fullness of Jesus Christ, through the power of the Holy Spirit, in the ministry of the Church until the end of time, when it will reach its plenitude or fullness. Paul develops his theological discourse under three sections: the divine pre-existence of Christ, historical existence of Christ through incarnation and the glorified existence of Christ in divine fullness.

The Divine Pre-Existence of Jesus Christ (the image of the invisible God)

We know how John so eloquently points out the pre-existence of Christ: 'In the beginning was the Word, and the Word was with God and the Word was God. He was with God in the beginning. Through Him all things were made; without Him nothing was made that has been made' (Jn 1:1-3). Paul writes about the pre-existence of Christ to the Colossians making the same statement of faith that everything was created through the pre-existent Son of God: 'He is the image of the invisible God, the first-born over all creation. For by Him all things were created things in heaven and on earth, visible and invisible, whether thrones or powers or rulers or authorities; all things were created by Him and for Him. He is before all things and in Him all things hold together' (Col 1: 15-17). The Pauline expression of Jesus as 'the image of the invisible God' is also seen in another Pauline text: The unbelievers cannot see the light of the gospel of the glory of Christ, who is the image of God' (2 Cor 4: 4). We find an analogous expression in the letter to the Hebrews: 'The Son is the radiance of God's glory and the exact representation of His being, sustaining all things by His powerful word' (Heb 1:3). We have to remember that, in the Biblical sense, an image is not just the faint copy of an original. When Paul uses the word 'image' it meant more than simple 'likeness'. Rather, being an 'image' means having the same essential nature of a thing. An image is both a 'manifestation' and a 'representation' of the reality or archetype. Through the image, the reality itself comes to expression. Hence, when Paul says that Jesus is the image of God, he states that Jesus is sharing the same divine nature with His Father. Also, Jesus perfectly reveals, manifests and expresses His Father to the world. In the letter to the Philippians Paul would explain the image as nature: 'He is in the very nature of God' (Phil 2:6). In this statement about the 'image' Paul seems to draw from the book of Genesis: 'God created man in His own image; in the divine image, He created him' (Gen 1:27) thereby referring to the first Adam. Later, Paul presents Jesus as the new Adam and states: 'Adam was a pattern of the one to come, Jesus Christ' (Rom 5:14).

In assigning the title 'the image of God' to Jesus Paul was attempting to say who Christ is. Paul declares that Jesus is not merely a reflection of God, but that in Him, so to speak, God comes to light and is expressed. It is as if Paul was responding to the famous question of Jesus to His disciples, 'Who do you say that I am?' (Mt 16: 15). His answer is Jesus is indeed the perfect representation and the manifestation of the divine glory, as the one and the only Son of God. In the face of Jesus, we see the divine glory present in visible form. He is the Image, the Representation, the Unveiling, the Manifestation of the invisible God, who has no manifestation save through His only Son. The declaration is not that Jesus became the image of God, but He is always the image of God. Jesus was the image of God, before time began and creation came into being. He will be the image of God in all the ages yet to come. At present also, He is the image, the One through whom the invisible God is always manifest to created beings. Whether they be principalities or powers in the heavenly places or things and persons of this world, whoever they may be and whenever they may exist and wherever their habitation may be, God is revealed to them through His only Son, who is His perfect image and likeness. As the eternal Son of God, Jesus is the originating Creator and the sustaining might in the universe in union with His Father and the Holy Spirit, as the one eternal Triune God. What is more, Paul also makes it clear that everything was created for Him (Col 1:15), thereby declaring that Jesus is the substance of not only the beginning of creation but also the end of creation and during the present time, He holds the creation together.

Historical Existence through Incarnation - Jesus, the Firstborn

Paul's next statement is that Jesus Christ who is the image/nature of God as the pre-existent Son of God, became the firstborn over all creation (Col 1:15). Paul also states in the letter to the Romans: 'For those God foreknew He also predestined to be conformed to the likeness of His Son that He might be the firstborn among many brothers' (Rom 8: 29). The author of the letter to the Hebrews writes, 'God brought His firstborn into the world' (Heb 1:

6). This terminology is derived from the Old Testament, where it is used to refer to Israel: 'The Lord said to Moses, 'You shall say to Pharaoh. Thus says the Lord: Israel is my son, my firstborn' (Ex 4:22). In another instance, in the book of prophet Jeremiah, Israel, referred as Ephraim is called the first-born: 'Thus says the Lord, 'I am a father to Israel, Ephraim is my firstborn' (Jer 31: 9). The Messianic King is also called as the firstborn: 'The Lord says, 'I myself make him firstborn, most high over the kings of the earth. Forever I will maintain my love for him and my covenant with him stands for ever' (Ps 89: 28-29). The name firstborn also reminds us of the special consecration of the male first born of the mother, whether human or animal, to God: 'The Lord spoke to Moses and said, 'Consecrate to me every firstborn that opens the womb among the Israelites, both of man and beast, for it belongs to me' (Ex 13:2). The animal was to be redeemed or sacrificed to God and the firstborn son was to be redeemed (Ex 34: 19-20). Paul points out that Jesus Christ, who is the sovereign Lord before creation, as the 'image of God' became the 'firstborn over creation' through His Incarnation as willed by His Father, through the power of the Holy Spirit (Lk 1: 35).

The term 'firstborn' primarily refers to the rank or priority. Paul, by naming Jesus as 'the firstborn over all creation' makes it clear that Jesus Christ, who is pre-existent, became a part of creation when He made flesh and dwelt among us' (Jn 1:14). That does not mean that Christ was created by God, at some point in history, to become a man. Paul had already sufficiently made clear that Jesus Christ is pre-existent and eternal by stating that He is the image/nature of God. What Paul is explaining is that that by His incarnation, Jesus, the divine Son of God became a perfect 'human' being as well. His becoming fully human makes Him a part of creation. Because Christ existed before all things and He created all things, He remained outside the realm of creation, before His incarnation. Therefore, He could not be the first in the human group until His incarnation when Jesus became a fully human person and entered the world of creatures and is first in rank and is supreme in the creation. After His incarnation, Jesus lives no more apart from His human nature, though He retains His divinity without any diminishing. Jesus is perfectly God and perfectly man, fully divine and fully human. Through His sacred passion and death and the glorious resurrection, Jesus, the firstborn over creation, became also the firstborn from the dead. Before the resurrection of Jesus, there were several instances when men were restored to life after their death as a sort of miraculous happening. Jesus Himself brought several dead persons back to life during His public ministry. But these are simply restorations back to earthly life and those restored persons died again. Jesus was the first person to experience resurrection as new and eternal life and thereafter to live forever. That is why, Paul calls Jesus the firstborn from the dead: 'Jesus is the firstborn from the dead, so that in everything He might have supremacy' (Col 1: 18). John also, like Paul, names Jesus the firstborn from the dead: 'Jesus Christ is the faithful witness, the firstborn from the dead and the ruler of the kings of the earth' (Rv 1: 5). Jesus is the first person to come back to life through resurrection, in accordance with the salvific plan of God, who in His holy will, has determined to redeem mankind through the death and resurrection of Jesus.

The Glorified Existence - Divine Fullness

The resurrection of Jesus imposed the divine seal on the act of redemption, inaugurated at the incarnation and accomplished on the cross. Glorified by the Father, Jesus, the Son of God, is constituted in His might (Acts 13: 33), Lord and Christ (Acts 2:36), Head and Savior (Acts 5:31), Judge and the Lord of the living and the dead (Acts 10:42). God has exalted Him to a position where every creature must adore Him and confess that Jesus is Lord (Rom 10:9). Seated at the right hand of the Father, Jesus has received the fullness of divine glory which is properly His as the Son of God, that now He communicates through the Holy Spirit, who continues the sanctification of humanity till the end of age. After the pre-existent Son has been manifested as the image, word, power and wisdom of God, in the history of salvation, the Holy Spirit enters human history and is revealed as the Counselor, the Advocate and the Gift of God. He kindles in the human hearts the divine fire of love that consumes sin, conquers evil, vanquishes death and empowers mankind and renews the entire creation, making all things new. As pre-existent Son, Jesus was the principle and substance of creation and now as the glorified Lord, He is the principle of new creation, accomplished through the power of the Holy Spirit. Salvation realized in the glorified humanity of Jesus is now in the process of realization in the believers who together constitute the Church, the Body of Christ. The superabundant sanctification existing in the glorified Christ is shared by the Church as His Body. That is why, Paul calls the Church as the fullness of Christ (Eph 1:23). However, the Church can become His fullness only progressively in the course of salvation history till the end of time. She has to continue to grow as the Body of Christ, bringing in new members in every age till she reaches maturity, attaining to the whole measure of the fullness of Christ (Eph 4: 13). Through the redemptive presence and ministry of the Church in the world, salvation is offered to the entire humanity and the creation itself is being liberated from its bondage to decay and brought into glorious freedom of the children of God (Rom 8:21). Men and women, from being sinful creatures as they are, are transformed into the image of Son of God, thereby becoming God's own children, through the sacramental ministry of the Church, especially in Baptism. The glorified Christ, now clothed in divine fullness, 'full of grace and truth' (Jn 1:14), communicates to those who believe in Him the inexhaustible abundance of the divine fullness. Indeed, 'from the fullness of His divinity, we have all received' (Jn 1:16), a share and participation as the children of God. Through His divine Son, the Father, fills us with the richness of His divine fullness in the Holy Spirit, according to His holy will.

Personal reflection – 'Jesus, the Fullness of Divine Glory'

Jesus is the image of the Father as His pre-existent Son. As human beings, it is impossible for us to understand all that implies in the divine life of the triune God. In His goodness, in the beginning of time, God created mankind in His own divine image. Our first parents did not preserve this divine image within them. As the result of their disobedience, the luster and the radiance of the divine image in them disappeared. As sin abounded in the world, the human beings became more corrupted: 'There is no one righteous, not even one; there is no one who understands, no one who seeks God. All have turned away, they have together become worthless; there is no one who does good, not even one' (Rom 3: 10-12; Ps 14: 1-3; Ps 53: 1-3; Eccl 7:20). Not the one who lets sin and evil to triumph over His marvelous creation, God initiated the process of restoration of humanity and the renewal of creation. According to His divine plan of salvation, in the appointed time, Jesus Christ came to the world and preached the good news of salvation and called upon the people to repentance and conversion. As expression of God's supreme love and steadfast fidelity, Jesus gave Himself up as a ransom to purchase us with His own blood. It is Jesus who brought the reconciliation of mankind and of the entire creation with His Father. Reconciliation implies a renewal and restoration not only of the human beings but of the entire creation to the friendship of God, the Father. Through the power of the Holy Spirit and by the sacramental ministry of the Church, Jesus continues to restore within humanity, the divine image, especially through the new birth of Baptism. It implies that Jesus makes it possible for us to have the precise disposition that God expects from us, through the sanctifying grace of the Holy Spirit, who, dwelling within us, helps us to love the Father as He deserves and to offer our utmost obedience and fidelity to Him as His loving children. Today, the adopted children of God who bear the divine image of God's only Son radiate the splendor of the Father, through a life of sanctity that shines in the midst of world's darkness.

We are God's own children

Jesus has restored the divine image in the sinful humanity by washing the sins by His own precious blood. He calls the entire mankind to the fullness of divine life. Therefore, every human person has the possibility to receive the sanctification of the Holy Spirit and thereby become a child of God. We are not isolated human beings, but members of one human race sharing in the one human nature. But this one human nature was radically affected by the first man and later, by the perfect man - Adam and Jesus Christ. Adam, the first man, disfigured the divine image within the human being through his disobedience. Jesus, the perfect man, not only restored the divine image in us but also sanctified us by the Spirit of truth and life so that we are now privileged to share in His divine fullness. What shall we do to Jesus in return for the extraordinary blessing He brought to humanity? As we strive and struggle in this world to be His loyal disciples, let us always remember that we ought to give Jesus the best of what we are and what we have, by way of knowing, loving and serving Him. First of all, let us make use of every opportunity to proclaim the good news of Jesus Christ to the world, to all nations and to all peoples so that they may receive the power of Jesus Christ and His Spirit, and through Him, the grace of sanctification.

In Jesus, God has called us to be His children and we may be truly His children only when we know Him as our Creator, love Him as our Father and serve Him as our Master. We can grow in our knowledge of God, the Creator, by becoming more and more familiar with the mind and heart of Jesus as we read His holy words in the scripture and pray to Him with the intimacy of a grateful friend and a disciple. We can love God, as our Father, by always remembering what He has done for us in salvation history and by appreciating gratefully His unsurpassable goodness and tender fatherly care for us, the undeserving sinful human beings. We can serve Him, our Master, by understanding and adopting authentic gospel values that He revealed to us through His only Son, so that His good news may always guide us as the light for our path. Since Jesus has restored the divine image in each one of us, we can love God and serve Him by our fraternal service to others, our brothers and sisters who bear the same divine image. In Christian communities, we are called to love and serve other members of the Church, with whom together we constitute the Body of Christ. It is the Church that Christ fills with His divine fullness and it is in the Church, especially through her sacraments that we are given a share in this divine fullness as the members of His body. It has great implication for our daily life as Christians. First of all, let us give great value and top priority to the worship and praise that we offer together to the triune God as the community of the disciples of Christ in the Church. The greater glory of God, the ultimate purpose of creation is served by our prayers of praise, thanksgiving and petition, not only as the members of a Christian community, but also as individual Christians. Our personal prayer is not a means of informing God with a list of petitions. It is rather a conversation with God that awakens our intimacy and love for Him as His ever grateful children. Among the practical effects of prayer are insight, illumination, comfort and conversion. A significant way of becoming Christ to other is to pray for them as Jesus prayed for His disciples. Let us always remember that our prayers have priceless value especially for those in need: the sick, the suffering, the frightened, the lonely, the betrayed and the misled. We must abandon the notions of God as being a distant majesty, observing us from on high. Rather, we know thanks to the revelation from Jesus that we can experience God's love and care as our father, helper, teacher, liberator and guide. He is mercifully present to all of us. His kingdom of love and justice, although not yet fully established, is already present in the world, inaugurated in the incarnation, redemptive passion and glorious resurrection of Jesus and now continuously expanding through the workings of the Holy Spirit. In loving God faithfully and loyally serving Him in this world we can be part of God's kingdom on earth and contribute to its growth and thereby making ourselves the worthy children of our loving Father in heaven.

The much loved preacher: There was a wonderful preacher of the word of God who used to impress and inspire thousands of people to love and serve Jesus with fervor and in fidelity. One day he told the story of a young man who used to be angry at those who prayed with much trust and love, deep down in their hearts. He considered them to be fools and whenever he could, he mocked them outside the Church. People, instead of getting angry, took pity on him, but could not convert him. One day, an old woman was fully immersed in prayer, in the Church. The young man thought he could mock her and tease her to his best and went near to her. The old lady challenged him to do something, she said he could never do and the young man accepted the challenge from her. She took him to the Cross hanging nearby and told him to shout at the top of his voice three times: Christ died on the cross for me and I don't care one bit. The young man repeated it loud first time, softly the second time, and just whispered the third time. Then to the surprise of the old woman, he knelt down and prayed. What is more, he prayed everyday. The preacher concluded: It is not a story but a real event. You know what! I am that young man.

Quote: By His first work of creation, God gave me to myself. By the work of redemption He gave Himself to me. And when He gave me Himself, He gave me back myself that I had lost - ***Bernard of Clairvaux***

Scripture reading for Day 38: Col 1: 9-23

Prayer for Day 38: Heavenly Father, we thank you for the privilege of being your children. In your kindness, use us for your glory!. Help us to see and seize the opportunities to serve you. Guide us to learn the worth of each and every person you have created in your image. Keep us from judging, labeling or belittling anyone, anytime!. Lead us in your way, to live as people who bear the restored divine image! Amen.

39

BEGINNING AND END

*I*n the book of Revelation, Jesus declares to John, 'I am the Alpha and the Omega, the first and the last, the beginning and the end' (Rv 22:13). It is significant that in this last book of the Bible John uses this title both to God, the Father and also to Lord Jesus Christ. John writes this statement at the beginning of the book: 'I am the Alpha and the Omega, says the Lord God, who is and who was and who is to come, the Almighty' (Rv 1:8). John repeats the same statement at the end of the book: 'I am the Alpha and the Omega, the beginning and the end' (Rv 21: 6). Alpha is the first and Omega is the last letter of the Greek alphabet. The phrase, equally applicable to God, also refers to Jesus. Thus, 'beginning and the end' expresses not only the eternity of Jesus Christ, but also His infinitude and the boundless Life that is in Him and that embraces all things as the source, yet transcending everything, as 'the Other', remaining beyond human comprehension as 'mystery', yet intervening at every step of humanity in 'history'. Eternally existent God, Jesus was, He is and He will be. In Him, the world has a beginning and end. His second coming as the Lord and the Judge of the world will bring to conclusion and to perfection what He began in the beginning of human history. Creation that took place through Him in the beginning of time finds its meaning and reference only in Christ and its final restoration and perfection at the end of time will have significance and purpose only in Christ, for He is the first and the last, the beginning and the end (Rv 22:13) and in Him, all things hold together (Col 1: 17).

In the Beginning

God is transcendental and eternal and He lives in eternity, but in relation to the world, He acts in time. The Bible, the holy book of His revelation to us, begins with the verse: 'In the beginning, God created the heavens and the earth' (Gn 1:1). It ends with the verse: 'Jesus says, 'I am coming soon'- Amen, Come Lord Jesus' -the grace of the Lord Jesus be with God's people. Amen' (Rv 22: 20-21). We see that both in the first and in the last verses of the bible, there is reference to 'time'. The first verse refers to the past act of God when He created the world. The last verse refers to the future act of return of Jesus when God, in His Son, would complete the fullness of the created world, including mankind. The last verse also refers to the present, here and now, when the grace of the Lord Jesus is with His people, guiding them through history. As in the beginning and in the ending of the Bible, throughout the pages of the entire Bible also, God is presented to us not in any abstraction as in the philosophical speculations and difficult discourses about His Essence, Being and Existence, but as the 'living and loving God' who acts with power and majesty and 'saves' with might and strength, out of His infinite goodness unsurpassable kindness, above all, out of His unconditional 'love'. In the Bible is revealed to us the salvation history that illustrates how the 'living God' of eternity is always 'loving His people' in steadfast fidelity with an enduring and everlasting love leading them to their eternal and abundant life with Him (Jn 10:10) as heirs in His kingdom.

While many ancient myths on the creation of the world present cosmic struggles and conflicts among the gods as the cause of the emergence of the universe, as we see in the Babylonian poem of creation with god Marduk as the hero, the Bible reveals the creator God in a radical and unique fashion. In the account of creation, the pre-existent God is presented as somebody who acts freely according to His own free will, in absolute freedom, thereby unrolling His divine plan. He alone, on His own, orders all creation. At each step of creation, Bible tells us that God 'said' and there it was, and God found it 'good'. An excellent artist God is, He loved every bit of His creative work- the work of His hands. For example about the creation of the light, the Bible says this: God said, 'Let there be light' and there was light. God saw how good the light was' (Gn 1: 3-4). God found all that He created, including the human beings very good. The Bible concludes the account of creation in these words: 'God looked at everything He had made and He found it very good' (Gn 1: 31). The entire creative work of God is oriented towards man, whom He made in His own image and likeness and blessed him with authority and dominion over all the other creatures (Gen 1: 28). The creation of man, in its turn, is oriented towards God's own divine plan of salvation, that Paul calls 'mystery' (Eph 1: 9), that is revealed progressively in human history till the Son of God brought us the fullness of revelation.

The cosmic time and the human time

Itself a creative work of God, 'time' serves as the framework by which God relates Himself to the cosmos and to humanity. The suggestion in the account of creation that God created the world in seven days, including His day of rest, points to the way God acts in relation to the world - 'in time'. We call the 'time' with reference to the cosmos as the cosmic time and the 'time' in relation to humanity as the human time. God established the rhythms that the entire cosmos obeys as can be seen in the case of the movements of the stars and the planets in the vast universe, resulting in the repetition of day and night and the recurrence of seasons such as summer and winter. Cosmic time is of cyclic nature and the material world follows the cosmic cycle. Humanity, though conditioned by the cosmic time, follows a different course, with events and episodes that do not follow the laws of repetition and recurrence as in the case of cosmic time, but a process of continuity, growth and progress. As a result, mankind is associated with the progress of culture and the growth of civilization. Enriched by the achievements of successive generations of human beings and safeguarding them for the future generations as the deposit of knowledge and wisdom, especially through memory and writing, mankind constantly moves ahead in continued progress in human time. Incidentally human time is divided in most parts of the world as BC (before Christ) and AD (after Christ). Great events that happened in the life of mankind, the numerous achievements that the mankind has accomplished as a community and the heroic deeds of so many individuals have been recorded by human beings for posterity. This human recording, we call 'history'. What is our Christian belief is that as God intervenes both in the cosmic time and in the human time and guides the destiny of the universe and the humanity, He acts according to His own mysterious divine plan, a definite design that existed in the mind of God for all eternity as His plan of salvation. The unfolding of the divine plan or the design of God is called sacred history. It is the Bible that has recorded for us the sacred history by which God has progressively executed His plan of salvation for humanity and the universe.

Sacred History

Sacred history, revealed to us in the holy Bible, is not about the cosmic events or the human achievements, but about the plan of God for the salvation of the world and humanity. It deals with the creation of the world and mankind, the election of the people of God, known as old Israel and the extension of His divine blessings to all the nations in a universal community named as new Israel or the Church, through whose instrumentality God brings to completion His divine plan for humanity as well as for the universe. The Bible, as seen in the first two chapters of the book of Genesis, places a primitive perfection at man's origin. In the third chapter of Genesis is illustrated for us how the first parents came to lose their wonderful existence of goodness and innocence and the joyful life of perfection and dominion that was offered by God as the result of His generous friendship with them. Their downfall happened not as the result of natural process or cosmic evolution but as the consequence of a conscious, voluntary and free act of the first parents who transgressed against God and His holy will, by siding with the Devil. Thus entered sin into the world and brought with it, evil, suffering, hardship and, above all, death to humanity and degradation and decadence to the universe. It is the first sin, the sin of the first parents that started a movement against God leading to the loss of goodness and the persistence of evil in mankind and in the world. At the same time, we know that where sin abounds, the grace of God overflows leading not only to the neutralization of the evil but also to the victory of the noble and the good in man and in the world over sin and evil. The mercy of God has initiated a counter movement of goodness and grace against the forces of sin and evil and in the sacred history what we witness as well as given the privilege to participate as active agents is the slow but sure triumph of the gracious movement of God over the movement of evil, of grace over sin, and of life over death.

In the sacred history, on one side, is seen the progressive development of evil, and of spiritual decadence, as seen in the sins of the world. It is first witnessed in the murder of Abel by Cain (Gn 4: 8-16), in the sins of ungrateful people during the time of Noah, leading to the destruction of these sinful men by the ferocious flood (Gn 7: 17-23) and in the dispersion of the proud and disputing people after building the Tower of Babel (Gn 11: 1-9). God chose the people of Israel and made covenant with them so that they might be a holy nation to Him (Ex 19: 6) through the observance of the Law. However, these chosen people also let Him down by their disloyalty and infidelity again and again. As the result of their sins, these chosen people would be exiled from their promised land and would be scattered among the Gentiles in foreign lands. They returned to the Promised Land only after God took pity on them, reformed them and renewed them as His people, thereby restoring His favor. But when the Son of God, at the appointed time, came to the world, the leaders of the chosen people would reject Him and His good news of salvation. Crucifixion of Jesus was the apparent and temporary triumph of sin in the world, at the hour of darkness.

In the midst of the progress of sin and evil in the world, we see also the counter progress of divine grace through the regular intervention of the ever 'living and loving God'. Even when God was destroying the world by flood, He chose Noah's family to be the source of human regeneration and to occupy the face of the earth and to multiply again in great numbers. Even after He dispersed the people to the corners of the world by the confusion of the languages, God gathered His faithful servant Abraham and led him to the Promised Land, promising him descendants as numerous as the stars in the sky. Even when the chosen people, the descendants of Abraham failed in their promises of obedience and loyalty, God guided them and preserved them in the Promised Land against their enemies. Even if they were sent in exile as punishment, God would lead them back and comfort them through numerous prophets. Even when the people of Israel rejected the savior of the world and refused to receive His gospel, God established the new Israel through the foundation of twelve apostles and disciples who were all Jewish men. They became the remnant of Israel foretold by the prophets with whom God would make a new covenant that will last forever. God would include the Gentiles in His promises through their union with the remnant of Israel in the community of the new and everlasting covenant, His Church. In Christ, both Jews and Gentiles together would constitute the new people of God, the Body of Christ that would reach the divine fullness in Jesus Christ on the last day. What is important to note is that the sin of the world could never destroy the plan of God that progresses steadily towards its fulfillment until the last day, when sin and evil will be fully conquered and eliminated. The definite and final victory of the divine grace over satanic evil and sin is the culmination of the sacred history, whose center is Jesus Christ, the Son of God. Salvation history moves towards the appearance of the divine redeemer as its center and His cross as the decisive moment. Through the cross, Jesus accomplished the sanctification of the world and began the mighty movement of restoration and renewal of all things that continues in the present age, until its completion at the end of time.

In the end of time

Already in Old Testament, the prophets spoke about the last day, which they called as the day of Yahweh. It meant the day of the final judgment of the world when the good people will be rewarded and the wicked punished. Referring to the punishment that awaits the wicked, the prophet Amos said: 'Woe to those who yearn for the day of the Lord. What will this day of the Lord mean for you? Darkness and not light, gloom without any brightness' (Am 5: 18-20). Prophet Isaiah observed in similar fashion: 'For the Lord of hosts will have His day against all that is proud and arrogant, all that is high and it will be brought low' (Is 2:12). Prophet Zephaniah announced: 'Near is the great day of the Lord, near and very swiftly coming. Hark, the day of the Lord! Bitter then the warrior's cry! A day of wrath is that day, a day of anguish and distress, a day of destruction and desolation, a day of darkness and gloom. For the Lord shall make an end, yes! a sudden end of all who live on earth' (Zep 1:14-18). Prophet Malachi warned: 'For lo, the day is coming, blazing like an oven, when all the proud and all evildoers will be stubble, and the day that is coming will set them on fire, leaving them neither root nor branch' says the Lord of hosts' (Mal 3: 19). Prophet Joel confirmed: 'The day of the Lord is coming, yes, it is near, a day of darkness and of gloom' (Jl 2:1). However, this day of judgment will also lead to the establishment of new heaven and new earth (Is 65: 17), where the good people, who loyally serve Him in the world will find the peace of the Lord for ever.

Jesus, during His earthly ministry, proclaimed to the people of Israel: 'The time has come. The kingdom of God is near. Repent and believe the good news' (Mk 1:15). The end of time, announced by the prophets, has begun in Jesus and will continue during the entire time of the Church. The coming of Jesus to the world has introduced a definitive moment of grace that is prolonged during the present time of the Church. It is a privileged epoch, the time of the Holy Spirit. This is the time of the proclamation of the gospel to all the nations, Jews and Gentiles alike so that all may receive the divine gift of salvation. There is a paradox at this present 'time' - on one side, the end of time has already arrived in the first coming of Jesus and in the ministry of the Church. On the other hand, we are waiting for the end of time at the future coming of the savior, Jesus Christ (Ti 2:12). This present time between the first and the second coming of Jesus, the time of the Church and the acceptable time of grace, marks the passage of humanity from death to life, from evil to goodness and from darkness to light in Jesus Christ, through the Holy Spirit. This is 'the acceptable time of God's favor, now is the day of salvation' (2 Cor 6:2), when each man is called to conversion and offered reconciliation through the light of the Gospel.

Now that the renewing Spirit has been already given to mankind, all of the creation longs for the final revelation of the sons of God (Rom 8: 19) that will come at the end of time, when Jesus Christ will come again to judge the living and the dead. Nobody knows when this end of time will come. It is a secret known to Father alone: 'No one knows about the day or hour, not even the angels in heaven, nor the Son, but only the Father' (Mk 13: 32). Also, 'It is not for men to know the times or dates the Father has set by His own authority' (Acts 1:7). Jesus Himself warns us to be always ready and watchful: 'You must be ready, because the Son of Man will come at an hour when you do not expect Him' (Mt 24: 44). Jesus further states, 'I will come like a thief and you will not know at what time I will come to you' (Rv 3:3). Paul also cautions us: 'You know very well that the day of the Lord will come like a thief in the night' (1 Thes 5:2). 'The hour has come for you to wake up from your slumber, because our salvation is nearer now than when we first believed. The night is nearly over; the day is almost here' (Rom 13: 11-12). When the end of time comes, both the cosmic time and the human time will come to their end and the salvation history will reach its fulfillment, and 'the redeemed people will live with God for ever in eternity, after the old order of things had passed away' (Rv 21: 3-4).

Personal reflection - 'Jesus, the beginning and the end'

We honor Jesus with the title, 'the beginning and the end' of everything, including human history. Jesus, the Lord of human history, has divided it as BC and AD, before His birth and after His birth. The present time is a decisive moment not only in human history, but also in salvation history. Now, though Jesus is seated at the right hand of the Father, yet He lives in the Church until the end of time (Mt 28: 20). It is the time of the Church and during this period, 'let us not become weary in doing good, for at the proper time, we will reap a harvest if we do not give up. Therefore, as we have opportunity, let us do good to all people, especially to those who belong to the family of believers' (Gal 6: 9-10). 'Be filled with the Spirit. Speak to one another with psalms, hymns and spiritual songs. Sing and make music in your heart to the Lord, always giving thanks to God the Father for everything in the name of our Lord Jesus Christ' (Eph 5: 19-20). 'Devote yourselves to prayer, being watchful and thankful' (Col 4:2). Praying and doing good are the ways of the disciples of Jesus, as they wait for the return of the Lord. For people who pray and do good, the end of time is not something to be feared but to be desired since it will bring to perfection all things in Jesus Christ. God alone is perfect and we are imperfect. He alone is eternal and we are finite beings. We have a beginning and end whereas God has no beginning and end at all. In fact, He is the beginning and the end. God made us, human beings, to glorify Him, and this we can do only by carrying out His holy will with the powers of intelligence and goodness, which He has graciously given us, even if it is only limited since we are finite beings. He loves us, not according to the level of our intelligence and goodness, but according to the degree we make efforts to co-operate with His grace. What is important is that we try each and everyday to become persons 'after God's heart'. God, in His wisdom and fatherly goodness, has given us a model in the person of Jesus Christ. Our divine savior, the Son of God, teaches us how to live in this world as human beings. He lived the greatest human life ever lived. Jesus became the perfect man who corresponded perfectly to the purpose that God intended for Him as a human being. God has a purpose for each and every one of us and that is why He has created us as human beings in a definite time and place. The eternal God who is present everywhere was with us at the beginning of our human life as our Creator. At present, He walks with us along the way as a loving guide and faithful companion at every step we make till our end of life. After our death, He will be there to receive us as the just Judge to reward us. We don't have to go looking for God or search for Him as He is ever present to us. Removing the layers of self-absorption and self-importance in our lives and seeking His holy will in whatever we do, we shall find Him all the days of our life and will be united to Him in heaven.

My chauffeur will give you the answer: There lived a great theologian who was a bishop as well. A priest drove him around as he went to give lectures on theological issues. Once the priest who drove him told him: 'Bishop, I have heard your lecture on the Holy Trinity so many times that I can repeat it word for word, exactly as you usually do'. The Bishop, when he had to do the next lecture on the Holy Trinity, asked the priest to dress up like a bishop and he dressed up as a priest and let his driver-priest deliver the lecture. The priest true to his assertion repeated exactly word for word the usual lecture of the bishop on the Holy Trinity. However there arose a real problem, when a person in the audience posed a very complicated question. Not knowing the answer, yet, trying to manage the difficult situation, the priest replied: 'The answer to your question is so simple that I will let my driver do it', and he sat down. The real bishop answered the question and concluded the lecture to the relief of his driver-priest. By ourselves we do not have the capacity to do what God wants us to do in our life in this world. But Jesus stands by us all the days of our life, from the beginning till the end, always helping us to do our best and to please God in all our ways, with the help of His heavenly graces and blessings.

Quote: Pray as if everything depended on God and act as if everything depended on oneself - ***Ignatius of Loyola***

Scripture reading on Day 39: Rv 22: 7-21

Prayer for Day 39: Lord God, we call upon you! Be among us all the days of our Life! In the day be our God, in the night be our Lord! In the city be our peace! In the nation be our joy! In our house, bring harmony and fellowship and in our children bring hope and trust! In our world, O Father of all, bring true love! Amen.

40

LORD

*L*ord' is the title, perhaps, the most used for Jesus Christ. In our prayers, we usually address Him as 'Lord Jesus Christ'. In Greek, the word is 'kyrios', in Hebrew it is 'adon' and in Aramaic it is 'mara'. The Greek word 'kyrios' signified power and authority, more precisely, the power to dispose of a person or object. The word 'kyrios' was used more as an adjective than as a noun in the classical Greek period (500-300 BC). Thus it was used to refer to the owner of a slave, of the ruler or conqueror of subject peoples or the head of a family or the master of a house, of the guardian of a minor, rarely though, the owner of property. It appeared as a title only from the 1st century BC, when it was applied to a goddess in Egypt. From this period on, the title was commonly used in Egypt, Syria and Asia Minor as an honorific designation of gods and kings, especially the deified rulers in Egypt such as Ptolemy XIV and Cleopatra. The Roman emperors were also spoken of as the lords, 'Kyrioi'. As the emperor cult was spreading from the East, it fulfilled a political rather than religious function in Roman Empire, promoting the loyalty to the sovereign ruler. For the Christians, their foundational belief is 'there is one God, the Father from whom all things came and for whom we live and one Lord, Jesus Christ, through whom all things came and through whom we live' (1 Cor 8: 6). Jesus, who was of 'divine state, having the very nature of God' made Himself a slave, being made in human likeness. He became obedient to 'death on the Cross'. Exalted by God, He received from Him that name 'which is above every name'. Now, His glorified humanity perfectly united to His divinity in eternal glory, Jesus exercises universal sovereignty as Lord (Phil 2: 6-11). His incarnation, passion, death and resurrection that took place for the salvation of the world together constitute the basis for the one and unique Lordship of Jesus.

In the Old Testament

The Hebrew word 'adon' signifies authority and the power to command and it differs from 'baal' which means ownership. In the Old Testament, 'adon' was used to refer to the owner of a slave, of a king or a husband, as a polite form of address. Applied to Yahweh, 'adon' stood for His kingship. The Lordship of Yahweh is not limited to the people of Israel whom He has chosen and over whom He is king (1Sm 12:12). Yahweh is the 'Lord of lords' because He is the God of gods, the mighty and awesome' (Dt 10:17). The psalmist sings, 'Praise the Lord of lords. God's love endures forever' (Ps 136: 3). As universal Lord, God exercises His dominion in every place for the benefit of His people. Moses said: 'The heavens, even the highest heavens belong to the Lord, your God, as well as the earth and everything on it' (Dt 10: 14). Two names express His authority: melek and adon. 'Melek' means 'king' as in 'My eyes have seen the King, the Lord of hosts' (Is 6: 5) and in 'For the Lord is the great God, the great King over all the gods' (Ps 95: 3) and in 'Tremble before God, all the earth; say among the nations: The Lord is King' (Ps 96: 10). The second name 'adon' means 'Lord' as in 'The Ark of the covenant of the Lord of the whole earth' (Jos 3:11) and in 'The mountains melt like wax before the Lord, before the Lord of all the earth' (Ps 97: 5). While human beings were addressed respectfully as 'adoni' (my Lord), for Yahweh, the word was 'adonai' to distinguish God from human beings, which is a solemn hymnic title, used more frequently in invocations especially in the Psalms and in the book of prophet Isaiah. At an early date in their history, the people of Israel began to abstain from the pronunciation of the name Yahweh in the belief that it was too sacred a name to be uttered by human beings. Thus, whenever, out of profound respect the name of Yahweh was no longer pronounced in the liturgical readings, 'adonai' replaced it. In the Greek translation of Old Testament known as LXX, Kyrios, the Greek equivalent of Adonai, translated the name 'Yahweh'. The title of Kyrios as used in the LXX version of the Old Testament, for this reason, can have two meanings: sometimes it designates the sovereignty of Yahweh over the heavens and the earth. At times it refers to the incommunicable name of the one true God.

In the New Testament

The background of the term 'Kyrios' in Hellenistic civilization impacted the use and meaning of the title 'Kyrios' in the New Testament, thereby signifying power and authority. That is why the use of kyrios in the Synoptic Gospels offers the meaning of power and authority and is used in this sense as a form of address of Jesus. However, it reflects also the Aramaic usage and means the respectful 'Sir'. Jesus wished to make people understand that, while being a son of David, He was superior to him and existed before him. In this way, He clarified the meaning of the title 'Lord' as addressed to the expected Messiah, that we know was Jesus Himself. He said to them, 'How is it then that David, speaking by the Spirit calls the son of David as 'Lord?' For he says, 'The Lord said to my Lord: Sit at my right hand, until I put your enemies under your feet' (Ps 110:1). If then David calls Him 'Lord' how can he be his son?' No one could say a word in reply, and from that day on no one dared to ask Him any more questions' (Mt 22: 43-46). Relying on this same psalm Ps 110:1, the infant Church proclaimed the lordship of Christ, which is made effective by His resurrection: 'Therefore let all Israel be assured of this: God has made this Jesus, whom you crucified both Lord and Christ' (Ac 2: 34-36).

The title of Lord was bestowed on Jesus, from the beginning of the Church, as is clear from the evidence of Paul, who recalls the primitive creed of the Christian faith: 'If you confess with your mouth, 'Jesus is Lord' and believe in your heart that God raised Him from the dead, you will be saved' (Rom 10: 9). From the beginning, the primitive Church addressed Jesus as 'Lord' and invoked every prayer to God, the Father, through Jesus Christ, the Lord. Paul was aware of the many lords honored in many cults of his day. Many shrines existed in Corinth for many gods. He states, 'For if there are so-called gods, whether in heaven or on earth (as indeed there are many 'gods' and many 'lords'), yet for us there is but one God, the Father, from whom all things came and for whom we live; and there is but one Lord, Jesus Christ, through whom all things came and through whom we live' (1Cor 8: 5-6). But attribution of Lordship to Jesus was not derived from Hellenistic environment or influence. The invocation of Paul in Aramaic as 'Marana tha' (come O Lord) in I Cor 16: 22, shows clearly that Jesus had been first designated 'mar', Lord, in His native tongue Aramaic and not in Greek, thereby pointing to the Jewish source than the Greek origin of this title for Jesus.

One Lord

In the place of tolerated pluralism, Paul insists on one God and one Lord (1 Cor 8: 6). It is not intolerance but affirmation of the uniqueness of Christ in consequence of His death and resurrection. It also reflects the background of uncompromising Jewish monotheism in which Paul grew up. Jesus is one Lord because God is one God. Paul transfers God's role in eschatological salvation to Jesus. He states: 'For there is no difference between Jew and Gentile - the same Lord is Lord of all and richly blesses all who call on Him, for 'everyone who calls on the name of the Lord will be saved' (Rom 10: 12-13). The distinctive application of kyrios to Jesus seems to be original with the early Christian communities. 'The Son of God who as to His human nature was a descendant of David and who through the Spirit of holiness was declared with power to be the Son of God, by His resurrection from the dead: Jesus Christ, our Lord' (Rom 1:4). The light of Easter and reflection on Scripture are the sources of the first Christian profession of faith: 'Jesus is Lord'. Paul states: 'Christ died and returned to life so that He might be the Lord of both the dead and the living (Rom 14: 9). 'We do not preach ourselves but Jesus Christ as Lord and our selves servants for Jesus' sake' (2 Cor 4:5). So, then, just as you received Christ Jesus as Lord continue to live in Him rooted and built up in Him strengthened in the faith as you were taught and overflowing with thankfulness (Col 2:6), for 'no one can say that 'Jesus is Lord' except by the Holy Spirit' (1 Cor 12:3). John testifies in the book of Revelation, 'On His robe and on His thigh He has this name written: King of kings and Lord of lords' (Rv 19:16). The title appears to be a liturgical invocation or acclamation of the Church. In its prayer, it preserved for a long time the primitive Aramaic invocation, Marana tha: 'Our Lord, Come!' (1 Cor 16: 22; Rev 22: 20).

Personal Reflection – 'Kyrios, Jesus and Doulos, the redeemed people of God'

Peter asks Christians 'to set apart Christ as Lord in your hearts' (I Pet 3:15). Paul declares, 'that at the name of Jesus every knee should bow, in heaven and on earth, and every tongue confess that Jesus Christ is Lord, to the glory of God the Father' (Phi 2:10-11. What does the word 'Lord' mean? When the Bible says that we must call Jesus 'Lord' to be saved, what does it imply? To understand it, we should know the definition of two words of the Bible in its original language. They are 'Kyrios' and 'doulos' and they mean 'Lord' and 'slave' respectively. In the time of Jesus and Paul, the 'Kyrios' (Lord) had absolute control over the 'doulos' (slave). The lord of slaves commanded everything about the slaves as when they ate, slept and worked. The 'doulos' was property of the 'Kyrios'. The submission of the slaves to their lord was total. Thus we are able to see the historic significance of the word 'Lord'. To call Jesus our Lord means we are His slaves. Our lives completely belong to Him and our loyalty and obedience to Him is total. Jesus is Lord because He is King over all. The Bible teaches that after His resurrection, God seated Him at His right hand and gave Him all authority and power over the universe: 'Then Jesus came to them and said: 'All authority in heaven and on earth has been given to me. Therefore, go and make disciples of all nations, baptizing them in the name of the Father and of the Son and of the Holy Spirit, and teaching them to obey everything I have commanded you. And surely I am with you always, to the very end of the age' (Mt 28:18-20). The early Church was absolutely sure that 'God made Jesus both Lord and Christ' (Acts 2:36). He is King of kings and Lord of lords (Rv 19:16).

We call this carpenter of Nazareth, Jesus, our Lord, because He reigns over the world. Jesus is Lord because He bought us with His blood, shed on the cross: 'You were bought at a price. Therefore, honor God with your body' (I Cor 6: 20). Jesus is our Lord because as a 'Kyrios' bought slaves with a price, so too Jesus bought us with His blood and became our owner (Kyrios). We became His slaves, 'doulos', when we were saved by Him. Now He seeks our good in everything. On our part, we have to live only for Him. We have to do His will in whatever we do in this world. Jesus set us free from the law of sin and death and the price that He paid was quite high. The only Son of the Father left heaven with all it's glory, to become a man like us and to die for us on a cruel cross. Now, since we decided to become Christians, we are 'doulos' (slaves) of our 'Kyrios', Jesus Christ. It was led by the grace that comes from the Holy Spirit that we chose to submit to the King of kings and Lord of lords in faith. Set free by the precious blood of the Lamb of God and thus saved from God's wrath against our sin, now we receive from Him the abundant life that He offers us gratuitously. Jesus is our Lord, the owner of our life and being, though, He is not like those owners of the slaves who abused and mistreated their slaves. Our Lord Jesus, who loved us to the point of sacrificing His very life, is only interested in our eternal good.

Jesus is our Lord and master. Paul reminds us that we should serve and obey Jesus and not sin: 'Don't you know that when you offer yourselves to someone to obey him as slaves, you are slaves to the one whom you obey - whether you are slaves to sin, which leads to death or to obedience, which leads to righteousness?' (Rom 6:16). In this world, in some way or another, human beings become slaves of someone or something. Often people think they are fully free human beings and are slaves to none. But the fact is most people are slaves to their own desires that may mean something or some persons. As Christians, God set us free from all that enslaved us. Through the sacrament of baptism, we became the slaves of the perfect Lord, Jesus Christ. Let us please Him in all our activities, in all our conversations and in all our thoughts, in all that we say and do. We should seek to do His will and not our own. The slaves did not want to displease their lords in anything, for fear of his wrath, that meant terrible punishment. Our Lord is not like the owners of the slaves who used and abused their slaves for their gain and profit. He is a good and kind master who seeks and desires only our good. What can we do in return for the wonderful kindness of the divine master? In all that we do, what we say and what we are, let us always seek to please Him. Paul tells us, 'Whatever you do, work at it with all your heart, as working for the Lord, not for men' (Col 3: 23).

Hosanna to the king

'When they brought the colt to Jesus and threw their cloaks over it, he sat on it. Many people spread their cloaks on the road while others spread branches they had cut in the fields. Those who went ahead and those who followed shouted, 'Hosanna! Blessed is He who comes in the name of the Lord! Blessed is the coming kingdom of our father David! Hosanna in the highest!' (Mk 11: 7-10). Jesus went to Jerusalem knowing fully well what awaited Him-betrayal, rejection, and crucifixion. The people of Jerusalem hailed Him as their Messianic King! Little did they know what it would cost this king to usher in His kingdom! Jesus' entry into Jerusalem astride a colt was a direct fulfillment of the Messianic prophecy of Zechariah: 'Rejoice greatly, O daughter of Zion. Shout aloud, O daughter of Jerusalem. Lo, your king comes to you; triumphant and victorious is he, and riding on an ass and upon a colt the foal of an ass' (Zec 9:9). The colt was a sign of peace. Jesus entered Jerusalem in meekness and humility, as the Messianic King who would bring victory and peace to His people. He would secure this victory and peace by His death on the cross and by His resurrection, central events in salvation history that would take place within a few days, at the time of Passover. Psalm 24 is another prophetic passage which echoes this triumphal procession of the King of glory: 'Lift up your heads, O gates! Be lifted up, O ancient doors, that the King of glory may come in. Who is the king of glory? The Lord of hosts is the king of glory' (Ps 24: 7-10).

Homage paid to the Lord

On previous occasions, Jesus always discouraged the people from raising messianic expectation about Him, since it got very much intertwined with the national aspirations of the people of Israel and political kingship. When people, after witnessing the miracle of the multiplication of the loaves, 'intended to make Him king by force, Jesus withdrew to a mountain by Himself' (Jn 6:15). In fact, before the beginning of His public ministry in Galilee, this was the enticing temptation of the devil who 'took Him to a very high mountain and showed Him all the kingdoms of the world and their splendor, and said: 'All this I will give you if you will bow down and worship me'. Jesus said to the devil, 'Away from me, Satan! For it is written: 'Worship the Lord your God, and serve Him only' (Mt 4: 8-10). Luke concludes the account of temptation of Jesus saying, 'The devil left Him until an opportune time' (Lk 4:13). Totally rejecting a political rule and Jesus made a conscious choice to be the humble slave of His heavenly Father, the suffering servant foretold by prophet Isaiah (Is 53) and sought to fulfill His Father's holy will by His suffering and death on the cross. He surrendered His life completely in the hands of His heavenly Father. It is an act of total trust and complete surrender, a model for us how to walk in the journey of faith.

The Lord of peace comes

After proclaiming the Gospel for nearly three years, during the course of His public ministry, Jesus saw that the appointed time has finally arrived to carry out the divine plan of His Father in Jerusalem, the eternal city, the place of his rejection, crucifixion and death. In order to fulfill the prophecy of prophet Zechariah about the coming of the king to the holy city seated upon a colt, Jesus took the initiative by sending two of the disciples to the next village to fetch 'a colt tied, which no one has ever ridden'(Mk 11: 2). He allowed the disciples to spread their mantles on the animal and He took His seat upon it. As He began His triumphant but peaceful entry into the city, there erupted spontaneous, solemn and enthusiastic homage. What a paradox! Jesus entered into the holy city, the King of kings and the Lord of lords, to reign on His cross. There were no soldiers line the road, nor were the spoils of war carried before Him. Instead of glittering swords borne by warriors ordinary folk carried the boughs of palm trees. In His joyous entry into Jerusalem, Jesus revealed the spiritual character of His kingdom- 'a kingdom of truth and life, a kingdom of holiness and grace, a kingdom of justice, love and peace. As He rode down the slope of Mount of Olives, the city of Jerusalem came into full view. The white marble turrets and the golden domes glittered in the rays of the sun. The sight of the city that would condemn Him to death and crucify Him five days later, and which would be razed to the ground and scorched in brutal massacre by the Roman legions fifty years later, stirred Him to the deepest sorrow and compassion. He wept for what awaited the city fifty years later, rather than what awaited Him five days later and His spurned heart lamented: 'O Jerusalem! Had you only known what would bring you peace! Alas, your enemies will dash you to the ground and you and your children within your walls. They will not leave one stone on another, because you did not recognize the time of God's coming to you' (Lk 19: 41-44). The Lord Jesus divine and human, full of goodness and love, rich in mercy and compassion stands at the door of our heart to enter and to bring peace, for He is the Lord of peace and joy. He is the true King who offers peace, joy, and everlasting life for those who accept His kingship. Let us give the Lord Jesus full reign in our hearts, in our homes and in our lives! And let the walls of our souls echo with the praise of His everlasting glory! Let the King of glory find a welcome entry in our hearts and homes, and into our lives, for He is the 'King of kings and the Lord of the lords' (Rv 19:16).

Jesus brings peace and reconciliation: Elsa Joseph was a Jewish woman who played violin for the concerts. During the Second World War, she was separated from her two daughters by the Nazis. After the war was over, she found out that her two daughters perished in the Nazi concentration camp of Auschwitz, after being gassed. She herself barely survived the miseries of another Nazi concentration camp. Elsa's response to the tragic news of the loss of both her children was to pick up her violin and perform in the concert halls in Germany. A mother who could forgive the murderers of her daughters, she spoke of peace and reconciliation among the peoples after each concert. Her message of peace rang aloud not only in Germany but also in Northern Ireland, in Lebanon and in Israel. Jesus came to the world two thousand years ago, and He comes again and again to every person as the Lord of peace, love and joy.

Quote: Jesus Christ has the decisive place in man's ageless relationship with God. He is what God means by 'Man' and He is what man means by 'God' - *J.S. Whale*

Scripture reading for Day 40: Lk 19: 28-44

Prayer for Day 40: O God! In your infinite goodness and love, you sent your only Son for the salvation of the world. Grant, we beseech you that we may receive Him in our hearts and be filled with His peace and joy. Help us to do your holy will as your faithful servants and serve you with a sincere heart all the days of our lives. We make this prayer through Jesus Christ, our Lord! Amen.

CONCLUSION

Our meditation on the forty names of Jesus completes a fruitful spiritual exercise. The entire focus has been on Jesus Christ, the Son of God. Reflecting on each of His names or titles enabled us to understand more who Jesus is, why He became man, how He lived among us as a human being, what message He preached as the good news of salvation, why He suffered the cruel crucifixion and died on the cross, and finally how God, His Father, raised Him up on the third day and exalted Him as the Lord and Savior. A focus on Jesus Christ draws attention also to our own lives as the beloved children of God. We reflect on who we are, why God created us and placed us in this world and how we have to live as devout and witnessing Christian people and what is our final destiny. Without the all important reference to Jesus Christ, our life as Christians will make no sense at all.

Let us examine what are the fruits of this spiritual exercise of the meditation on the forty names of Jesus. First of all, it enables us to deepen our faith in Him. As we receive Him as our personal Lord and Savior and understand what such faith implies for our daily lives as the Christian people, we find right meaning and great purpose for our life in this world. As human beings, no doubt, we have to face many challenges and encounter numerous problems, undergo recurring temptations of sin and experience occasional failures of human weakness, all an inevitable part of our human existence on earth. However, in spite of our shortcomings, we never give up trying to be good Christian people as we seek to please our heavenly Father in all the things that we do. Jesus assumed our human condition, lived as a human being and met with the same challenges that we daily face. Yet, He was totally dedicated to His Father and His steadfast fidelity and unwavering obedience to His Father's holy will is indeed a great example for us that can strengthen our resolve to love and serve God, our Father, in spite of falling short many times. Jesus became the beloved Son, in whom God was well pleased (Mk 1:11). As the loving children of God, to please our Heavenly Father, all that we have to do is to follow Jesus with a strong and firm faith, thereby to carry out the holy will of our Father in heaven more joyfully. Also, the victory of Jesus over sin, evil and death inspires us to never lose courage in the midst of our struggles but to remain fully focused on our journey towards our promised land, always with a strong and unwavering hope. This is very important to us, because a hopeless man is a dead man. The meditation on the holy names of Jesus invigorates our hope in our great and glorious destiny.

With faith deepened and hope strengthened, we are empowered to love our heavenly Father as we should do, not only as His creatures but also as His children, the unique privilege that we received through Jesus, His only Son. Loving God involves trusting Him fully and surrendering our lives totally because He cares for us and seeks our good in all that He makes of our lives. It also obliges us to seek to do only what pleases Him. We understand that authentic worship of praise and thanks from a grateful, humble and loving heart pleases God and that is what we should seek to do in all our acts of worship in the church and at home, any time and anywhere we pray. Also, fraternal service, as kindness to all and charity to the needy, inspired by the unconditional love of God and guided by the noble divine Spirit within us, is also equally pleasing to God. In this way, loving God and serving neighbors constitutes the authentic spiritual sacrifice of a Christian who offers worship in spirit and truth (Jn 4: 24). Meditating on the holy names of Jesus empowers us to consecrate our entire lives as a significant spiritual offering to God and to fulfill our daily tasks accordingly with utmost dedication. Our earthly existence is meaningful in so far as we know God, love Him and serve Him. For us Christians, it means also knowing Jesus, loving Him and serving Him, since He alone leads us to God. Knowing Jesus involves a process of understanding of the person of Jesus that in turn leads to an existential relationship with Him, whereby He becomes our unfailing friend and trusted guide in our earthly journey. As a result, as Christian people, we find great peace and much joy in loving and serving Him and dedicating our lives fully and totally to Him. After serving Jesus faithfully till our last breadth, when we go to meet Him at the end of our earthly life, He will joyfully welcome us at the gates of heaven saying: 'Well done, good and faithful servant! Come and share eternal happiness with me! (Mt 25:21).

Printed in the United States
49816LVS00004B/97-510